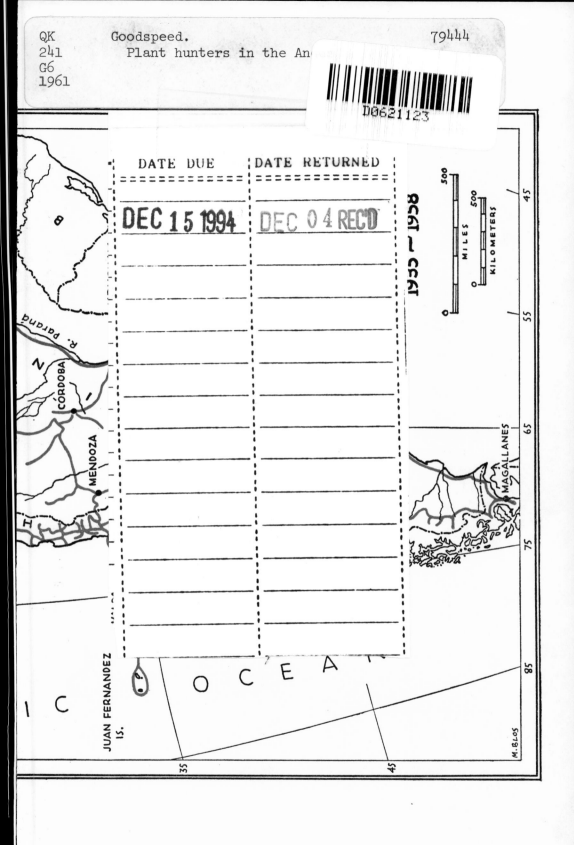

DATE DUE	DATE RETURNED
DEC 15 1994	DEC 04 REC'D

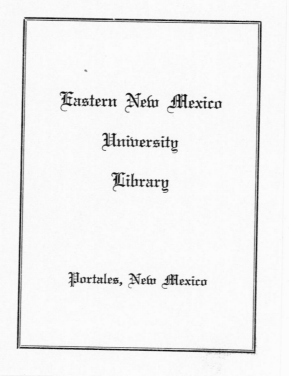

PLANT HUNTERS IN THE ANDES

T. HARPER GOODSPEED

PLANT HUNTERS IN THE ANDES

1961

Berkeley and Los Angeles

UNIVERSITY OF CALIFORNIA PRESS

UNIVERSITY OF CALIFORNIA PRESS
BERKELEY AND LOS ANGELES, CALIFORNIA
© 1941 AND 1961 BY T. HARPER GOODSPEED
LIBRARY OF CONGRESS CATALOG NUMBER: 61-7533
SECOND EDITION, REVISED AND ENLARGED
PRINTED IN THE UNITED STATES OF AMERICA

THIS VOLUME IS DEDICATED TO THE
MEMORY OF HARVEY E. STORK AND
TO THOSE OTHER NORTH AND SOUTH
AMERICAN ASSOCIATES AND ASSIST-
ANTS WHOSE LOYAL AND EFFECTIVE
COÖPERATION HAS BEEN RESPONSIBLE
FOR THE SUCCESS OF OUR ANDEAN
PLANT HUNTING.

PREFACE

T HE FIRST edition of this book appeared twenty years ago. It contained an account of certain of the accomplishments and experiences in Peru and Chile of members of the first two botanical expeditions sent to South America from the University of California Botanical Garden in Berkeley. It was translated into Spanish—word for word and therefore badly—and published in Buenos Aires in 1944. A British Empire reprint was published in London in 1950.

Since 1941 four additional expeditions have collected plants and mapped vegetation not only in Peru and Chile but also in Colombia, Bolivia, Argentina, and Uruguay. The present, second, edition includes much of the original, revised and supplemented, together with a number of new chapters—the whole serving, in some measure at least, to complete the record of our plant hunting in the Andes which has covered a period of more than twenty-five years.

The first two expeditions were made possible, in part, by grants-in-aid provided by scientific and other institutions in this country and abroad and by agencies of the federal government—assistance acknowledged in the first edition. To that list should now be added the Chicago Museum of Natural History, the New York Botanical Garden, Associates in Tropical Biogeography (University of California), the Madison Foundation (San Francisco), and the Cactus and Succulent Society of California. Throughout, the generosity, often repeated, of the late Lora J. Knight and of some three hundred fifty other private individuals has alone permitted the full realization of our South American plant-hunting proposals.

I gratefully acknowledge renewals of the Fellowship grant from the John Simon Guggenheim Memorial Foundation referred to in the first edition and also a subvention from the same source which assisted in the publication of certain of the scientific products of the expeditions. The sustained coöperation of W. R. Grace and Company in allowing reductions in passenger fares and in transportation, gratis, of expedition equipment and collections between California and South America has been of great importance. Assistance of many kinds consistently offered by agencies of the government and by colleagues and scientific institutions in the South American republics in which we worked was indispensable.

Reference should be made to the assistance furnished by the Botanical Garden and the Herbarium of the University of California, (Berkeley), in preserving and in distributing to similar institutions at home and abroad the large collections of living and dried plant material returned by the expeditions to Berkeley. In this connection the coöperation of Robert D. Dutton, Manager of the Botanical Garden, and of Dr. Herbert L. Mason, Director of the Herbarium, is acknowledged with thanks. Finally, I am indebted to the editorial staff of the University of California Press for advice and encouragement during the preparation of this volume.

The photographs reproduced were, with few exceptions, taken by members of the six University of California Botanical Garden expeditions to the Andes.

T. H. G.

CONTENTS

1

WHY, WHO, AND WHERE?

*The squash grew from the earth above
Earth-Mother's navel, the beans from the
earth above her feet, and tobacco from
above her head—thus it soothes the mind
and sobers thought.*

IROQUOIS TRADITION

THE SENIOR CLASS stood in broken ranks on College Hill waiting to
begin the march to the First Baptist Meeting House where we would
receive our last official gift from Brown University—that short roll
of white paper tied with a knot of brown ribbon. Relatives and friends
pressed upon us with greetings and congratulations. In the crowd I
saw one of my freshman fraternity brothers. Hailed and instructed,
he left for the Chapter House in search of any mail that might have
come that morning for me.

Among my letters was something that I had given up hope of receiving—notice of my appointment as Assistant in the Department of
Botany at the University of California. That was a little more than
fifty years ago, and, although from time to time I have wandered far
afield, my connection with the University of California has been continuous and my regard for it increasing. Quantitatively it was a small
institution in 1909, but in things of the mind and spirit it had already
reached a high plane.

When I came to California I had little idea that I was taking the first
step in the life of a plant hunter. There was no way of anticipating

that ahead of me lay adventures on the Andean eaves of the world and on the Pacific and Atlantic shelves of the southern continent below them. Nevertheless, on the second day after my arrival in Berkeley my plant hunting in the Andes began—with my introduction to *Nicotiana*. That introduction was, eventually, to be largely responsible for my leading six botanical expeditions to South America. This book describes them, in part.

In retrospect those six expeditions call to mind long minutes of earthquake, hours of shipwreck, days of danger and privation in deserts, jungles, and snow fields and of sickness, loneliness, and the depression that follows long contact with primitive ways of life in uncongenial climates. Extended over a total of more than four years these experiences furnish an illustration, not the first and not the best, of how sustaining scientific curiosity can become. I have often wondered at my temerity in assuming, time after time, responsibility for the well-being of a total, in addition to my wife, of fifteen associates, one or another of whom worked, at my request, in territories where I knew in advance that distress of body and mind might lie in wait anywhere, any time.

The reverse of the shield, preëminent in remembrance, shows many days filled with intense satisfaction in scientific achievement and discovery, scenic wonders far beyond expectation, periods of comfort and relaxation in delightful surroundings, and rewarding association with new-found friends of both high and low degree.

When you ask the why and the where of the story which is to follow, we come back to the plants which led me on. *Nicotiana* is the name given to an aggregation or genus of flowering plants belonging to the Solanaceae or Nightshade family. To this large and cosmopolitan, plant family also belong the potato, the tomato, the pepper (but not the one in the pepper shaker), and many less familiar plants. So far as *Nicotiana* itself is concerned, its chief claim to fame is the species *tabacum*, the tobacco plant, commercially one of the most valuable of crop plants. But in addition to *tabacum* there are some sixty other species and many varieties classified under *Nicotiana*. Of them, one or two have some agricultural, a few considerable horticultural, and the remainder botanical importance.

My introduction to *Nicotiana tabacum* as a living plant (for my smoking began long before) was arranged by the late Dr. W. A. Setchell, one of the world's foremost botanists, at that time and for many years thereafter Chairman of the Department of Botany at the University in Berkeley. The size of his pipe and the volume of his smoke had awed the undergraduate long before my advent on the campus. It was in part his enthusiasm as a smoker but far more his scientific curiosity and a keen collector's instinct that led him to make, first, a collection of tobacco pipes from near and far; second, a collection of the early literature on and broadsides against smoking; and, finally, the start of a living collection, in the University's Botanical Garden, of the many cultivated varieties of the tobacco plant and of its numerous wild relatives.

That first morning in the Botanical Garden the professor showed me plants of "Havana," "Maryland Broadleaf," "White Burley," and many other tobacco varieties, most of which were of lesser agricultural and greater botanical interest. Some were low-growing but many were over six feet in height and portly. There were large- and small-flowered races, white, red, and pink. Some varieties bore stalked or petiolate leaves, others unstalked or sessile ones; some leaves were slender and sharp-pointed, others blunt at the apex and wide behind it. The professor showed me why shape is one of the things important in the selection of tobacco leaves for making cigar wrappers, because one shape will cut more wrappers without excessive waste than another. He pulled down an old branch, long out of flower, and from the dry, open capsules at its end, poured into my hand thousands of the minute dark-brown seeds which the tobacco plant produces.

Near by was another species of *Nicotiana* called *rustica*. It was actually the first sort of tobacco cultivated in the Colony of Virginia, where the white man obtained the seeds from the little gardens in which the Indians were growing it along with their corn and beans and squashes. It was not long, however, before the colonists replaced *rustica* with the far more desirable species, *tabacum*, which came to them from Indian cultivation in the West Indies and has ever since been the tobacco of commerce. For some time, *rustica* has again assumed some agricultural importance as a high-yielding source of nicotine sulfate for use in insecticides.

Then the professor showed me his collection of "wild" species of *Nicotiana*, those which, at that time, had little or no importance agriculturally but were allied in form and structure to those that had. First I saw the native North American species that came from the Great Plains, the Southwest, and the Pacific slope and were, most of them, smoked on ceremonial occasions by the Blackfoot, Crow, Navajo, Comanche, or other Indian tribes. Then there were species from Australia and one or two from islands in the South Pacific, relatively small plants with white flowers, often highly fragrant.

Because of man's intervention it is today hard to say just what were the original areas of distribution of the Australian species of *Nicotiana*, all of which I was, later, successful in assembling in the Botanical Garden. Many years ago, in Australia, cattle were driven over long distances to market or to seasonal pasturage and the minute seeds of trailside Nicotianas were caught in their rough coats and carried far away from their native homes, to grow and mingle and hybridize with cousins that were originally distant both geographically and botanically. We shall see later that in South America also man has succeeded in altering the extent of natural distribution of the Nicotianas.

Finally the professor and I came to the garden beds in which he was growing the many species native to South America. Towering high above its relatives from other continents was the great "tree tobacco" (*N. tomentosa*) of the Andes. We shall come across it in a later chapter growing to a height of forty feet where the jungle disappears and the Peruvian cordilleras rise to their supreme altitudes. What I saw on that first day in the Botanical Garden was a monstrous bush, twenty feet high, with many stems from the base, all clothed with large, coarse leaves and bearing at their tips pyramids of pinkish-white flowers. It grows happily and vigorously in the Berkeley climate until an unusually heavy frost occurs.

Near the base of this giant *Nicotiana* was another species, smaller, which produced flat-topped heads of long, slender, tubular white flowers, very fragrant. It is a native of Andean foothills in northwestern Argentina. Sometimes under its Latin name, *Nicotiana sylvestris*, it is listed in seedsmen's catalogues, and it may be seen now and then in gardens other than botanical ones.

There were other Nicotianas from the Andes and from the east and west coasts of our sister continent. In the pages that follow we shall come across them, as well as others not known to exist until we discovered them, and they had best be described in their own native setting.

My introduction to *Nicotiana* so many years ago resulted in a permanent alliance, and my study of her and her relatives still continues.

This study has taken me to many pleasant places and put me into touch with colleagues all around the world. It sent me to Sweden when the demoralization of German science that immediately followed the First World War had made Botaniska Institutet of the University of Stockholm the most famous headquarters in the world for research in the anatomy of the cell; it has often sent me to botanical centers in England, France, and Germany.

How vividly I remember those first Nazi salutes during one long stay in Berlin! By special dispensation my fifteen-year-old son had been admitted as a full-fledged student in a famous boys' school originally built by Kaiser Wilhelm in order that the sons of his provincial ministers might live and be educated in the capital. For the spring holiday my son was invited to go home with a schoolmate whose family owned one of the great estates in East Prussia. I went to the school to see the two boys off on their train for the country. Crowds of young Germans were pouring out, loaded with bags and rucksacks and filling the street with noisy holiday exuberance and shouted good-byes to classmates and teachers. But many of these good-byes were not alone spoken ones but ended in arm-raised, palm-fronted salutes. This was something new and seemed very foreign to a Germany that had shown me only evidence of glorying in its freedom from military etiquette, as well as from "*Verboten*" signs. How little I realized on that spring morning that the raised arms I saw represented outward allegiance by German schoolboys and their teachers to a formula designed to breed the ultimate in "man's inhumanity to man."

Still on the trail of *Nicotiana*, I was in Germany again six weeks before "Munich." How often history repeats illustrations of the "fact blindness" of men and nations; that inability or unwillingness, inconceivable in retrospect, of human beings and their leaders to interpret the evidence before their eyes in terms of the result which it so clearly indicated and then to formulate their plans and direct their activities in accordance with the facts. Berlin that summer was full of facts—not alone sidewalks crowded with soldiers equipped to fight and camouflaged motor transport for troops and guns on many streets but, more disturbing, an all-pervading atmosphere of expectation among the young and anxiety among the old, which you felt almost like the hush that immediately precedes the storm. How could the world have been so blind?

My almost lifelong study of the Nicotianas had a single underlying objective. I proposed to produce, if possible, a picture of the ways in which, over the long stretches of geologic time, the various present-day species of a characteristic genus of flowering plants—and *Nicotiana* is one—had their origin; of how and to what degree they are today interrelated; and of the various avenues along which in the future their evolution will be directed. To this end I finally succeeded in assembling in the University of California Botanical Garden in Berkeley the world's largest and most complete living collection of *Nicotiana* species. Growing side by side under equivalent conditions, their likenesses and distinctions in form and structure have been estimated. Hybridization between species and varieties and study of the behavior of hybrid progenies have extracted from the living plants much evidence concerning their origins and relationships. More fundamental and precise is the evidence from the cell itself and the revelation under the microscope of the character and behavior of the chromosomes, bearers of the heredity potentialities, in species and hybrids. In the desire that the picture should be not only most complete and accurate but also most realistic, I have gone again and again to South America in order to see growing in their native state the most numerous and the scientifically most significant Nicotianas.

In museums in North America, Europe, and South America I read on the labels attached to the pressed specimens of *Nicotiana* species the localities where, over a period of more than one hundred years, the pioneer plant-collectors in South America had found them. I was, thus, directed to those areas where I might hope to find them again on the foothills and higher slopes of the Andes from near the equator south almost to Cape Horn, along the coasts of Peru and Argentina, and in parts of Chile and Brazil.

A few of the museum specimens were exciting. They had been collected in areas, especially in Peru, from which Nicotianas had not before been reported. Some were labeled "new species?"; some others were identified, incorrectly, as well-known species. This meant that there certainly were little-known and unnamed Nicotianas in South America waiting to be re-collected. If I could find them again and from their seed add them to my living *Nicotiana* collection, it should be possible to establish their identity and determine their relationships. More than this, did not these "new species?" hold out the promise that additional and entirely unknown Nicotianas awaited discovery off the beaten track in South America? Later chapters tell of failure, sometimes repeated, and of ultimate success in the rediscovery of those "new species?" and of the fulfillment of the promise they held out.

The objective of my long-continued studies of *Nicotiana*, referred to in a previous paragraph, has been attained in the sense that a few years ago I produced a monograph which condensed the products of all my research at home and abroad and presented my conception of how the Nicotianas became what they are today. It is a long treatise, documented with many drawings and tables, and has practically no popular appeal. Its publication was, naturally enough, a source of satisfaction to me. I am happy that reviewers have dealt generously with the book. It has also produced various sorts of heartening scientific recognition.

From the beginning there was no dollar sign attached to the search for the wild relatives of the tobacco plant. Why, then, you may ask, spend time and money, and subject yourself and others to privation and danger in a far-off land, on such a thoroughly "impractical" quest? There is only one reply, the one that has been valid since man began to think—the pursuit of knowledge can become an end in itself.

Actually, however, our plant hunting in South America has had considerable practical significance. Modern crop plants and ornamentals are descendants of "wild" ancestors, some of which in prehistoric time and others more recently were brought under domestication. Following initial recognition of their value—as food or otherwise—conscious selection was undertaken, by early man and his descendants, to improve their desirable qualities. Among the results was the production of varieties showing significant increases in yield, larger or finer fruits and flowers, and adaptation to climatic extremes. However, along with such important improvements an increasing susceptibility to plant disease has often appeared. Many years ago it was suggested that long-continued and successful selection had at the same time eliminated or reduced the disease-resistant characteristics which the original wild ancestors might have possessed. Therefore, if the descendants of those ancestors could today be found in their native state and if they still retained those characteristics, then the plant breeder might be successful, through hybridization, in reintroducing disease resistance into the improved varieties. This expectation has more than once been realized.

The relation of all this to my Andean plant hunting is the fact that we were able to collect and send back to the plant breeder the seeds of the native South American descendants of the original ancestors of such outstanding crop plants as tobacco, potatoes, and corn, and of tomatos, beans, and peppers also. With regard to the present-day and continuously more improved commercial tobacco, our research at the Botanical Garden in Berkeley indicates that it (*Nicotiana tabacum*) is actually a hybrid that must have originated, perhaps in remote past time, from the cross-pollination of one of the Nicotianas then in existence in the Andes with another and quite different one growing not too far away. There was clear indication that the descendants of those species which had been parents of this ancient hybrid could still be found in the wild state in Peru, Bolivia, and Argentina at middle altitudes or higher.

Losses from plant disease in the tobacco fields of our southern states alone (not to speak of the tobacco grown elsewhere in this country, in South Africa, and in other parts of the world) have at times reached many millions of dollars. Obviously, then, seed of wild Andean Nicotianas—particularly of those from which the tobacco plant was derived —should be collected in the hope that the plants grown from them would prove resistant to disease. If so, there was a chance at least of reducing tobacco-crop losses. It took a good deal of doing and a good deal of time but we got the seed.

Two native South American Nicotianas and a native Australian one have proved to be most important in reducing plant disease losses in the tobacco fields. Each of those three "wild" Nicotianas is resistant to one of three destructive diseases caused by fungus, bacterial, or virus infection. Hybridization of the three with commercial races of tobacco was followed by years of selection and recombination. The result has been the production of strains of tobacco plants in every way desirable as a commercial source of what we smoke and also highly resistant to all three diseases.

This outstanding result has been accomplished by a highly trained and dedicated group of geneticists working at the research station of the United States Department of Agriculture at Beltsville, Maryland, and their associates in agricultural experiment stations in tobacco-growing areas. Our farmers are well aware—as the general public should be—of the extent to which major improvements of many kinds in the plants and animals produced for our consumption have come from the extensive and long-range breeding and other programs under way at Beltsville.

There, a few weeks ago, I had an opportunity to meet some of the men responsible for the success of the tobacco disease-resistance program and to see some of the resistant plants. It was a source of great satisfaction to realize that, in some small part at least, those plants which are of such great potential importance in an almost world-wide agricultural operation were a product of my many years of *Nicotiana* research.

I was brought up at the extremity of our family's mid-Victorianism and New Englandism. As the only child in a clan that included a number of quite adult aunts and uncles, I was the recipient of frequent admonitions of many kinds. One I particularly remember because I resisted it successfully was to "turn out your toes"—considered essential to proper deportment sixty years ago. I also remember becoming ingenious in lightening the severity of strict Sunday observances. In general I probably managed to be something of a thorn in the family flesh. Less easy to resist was the insistence upon doubling up on things. It became a matter of conscience never to do one thing at a time if more than one could be accomplished, and remarks were made about "letting your head save your heels." It got to the stage where you felt guilty in going up or down the stairs unless there was something to carry in addition to yourself. There is no limit to the ramifications of this tendency not to let well enough alone. I believe that it all must have been an oblique application of the New England hatred of idleness. At any rate, an effect was produced and I have always been afflicted with a tendency to pyramid my activities.

You will, therefore, not be surprised to learn that my Andean plant hunting has had more than one objective. Study of the wide geographic distribution of *Nicotiana*, and particularly the search for previously unknown species, was its primary objective. A second objective originated in commissions I accepted from other botanists to do a little private hunting for the particular South American plants they needed; from the United States Department of Agriculture to collect seed of native races of all crop plants of which the ancestors were Andean; from garden clubs and others to bring home as many plants of proved or potential ornamental importance as we could find. As if this were not enough of a program, I decided, in order to share with botanists throughout the world the results of our South American plant hunting, to make, if possible, four or more dried and pressed specimens of every one of the various kinds of plants of scientific interest, in addition to *Nicotiana*, that we came across. Certainly the shades of my ancestors have no reason to complain.

I needed help to carry out successfully the plant-hunting program just described—not ordinary people to go with me to South America but trained collectors or, at least, those who had a botanical background and, if possible, some experience in adjusting themselves to foreign and unfavorable environments. A minimum of newspaper publicity concerning our plans for South American plant hunting was enough to bring out the volunteers.

From all over the United States, young and old, male and female, they wrote to me intimately about their physiques, moral character, adventurous spirit, love of flowers, and burning desire to see South America. All this they would freely and willingly devote to the success of the expeditions in return for traveling expenses and a reasonable salary. Some of them gave me their advance picture of what we would be doing in South America. It was apparently to be a glorious safari—native porters in a straggling line winding through the untrodden wilderness, flanked with swarms of bronzed and hardy botanists gathering in the rare and beautiful vegetation. One volunteer, employed at the moment in a lumber camp, saw himself chopping down the tall and stately forest trees of the high Andes so that we might gather their topmost blossoms. A young lady, expert in the manipulation of business machines of all sorts, was to make a charming picture seated at the door of her tent on the mountainside and running her fingers rapidly over a battery of calculators. Otherwise, she predicted serious errors in our accounts. By their letters, these and many more volunteers demonstrated that the pioneer spirit is with us yet—we still long to "live adventurously."

One volunteer called upon me personally. He was an amazingly versatile gentleman. First he told me that he was a construction expert. Before I could stop him he had built me quite a village, which he said would be essential as headquarters in the Andean fastnesses for the dozens of collectors, packers, cooks, and body servants we would be taking along. His opinion of the importance of our expedition suffered visibly when I finally had a chance to explain that not more than two or three of us were likely to be in any one part of the Andes at any one time. He then revealed the fact that he was an embalmer. Pointing an accusing finger at me, he said, "Have you considered death and what you would do about it?" Without giving me time to ponder this sobering question he poured forth such a flood of statistics on the causes and incidence of accidental death as would deter the stoutest heart from venturing any distance from his hearthstone. Before I recovered from this gloomy prospect he took me into the mortician's confidence concerning rates of decay in cadavers, with special reference to cause of death, temperature relations, and other depressing details.

In other words, it appeared that each member of the expedition should, like the immortal Sarah, travel with a coffin; our friend, the volunteer, being on hand to counteract decay and dissolution as one after another of us died an unnatural death. I never thought to ask him what would happen at the end when he found himself alone with his coffin. But this was not all. Our combined construction expert and embalmer was also an airplane pilot and thus was able to add the capstone to the arch—he would fly each product of his handiwork to civilization, thence to start its journey home to its relatives. He explained that for legal as well as sentimental reasons the relatives probably would insist upon receiving the remains. I have never understood why such a versatile man, so serious minded, so conscientious, with so picturesque an imagination, should have been on government relief!

During the first three Andean plant huntings my wife Florence was, for me, a most important expedition member. Her acquaintance with *Nicotiana* had begun many years before at a time when I had no other help but hers in working with my accumulating collection of tobacco relatives. In South America, with enthusiasm she renewed her contact with them on their native Andean mountainsides and, despite the start of a losing struggle with a malignancy, insisted upon assuming a share in some of our many activities. Betty and I were married some years later and have enjoyed a period of study in Europe and a long sojourn in South America during the sixth expedition there. I am grateful for having, a second time, a companion who has unshakable confidence in the ultimate triumph of the good, the true, and the beautiful and a fellow traveler who anticipates only pleasure and profit and therefore finds them always.

During the first and comparatively brief expedition of 1935–1936, Mrs. Ynés Mexia and Prince Egon von Ratibor were with me as assistants and collectors. Mrs. Mexia was a remarkable woman. Relatively late in life she began her travels in Mexico, Alaska, and South America, which had as principal objective the collecting of plants in remote and almost inaccessible regions. She had collected extensively in Brazil, Ecuador, and Peru before she joined the expedition. While Mrs. Mexia was with us she collected intensively, particularly in Peru and the foothills of the Argentine Andes. She was the true explorer type and happiest when independent and far from civilization. Her death was a distinct loss to botanists, who had learned much that was new about the vegetation of the territories in which she collected.

Prince Egon von Ratibor, or "James West," as he was known to a large circle of acquaintance in California, was a valuable member of the expedition. The breadth of his botanical interests and knowledge made him a most discriminating collector. His enthusiasm for the plant hunt was boundless and infectious. The rougher the terrain, the better he liked it, because the fatigue and hazards involved probably meant that it had not before been botanized. He continued to collect in Peru, Bolivia, and Argentina until his return to Germany in 1938. He died there some years later.

The second expedition, in 1938–1939, was a far more ambitious and extended affair than the first. I was convinced that in the Andes and near by there was much *Nicotiana* collecting of the most important sort still to be done. The vital collecting areas were spread over a great north-and-south distance and in many of them, distant from one another, the best collecting seasons coincided. Therefore I took a large party with me and subdivided it into small, mobile units, so that collecting might go on simultaneously over a large stretch of the Andes, the coasts, and the plains. In this way it was possible to cover all or most of the important areas in a single year.

One of the units operated exclusively in Peru. It was led by the late Dr. Harvey E. Stork, for many years Professor of Botany in Carleton College. He was the ideal combination—a highly trained and enthusiastic botanist, an experienced collector, a skilled photographer. With him in Peru were Ovid Butler ("Bob") Horton and Dr. César Vargas Calderón. Bob had just graduated from the University of California, where he had done some work in botany. Physically he was a bit on the short and slight side, while Harvey was the reverse. Thus they complemented each other physically and in every way made a good team. César was the Professor of Botany and Director of the Botanical Museum at the University of Cuzco, in the Andes of southeastern Peru. He still holds that position and in the intervening years has become an acknowledged authority on the vegetation of the Peruvian Andes. During those years we have been continuously in touch via my frequent visits to Peru. Two years ago Betty and I were with him in Cuzco when its ancient university presented me with an honorary degree. The gold medallion hanging from a blue silk ribbon that was placed around my neck as a symbol of that honor is among my most cherished *recuerdos* of South America.

Another unit was assigned to Chile. At the beginning Drs. Carlton R. Worth and John L. Morrison represented the Chilean party. Later on, Rodolfo Wagenkneckt, a Chilean naturalist, joined them. Carl was on leave from the faculty of Rutgers University. He had a special interest in alpine plants and had collected and studied them in the Rocky Mountains. John was completing work for his doctorate at the University of California; he has for some time been Professor of Forest Botany at Syracuse University. As we shall see, he acquitted himself well on a number of difficult collecting assignments.

The third unit collected along a winding path which began in Peru, traversed Bolivia and Argentina, reached Magellan Strait, and then turned back into southern Chile. The leader of this unit was Walter J. Eyerdam, of Seattle. He is the unadulterated collector and explorer type, with a flair for natural history in general and for shells and plants in particular. With him was Dr. Alan A. Beetle, who is now Professor of Agronomy in the University of Wyoming. With Walter and Alan on their Patagonian adventure was a young Argentine, Eduardo Grondona, at that time an advanced student of botany in the University of La Plata.

The various North American members of the six Andean expeditions have traveled to the south both by sea and by air. Our six companions on the second expedition sailed from San Francisco on the Grace Line's freighter *Capac* for Callao, Peru. During the forty days at sea they improved such proficiency as they had in the Spanish language, and studied maps of the areas in South America where they were to collect and such few books of reference as were then available dealing with the vegetation of those areas. The ship stopped often in Central American ports and, when possible, they went ashore to botanize. I met them in Peru, having arrived there somewhat earlier via Europe and the east coast of South America.

In addition to the expedition party, which occupied practically all passenger space on the *Capac,* there was an American mining man aboard who claimed to have had large South American experience. He immediately saw to it that the most impressionable members of the party were properly prepared for what they were to encounter in the mountains and jungles. On the second day out of San Francisco one of them wrote in his diary: "He told me about some of his terrible experiences among the wild Indians of eastern Peru and Ecuador. He said that a German professor with a good head of hair and a fine large mustache made a trip among the head-shrinking tribes. Nobody knew what happened to him until a few months later his shrunken head was offered for sale in a curio shop in Guayaquil. He also told about the old Quechua Indian who used to work at the Cerro de Pasco mines in Peru. Every day when the noon whistle blew he solemnly urinated in his hands, washed his face, smoothed down his hair, and was ready for dinner. Quite a simple procedure to be sure."

Now, I have heard these identical tales more than once in the smoking rooms of west coast liners when an old timer found the proper audience of tourists. Of course, they may be true.

For a year and a half, beginning a month after Pearl Harbor, I acted as representative of the Department of State's Committee on Inter-American Artistic and Cultural Relations, directed by Nelson A. Rockefeller. My assignment was to coöperate with South American educational institutions. This proved to mean that I gave courses of lectures on botanical topics in universities in Colombia, Peru, Chile, Argentina, and Uruguay and talks, illustrated with films and lantern slides, to audiences of various sorts about such things as our National Parks and botanical gardens, the relation of scientific research to the improvement of agriculture, and student life in North American universities. There were a number of others from the United States who were similarly engaged in South America during a period when this country sought improvement in inter-American relations on all fronts leading, hopefully, to declared support of the Allied war effort by the nations of the other America.

My Spanish was by no means perfect but my more than one hundred and fifty audiences were uniformly courteous, although I detected a smile or two now and then. In this connection, you should realize when traveling abroad, and particularly in Latin America, that your local contacts will feel complimented if you try to do the best that you can in their language. Anyone should be able to acquire at least a smattering of another tongue, and being willing to use it makes a small but real contribution to mutual understanding and good will so essential if the Free World is to survive.

During 1942–1943 I did as much plant collecting as my lecture appointments permitted. As will appear in a later chapter, I had the assistance of Roy D. Metcalf in Colombia and Peru and in the former that of Dr. José Cuatrecasas also. In Argentina Dr. Adrian Ruiz Leal, of Mendoza, made collections of *Nicotiana* in the foothills of the southern Andes. Those various plant-collecting efforts and accomplishments constituted the third Andean Expedition.

The impulse toward a fourth expedition came in 1946 from an invitation to lecture at the University of Colombia. In Colombia, as elsewhere in South America, there is a federal university which is charged with directing higher education throughout the republic; apart, of course, from instruction in private institutions maintained by religious and other groups. My lecturing in Colombia included not only Bogotá, the capital and headquarters of the University of Colombia, but also the Agricultural College in Medellín and the School of Subtropical Agriculture located at that time in Cali. With the assistance of members of the staffs of those institutions I was able to supplement the information concerning the orchids native to Colombia obtained earlier by Roy and Dr. Cuatrecasas. Later I spent some time in Peru and, primarily through the coöperation of Felix Woytkowski, our fourth series of plant explorations there was successfully continued until 1948. More concerning Felix, and his plant hunting, is contained in a subsequent chapter.

Our fifth expedition, in 1951–1952, was confined almost entirely to Chile, and our sixth, 1957–1958, to both that republic and Peru. There was, again, a reason apart from plant hunting that led to the organization of my two most recent South American plant-hunting forays, and it was the same in both instances. In 1943 during our prolonged stay in Chile a movement was on foot to establish a Chilean National Botanical Garden in which elements of the remarkably diverse floras of the nation might be brought together to aid in their scientific study and also to serve as a tourist attraction. Because of distinct differences of opinion, locally, concerning the proper site for the proposed institution, I was asked, as a foreigner with no axe to grind and with experience in botanical garden development and maintenance, to make a recommendation. I did so and negotiated with the owners of the property, who ultimately gave it to the Chilean government. It is a four-hundred-acre tract in the low coastal hills near Valparaiso and nearer Viña del Mar, the so-called "Monte Carlo of South America." Years before, it had been in some part landscaped and planted with exotic trees and shrubs by a wealthy Chilean, and subsequent owners had maintained it remarkably well. It has long been attractive to citizens of the near-by cities, and today, somewhat more developed and better cared for, it is decidedly worth a visit by tourists who have some interest in ornamental horticulture.

Following my selection of the site I was asked to redesign certain portions, suggest the proper development of others, and estimate the annual budget necessary for proper maintenance. This last item gave the government pause and for some years only the irreducible minimum was appropriated. Meanwhile, a local group had become enthusiastic about the scientific, economic, educational, and touristic potentialities of a well-developed and well-maintained National Botanical Garden, and at their instigation I was twice officially invited to return to Chile. I was supposed to propagandize in favor of the project and to push such development as the available funds permitted. The two invitations were followed by the organization, respectively, of the fifth and sixth expeditions.

During both these expeditions, Paul C. Hutchison was my principal collaborator. He is a botanist on the staff of the Berkeley Botanical Garden and from boyhood days has had an enthusiasm for cacti and other types of succulent plants. This predilection resulted, under his direction, in the accumulation at the Garden of the most scientifically important collection of those plants in existence, to which our collections in Chile and Peru have made significant additions. He has become a widely recognized authority on the members of the prickly tribe and is preparing monographs dealing with their character and widespread distribution in Peru and Chile. With Paul in Peru during their recent six months' collecting was William H. ("Bill") Marshall, a Berkeley photographer. Between them, in addition to the important collections of plants they made, over ten thousand negatives—black and white, and Kodachrome—were exposed. Traveling almost exclusively in a specially equipped pickup, they covered almost as many miles from one end of Peru to the other and spent some time in Bolivia also. Their experiences, sometimes unique, in the Peruvian hinterland deserve more attention than limitation of space permits me to give to them in the following chapters.

While Paul and Bill were at work in Peru, Walter renewed his contact with and collecting of the Chilean floras which had begun twenty years before when, as already mentioned, he was a member of the second expedition. I had asked him to meet Betty and me in Valparaiso and spend some months in botanizing the South Chilean vegetation.

In addition to "official" expedition members there were many others in South America who assisted in various ways in forwarding our plant-collecting projects over the past twenty-five years. I am particularly indebted to Drs. Edwyn P. Reed, G. Looser, R. Ferreyra, and R. Aspiazu and Sr. A. Garaventa. In the pages that follow, reference is made to most of them and to their coöperation.

It would be fruitless to attempt an estimate of the total number of miles traversed on land, sea, and in the air by all of us who have shared in the six Andean expeditions—the map showing the combined expedition routes will permit you to do so, if you are so inclined. Certainly, you would have to travel round-trip by air from San Francisco to New York a good many times to log an equivalent total. Of plant material taken in South America and returned to the University of California, the total approximates 100,000 pressed specimens, including duplicates. There were also over 500 packets of seed. Both the specimens and the seeds have been shared with botanical institutions at home and abroad but the most complete collection of what we took will be found in the University's Herbarium and Botanical Garden in Berkeley.

As the map shows, we have crisscrossed Peru in all directions— along the arid coastal plain, from coast to cordillera, in and out of the *montaña* or tropical rain forest. Lima was always a general headquarters and Cuzco a secondary one. We met president and peon, Indians and mixed-bloods, a few compatriots and more Britishers, Germans, Japanese, and Italians. We were charmingly entertained by cultured Peruvians, received many attentions and much valuable assistance from the government, and were usually accepted by the Indians of the Andes and the jungle without particular interest or show of feeling. We learned something of the social and economic problems that face a semitropical country in which the Indian element represents over eighty per cent of the population, where foreign capital has built and controls essential communications and industries, where agricultural labor is exploited, and where lack of adequate transportation facilities still hampers extraction from mountains and forests of much of the great wealth they are known to possess.

In Peru the botanist finds a wide choice of climate and vegetation: first, a coastal desert, containing a remarkable fog-supported winter flora on hills that rim the sea; next, the Andean complex, with foot-hills both dry and moist, an unusually high snow line, great river gorges, and lofty, semiarid plateaus; and, finally, the vast tropical rain forest, with its wealth of lush vegetation. Chile too, has an arid coast line—eight hundred miles of it south of the Peruvian border. The central Andes, which Chile shares with Argentina, rise to supreme heights and along their tremendous north-south extension exhibit wide variations in climate and floras. Interestingly enough, Chile possesses on her southern coast the temperate equivalent of the Peruvian jungle and one of the few extensive temperate rain forests in the world. Between the arid north and wet south and just below the highest point on the Andean backbone of the continent lies the heart of Chile, with its Mediterranean or, if you will, Californian climate. Chile, like Peru, will always be a magnet drawing plant hunters toward her from near and far.

We have worked along more than half of Chile's twenty-eight hundred miles of coast line. Most of the rest is the excessively humid archipelago and narrow Andean coast of the republic's southern extremity, which held little of importance for us. We collected in Chile's highlands and lowlands, on the margins of her deserts, in her wet forests, and in the glorious climate of her central zone.

Approximately six and a half million people live in Chile. The majority possess Spanish-Indian blood, but Chile has no social prob-lem comparable to that which Peru's large Indian population presents. In both Peru and Chile much of the small "upper class" is of Spanish descent. In Chile there is something of a middle class, predominantly of foreign ancestry. To no such extent in Peru can one speak of a middle class interposed between the Indians and the descendants of the conquistadors. In contrast with Peru, a significant portion of the "upper class" is of British, Irish, and German origin.

The coöperation of private citizens and officialdom that we en-joyed in Peru was also offered to us in Chile. As a vacation land,

Chile offers, in particular, her southland where the dense forests of the Andes continue their sweep toward Cape Horn through a marvelous land of snow-covered volcanic peaks and lakes, rivers, and waterfalls—a fisherman's mecca. There is no more magnificent area in the world than the central Andean highlands that culminate in Aconcagua, the highest mountain in the two Americas; in the southern winter it is a skier's paradise.

Apart from modern, gay, and charming Buenos Aires, most visitors from the United States know almost nothing of Argentina, that mighty land that spreads westward from her capital to the Andes, north to the warm, moist borders of the semitropics, and south to the cold, blustery Magellanic Provinces. Therefore, of course, they have no idea that some significant geographic analogies can be drawn between "the Argentine," as the British like to call it, and their homeland. For example, Argentina's sub- to semitropical areas may be likened, in varying degrees, to Florida and the adjacent states and to part of California; upper Patagonia to our Southwest; the northern portion of her South Atlantic coast to the southern section of our North Atlantic one; her Paraná River to our Mississippi; her Andes to our Rocky Mountains. To stretch the parallelism to include descendants of ancient floras, Argentina has her Araucarias and we have our Sequoias. These analogies and the progressive and independent attitude of her people are responsible for the considerable appeal which Argentina makes to North Americans who have opportunity to know her rather intimately. They also give, in terms of our own geography, a generalized picture of the types of terrain that the plant hunter encounters there.

We have come to know a fair cross-section of the land and the people of Argentina, besides seeing and studying the vegetation of all the geographical subdivisions already mentioned. As elsewhere in the other South American republics where we worked, high and low alike were kind and helpful. Colleagues in universities and other institutions placed at my disposal their technical advice and knowledge of the botany of their areas, as well as the valuable collections of plants in their fine museums.

Argentina has an area equal to almost one third of the United States and greater than Peru and Chile combined, with a population somewhat greater than the combined populations of those two republics. In the Western Hemisphere only New York exceeds Buenos Aires in population, which means that altogether too large a proportion of Argentina's people live in the *Capital Federal*. Most are Argentine-born and of European descent. The British community is numerous, as are both the Italian and the German communities.

Some important collecting was done in Bolivia, but very little in Paraguay and Uruguay. At different times, the Prince, Walter, Paul, and Bill spent a total of over three months in various parts of Bolivia.

Bolivia, like Peru, contains abrupt transitions between exceedingly different climatic zones. As a result, there is a series of distinct and interesting floras. At the proper season, much of the six thousand square miles of twelve-thousand-foot plateau, or *puna*, shows a transient vegetation containing many strange and often beautiful plants adapted in form and structure to meet the demands of a semiarid alpine environment. Then there are the *valles*, or highland valleys; the tropical valleys, or *yungas*, where the northern mountains are drained by the Amazon; the fertile Chaco to the south; and, dominating all, the two majestic Andean ranges, with peaks rising to twenty thousand feet.

Now that the "why," "who," and "where" have been answered, we can proceed with our far-flung quest for the South American Nicotianas and for the multitude of other plants of scientific, agricultural, and ornamental importance that await the plant hunter in the Andes.

Harvey finds that the flower stalk of the lost *Nicotiana* of the northern Peruvian Andes measures almost five feet in length.

Flowers of the South American wild relatives of the tobacco plant (left to right): *Nicotiana longiflora, rustica, noctiflora, glauca, sylvestris, glutinosa.*

The Journal of Business		Journal of Human Resources	
JULY '94	80Q0194	SPRING '94	79Y0663
APRIL '94	78N0278	WNTR '94	76Z0325
JAN '94	76N0002	FALL '93	75Q0254

Journal of Business Strategy		Journal of International Business Studies	
JULY-AUGUST '94	80Q1324	SUMMER '94	79V0821
MAY-JUNE '94	78Z1351	SPRING '94	78P0283
MARCH-APRIL '94	77S1372	WINTER '93	75U0499
JAN-FEB '94	76Y0777		
NOV-DEC '93	75Q1046		

Journal of Commercial Lending		Journal of Management	
JULY '94	80N0002	SUMMER '94	80S0393
JUNE '94	79S0002	SPRING '94	78P1077
MAY '94	78U0138	WINTER '93	75U0282
APRIL '94	77X0002	FALL '93	74W0599
MARCH '94	77N0034		
FEB '94	76U0002	Journal of Managerial Issues	
JAN '94	75W1885	SPRING '94	78N0002
DEC '93	75P0002		
NOV '93	74W0161	Journal of Marketing	
		JULY '94	79Z2287
Journal of Consumer Affairs		APRIL '94	77V2404
SUMMER '94	78T0519	JAN '94	75Z1210
WINTER '93	74X0002		
		Journal of Marketing Research	
Journal of Consumer Research		MAY '94	78S4035
JUNE '94	79Q4042	FEB '94	76X2380
		NOV '93	74W3221
		Journal of Money, Credit & Banking	
		MAY '94	78U0516

2

THE LOST NICOTIANA

IN THE BOTANICAL MUSEUM in Berlin-Dahlem I once came across a folder full of pressed specimens of *Nicotiana*. The label on the folder read, "Unnamed Species." Some were not Nicotianas at all. Others were, and I was able to name all but one of them. It was a *Nicotiana*, right enough, but entirely different from anything in the genus I had ever seen or heard about. A collector's label was attached, and it read, in German: "Weberbauer, No. 7015, collected on the grass-steppe, at 12,500 feet, between Huamachuco and Angasmarca, Peru, July 6, 1914." In pencil on the corner of the label someone had written, "*Nicotiana thyrsiflora.*"

There was no such name recorded for a *Nicotiana*; the collector I knew only as the author of a book about the plants of Peru; the place where he had collected it meant absolutely nothing to me. How far beyond my imagination, that day in the German museum, was the sequel to this first acquaintance with *Nicotiana thyrsiflora.* How could I have imagined that I should come to know Weberbauer intimately; that he should try, and try again, and finally fail to get for me the seed of this totally unknown *Nicotiana*; that I and my associates should go to Peru in search of it, and that this search should continue over a number of years and mean long days of hardship, frustration, and bitter disappointment before it was successful?

From that moment I first saw it as a dried specimen, I knew that I must have the seed of *Nicotiana thyrsiflora* so that I could grow it, see it as a living plant, study it, and compare it with its relatives already growing in the University's Botanical Garden. I wrote to the collector, Dr. Augusto Weberbauer, and finally he replied. He told me that

21

many years before, on a collecting trip into the high plateaus of northern Peru, he had seen only a plant or two of something that he had not even recognized as a *Nicotiana*. He collected it, dried and pressed it, and sent it to Germany to be named; but until I told him that I had discovered the plant in the Berlin museum he had had no news of it. He kindly offered to try to find someone in the remote region in which it grew who would try to get seed for me. The implication was, however, that there was not much hope of success— and so it proved. More than a decade was to go by after I saw the dried plant before I saw a living one.

The territory in which this elusive *Nicotiana* was first found and where over twenty years later it was rediscovered, first by the Prince and again by Harvey and Bob, is not tourist country. From the northern desert along the coast the land rises steeply into the high altitudes of the western range of Peru's Andes. Behind this outermost range are the plateaus, or punas, through which the mighty Rio Marañón has dug a monster gorge, almost at the beginning of its long journey to join the Amazon and then flow on to the Atlantic. These high punas are cold and wind-swept. They can support only the hardiest of plants. But in the bottoms of deep, steep-walled valleys that intersect them is the jungle, for this *Nicotiana thyrsiflora* country lies only eight degrees south of the equator, and that means that all life at seven thousand feet and below is tropical. Early one December, the Prince went into this north Peruvian hinterland. He was to make the first attempt to rediscover *Nicotiana thyrsiflora*.

In Trujillo, on the coast, the only transportation eastward was a big open truck loaded with dynamite and headed for the mines near Parcoy, on the far side of the Marañón. Concerning the long, rough journey, the Prince wrote, "To get an unrestricted view of the countryside, I rode all the way on top of the dynamite rather than in the cab with the driver. At 3:00 A.M. we pulled into our destination, Huamachuco. It was too late to rouse the staff of the hotel; therefore I slept in the fiendishly designed cab of the truck."

He had letters of introduction to leading citizens of Huamachuco, and one of them worked to the extent of eliciting a promise to find a horse, a mule, and a guide for the *Nicotiana thyrsiflora* hunt. "But," said his new friend, "it will take time, *Señor*, it will take time. Perhaps the day after tomorrow all will be arranged."

On the third morning the cavalcade was organized—the Prince on a small, anemic horse; the plant presses and other baggage on the back of a tiny burro; and Pedro, the Indian guide, on foot. As their trail wound up the hillside out of the city, the general debility of the horse and burro immediately came to light. When at last the top of the first steep ascent was reached they abruptly halted, with heaving sides and drooping heads.

From this first eminence the view was superbly expansive. To the north a sea of green ridges rolled away toward a misty horizon, beneath which lay the Ecuadorian border. To the east, the high ranges behind the Marañón rose abruptly from vast tablelands. Far to the south a great white mass, the Cordillera Blanca, hung suspended above a foreground of cloudy ranges, themselves mighty but insignificant by comparison.

That first day they rode and walked slowly toward the twelve-thousand-foot plateau. Somewhere on it the plant they sought should be waiting for them. For many miles there was no human habitation. At dusk they found a group of miserable huts on the shores of a little, dark glacial lake. It lay in a cup formed by black, rough cliffs so steep and so high that only at noon could the sun illuminate its waters. In the gathering darkness it thoroughly deserved its name, Laguna Negra.

Pedro hailed the huts, and from one of them slowly and cautiously appeared three incredibly dirty young women. They were very shy, almost like wild creatures. Clearly, they were terrified almost out of their wits by the sudden appearance of perhaps the only strangers they had ever seen. No persuasion on Pedro's part could gain permission for himself and the Prince to occupy one of the huts during the freezing night that was already descending upon them. After some search they found, at a little distance, a shedlike pigsty. It was inhabited by many black pigs. The Prince remarks in his diary, "They were not at all unwelcome as foot warmers, for the night was windy and bitterly cold. Next morning when I tried to perform my ablutions in the pigsty trough there was a quarter inch of ice to break."

The next day was a severe strain on all of them. A thirteen-thousand-foot pass had to be crossed. The cold wind that had arisen during the night continued to blow with steadily increasing violence. They were now where *Nicotiana thyrsiflora* had been collected by Weberbauer. But despite a sharp lookout and many digressions from the trail into promising *quebradas*—draws and deep ravines—they saw nothing that even faintly resembled the plant they were hunting. Beyond the pass the country looked very unpromising. Open, rolling expanses were covered as far as the eye could reach with nothing but stiff, coarse grasses.

That night they were hospitably received by a friend of Pedro's who lived with his family in a large, low mud dwelling. All the next day they searched without success for *Nicotiana thyrsiflora*. In the afternoon the terrain gave more promise, with less grass and more rocky, broken hillsides. A few strange and charming alpine shrubs and herbs were in flower. These the Prince collected. They served somewhat to relieve the discouragement that was beginning to oppress him. Again that night they found a friendly Indian family and slept warm, if not altogether in comfort. The evening meal consisted of boiled *cui*, or guinea pig, served with the small, yellow, nutritious potatoes of the Andes and a hot peppery sauce. The whole was washed down with *chicha*, the homemade corn beer of the Peruvian highlands.

It is depressing enough to go out into the chicken yard and slaughter a hen who from long acquaintance treats you as a friend, but sadder still is it to wring the neck of a bedfellow. For the Andean guinea pigs are often bedded down on the dirt floor of the hut with the members of the family. In one corner is placed a pile of the stiff but succulent leaves of Puyas and Pitcairnias, members of the Pineapple family, on which the guinea pigs are fattened and under which they live and breed. All night long the little demons squeak and scratch and rustle among the spiny leaves. Periodically, they dash out from their home in the corner to investigate the hands and faces of family and guests bedded down on the floor. With sharp claws, unfamiliar odor, and snuffling noses, they trot back and forth over faces and any other exposed surfaces. Their unwelcome attentions, added to those of innumerable fleas and other unidentified bloodletters, make sleep hard to capture in the fetid air of native Andean habitations. Only extreme fatigue will bring oblivion.

The next morning the Prince was treated to a typical Indian breakfast. It was eaten under a small arbor which served as combined kitchen and dining room. The family and their guests squatted in the dirt around three half-gourds. One was full of coarse barley meal, another held a thick gruel made of boiled potatoes, and in the third was a thinner barley soup. Wooden spoons, not enough to go around and therefore shared, were handed about. The spoon first was wetted in one warm liquid or the other and then dipped into the dry meal. Or, using a different technique, a mouthful of meal was taken and then moistened by a spoonful of potato or barley gruel. More than once I have found this to be a hearty and sustaining repast. Hygienic considerations make it hard for me to swallow.

There followed three days of fruitless search for *Nicotiana thyrsi-flora* and long, hard climbs on bad trails. The Prince was thoroughly tired and discouraged. The little horse was fast giving out and could be ridden only for a short time and then only on level ground. The burro began to exhibit every meanness he had inherited from a long line of reprehensible ancestors. Pedro was beginning to be restive and ill-humored. He continually complained of sore feet and insisted upon starting home. Actually, it was the fear of running out of *coca* which afflicted him. His supply of those dried leaves from which he chewed cocaine was low and without them he was lost. Altogether, the Prince knew that he could count on only one day more in the high country. In desperation he sought the advice of a quizzically keen, morose old Indian whom they met along the trail and who, after some urging, was willing to use a little Spanish. The Prince repeated over and over again the best and simplest description of *Nicotiana thyrsiflora* that he could devise. But the old Indian only shook his head. Finally, however, he pointed out the direction of a trail which he said would lead them toward the gorge of the Marañón. Along this trail he seemed to think that considerable vegetation was to be found.

The trail which the Indian had designated led them rapidly to still higher ground. Again the view was magnificent. In the foreground, beyond the barren, rocky ridges, a partly wooded quebrada sloped down to a curiously formed, isolated hill. Behind it rose range upon range of purple mountains gradually increasing in height until they merged into the enormous, craggy mass of the Ancash cordillera. In the farthest distance the glittering apex of Huascarán towered twenty thousand feet into the pale-blue sky.

The country rapidly became wilder and extremely rough and broken. The Prince examined carefully every likely spot where, in the protection of high outcroppings of rock or in the narrow bottoms of steep quebradas, some vegetation managed to maintain itself. As the day wore on they approached the summit of Tres Cruces Pass near the Marañón. It had been agreed that once there the hunt would be abandoned.

Now the trail became almost vertical and terribly rocky. With heads down, man and beast tramped doggedly onward and upward. Automatically, but without much enthusiasm, the Prince at every few steps glanced first to the right and then to the left to note the vegetation. One such glance showed him a group of low shrubs and growing up through them what looked to be a giant yellow-flowered foxglove. He was so tired, so convinced that the hunt had completely failed, that at first this extraordinary plant, so different from anything he had seen on the punas, failed to interest him. Then he stopped and looked again. Instantly he knew that he had found *Nicotiana thyrsiflora.*

It stood seven feet high, a tall wand, leafless for the upper half of its length and covered below with long, narrow, wavy-margined, somewhat twisted leaves. The top of the stem was enlarged for two feet into a mass of small yellow flowers tightly fitted together. He had come across nothing like this during the previous three days. Such a large and distinctive plant would have been seen literally for miles across the almost level plateaus he had been traversing. So, at least, he had the satisfaction of knowing that he had not overlooked the object of his plant hunting. In addition, he realized that the living plant was quite different from the mental picture of it that I had drawn from the dried, pressed specimen in the Berlin museum.

However true it may be that the charm of anticipation often exceeds the joy of realization in most human affairs, this relationship is always reversed in plant hunting. For a dyed-in-the-wool collector there is nothing so solidly satisfying as the termination of a successful quest. All the strain and weariness, all the aggravations small and large, all the defeats and disappointments, are instantly forgotten. His eyes gleam, he gloats, he begins to whistle, he may even indulge in a bit of affectionate profanity. If some snake-bite remedy is handy he is likely to take a drink—or even two. The Prince never told me just what happened when he found his plant, except that he promptly gave Pedro a sol by way of *gratificación*. Probably his satisfaction was tinged with a shade of disappointment because this one plant of *Nicotiana thyrsiflora*, the only one in sight, did not bear any ripe seed. He knew that it was the seed that I wanted.

The afternoon had gone and the evening winds began to blow chill across the alpine moors. All day the trail had passed only one or two deserted and tumble-down huts. Pedro had never been so far from home and had no knowledge of human habitations in the neighborhood. Hungry and cold, they lay down. In such shelter from the icy wind as bunches of tall, rough *ichu* grass provided, they tried to sleep. With the first light, the hunt for seeding plants of *Nicotiana thyrsiflora* was continued, with absolutely no success. Indeed, they found only one other specimen. It was a poor thing, not in flower and with only a few empty seed capsules left over from the previous year's blooming.

I am certain that if the Prince had been alone or free to remain near Tres Cruces, nothing would have kept him from continuing the search. But Pedro had broken down completely. Long-continued and unaccustomed exertion, lack of food, the severe exposure of the previous night, and, especially, many hours without coca, had left him in such a weakened condition that without help and encouragement he could never have reached Huamachuco. There was nothing to do but strike across country at the best pace Pedro and the animals could maintain in the hope of reaching civilization before nightfall. They made it, but it was a bad day for all of them.

In Huamachuco the condition of Pedro as well as that of the horse and mule excited so much public comment that it was hopeless to seek other animals or another guide. Who could be expected to go out again with this "gringo loco" to climb about in impossible places hunting for nothing more exciting than weeds? And so, with reluctance and keenly disappointed at his failure to fulfill the most important part of his assignment, the Prince returned to Lima.

I did what I could to cheer him up. I proposed another trip to the *Nicotiana thyrsiflora* country at a better season, but he was inconsolable and worried himself into a decline. I tried to persuade him to forget plant hunting for a month or more and, in particular, urged him to stay out of the high country for a while. But he must have known that hard work was his only salvation. At any rate, when next I heard from him he was in the Andes of southeastern Peru and full of enthusiasm for the collecting there.

In remote and dangerous regions and at high altitudes, where your only contact is with primitive people, the psychological hazard of plant hunting can often become more acute than the physical one.

A fine physique and some enthusiasm for the work are not enough. It is difficult to tell in advance whether one possesses the necessary combination of steadfastness of purpose and adaptability of mind and temper that will enable him to carry on under adverse conditions for months on end. Almost complete intellectual isolation, added to continuous physical strain, ultimately comes to make heavy demands on the disposition.

The rediscovery of *Nicotiana thyrsiflora* by the Prince was quite a triumph, but without seed of this strange species which, so far as I could tell, was truly a rarity in a most isolated subandean region, all I actually had was a pressed and dried duplicate of the specimen I had seen in a Berlin Museum. With seed I could grow the plant in California, establish its identity and relationships with the other South American Nicotianas, and assign it a position in the picture of the origins and evolution of the Nicotianas which I was anxious to complete. In other words, it was essential that another attempt be made to find *Nicotiana thyrsiflora*. As we shall soon see, a few years later Harvey and Bob made it.

They traveled by plane to Trujillo. No wonder air travel is so popular on the west coast. Across its deserts and over its high mountains, flying not only reduces the time of your journey by hundreds of per cents, but, even more important, it reduces to a minimum the discomforts and dangers of overland travel through exceedingly inhospitable country. Of course, there are sometimes plenty of bumps in air pockets, more than one hair-raising sideslip, and for a few moments at a time extreme altitudes that seem to make the heart go "dot and carry one." But when these disquieting things happen, you just look down and visualize what a traveler would have to endure on the hot sands or across the lofty mountain passes that you see passing in review below you.

On the morning following their arrival in Trujillo they arranged for transportation to Santiago de Chuco. This would bring them well up into the mountains and also into the *Nicotiana thyrsiflora* country. For the first few hours, the wide and moderately good gravel road ran through hot, boulder-strewn desert, which was decorated only with columnar cacti. Then they began to climb up a valley wall and the road became a shelf clinging to rock cliffs. With even this first slight increase in altitude, trees and shrubs, but no herbs, began to appear. Low algarroba trees (*Prosopis*) were common and in places grew in grovelike aggregations. Among them they saw *palo santo* and *Bombax*, which themselves made small groves in places. *Acacia* and *Capparis* were among the more scattered elements of the vegetation. Higher still, and now well into the mountains, the road entered the "rainy-green" shrubland. This grew more and more dense and finally merged into a region of evergreen shrubs and perennial herbs with which the valleys in particular were entirely filled.

Near one of the villages in which they stopped, a yellow-green-flowered herb attracted their attention. It proved to be the first tobacco relative they had come across on their trip into northern Peru. It was *Nicotiana paniculata* and its discovery there was the first evidence that this species grew so far north and in country well behind its characteristic coastal area of distribution. In the middle of the afternoon the shrubland was left behind and the road flattened out onto the cold, drizzly, monotonous puna.

At the American-owned mining camp of Shorey, the road forked. On the left it turned northward to Huamachuco, to the right toward Santiago de Chuco, their destination, and, according to agreement in Trujillo, the destination of the truck also. But, in the offhand manner of Peruvian mountain transportation, the original understanding had no validity. The truck was going to turn left to Huamachuco, and Harvey and Bob could get off and wait for another truck to come along that might take them to Santiago de Chuco, or they could stay aboard, or they could go to blazes, just as they pleased!

They disembarked. Their baggage was tumbled by the roadside and the truck rumbled away. On such occasions, Harvey could always be relied upon to repeat a refrain he had learned in France in 1918: "We might as well be here as where we are." On other occasions, particularly when the going had become rough and the situation needed to be enlivened, he was likely to call for a momentary halt and inquire of his companions: "Are people older in the mountains than they are in the summer?" This was usually good for a laugh, or at least a grin.

Actually, they had fallen into the lap of luxury. The Shorey camp was idle and under the care of a mining engineer, Ricardo Schuster, to whom Harvey had a letter of introduction. The warm Schuster home with its warmer welcome provided a striking contrast to the cold, foggy, desolate out-of-doors at this twelve-thousand-foot elevation. While the afternoon light held, the botanists went out onto the puna and collected a few species of grasses, a gentian, and several composites that eked out an existence by keeping close to the soil. A few llamas and chickens represented the only animal life. At six o'clock an elaborate tea was waiting for them. At nine came a wonderful chicken dinner. With stories and reminiscences the cheerful party lingered over the dinner table until after eleven.

Don Ricardo told them that possibly a truck would be coming through for Santiago de Chuco that night. But when midnight arrived without its making an appearance, beds were prepared in a spare room and the *botánicos* turned in. The room was very cold. They put on all the sweaters and the wool socks in the duffel bags and were dozing off when Don Ricardo came in to announce the arrival of the truck. Half awake, they pulled themselves and their belongings together. Then came prolonged farewells by the family, all of whom had dressed and come out to see them off. Finally they climbed into the large covered truck among freight and other passengers.

The heavily loaded truck got slowly under way. As it left the mining settlement there was a terrific crash and it came to a dead halt. To the passengers inside, the crash sounded like an exploding bomb. However, nothing had really happened except that the road passed under a viaduct designed for hauling ore and the roof of the truck was an inch too high to clear it. After much maneuvering they managed to start on again. From that point the truck followed precarious shelf roads where they prayed that the driver was keeping thoroughly awake. At three in the morning he brought them safe and sound to the hotel in Santiago de Chuco.

The morning sun showed Santiago de Chuco to be an extensive city of low buildings with red tile roofs, eucalyptus trees forming a fringe, and a colorful but very dry mountain landscape. It certainly was no place in which to linger. The near-by vegetation was poor and dry, and collecting was not promising. Local information suggested that the Cachicadán area, five hours farther on, was much better. But this meant horses to ride and a mule to carry the collecting equipment, and in Santiago de Chuco almost all such animals had long since been driven off to higher mountain valleys. Harvey and Bob therefore appealed to the city authorities, who actually had a brilliant suggestion to offer. In Cachicadán, they said, there was a Señora Haggenmüller, *una famosa botánica,* who would know what to do. Also, near

Cachicadán the grazing was good and undoubtedly the *bestias* there were more *valientes*. Finally, there was a telephone line to Cachicadán and a messenger could be sent to find the *señora botánica* and bring her to the telephone.

In the Andes the maintenance of a telephone line is a problem because stealing wire of every sort is a recognized outdoor sport. Only the authority of the government can cope with this situation, and therefore its lines are the only ones that connect all the larger communities. In Santiago de Chuco an elderly lady was in charge of the mysteries of the telephone, the operation of which attracted a number of loafers who crowded the door of the dirt-floored office when Harvey went in. With unexpected efficiency on the part of the operator, the desired connection was completed in about two hours. Señora Haggenmüller proved anxious to coöperate and promised to send horses and mules the next day if possible or on the day after that for certain.

True to the "for certain" promise, a *mozo* arrived with two saddle horses and a pack mule. They loaded up immediately and were off. The airline distance to Cachicadán was not great but the road was extremely circuitous. It threaded in and out, zigzagged down into a steep gorge and then climbed out again, always presenting superb mountain views against white clouds in an intensely blue sky. As they slowly approached Cachicadán, more vegetation appeared. A yellow-flowered *Stenolobium*, a member of the family to which the trumpet vine belongs, was the dominant shrub, and both red and blue Salvias mingled their spots of color with the yellow tufts of Calceolarias.

Cachicadán was a small place surrounded by magnificent mountains. The houses were scattered on a hill slope and embowered in a eucalyptus grove. Hot springs bubbled up from the different rock formations; near one was a bathhouse and a pool through which hot water ran continuously. Here was one place in the Andes where bathing was popular, despite the fact that it was always difficult to get the water cool enough. The temperature of the pool was regulated by going upstream and diverting either the hot or cold water into other channels until the amount entering the pool was just right.

While her husband was employed in mining operations in various parts of Peru, Señora Haggenmüller led a busy life. It was hard to believe her laughing claim to sixty-five years. Her first duty was the maintenance and management of several small farms located in various areas on the mountainsides. She rode among the surrounding neighborhoods as a sort of agricultural adviser, efficiency expert, homeopathic physician, and Good Samaritan in general and in particular. She maintained excellent gardens in which many introduced as well as native plants were in bloom. There were gentians, valerians, and mints which she used in her medicines. The red *floripondio* (*Datura sanguinea*) and two varieties of the white species (*Datura arborea*), one scented much more strongly than the other, were flowering. Most attractive were several kinds of passionflower which she had introduced from the mountains. Two plants of cultivated tobacco were in bloom. She took a great interest in foreign plants, and remarked that for a long time she had wanted to experiment with various species of *Eucalyptus* and some of the conifers in addition to the cypress which she had been growing. A month later a collection of the seeds she desired was on its way to her from California.

She had great faith in the healing properties of various herbs. On a near-by mountain there were so many of her medicinal plants that she had named it *Cerro Botica* ("Apothecary Mountain"), and this name was used by the natives. She referred to plants in terms of what they were good for rather than by name, although she had also native Quechua designations for most of them. She frequently encountered the use of an abortifacient herb among the mountain women endeavoring to exercise population control. Unfortunately, its use is dangerous and frequently results in a violent contraction of all the muscles of the body, often with fatal consequences. But if she is called in time, an antidotal herb tea of hers will pull the patient through. She seemed reluctant to identify the plants she used and apparently considered them to be a professional secret. She was known for miles around and was highly respected and even revered by the native families, many of whom she had helped in sickness and in health. Everyone called her "La Gringa" and her daughter "Gringa Irma," since they were the only foreigners anywhere in the neighborhood.

The most extraordinary plant in the señora's garden was *Nicotiana thyrsiflora* and the very thing, of course, that Harvey and Bob were looking for. It appeared that years ago, following my original request to Dr. Weberbauer for seed, she had found a colony of this little-known species of *Nicotiana*. She collected seeds and sent them to

Lima. They arrived moldy and lifeless and so had not been forwarded to me; but some of the seed she had saved to grow in her garden. The señora agreed to lead the two botanists to the plants she had found. In other words, the search for *Nicotiana thyrsiflora* was practically at an end almost before it had begun.

At daybreak next morning two horses were waiting at the *pension* for Harvey and Bob. With Señora Haggenmüller, who was mounted on a fine white mare, they were soon off to see *Nicotiana thyrsiflora* on its native heath. Running behind, now and then taking a short cut across zigzags in the trail, was her faithful peon. She had taught him her plant lore, and often entrusted him with collecting the potent roots and leaves when her pharmaceutical supply needed replenishing.

Starting from an elevation of nine thousand feet, the route led up quebradas and across ridges to higher altitudes. Now and then they passed tiny mountain-slope fields of maize, *habas* (beans), *papas* (potatoes), and *ocas* (*Oxalis tuberosa*). From earliest times ocas have been cultivated in the Andes. The tubers are not large and tend to be more watery than potatoes, but they are quite nutritious and sustaining. But any love for ocas depends upon acquiring a taste for their rather peculiar flavor. Sometimes in the middle of a plantation there would be a pile of boulders supporting a crude wooden cross. Thus the Church left its mark, even on these remote mountainsides. Without the cross the crop might not succeed.

Occasionally they passed a shy Indian shepherdess watching her sheep, one or two or several, never a large flock. Inveterate spinners are the *serranas* (mountain women) throughout Peru. While they tend their sheep, they continually twirl a wooden spindle to fashion a remarkably fine thread from the mass of wool carried in the shawl over their shoulders. The education of the little girls consists in learning at the mother's side the few household arts that will meet the simple requirements of daily existence in the cold, cheerless puna country. Spinning is one of the most important of these arts. Often a little tot of not more than five stands at her mother's knee with a smaller spindle, spinning thread not so smooth, perhaps, as her mother's but strong and serviceable. These little folk of the steppe do not look like children; rather, they are miniature "grownups." Their garments are cut and fashioned like those of their parents. They act like adults. Seldom do you see them at play in groups, and laughter is almost as unusual with them as it is with their elders. Sometimes one wonders whether they have any more voice than the llamas pastured on the mountainsides.

In protected valleys above Cachicadán there were shrubs and small trees. The most familiar in appearance was the Peruvian alder, *Alnus jorullensis,* which supplied most of the fuel used in the village. From the introduced Eucalyptus some wood was obtained when older trees died or branches were shed. A small tree, attractive because of its reddish, papery bark and its unsymmetrical habit of growth, was the *qqueuña (Polylepis incana).* Buddleias also occurred, white on twig and underside of leaf. A low St.-John's-wort, *Hypericum laricifolium,* with needlelike leaves, was everywhere underfoot in the grassy steppe.

The señora then led them gradually upward, still higher into the mountains. Finally she turned her horse into a sheltered valley. She called it "Inca Corral" because all about were the ancient ruins of neatly constructed stone corrals. In the shelter of these Inca walls they found *Nicotiana thyrsiflora*—not one plant, but many plants. Some were small and misshapen, probably because in their youth the goats and sheep that frequented the ruined corrals had trampled them. Others were in their prime, large, vigorous, and much branched. One was almost ten feet high. The inflorescences were sometimes over four feet long, packed with hundreds of flowers. There was abundance of ripe seed. With great satisfaction in the knowledge that the *Nicotiana thyrsiflora* hunt had at last been brought to an entirely successful conclusion, Harvey and Bob leisurely collected the seed, put abundant specimens into the presses, and took many still and motion pictures of the plants in their native environment.

They would now have been glad to return to Cachicadán. The señora, however, had not the slightest idea of going home. It was not even time for luncheon and there was a great deal she proposed to show the visiting *botánicos.* Now that the *Nicotiana thyrsiflora* business was over, she was impatient to be off. Her enthusiasm was so infectious that Harvey and Bob began actually to look forward to the long day in the saddle, which she obviously proposed.

She took them eastward into higher country, through lofty mountain passes, and along the margins of deep ravines. They toiled slowly up onto a saddle between two peaks. On the steep slope hung Inca or pre-Inca terraces, buildings, and fortresses, only partially in ruins. Into the face of smooth cliffs, recesses had been hollowed out by the pre-Columbian inhabitants of this high, exposed, and forbidding mountain retreat. These recesses extended some three feet into the solid granite and were two to three feet square. Did the ancient people use them as places of storage for products of their agriculture, or were they rock tombs? Near by, a vertical depression had been cut into a wall of rock. It was so situated as to command a wide and unobstructed view over the countryside. Large enough to shelter a small man from the rain and wind, was this a stone sentry box from which the approach of an enemy could be seen? Or, in those long-forgotten days, did an overseer stand in this niche to direct and keep to their tasks the agricultural laborers who were cultivating the soil in the narrow terraces below his feet?

In Peru, the innumerable and usually well-preserved evidences of ancient civilizations constantly give rise to speculations concerning the particular significance of certain of these remaining evidences of highly developed and utilitarian cultures. One of the questions that always occurs even to the most casual observer is why so many of the ancient peoples of Peru and the adjacent regions lived exclusively in the high mountain ranges, where life must have been far more difficult than in the lowlands. More than this, why did they so often select as sites for their settlements the steep walls of river gorges or narrow saddles between lofty peaks and ridges? On, or over these, with infinite toil, they had to build terraced fields of imported soil on which their meager alpine crops could be grown, and to them water had to be brought in aqueducts from higher, snow-fed streams and lakes.

The botanists made a halt for luncheon among the caves and ruined terraces. Then on the señora went, still farther across the apparently trackless ridges and quebradas, always climbing. Soon they left the rocky defiles and rode across the puna. At once, strange, massive monuments began to appear, monolithic monuments each of which must have weighed several tons. Near them were many rectangular basins carefully carved out of the basic rock surface of the moors, some of them seven feet square and three feet deep. Each had once been covered with a great slab of granite, fashioned exactly to fit its basin. Often the cover stones had been raised and thrown to one side. In one case the cover had merely been propped up along one edge. All the basins were empty.

According to the señora, only one archaeologist, a German, had,

up to that time, made a study of these moorland relics. He had concluded that the race that left behind these evidences of its presence
and accomplishments was very different from that which culminated
in the Inca civilization, destroyed by Pizarro. He thought of them
not as sun worshipers like the Incas, but as moon worshipers. Harvey's
diary should be quoted at this point:

"I think the German was off the track. How could any race which
undertook to live on those cruelly cold alpine plateaus have failed
to worship the sun? We certainly welcomed every one of its infre-
quent rays. Or were these ancient puna dwellers superromantics, ever
living in a dreamy, moonlight-and-roses reverie. Roses, certainly not,
in this bleak climate, but possibly the Lobelias and gentians which
were blooming in recesses of the ruined monuments. They spoke to
me of days long past when they had been cherished and protected
by a simple people who lived close, all too close, to nature. Perhaps
they used them in their medicine, as the señora today brews from
them some of her herb teas. One she called *corpus hui macho*, effica-
cious in male diseases of the blood and kidneys, the other *corpus hui
hembra*, effective in similar diseases of women. The latter species was
Gentiana stricticaulis."

The botanists were tiring fast. But on the homeward journey,
which was almost as difficult as the outgoing one, they were able to
give more attention to the general character of the country they had
been traversing. There was an intangible something in the aspect of
those remote alpine moors, rocky mountainsides, and pinnacled peaks
of which they began to become conscious—something infinitely elemental and primitive, something with a spiritual quality. It brought
detachment from the ordinary concerns of life. In part this may have
been the influence of a continual series of magnificent, unrestricted
mountain panoramas.

On one side of the trail and then on the other side superb landscapes were always before their eyes. As they topped a lofty ridge and
looked to the south, the panorama held them spellbound. It was almost
the same scene at which the Prince had marveled some years before,
except that they saw it just as the setting sun turned all the foreground into shadow—the white head of Huascarán, seventy miles
away it must have been, and on its left the *Piel de Gato*, or Cat's
Skin, black mountainsides splotched with snow fields, and on its right
the snowy crests of the Cordillera Blanca.

Mountain views were an old story to the señora, and she finally tore them away from this one. With no abatement in vigor and enthusiasm, she pushed on. On the steepest, roughest parts of the trail the tired horses had to be led or dragged along, and the two North Americans were panting for breath much of the time. But not the señora. She talked continuously about the vegetation, the ruins, and the geology of this countryside which she thought of as her very own. When they rode into Cachicadán long after dark, she said: "You are no doubt tired and anxious to rest, so I will not detain you. I still have much work to do." What a rebuke to a retirement plan for sixty-five-year-olds.

I had suggested to Harvey that if their *Nicotiana thyrsiflora* hunt was successful I wanted them to spend additional time in northern Peru to determine something about the geographical range of this practically unknown species. To this end he and Bob decided to make for the city of Hualgayóc, one hundred and twenty-five miles north of Cachicadán and less than half that distance from the Ecuadorian border. To get to the north from Cachicadán they had to return by truck to the coast at Trujillo, travel north to Pacasmayo—an attractive community near the sea, and thence inland to the dry, dusty, not so attractive town of Chépen.

Not the same day, of course, but actually on the *mañana*, the truck in which they had taken passage from Chépen to Hualgayóc started eastward. At the beginning it took them up the valley of the Jequetepeque (pronounced Heck-e-te-*peck*-e) over a road like the one along which they had traveled from Trujillo to Santiago de Chuco. The first night out was spent at San Miguel. In the afternoon of the next day the road left the dry shrubland and came into the high puna they were beginning to know so well. The air was hazy and the sun glowed red through the smoke from distant grass fires. In the dry season herdsmen burn the grass that grows on the steppe, so that when the rains come their llamas and sheep can have better grazing on fresh tender grasses.

A long stop was made for generator repairs on the chilly puna near a village of grass huts constructed by laborers doing pick-and-shovel work on the road. The rest of the trip to Hualgayóc was punctuated with frequent stops, for in spite of all the driver's tinkering the generator refused to show any charge. It seemed obvious that the field or the armature or both were burned out, but nobody could tell the *chófer* anything. He maintained that air of aloofness characteristic of chauffeurs at home and abroad. Nevertheless, he was quite happy to have a gallery of passengers who, with respect and with awe, watched him take the generator apart and then put it together again. To his audience of countrypeople an engine was a bit of manmade magic which would respond only to the will of a superior magician.

As the truck coasted downhill from the puna into the narrow streets of Hualgayóc, the late afternoon sun shone redder still through the smoke and cast an eerie light over the grass-thatch roofs. More than two hundred years had written their record in the cobbled streets and on the ancient dwellings. As the city accumulated antiquity it also accumulated dirt. On the thatch, which was Hualgayóc's most conspicuous and characteristic architectural feature, successive crops of weeds and grasses had come and gone. They had left behind a quantity of humus, which in the dry season sifted down as a brown powder into the streets. But with the coming of the rains there would be a sudden transformation and Hualgayóc's roofs would all be green.

The streets were unbelievably narrow. They had been laid down in a period of Peru's history when there were only two kinds of people, peasants on foot and noblemen on horseback. Therefore the streets needed only to be wide enough for horsemen, foot passengers going to the wall or under the hoofs of the horses as the case might be. There are other cities in Peru that preserve an atmosphere of the Middle Ages, but none can surpass Hualgayóc in the impression of antiquity that it makes upon the foreign visitor. Every vista along its streets carries unreality, but with the authenticity of a Hollywood unreality. An artist with easel or camera might prowl about for days and find always new and appealing compositions, as light and shade play over this quaint old "City of Thatch" and its flanking mountain walls.

So far, Harvey and Bob had seen nothing of *Nicotiana thyrsiflora* along the road. Since the generatorless truck was going on twelve miles beyond Hualgayóc to the town of Bambamarca, they decided to stay aboard in order to see still more of the countryside. The driver had done something so that his engine would start, but that was about all. After a few miles along the road, he decided that more repairs were required. This time he hauled out the generator and fan assembly, gazed at it with passionate resentment, and then, with profane comments, threw it into the back of the truck. He thereupon became doubly an optimist. First, he hoped to keep the engine cool without its fan by coasting all the way to Bambamarca. Second, he hoped to get there in daylight since now he had no headlights. Hualgayóc lies at an elevation of twelve thousand feet and Bambamarca is about three thousand feet lower; but coasting is perilous on a narrow mountain road in Peru where it is often necessary to come to a dead stop in order to make a hairpin turn. In addition, it was not all downhill and there were places where the road had to climb over small ridges.

Coasting out of Hualgayóc, in the open shrubland where goats and sheep were browsing, Harvey and Bob saw a plant or two that looked like *Nicotiana*. As the truck reached some old Italian mines, the driver halted to cool the motor and take the generator to the mine shop on the chance that it could be repaired. Meanwhile, botanizing on the mountainsides was in order. They found two more clumps of the same *Nicotiana* that they had just seen. The plants were badly damaged by grazing animals but what was left of their leaves looked like those of *Nicotiana thyrsiflora*. The driver returned, shook his fist at the generator, threw it back again into the truck, and the party was off once more. From then on they often saw the Nicotianas, but all were low and bushy and none had the vigor or foxglovelike inflorescences so characteristic of the plants at Cachicadán. It was getting dark and the other passengers became fearful of negotiating in the coming darkness any more of the difficult road than was absolutely necessary. They could not be blamed, because it had become another of those narrow shelves hollowed or built out from steep cliffsides. The sheer drop on the outside of the road was anywhere from five hundred to a thousand feet. Obviously, the chófer could not stop for plant collecting.

The truck crept slowly toward the lights of Bambamarca, far below. Bob impersonated a headlight by hanging out one side of the truck and flashing his spotlight. Sometimes, where the road was particularly narrow or otherwise especially treacherous, a passenger or two climbed down and walked ahead to pick out the best ruts for the truck to follow. It was a fine clear evening. The distant hills were illuminated by the grass fires. On the whole, they considered it quite an experience, enjoyable in a way and also not so enjoyable.

Next morning in Bambamarca they hired horses and rode back along the road to examine and collect the Nicotianas seen the previous evening. The day was clear and bright. The haze from the burning grass had been dissipated during the night. Dry hills supported dusty shrubs, a few in flower. It was a *Lantana-Rubus-Eupatorium* type of vegetation, which looked weedy now but gave promise of a botanically interesting countryside when the rains set in. The formations were mostly limestone—some chalky, some dolomite—and the boulders were wind- and sand-etched. Now and then groups of boulders simulated tombs, and at a distance spots on the mountainsides suggested burying grounds. Sometimes whole mountainsides showed regular furrows, as though white clay had been turned up by a plow, where the layers of limestone were tilted on edge and irregularly weathered. The lower hills were superbly colored—red hills, vermilion hills, chalk-white hills. To the south they saw a few extraordinary rock pinnacles formed by differential weathering and colored white and scarlet like some of those in Zion and Bryce national parks. Now and then on the hillsides there were pure stands of the cosmopolitan bracken fern, but it was quite dry and weather-beaten and stood only knee high.

The Nicotianas proved to be *Nicotiana thyrsiflora*—there was absolutely no doubt about it; but only one out of hundreds was equivalent to those they had seen near Cachicadán. The rest were large shrubby growths without a prominent main stem. This was due largely to injury by sheep and goats and llamas. The branches and stems were quite brittle and probably were annually broken off in quantity. They were constantly exposed to hot, drying winds, in contrast with those the señora had found for them that appeared to seek protection from wind. They had now established a northern station for this *Nicotiana*. How much farther north, perhaps well into Ecuador, it can be found I do not know.

As soon as the *Nicotiana* had been taken care of, with the necessary seed collections and specimens and photographs, they turned to some general plant collecting. It is peculiar how an absorbing hunt for some one particular plant will almost completely blind the collector to the near-by presence of other, perhaps equally interesting or attractive, species. Thus, they had entirely overlooked a fine orange-flowered *Stenomesson* on the ride out from Bambamarca. But on the return journey they saw it in quantity blooming along the edges of the road-cuts above their heads. Promptly dismounting, they dug two sackfuls of the bulbs. The tying of the sacks to the saddles was just completed when they heard a truck coming around the turn of the road behind them. The horses had been hired from an outlying hacienda and even the sound of a truck made them nervous. There was not enough room for the truck to pass, even if the horses had been willing to let it approach them. For a number of miles there would be no chance either to climb the cliff on one side or to descend on the other. Going downhill, the truck had picked up considerable speed, and the truck driver gave no indication of being willing to slow down. In other words, there was nothing to do but keep well ahead, and the horses agreed entirely with this proposition. They immediately went into a gallop and ran away from the rumbling menace behind them. Flopping plant presses, camera cases, and sacks of bulbs only added to the consternation of the horses and their riders. It became a mad race. The horses were so terrified that anything might have happened. Just as Bob and Harvey were about to be unhorsed, a level stretch of brushland appeared beside the road. They pulled the horses out into it, and the race was over.

This was their first and last gallop in the highlands. Usually one has to exercise all his ingenuity to get much in the way of motion out of the underfed, lazy Andean four-footed type of transportation.

As they approached the town they began to think that "all roads lead to Bambamarca." Along every mountain trail the Indians, dressed in fiesta costume, were converging on the town. The women carried children in the shawls on their backs and bundles in their arms; the men carried packages and jugs. It seemed impossible that so many people could come from the neighboring mountains, which always appeared to be sparsely populated. But they kept on coming and coming until late into the night. The next morning still more drifted in. Upon inquiry it appeared that this was the Sunday when an especially grand fiesta occurred at the near-by Hacienda de Chala.

The Bambamarca market that Sunday was one of the greatest of the year. Not only the plaza but all the streets of the town were crowded. The women wore multicolored full woolen skirts, shawls, and silly little white straw hats. The men were draped in cinnamon-brown ponchos with huge white hats above. Almost all of them were full-blooded Indians.

Hundreds of women squatted on the ground in the plaza with their wares spread out before them. Whether they sold anything or not seemed to make no difference. The main business was gossip with friends and neighbors. Only a few kinds of commodities were on sale, but most of these were displayed in quantity. There were piles of potatoes, some dark-red, some light-red, some yellow, but all small in size. There were mounds of white, mealy pellets, representing what was left of potatoes that had been frozen in the high mountains and then washed and dried. These dessicated potatoes produce what is called *chuño*, a staple article of diet in the puna country and elsewhere in the Andes. For fifty centavos (in those days about ten cents, U.S.) you could buy a bundle of rye straw sufficient to make yourself a new hat. Little heaps of powdered aniline dyes attracted the mountain women who had spun enough yarn to weave a new skirt and were hoping to make the neighbor ladies jealous with the brilliance of its rainbow hues. For the men's ponchos the somber brown dye extracted from the native walnut, *Juglans peruviana*, was good enough.

There were piles of dried corn, the ears always small, but brightly colored. There were little bundles of green alfalfa and of green barley straw for those buyers high enough in the social stratification to ride on their own ponies or donkeys. Pigs, goats, sheep, and chickens were for sale "on the hoof." One woman's sole stock in trade consisted of six heads of teasel, the thistlelike heads of *Dipsacus fullonum* used in carding wool. This plant, a native of Europe, has been carried over the world wherever wool is produced. The teasel market appeared to be on the bearish side. In the morning she had six heads, at noon she still had six. Profits in general must have been meager.

In the larger stores of North American cities, tired shoppers may refresh themselves at the soft-drink counter or in the lunchroom. In that respect the Bambamarca market was up to date. For five centavos you could buy a "pickup" in the form of a ladleful of *caldo*, a soup with ingredients you knew better than to investigate. For another five centavos there were plate dinners with choice of boiled potato, rice, hunk of *charqui* (jerked meat), leg of guinea pig, or even a morsel of chicken. The men always found it necessary to wash everything down with another five centavos' worth of *chica*. For the foreigner, the safest bet was a small ear of corn on the cob, called *choclo*, which also cost five centavos.

The "gringos" were much interested in this remarkable concourse of mountain people, and in their wares. The Indians were equally interested and stared silently but raptly at the two oddly dressed, pale-skinned foreigners who were so restless and who kept continually pointing their mysterious cameras at somebody or some thing. Children cried when they saw them and ran away; dogs barked at them; a gang of older and bolder children followed them about. Some of the men knowingly explained to one another that the people of Bambamarca were being highly honored; undoubtedly their faces would soon be shown in the cinema palaces of the world. A policeman offered his assistance in making the grand spectacle appear in its best light. For him this market was the most important event of the year. He considered it well worthy of being pictured to all foreigners not fortunate enough to visit the Bambamarca *feria* on this, its grand fiesta day.

In the afternoon the crowds gradually drifted out of town, over a bridge and up a hill along the trail that led to Chala, center of the celebration. Grogshops along the way did a riotous business, even though most of the celebrants carried their own jugs of chicha. A Peruvian Indian's idea of "whoopee" is to acquire a fried guinea pig and a gallon of chicha and then foregather with his neighbors similarly provisioned. When between twelve and fifteen hundred are thus congregated, that makes a rattling good fiesta. Chicha provides the Indian with a feeling of balmy contentment. All's well with that world with which on ordinary days he must contend. His face muscles relax into a smile. He may go so far as to laugh boisterously, slap his neighbor on the back, and even embrace him. Although he is ordinarily uncommunicative and often sullen, chicha makes the Peruvian highlander positively loquacious. The jabbering of hundreds in their strange, guttural Quechua tongue reminds one of the din produced by colonies of parakeets and macaws in the Amazonian forests. There was dancing everywhere—most of it go-as-you-please, or at least not conforming to any set pattern. Some couples, however, danced the graceful handkerchief dance, *la marinera*.

Next day, while the town was holding its head and beginning to sober up, Harvey and Bob left Bambamarca and headed north to Chota. They were outfitted with two saddle horses, two pack horses, and a general nuisance who called himself their guide. The country between the two towns, indeed the whole expanse of mountains and valleys roundabout, was almost completely barren. For centuries it had been grazed and cultivated. No doubt, in the remote past even more intensive cultivation had been practiced. Many of the hillsides were red and yellow where erosion had carried off the surface soil and exposed the rocky substratum. Again there were square miles of limestone outcrop weathered to a fairly even level, with giant furrows and ridges. Prominences like tombstones appeared again here. At a distance the gray rock masses could sometimes be mistaken for flocks of sheep pasturing on the mountainsides.

They passed rows of scattered stones that indicated the course of ancient fences, as did also lines of barberry and a species of *Mutisia*, a member of the Sunflower family. Barberry is common throughout the Peruvian Andes, and some of the spinier species are used in hedges. A shrubby *Mutisia* with long thorns is often built into barricades against grazing animals. The most successful plant along the trail was *Iochroma grandiflora*, long ago introduced into horticulture and much esteemed in frostless climates, particularly for its masses of tubular, rich purple-blue flowers. It stood out, a vigorous, dark-green shrub, among the thickets of *Baccharis* and brambles in rocky quebradas, along old stone walls, and even in heavily grazed pastures. About the hovels of shepherds and covered with white bloom was a small elderberry, *Sambucus peruviana*.

In fence rows and along streams near Chota, the most common tree was a cherry, *Prunus capuli*. Its fruit has a large pit and little flesh, and is sold in the markets throughout the Peruvian Andes. A species of *Duchesnea*, which they found on dry hillsides, bore fruits like our wild strawberries, but its petals were yellow rather than white. Twining in hedgerows was a *Passiflora* or passionflower. Its blooms were gorgeous, with large scarlet petals and dark-purple corona fringe. The Indians call this striking flower *ccoto-ccoto*, in the belief that if you pick it you will become goiterous. A fine pink-flowered *Passiflora*, which they saw first in Cachicadán and was there called *pfuro-pfuro*, which in Quechua means "feather," also grew about Chota, and its common name was the same as that of the red-flowered species. Goiter is, and has for centuries been, all too common in the Andean valleys remote from the sea.

They had barely arrived in Chota before it was discovered that bubonic plague had broken out. One victim had died three weeks before, a second one on the following week, and a third had just succumbed, all in one family. The *botánicos* decided that a stay in Chota was undesirable, but the hotel proprietor, with an eye to prolonging the visit of such well-paying guests, scoffed at the report that *bubónica* was actually in town. He insisted that it was silly to dignify a bit of influenza by such a name. But the cat popped out of the bag when without warning the district health officer arrived from Cajamarca and put up at the hotel. At once he ordered the Indians and townsfolk to kill all their guinea pigs because, together with rats, they were known to spread plague. So everyone feasted on guinea pig. The rats, more difficult to deal with, remained at large. The stricken family was moved out of town to a hovel on the riverbank, and all their bedding was burned.

In larger centers of population in Peru, an outbreak of bubonic plague is usually caught in time to prevent a serious epidemic. But when, years ago, it appeared in isolated communities far off in the Andes, there was a different problem. A death, irrespective of the cause, was made the occasion for a gathering of the clan from near and far, together with as many neighbors and friends as were permitted to share the liquid refreshment provided for the prolonged wake. If the deceased had been a plague victim the fleas and other vermin leaving the cadaver might thoroughly infect the celebrants, who went home to carry the disease to a dozen or more small mountain communities. In a short time a large area might be involved, and the health authorities would find it difficult to cope with the situation.

Harvey and Bob were headed for Sócota, via Tacabamba, with their horses, mules, and so-called guide. They left Chota on a trail along the river. The hillsides were covered with a shrub vegetation, most of which would have been in flower had this not happened to be one of the rare seasons when the rains were very late in arriving. Among a few species in condition to be collected was a *Bejaria*. It looked much like Azalea and the plants were brilliant with bright-pink flowers. *Embothrium grandiflorum* showed some of its pastel-pink flower clusters, but not the gorgeous ones we were to see later in the Andes of southern Peru. *Puru-puru, Erythrina* trees, were common. The hard scarlet beans they bear are prized by the Indians, who string them to make attractive necklaces.

This by no means complete account of the search for *Nicotiana thyrsiflora*, at long last entirely successful, will terminate with the following excerpt from Harvey's diary:

"Having established ourselves in Sócota, we decided to collect up a small river which flows near by into the main stream. We asked the padre if we could find a *muchacho* who would carry our plant press.

He agreed to speak to the director of schools about it. After a little while he returned to say that he had located the director in a poker game and that, rather than recommend a boy, the director himself would accompany us, but not just yet. We should please wait until after lunch. Ultimately, word came from the director that the *alcalde* or mayor and also the recorder of the town would like to go along. All we had asked for was a boy to carry a plant press; now it appeared that we were to have an official entourage. This meant that, after all, we would carry the plant press ourselves; those august officials could certainly not be expected to carry anything. Menial tasks of any sort were not for them. However, when three members of the gentry and the flower of officialdom showed up, they brought with them a servant to do the carrying. Before starting, the director made a further request. Another friend of his would like to shut up shop and come with us if the *exploradores* had no objection. Of course, we consented and were soon joined by a shifty-looking character who had come from Spain some years ago to this remote spot.

"After the going got a little hard, up the river, the mayor produced two sticks of dynamite from his pocket and said that he thought he would like to stop a while to fish. The Spaniard stopped with him. We continued botanizing upstream. The school director and the recorder proved to be good sports on a long climb with hard going through brushland. Cassias, Solanums, Crotons, yellow-flowered Jussiaeas, and the rank *Ambrosia peruviana* were among the plants we collected. This last is a vile weed in many parts of Peru. It even gets into the cultivations of the east coast of South America. In practically all respects it is the counterpart of our ragweed of bad repute among hay-fever sufferers, except that it grows several times larger and in favorable situations may be as tall as a horse. On dry hills throughout this region *Dodonaea viscosa*, a member of the Sapindaceae, or Soapberry family, is very common. It has a wide distribution throughout the Peruvian mountains, and is used for making mattresses. The leaves, as the specific name indicates, are viscid. When growing on dry hillsides they are not moistly viscid, but just viscid enough so that, if the twigs and leaves are gathered and made into a bed, the whole mass sticks together and can be picked up and handled as a mattress.

"We had expected to hear the dynamiting of fish by the alcalde and the Spaniard, but the afternoon wore on and nothing happened. On our return that night, the padre asked me whether the alcalde had taken any liquor with him. I said that all we had seen was dynamite, but that he might have had something else in his pocket. The padre felt sure that there must have been some alcohol along because the alcalde had fallen in the river and the Spaniard had brought him home soaking wet. He was now in bed, preparing to come down with pneumonia.

"As we sat before the cabin that night, frogs were attempting a few uncertain croaks in the quebrada below. An old man passing by said to us, 'They are announcing the coming of rain.' The frogs were not wrong. In the night we were awakened by the patter of rain on the roof, thatched with sugar cane. Ordinarily it might have been conducive to sleep, but the thought of the slippery clay roads which we must travel for four or five days to get back to civilization took some of the poetry out of the situation, as did also the ominous drippings that were beginning here and there about the cabin. I fared better than Bob did, for one of his boots was exactly under a drip and in the morning he poured a pint of water out of it."

3

MEADOWS ON THE DESERT

Not many places on this earth are as dry as the deserts of the west coast of South America. From that point where the rim of our sister continent lies farthest west, several degrees below the equator, a barren waste of sand and exposed rock stretches down to the middle of Chile. It averages fifty miles in width, washed by the Pacific waters on the west and bounded by the imperial Andes or their foothills on the east. In much of this coastal wasteland appreciable rainfall is almost completely unknown, for the cool Humboldt Current upwelling along its shores so chills the winds from the southwest that they give up their moisture at sea and become dry as they blow over the warm land. They lift and carry the desert sands, piling them into the ever-shifting, crescent-shaped dunes and carving the basic rock where it juts out to form the foothills of the cordillera.

When I tell you that in the midst of this rainless desert I have often, over the years, walked through fields of filmy-leaved flowering plants in water-soaked boots and with clothing wet by the dew from a mantle of delicate vegetation, you will shake your head. Nevertheless, it is true, for there are a few small areas on the deserts of Peru, and of Chile also, where dense fogs hang almost continuously over the coastal hills and plains during the late southern winter, with the result that the land is shaded from the rays of the sun and the soil becomes moist and even boggy as the saturated air condenses. On these wet spots in the desert a short-lived vegetation springs up, like the woodland wildflowers that flourish in the springtime through our Temperate Zone forests. These "meadows on the desert" the people of the west coast call *lomas*.

48

In September the Peruvian loma vegetation is usually at its height. Twenty years ago the flora of the lomas had not yet been adequately studied. Therefore, on our second expedition I planned the arrival in Lima of my North American botanical assistants and collectors for early September, even though the best collecting season in other parts of Peru and Chile usually begins a month or so later. After a day or two in the "City of Kings," two of them, Walter and Alan, began their long journey across Peru, Bolivia, and Argentina, a journey which was finally to carry them almost as far south in South America as it is possible to go. Carl and John were soon to be on their way down the South Peruvian and North Chilean coast. Just before they left, we saw our first loma together.

In those days the dean of South American botanists was the late Dr. Augusto Weberbauer. For many years he had studied the plants of coast and cordillera, of the desert and the jungle. His wide knowledge of the Peruvian floras produced dividends in a famous book dealing with the plant geography of his foster fatherland. When first I met him, he looked to be a little, frail, old man. But how thoroughly he tired me out, then and later, when we went together for plants into the Andean foothills. He most willingly directed us on numerous collecting trips near Lima. During the foggy winter he always took visiting botanists to the loma de Atocongo. There, on the hills east of the coastal town of Lurin and an hour or two by train or automobile south of Lima, he exhibited to them one of the vegetationally rich Peruvian "meadows on the desert."

On our first botanizing at Atocongo a caravan of automobiles with geologists, botanists, zoölogists, and others aboard wound out of the city, ran through the green, irrigated fields that surround it, and soon reached the sandy, barren coastal desert. After some twenty miles along a good highway, they passed the famous ruins of Pachacamac. Many tourists go there to see the little that remains of what was one of the most important coastal settlements during the pre-Columbian era in Peru. Years ago they were permitted to poke among the potsherds, and everywhere they found evidence that Pachacamac was a vast necropolis in Inca or pre-Inca days. In the hotel lobbies of Lima there were hanks of hair, teeth, bits of pottery, and fragments of burial cloths being gloated over by grave robbers who received the envious glances of other tour members who had not invested in the Pachacamac side trip. How many of those grave-despoiling compatriots of mine realized that the perfect preservation of the antiquities they found at Pachacamac was proof that, for many hundreds of years at least, the central Peruvian coast must have been as completely arid as it is today?

Even at a distance the foggy hills near Lurin had a green sheen—so by contrast with the prevailing tan-to-gray elsewhere along the dry coastal hills—and in a sheltered valley the lower slopes showed scattered delicate plants of *Oxalis, Cryptantha, Plantago,* and a *Drymaria.* All were but a few inches high and most were in profuse bloom. They had none of the characteristics of desert plants. The leaves were thin, without heavy cuticle; nor were they gray in color as are the hairy leaves of many plants of dry terrain. A day's bright sun would have laid them low. But at that season there are no days of bright sun. There may, perhaps, be faint sunshine for an hour or two in the morning; then fog clouds sweep over the desert and in the afternoon the mists descend and dew glistens on the vegetation and on the sand. Higher up in the valleys between the hills, the plants were larger and the earth greener.

The botanists, led by Dr. Weberbauer, started up into the green hills. Slippery climbing soon brought them under the low ceiling of dense fog. Then, suddenly, it engulfed them and immediately blotted out the sandy wastes and lower hillslopes which they had just been traversing. Don Augusto, using his omnipresent cane as an alpenstock, scrambled ahead with the greatest enthusiasm. Only when he had reduced the visitors to gasping impotence would he stop for a few minutes to give them time to recover and to hear a short lecture on the remarkable vegetation through which they were passing.

The soil was beginning to be distinctly boggy. Small trees appeared, singly or in scattered groves—*Lucuma obovata, Carica candicans,* and a species of *Acnistus.* From their branches hung festoons of epiphytic bryophytes, ferns, and Peperomias. Clustered in their protection or in crevices of rock outcrops were species of *Calceolaria* (the slipperwort), various Begonias, and other charming plants. The scent of the Peruvian heliotrope was heavy in the moist air. In the shelter of boulders they saw *Begonia octopetala* in bloom and growing far larger and more vigorously than it does in those North American gardens to which it has been transported. Altogether it was unbelievable—a luxuriant, flowery garden, and not much more than a center fielder's throw from one of the driest deserts on the surface of the earth! It was certainly enough to make botanists forget the lunch hour.

According to previous agreement the whole party was to reassemble at one o'clock. A sumptuous *asado* or barbecue had been prepared with *cabrito* (broiled kid) as the *pièce de résistance*. No one thought of waiting for the botanists who had disappeared in the fog. Students being much the same the world over, there was a great deal of lighthearted merriment, some pommeling, and a few practical jokes. Reminiscent of the organized cheering of our universities were their "chants" which ended with the name of one or another of their professors, except that in North America cheers are for the team and something else is for the faculty. Three o'clock came, luncheon was long since over, a few enthusiasts had gone on to the hills to collect specimens, and others had sought shelter within the cars from the penetrating moist cold, when from out of the mists appeared Dr. Weberbauer and his entourage. Cheers and groans greeted them. The students were, of course, unanimous in their decision that they had lost their way in the fog-shrouded quebradas. We never did discover whether they actually had been just a little bit lost or whether their enthusiasm for the strange and unexpected vegetation had led them too far afield.

Over sixty different species of flowering plants and a number of mosses, ferns, and fern allies had been collected in the foggy meadows. Although from a distance they gave the impression of grasslands, there was actually but one species of grass in the whole collection. The only foreign plant that had come to settle in that out-of-the-way place was a "sow thistle."

Everyone said that it had been an unusually dry year on the northern coast of Peru, with thin fogs which would not support the "meadows on the desert." On the other hand, the lushness of the middle Peruvian loma at Atocongo somewhat discredited these reports, and the diversity of their flora was beyond expectation. Therefore I suggested that Harvey, Bob, and César try a scouting expedition as far north as Chimbote, some two hundred and fifty miles above Lima on the coast. To see more of the countryside, they went by road in a *colectivo*.

In Peru, a colectivo is likely to be a more or less defunct automobile or springless truck which is always ready to carry whatever passengers and cargo can be assembled for transportation to any given destination. In this case an old Buick touring car had collected eight passengers, two live chickens, bed rolls, plant presses, and sundry boxes and packages in addition to the driver. The starting time was announced as nine-thirty. The driver postponed it until ten. At one-thirty he got around to strapping some extra tins of gasoline on the running board. At two-thirty he checked out at the office of the *guardia civil* and finally made a start.

Northward from Lima, the colectivo bowled merrily along through the cultivations of the Rimac Valley, thence out into the sand and over rocky ledges. At times it skirted the coast to give glimpses of beach, where white surf separated the red and yellow sands from the blue waters of the Pacific. Where the coast was abruptly rocky, the highway rose well above the sea and looked down upon vast clouds of guano birds following luckless schools of surface fish—not hundreds or thousands but millions of birds.

At that time the fine automobile road, a segment of the Pan American Highway, which the colectivo traveled north from Lima had been completed only to a point north of Supe. It mostly followed the coast, and this means that it was built on desert sands. On this same highway we once had the following unforgettable experience, conceived in imagination and almost ending in reality.

A well-developed hair-trigger imagination doubtless adds to the enjoyment of life. Unfortunately, however, you cannot turn it off at will. This we learned many times on South American roads. Long exposure to critical situations—made doubly harrowing because you envisage, instantly and crystal clear, their potentially fatal consequences—should ultimately discourage imagination, because only rarely are these situations followed by the dire consequences that you conjure up. I agree, but somehow this entirely logical deduction fails to come into one's mind when an apparently critical situation arises.

Through the courtesy and coöperation of La Molina Agricultural Experiment Station, near Lima, we were often given the use of a big station wagon for our collecting trips into the Andes and along the coasts. An efficient driver came with the machine. Including him, that April morning, our party numbered seven. First, there was Dr. Weberbauer. He was to guide us to a special collecting ground in the foothills behind the coastal town of Huacho, somewhat less than one hundred miles north of Lima. We, together with Harvey, made up the *norteamericano* contingent. Then there was Miss Agnes Johnson, a charming little English lady long resident in Peru and a talented artist, and Dr. Rufino Aspiazu, who had retired as one of the leading physicians of Lima and was—and still is—an accomplished amateur botanist. We were a very jolly party.

This Cuzco Indian girl and her companion, with wooden hoe on shoulder, start for an Andean potato field. Their colorful ponchos, at least, are not too ragged.

Often the little but nutritious Andean potatoes are frozen, dried, and powdered.

In the Peruvian Andes the Indians rarely smile except at a fiesta. Pisac, near Cuzco.

A serrano and his wife stop for a snack along the road to the Huancayo market.

A religious procession circles a Cuzco plaza.

The record of years of encounter with the stern realities of Andean life is written deep on the features of this tattered patriarch.

An embossed silver staff designates this Peruvian Indian as an honorary alcalde who aids in policing his district.

The winter fogs had not yet begun to blanket the coast, and the wasteland that presses upon the irrigated fields near Lima shimmered in the heat waves which rose against the hazy outlines of the Andean foothills to the east. After a few miles across dry plains, the highway rose gradually along sandy oceanside bluffs. Soon the sea was some hundred or two hundred feet below us and the road became nothing but a step hollowed out of the steep side of an immense sand dune, the bottom of which was the ocean beach. The road was a little more than two cars wide. On the dune side the sand was constantly sifting and blowing down onto the road surface. On the outside it was just as constantly falling away down the almost vertical slope to the water. There was no railing along the edge. To keep the highway in repair, and even passable, a large crew of road men was always at work. Most of them were sweepers armed with large homemade brooms. All day long they moved back and forth on the inner side of the highway, sweeping back the sand which never ceased to slide down from the dune overhead.

We had the inside lane on the way to Huacho and only when the car swung wide to pass a group of sweepers did we have a momentary look over the outer edge of the road to the surf breaking far below against the foot of the dune. This sand-swept portion of the highway wound for a considerable number of miles in and out as it followed the contours of the dune. Sometimes its surface was of normal width, and sometimes the sand had got ahead of the sweepers and made the single passable lane near the outer edge dangerously slippery.

One of our party thoughtlessly remarked that this stretch of highway must be an unpleasant one to negotiate in the dark. Forthwith my imagination and, as it later proved, that of all the rest of the party except the driver, went to work. I could almost feel the darkness, the back wheels bumping off the pavement, the car's sudden downward lurch, one or two turns in the air—"No, no; this won't do, snap out of it." But the seed had been planted, and the tag end of imagination kept slyly insinuating a menacing picture long after we left the road around the dune and were again bowling across the level, arid plains.

We had a thoroughly good and profitable time in and near Huacho. The prime collecting ground to which Don Augusto was to lead us turned out to be too dry. Still, we found much of botanical interest there. I was surprised to see *Nicotiana glutinosa*, a tobacco relative, growing so far north of its center of distribution in the foothills east of Lima. We collected seeds of a *Caesalpinia*, or related genus, which was in full flower and was the most conspicuous or, at least, the most colorful element in the rugged quebradas along the base of the mountains near the coast.

On the following day it was well into the afternoon before we loaded ourselves and our miscellaneous spoils into the station wagon for the journey back to Lima. The day had been unusually hot and, as we rolled through the desert on the narrow strip of paved highway, mists began to rise from the cooling sands and more than a mist rolled in far ahead where the highway approached the sea along the great dune. Conversation had been lively for the first half-hour of the ride. Gradually the combined influence of a good, abundant, and somewhat vinous dinner, the rush of cooling air, and the monotony of the landscape induced a comfortable lassitude and even a snore or two; in other words, a series of delayed siestas was enjoyed.

When I awoke the sun was setting—a red ball sinking fast into the ocean's horizon, but only dimly seen through the gathering fogs. The broad, dry plains, a patchwork of vivid yellows, browns, and reds under yesterday's bright sunlight, now were gray and misty and exhaled a chilling breath. My return to consciousness was immediately followed, or perhaps preceded, by a premonition of what lay ahead on the breasts of the great sand dune. I realized that we would begin the miles of sand-strewn dune just as the uncertain light of early evening was being replaced by the treacherous blackness of a foggy night. In imagination I saw the slow and cautious negotiation of every foot of those miles. I could almost hear the sound of the breakers, a constant and menacing reminder of what lay directly below the outer lane of the highway along which we must travel. I remembered other night rides in this same car and with this same driver. These had been rides along level, safe valley roads. But how dim the headlights had been! Worse than that, it suddenly came to me that the station wagon had no headlight dimmer, and that this driver had always slowed down and put out his lights when a car approached from the opposite direction. I wondered whether he would be willing to disobey the dimming law on that bad stretch of highway which we were so rapidly approaching. How many other dangerous and terrifying contingencies my imagination conjured up as the light began to fail and the road turned toward the sea, I cannot remember. The most serious one I had not thought of, but it was not long in making itself manifest.

The car rounded the first of the broad curves on which the highway crossed the surface of the precipitous dune. We could see for miles ahead. In a long, broken strand, sometimes two or three together, sometimes singly, the headlights of approaching cars were strung out all along the dune shelf. Yesterday there had been almost no traffic on this part of the highway. Then I remembered that this was Sunday night and that we were traversing the only road upon which weekend revelers from Lima could return to their northern homes.

The harrowing uncertainty, insecurity, and final terror of that next hour—for it took us that length of time to cross the relatively few miles of dune—each one of us will always remember. Since the road sweepers had stopped work long before sundown, there had been time for the sand to work its way down and far out into the roadway. In some areas it had crossed the road. Driven by a rising wind, the fog swirled about the exposed ridges and rushed up the sandy valleys. Sometimes sand filled the air to decrease visibility almost to the vanishing point. The ineffective headlights cast only a faint glow on the pavement a few yards ahead of the car. At intervals twin spots of light suddenly blazed in our faces out of the murk. They always seemed to rush toward us head on, and each time I was certain that our quick turn toward the outer edge of the road would carry us over the precipice to the breakers, whose muffled roar was always in our ears. But each time, by what seemed a miracle, the two cars brushed past each other and we were still on the road.

I sat in the front seat next the driver and watched his quiet intentness, his complete absorption in the task in hand. Never faltering, he was apparently sustained by a complete faith in his ability to meet the hazards of our position. I had almost lost the power to look ahead, and I soon gave up the attempt to force my eyes to the side where there was no road and death lay in wait. My attention was fixed on those hands that held the steering wheel. I watched them periodically tighten and then slowly move round as he drove to one side or the other to pass an approaching car or avoid the sand where it had formed small drifts on the roadway. I would just begin to draw from his steadfastness a little confidence and then it would drain away when I saw the wheel begin to turn to the right. A dozen times I thought I felt the right wheels leave the pavement. At such moments, dumbly, supinely, I waited for the first sickening tilt of the heavy car as the sand gave way and we began our plunge over the cliff.

Gradually the fog blew away and the road became more visible.

I knew that we had passed the center of the dune, because in the faint light from the clearing sky the dark silhouette of the great mass of sand was gradually lessening in height. Our driver relaxed a trifle and began to improve on the snail's pace we had so long been maintaining.

Suddenly a car came up behind us very fast. Its insistent horn demanded more room on the left. We slackened speed and cautiously worked over toward the edge. Behind us the horn was still insistent, but we could give no more room. Then the car's angry and perhaps drunken driver, still at the top of his noise, pulled up beside us and began to pass. Just as he cleared our front wheels he viciously swerved to the right, across our bows; our driver wrenched at the wheel to avoid a crash. Instantly we were headed for destruction.

It may have been the sudden change in our situation from relative security to terrible danger, or perhaps the long strain which he had endured had unnerved him; at any rate, something made our driver lose control. At once the front wheels bumped off the pavement and before I could get them back on the road again the rear ones began to skid dangerously. At this, the driver recovered from his momentary lapse and our combined hands on the steering wheel succeeded in straightening out the car; but not until we had run for fifty feet with front and rear right wheels alternately on and off the road. A dozen times we must have been only inches from the brink of the precipice.

Fortunately, we were almost off the dune shelf. In a few moments the lights of Lima glimmered in the distance. On an easy downgrade the car rolled out along the plains. Someone spoke, someone answered, then everyone was talking at once. We began to realize that for an hour not a word had passed our lips. But talking was not enough. Harvey began to sing. "There's a long, long trail," and we all joined in, the driver humming quietly under his breath. It was our heartfelt hymn of thanksgiving. Another and another song followed, and noisily we rode into Lima.

We return now to Harvey, Bob, and the other passengers in the colectivo pursuing their journey to the northern Peruvian coastal lomas. While the smooth road lasted they were in high spirits and conversation was brisk and free. The North Americans concluded that some of it might even be a bit ribald, to judge by the roars of laughter that followed stories told in a Spanish vernacular too rapid for them to understand. Even the driver loosened up. At first he had been sullenly uncommunicative, following an argument with one of the women in the front seat. She had refused to pay extra fare for transportation of her two hens which, with legs tied together, she had crowded under the front seat, but which preferred to flop around between the driver's feet. He had told her that it was not the extra weight he minded but that there was a decided nuisance angle involved. The woman, however, refused to argue, and each time he showed signs of anger she would take the fowls into her lap and stroke them, as if to smooth the feathers of the whole situation. As the afternoon lengthened, the rest of the passengers saw the humor of the situation. After a while the driver began to thaw and finally joined in the laugh that followed the woman's proposal to give him all the eggs the hens would produce in the course of the trip. A louder laugh went up when she added that, considering the age and generally unreliable appearance of his vehicle, this was likely to be no small consideration by the time they arrived at their destination.

The west coast desert of northern Peru is often crossed by larger or smaller streams. They originate in the Andean snows not so far to the eastward and with considerably decreased flow manage to reach the sea. The soils of the lower reaches of these river channels are deep with alluvium. Desert valleys in Peru, as elsewhere, bloom like the rose when water is made to flow through them in irrigation ditches. Inca and pre-Inca civilizations must have flourished in these fertile valleys, for in and near them are always the ruins of adobe hamlets, villages, and even cities, often guarded by watchtowers and fortresses.

Modern civilization has replaced that of pre-Columbian times in these valleys. Along the larger streams, which may continue to flow even at the end of the dry season, there were settlements built upon or beside the ancient ones. These modern communities had a sameness of landscape—adobe and galvanized houses, too few of the hardy shade trees that will flourish in the dry air of the desert, and sandy streets narrower than was justified by the ample room for a townsite. However, being near the sea and therefore in touch with a wider world, the people of the coastal towns were not so impoverished of ideas as those who lived in the high, isolated Andean valleys of Peru.

Next morning a good road led the party northward to Paramonga, where the river of that name has spread wide plains of alluvium which are green with checkerboard fields of well-irrigated sugar cane. As one leaves this fertile valley for the dry hills to the north there stands on a prominence a picturesque ancient *fortaleza*, or fortress, visible for miles around. After many centuries its sturdy red walls and terraces are still in good condition.

Today, an excellent highway has been completed almost to the Ecuadorian frontier, but at the time when our *botánicos* were voyaging north via colectivo the pavement weakened, faltered, and finally vanished into a stretch of soft, wind-blown sand. Thereupon, the driver, with a sigh of resignation, extricated himself from behind the wheel and proceeded to let some air out of the tires. Then he raced the engine through several spurts like an aviator about to take off and was ready to match his wits against the sand. From that moment he became entirely uncommunicative and refused to pay the slightest attention to questions of anxious passengers. Like a ball carrier running in an open field, he required all his wits to determine which tacklers to avoid and which to charge. Some dunes have a hard crust which bears the weight of an automobile, and others are powdery and lead only to grief. Most of the time he guessed right and the passengers voiced approval, even admiration. Sometimes he guessed wrong, and then the rest of the colectivo team paid for his mistake. The men disembarked to help push. The fat women also disembarked, to make the task of the men lighter.

To extricate the car, the sand in front of the wheels had to be dug away with the hands—no one bothered to ask why the driver had forgotten to bring a shovel—in the manner of a dog trying to expose a subterranean woodchuck. Thereafter they all fell to and pushed, and then trotted after the car until it dared to halt on firmer packed sand. At some of the stoppages where they happened to be in hilly country, the task of getting under way again was not so laborious. On the sandy hillsides there were patches of a silver-gray desert plant, *Tillandsia straminea*. The driver and male passengers would collect a large pile of these plants and then feed them to the sand in front of the wheels. It was remarkable how much traction they provided.

This *Tillandsia* is common on all the hills of this rainless region and in fact through most of the length of the Peruvian coast. It is a relative of the "Spanish moss" and the pineapple, has almost no root system, and holds its place only by virtue of the sand that drifts about its base to anchor it. It takes moisture from the air on occasions when dew forms, and this it conserves very efficiently. In the middle of the day when the sun sometimes dispels the fog, the reddish flower-shoots droop; but in the morning they are again erect, looking cheerful and vigorous. Sometimes whole fields of these plants have died and partly carbonized, and their black skeletons contrast sharply with the silver-gray stretches of their living relatives. Otherwise, for many miles, the desert landscape shows no contrasts. On some level areas, particularly where the sand holds a little clay, belts of *Tillandsia* spread out at right angles to the direction of the prevailing wind and lean toward this wind which brings them moisture. From an elevation and at a distance these belts of silvery gray produce the effect of waves upon the desert.

There being no appreciable root system, *Tillandsia* transplants easily. Travelers have taken advantage of this fact as a means of erecting living memorials to those who have been no match for the desert road, which must have taken a heavy toll in the days of slow travel by horse or burro. Usually in Peru a wooden cross is built by the roadside where a traveler has died. But in the desert there is no wood, and so here and there the name of the departed is spelled out in Tillandsias. Once, in the past, when travel over the coastal sands was less regular than it is today, a luckless colectivo was stalled for two or three days near a considerable hill. By way of diversion the unfortunate passengers recorded in *Tillandsia* the impression their surroundings made upon them, and one could clearly read in green characters on the hillside the word INFIERNILLO, which is to say, "Little Hell."

Aside from *Tillandsia* and some of its close relatives there was, that year, little to excite the *botánicos* along the highway. Occasionally they saw a few cacti, and now and then a low valley showed some deep-rooted woody plants. Plains close to the sea supported a carpet of resistant plants, principally *Distichlis*, which bind the sand and hold it temporarily in place. Otherwise, the north Peruvian coastal shelf lacked detail. It was a world of cloudy sky, blue sea to the west, wind-eroded foothills to the east, and behind them a purple mountain wall rising straight up and up into the clouds. Travelers never cease to marvel at the steep slope of the western walls of the Andes. Fifty miles from the ocean stands this great backbone of the continent, a continent which, beyond the Andean crest, slopes for thousands of miles eastward to the Atlantic. And the descent below sea level from the Pacific shores is equally abrupt, so that near the western mainland of Peru some of the world's great deeps occur.

As the Buick chugged through the sands to Chimbote, they constantly kept a lookout for evidence of loma vegetation. Sometimes at a distance a hillside looked to be green but on closer approach proved merely to be covered with greenish shales. These and parti-colored

rock formations northward from Chancay lend a picturesque, somewhat bizarre atmosphere to the landscape, which is reminiscent of the
Bad Lands and even of the Grand Canyon of the Colorado or Bryce
Canyon. The sands are mostly fine and exhibit a rounded grain under
magnification. The rocks protruding from their sandy beds are shales
of different colors and conglomerates, with here and there an outcrop
of amorphous rock which looks like rhyolite. But there were a few
spots genuinely green with loma vegetation. These they noted down
to be visited on the return journey, for they proposed to make it in
a hired automobile which would stop upon demand.

On the second night the colectivo discharged its weary human cargo
at its destination, Chimbote. The passengers had acquired a considerable physical, if not intellectual, intimacy during the rough desert
journey, but they parted silently and with no regret. Each one was
anxious to forget not only the hard bottom of the colectivo but also
the sharp elbows of his companions in discomfort. Even the jovial lady
of the hens was too weary to fire a parting shot at the driver. But the
hens were equal to the occasion. Heads down, they continued to
squawk and thrash about as, slung over their mistress's shoulder, they
disappeared up a dark Chimbote street. The botanists sought the hotel.
It proved to be relatively modern and quite comfortable. Next morning they saw Chimbote's natural harbor, one of the best on the west
coast of the continent, and then went into the hills to the east. Only
here and there did they see evidence that vegetation had existed even
in wet years. Along the Santa River to the north they collected some
shrubby plants of the *Baccharis* and *Tessaria* type and various introductions from the Andes and from Chile and Ecuador, as well as some
cosmopolitan weeds of the sort found wherever civilization reaches.
For the return trip to Lima they negotiated in Chimbote with owners
of private automobiles. Finally, one who had an apparently sandworthy
Model A Ford was willing to listen to reason in the matter of charges.

Even the definitely green lomas which they found on the return
journey were disappointing. Once in a while there were stretches of
vegetation, all in flower. In the Lachay lomas considerable areas were
gay with yellow- and also white-flowered species of *Loasa*. Only at
Pasomayo did the fog vegetation carpet the hillsides all the way down
to the ocean beach. The yellow *Loasa* was there, again forming sheets
of color; at a distance, it was hard to believe that the slopes were covered with something other than our common yellow mustard. The

yellow *Loasa* fields were spotted here and there with the blue of a *Solanum* in flower.

As their Ford brought them closer to Lima and the end of our first north coastal plant hunting, the moister and even some of the drier hillsides and small plains in the coast range began to show bulbous plants, notably such amaryllids as *Stenomesson* and *Zephyranthes*. For miles the wasteland would be pitilessly barren; it was inconceivable that any living thing, animal or vegetable, could long exist there. Then, for no reason at all, a thousand, ten thousand, slender green stalks thrust themselves up out of the sand, each with a tassel of orange or scarlet trumpets hanging from its nodding tip.

Following this first period of collecting on the Peruvian "meadows on the desert," members of later expeditions have passed through them, north and south of Lima, on their journeys to the highlands that rise so abruptly to the east. Thus, our most recent loma collecting has been incidental but always rewarding. My distinguished friend Dr. Ramón Ferreyra, who succeeded Dr. Weberbauer as Professor of Botany in the University of San Marcos and heads the botanical section of Lima's Natural History Museum, devoted himself for a number of years to a really intensive study of the lomas. He examined thoroughly both those already known botanically and, in addition, some that we and others who have been attracted by the unique character of this desert vegetation had failed to find. His recently published report reveals a larger number of plant families and many more species than had previously been recorded.

4

CITY OF THE KINGS

Beginning with its founding in 1535, Lima, City of the Kings, became for many years the gateway to South America for the Europeans. It was the front door through which the first entrance to the other America was effected. Glancing at a modern map of the western world you would scarcely point to Peru as a geographically logical first approach to South America from Europe. Yet it was there that the conquistadors, from Panama, first came. In succeeding decades, overland and coastwise expeditions ramified from Lima into much of the rest of the continent. The Church sent its missionaries there. Thence, they carried on, eastward and southward, over the Andes and through the jungles into what we today call Bolivia and Argentina.

I have always had a certain affection for colorful, friendly, and increasingly progressive Lima. Someone has said that, geographically and otherwise, it has little excuse for existence; that it is unproductive and lives parasitically upon the wealth created in other parts of Peru which, therefore, are unable to enjoy equivalent prosperity. So long as human beings prefer to herd together and create large centers of population, some products of this disposition will always grow up in places where they may not belong. In a Latin-American sense Lima has become, in relatively recent years, a capital in which to take pride. Unfortunately, this has meant that modern improvements have encroached all too effectively upon many authentic remnants of Spanish Colonial architecture and thereby have altered an atmosphere which at one time was distinctly reminiscent of the days of the conquistadors.

Lima, when I first knew it, was a city of vivid contrasts. In newer suburbs one saw elegant homes, the architecture of some of them having a modernistic, functional feeling. In older suburbs there still remained adobe huts with straw-thatch roofs. One of the commercial gardens maintained glasshouses in which orchid seedlings were grown on agar in hundreds of sterile flasks, the last word in orchid culture. In a field just beyond, oxen were drawing crude plows. In the matter of transportation, passengers could travel in big autobuses. But once in the suburbs these fast buses often had to dispute the right of way with files of laden burros, and sometimes llamas, whose ponchoed and barefooted owners plodded stoically beside them. In Lima many nationalities and races have met and mingled. It has been said that in no other South American city does one encounter so many hybrid types —creoles, mestizos, mulattos, quadroons, quintroons, chinos, zambos, cholos, and chino-cholos.

During most of our early sojourns in Lima we lived in the original Hotel Maury, in part at least one hundred years old, and famed for its cuisine. We also liked its large, airy suites of rooms and always chose one which had a long gallery overhanging a busy and characteristically narrow thoroughfare. On our gallery we dried plants, and the dwellers in the improvised penthouses across the way must still be wondering why the *norteamericanos* were forever laying out gray felt blotting papers where they would catch the maximum of hot Lima sunlight, and then picking them all up again. When quantities of wet plants began to come in by airplane, the sun did not dry the felts fast enough. Then we needed an electric stove and hung the plant presses over the heat, doubtless to the still further mystification of our vis-à-vis. Now rebuilt, the "new" Maury is modern in every respect but lacks completely the charm and atmosphere of its ancestor.

The things we saw at night from our gallery were most entertaining. On one occasion we were awakened by noisy talk and snatches of song. We looked down to see a street deserted except for an intoxicated youth. Now, in the Latin America we know, it is rare to see an adult so drunk that he will make an unfavorable exhibition of himself in public. Therefore I was suspicious that this was a case of youthful "arm waving" or that the noisy person was a foreigner, possibly a compatriot of ours. Although his identity was never revealed, my first suspicion was confirmed by the character and effect of the technique which a policeman applied. He appeared from nowhere, walked for a few steps behind the noisemaker, and then applied a vigorous kick to the right spot. The victim stopped, looked around, sized up the situation, and walked off a bit unsteadily but very quietly. Apparently shock is one of the remedies for "arm waving."

It was this same policeman who was in view on a subsequent night when the heat drove us from our beds to the gallery for a breath of air. We pulled chairs close to the long line of open windows and, with elbows on the sill, rested heads on arms and looked down to the dark street. It was very late. Everything was peaceful and quiet; delicate, refreshing drafts of cool, sweet air were drawn past us from the Plaza de Armas. Half awake and half asleep, we gradually became aware of an unfamiliar, elusive, intermittent sound. It was as though someone was periodically drawing a large wood-rasp lightly across a resonant timber. The sound seemed to come from around a near-by corner and to be slowly drawing closer. We looked at each other inquiringly and then turned our heads toward the corner. After a moment or two a small block of kindling wood slid out into the intersection of the two smoothly surfaced streets, and behind it appeared our policeman. He was walking his beat very slowly and, like a small boy employing similar means to add interest to running an errand, was kicking this bit of wood ahead of him. Sometimes he kicked for distance, sometimes for accuracy, and sometimes he merely tried to regulate his stride so that the kick would become an integral part of it. As the little billet skittered over the street, it made a pleasant noise—not loud enough to disturb sleeping citizens but sufficient to echo faintly up and down the empty street. We followed it until our eyelids began to droop.

On one occasion, when we were about to sail from Valparaiso for Peru, our Chilean friend "the General" brought to the stateroom a large brown native tarantula ensconced in a round wooden cheesebox. I remember that Florence had admired a preserved specimen she had seen in the General's insect collection. His presentation to her of this live spider was one of his practical jokes. Florence, however, chose to look upon his parting gift as a challenge to the quality of her scientific curiosity. In other words, by appearing to take it for granted that this was a bona fide *recuerdo,* and one that she was supposed to guard and cherish, she gave the General no satisfaction. She gravely inquired concerning the food and other requirements of the fearsome-looking, many-legged, hairy beast, big enough to cover a good-sized soup plate when extended. Obviously the General was not sure whether Florence was serious or whether his leg was being pulled. I was, however, quite certain that she had already decided to introduce this delightful little stranger into our cabin; and so it proved. The name "Edwyn," after the donor, was promptly bestowed upon the tarantula, with "Edwina" held in reserve should subsequent evidence necessitate its substitution.

For the next four months we traveled with "Edwyn," not he with us. His daily requirement of two or more live flies or moths kept us on the alert. Since on ships, trains, and in hotels rather violent objection to Edwyn's presence might be anticipated, we could not reveal his identity by enlisting the aid of the crew, the brakemen, or the porters in catching his food. Therefore, we went about armed with a small net and a ventilated bottle and, by dint of making ourselves unpleasantly conspicuous in public places, managed to keep Edwyn well fed.

The Plaza de Armas was my principal hunting ground in Lima. Early in the morning, before the city loafers had occupied the benches in the plaza, I swept the edges of grass plots with our net and rushed about wildly when a particularly promising insect buzzed past. Sometimes I seemed to detect a puzzled expression on the bronze face of Pizarro as he looked down upon our activities from his high pedestal, which in former days stood on the steps of the Cathedral. Early-rising citizens were equally in doubt about us, but probably thought that, like most "gringos," we were a little mad; in this case, harmlessly so.

After successfully passing through New York customs office concealed in a voluminous knitting bag, Edwyn rode in a glass-topped tin candy-box from New York to Berkeley. Except for the rubbing off of some of his auburn hair, he appeared to be little the worse for his long automobile journey. At home in Berkeley he lived happily for more than a year in a large glass-sided box filled with sand and vegetation and covered with wire netting. He and Florence became devoted friends. At the sound of her voice he rose up on a number of his hind legs and waved a welcome with his feelers. The next summer we were away from home for two months, and, despite the meticulous, if somewhat unwilling, attentions of our son, poor Edwyn died. A broken heart was doubtless responsible, because a tarantula, like Long John's parrot, "lives forever, mostly." I should, perhaps, have said that Edwyn was a nonpoisonous species, technically known as *Mygale rosea*.

When I first saw it, Lima's Plaza de Armas, even though a bit untidy, had a certain dignity and charm which it now lacks. Long since, it lost, and along with them a certain feeling of spaciousness, its big, graceful palms, and the shade trees that replaced them have never been too happy. Today you can, if the sun is unpleasantly hot, go around two sides of the Plaza under galleries. A third side contains the Cathedral and the Archbishop's Palace. It is pleasant to step for a moment into the cool interior of the Cathedral and watch the far-off, silver, candle-studded high altar take form as your eyes gradually become accustomed to the semidarkness. You enter through tremendous, round-topped, ancient wooden doors, many inches thick and studded with decorated iron bosses. Perhaps they hung at the entrance of the more magnificent cathedral built during the early years of the viceregal regime and later thrown down by one of Peru's most destructive earthquakes. For some reason, I never got around to examining the famous glass casket in which tourists are convinced that they see the mummified remains of Captain Don Francisco Pizarro. Perhaps they do, but the religious paintings from colonial days and the splendid silver altar with its appropriate decorations seemed to me considerably more attractive. Some claim that the precious metal covering the altar represents part of the treasure with which Atahualpa's followers believed that they were buying the Inca's freedom.

Beyond the Cathedral you walk beside the ornate but architecturally interesting Palace of the Archbishop, with its beautiful, intricately carved, black wooden balconies. The Cathedral and Palace fill one whole side of the Plaza. On the fourth side is the low, spreading Presidential Palace, with its big cobbled forecourt behind a decorative, but thoroughly businesslike, high stone-and-iron fence. Tourists, strolling citizenry, and country visitors to the capital always pause to gaze through the bars and past the soldiers standing by the gates at the coming and going of government officials and at the occasional automobile that has been passed by the guard and has rolled up to the presidential steps.

Until the last decade or so, except for the tops of two or three modest office-buildings Lima's sky line was smooth. Today it is sharply serrate. Here and there in the center of the city and near by are numerous large, tall structures, most of which house departments of the national government. On the whole, they are good-looking; hopefully, they are also well built, because Peru is an earthquake country. It is said that during the previous presidential regime Lima was a happy hunting ground for contractors, including North American ones. This reminds me that I was told the following rather remarkable tale which was said to bear upon the unpleasant nature of Vice President Nixon's reception in Lima not so long ago.

The University of San Marcos, founded by a royal decree signed in 1551 by Charles V of Spain, and either the first or second-oldest institution of higher education in Latin America, has its main headquarters near the Plaza San Martín, the hub of Lima's business district. It is a long, low, rather ancient, and exceedingly well-worn building consisting of a number of patios and inner courtyards surrounded by cloisters and second-story galleries, together with a crypt containing the remains of Peruvian heroes. It is sometimes referred to as the "Peruvian Pantheon," and certainly it is looked upon locally with respect and even veneration.

Over ten years ago my friends on the San Marcos faculty were enthusiastic about a project to build a *Cuidad Universitaria* on a tract of land in the suburbs along one of the avenues leading to Callao, Lima's port city. As in the Old World, so in South America each of the various "faculties" or departments of instruction of a large city university is likely to be housed in a different building, all separated by considerable distances one from the other. The notion of bringing all or most of them together on one campus, as we do, has for some time been popular in South America and there have been established a number of such "university cities." I know the one at Bogotá and another near Tucumán, in Argentina.

I feel sure that the proposal to build a *Cuidad Universitaria* was long known to the faculty and students of San Marcos and to the general populace in Peru's capital. When I saw the site some months before Vice President Nixon's visit a number of sizable buildings for instruction and research either were almost completed or had their foundations laid.

In view of what I have just said, it is hardly conceivable that the following rumor could have gained any credence in Lima, but apparently it had. Considerably before Mr. Nixon's South American good-will tour, the story went from mouth to mouth that through the connivance of certain officials of the Peruvian government and certain building contractors from the United States a secret scheme was being cooked up to abandon the University of San Marcos, including the pantheon, and rebuild it somewhere outside the city—with strong intimations that graft and corruption were involved. All this, mind you, as though up to that time no one had ever heard of the university city proposal.

South American governments, with some reason, always assume

that students are an initial, if not major, source of political unrest. Often the government in power has for "political reasons" closed the University of San Marcos, sometimes for months, and the same thing has occurred elsewhere in South America. Certainly, Latin-American undergraduates appear to take a far greater interest in local and national political issues than do North American ones, and economic and environmental factors predispose them to be readily and effectively propagandized. Thus, those Communist-inspired disruptive forces constantly at work in Peru, as everywhere in South America, saw in the rumor just described, and which they doubtless originated, a means of inciting unrest among San Marcos's undergraduates which could be directed either against the Peruvian government or against the United States. As soon as the Vice President's visit to Lima was announced, the choice was clear.

This, then, was offered as an "explanation" of why students were reported to be prominent in the obviously organized effort to show disrespect to Mr. Nixon, and in reputable quarters in Lima it is believed to be true. Do not forget, however, that in the United States the young hoodlum element usually attaches itself to our undergraduate demonstrations and is, more often than not, responsible for any serious breach of the peace. I have no doubt that Lima's "juvenile delinquents" were the more vociferous in the discourtesy shown our Vice President.

I cannot vouch for the truth or significance of what I have just written; nevertheless, similar and equally fantastic sequences of events have in the past been proved to occur in Latin America. They point to how delicately poised are current inter-American relations. We must make every effort not to become restive under the necessity of continually having to reëstablish our *bona fides* in South America when we know that fundamentally, and actually in practice, we are people of good will. Obviously, good will and good works are not paying the dividends they should. Perhaps when we begin to make a more conscious and sustained effort to understand the temperament and aspirations of our neighbors to the south they may. Of course, this same statement has been made, over and over again, by others, but each time during the past twenty-five years that I have lived in South America its validity has been increasingly impressed upon me.

In Peru, as elsewhere in South America, my companions and I have been fortunate enough to know rather intimately a considerable number of Latin-American families. They entertained us in their homes, coöperated with our work when they could, and brought gifts when we departed. We have mutually kept in touch via their friends who have visited California and our friends who have been in South America. Many of my sustained contacts have been with colleagues in universities or persons in technical branches of government service. Such people are likely to be well informed and tolerant, and I have found them willing and even anxious to get to the bottom of the intellectual and temperamental distinctions between us and to seek common ground.

On the other hand, some of the North Americans I have seen in action in South America could hardly be called ambassadors of good will. I do not refer to the touring compatriots who, in hotels throughout the world, make loud complaint—how those raucous voices ring out!—about conditions of life and travel, and who thereby do little more than exhibit their own ignorance and provinciality. Every nation breeds such people. I have had reason, however, to become disgusted with resident North Americans who insisted upon patronizing, and worse, the citizens of the countries in which they are living. The fact that our fellow citizens have usually consumed too much alcohol before indulging in actual discourtesy does not excuse them; indeed, their overindulgence only adds to the resentment of those who suffer at their hands.

To me the archaeological collections in Lima have always been singularly attractive. Years ago, through the kindness of the late Dr. Julio Tello and of Dr. Luis Valcárcel, Peru's well-known archaeologists, I enjoyed a number of personally conducted tours through the archaeological and anthropological museums. Often, since, I have spent long hours there and, also, at excavations under way at sites near and far from Lima, examining or searching for *huacos*, those remarkable jars and pots found in Inca and pre-Inca burial grounds.

Long before the possibility of visiting Peru had occurred to me I saw an illustration of a piece of Inca pottery that I never forgot. It showed a huaco, almost spherical in shape, on the surface of which was depicted an Inca noble sitting in the middle of a raft that was being propelled by swimmers. The feeling for form and composition, the perfection in the proportions of the figures, and particularly the entirely natural manner in which the swimmers flowed over the rounded surfaces of the jar prepared me for the even more remarkable evidences of pre-Columbian ceramic art to be seen in the Lima collections. The quality of Chimu pottery portraiture is extraordinary, but I spend most of my time in front of the cases that contain the smooth, beautifully colored huacos that come from Nazca on the South Peruvian coast. I have one that is decorated with a broad band of reddish-brown flamingos on a white background, and another, more complicated and less sophisticated, that shows faces of monsters, geometrical designs, and, at the bottom, a ring of jolly little mice.

I have, however, always been particularly concerned with the representations of plants and plant products to be found among the Inca burial ceramics and the evidence they give of the extent to which the ancient peoples of the Andes employed and improved their native food plants. There are huacos in the form of potatoes, corn, peanuts, squashes, pumpkins, melons, and papayas. Others represent pre-Columbian food plants that either are not now consumed in Peru or have not been extensively cultivated elsewhere. In addition, there are representations of a number of plants that are difficult to identify and may no longer exist in the Peruvian and Ecuadorian Andes. The collections of wonderfully well-preserved plant products, found with the mummies and huacos in the coastal burying grounds, are also important. There is a good deal of research in Peruvian ethnobotany still to be done.

Until recently, the botanical collections in Lima have not been as large or well maintained as they might have been in terms of the diversity and the scientific and commercial value of the Peruvian floras. The situation is beginning to improve greatly, in both regards, owing to the enthusiasm of Dr. Ramón Ferreyra and his associates at the Museum of Natural History. Of importance to visiting botanists is the better organization of the valuable collections made by the pioneer naturalist Antonio Raimondi, who arrived in Peru from Italy over one hundred years ago and began almost at once a series of journeys and explorations that continued without interruption for twenty years and, ultimately, provided him with a more comprehensive view of the geology, geography, and botany of all parts of Peru than any other single investigator has since obtained. He is, perhaps, best known for his map of Peru and for his geological studies. His botanical contributions include a collection of more than twenty thousand dried plant specimens.

The unwearied activities and sustained enthusiasm of the early naturalists in South America put the modern plant hunter somewhat to shame. We were wafted by train, automobile, or airplane over hundreds of miles of the difficult country that our predecessors spent weeks or months in traversing on horseback or on foot. Only in the most remote areas did we have to adjust ourselves to the primitive conditions of life that Raimondi encountered almost as soon as he left the few centers of coastal civilization. There were occasions when he spent between two and three years at a time away from his Lima headquarters, engaged upon intensive studies of the natural history of some particular area in Peru. The present-day plant hunter would hesitate to engage himself to carry out an equivalent program under the conditions of life and travel that Raimondi had to endure.

Considerable contributions to knowledge of the vegetation of the Lima area can still be made, although for two hundred years botanists have headquartered in the City of the Kings. They did not, however, spend much time in the surrounding countryside, but looked forward only to pushing eastward, up the valley of the Rimac, to gain the Andean heights. Therefore, during various seasons of the year, we have made many one- and two-day collecting trips out of Lima and worked the floor and walls of the Rimac Valley up to fourteen thousand feet. At the beginning I was particularly concerned about two Peruvian tobacco relatives which Linnaeus himself had named. He called one of them *Nicotiana paniculata* and the other *Nicotiana glutinosa*, and his dried specimens of both had been collected near Lima. Apparently the early plant hunters sent seed, as well as dried, pressed specimens, to Europe, because these two Nicotianas have been grown in botanical gardens for a hundred years at least. Peculiarly enough, however, my search in European museums for later collections of *N. paniculata* and *N. glutinosa* in the original locality had been largely unsuccessful. In other words, there was little evidence that today these species were elements of the vegetation in the neighborhood of Lima. The fact that we found them in great abundance in the lower Rimac Valley confirmed my impression that botanists had paid relatively little attention to the Lima region.

We collected *Nicotiana paniculata* many times in the Andean foothills of central and southern Peru, rarely in the north, and, except where the soil was rich and moist, it corresponded in appearance to the plant Linnaeus named. In very dry locations, however, it was diminutive and differed from Linnaeus's plant in general appearance. At higher altitudes in the Rimac Valley this Peruvian *Nicotiana* disappeared, to be replaced by *Nicotiana glutinosa*, the other species that had originally been described as growing near Lima but had hitherto been overlooked. Like *N. paniculata*, it grew rank where soil conditions were optimum and was reduced to pygmy stature on dry, thin soil. Too often, undiscriminating botanists have described such variants of well-known species, and particularly the diminutive ones, as new species. One of the greatest sources of satisfaction in my Andean plant hunting has been the opportunity to see large numbers of plants of many *Nicotiana* species growing in their natural habitats and exhibiting the extremes of their responses in form and structure to differences in environmental conditions.

The Río Rimac flows through Lima on the last of its journey from cordilleran sources to the Pacific. Along its first broad and then narrower valley the paved highway and the railway run side by side up into the high altitudes. For twenty miles inland, and until you have ascended about three thousand feet, unirrigated areas in the valley bottom and the slopes of Andean foothills are almost as arid as the coast itself. Such terrain abounds in desert and rock plants. At somewhat higher altitudes there are spring and summer rains, and, except in the long dry season, the mountainsides are green, sometimes all the way down to the floor of the valley. The trip from Lima to the town of Matucana (elevation 7,400 ft.) and return carries one through both desert and hillside vegetation, and can be accomplished by automobile in one day.

The first time we went to Matucana, the Prince was in the party. Cacti were his long suit, and he was overwhelmed by the number and variety of those that infested the Andean foothills. He was, for the first time, surveying a cactus enthusiast's paradise. There were tall and slender cacti, large and powerful ones; barrel-shaped ones, both little and big; green ones and gray ones; smooth ones and woolly ones. Best of all, many were in flower and some in fruit.

The collecting of cacti takes time and some apparatus—heavy gloves, metal tongs, and, particularly, cartons or similar containers in which to transport the prickly prizes. Since we had none of these things on the reconnaissance by automobile to Matucana, the Prince was only tantalized. I was, therefore, prepared for his suggestion that the two of us go back again to the cactus country, via the train, stop here and there at stations near which cactus collecting looked good, go on by the next train, and ultimately end at Matucana for the night. Concerning what would happen after that the Prince was rather vague. I told him that the scheme sounded good, but that I would not become a party to it. I felt confident that the best collecting would appear near the loneliest and dirtiest station on the line and that his collecting enthusiasm would lead us so far away that only nightfall would bring us back to it, too late to catch a train to Matucana or anywhere else. I had not attempted to spend the night in an isolated Peruvian railway station and I did not intend to do so. After dark, inebriated citizens and cur dogs are invariably drawn toward country railway stations. This always involves an unnatural increase in the flea population and I could foresee a hasty retreat to neighboring mountainsides, there to recline among cacti on a rocky slope. No, decidedly; the Prince should conduct the proposed excursion by himself; and so it was arranged.

Two mornings after our automobile trip, the Prince took the earliest train which left Lima for the Andean foothills and their cacti. Anticipating much climbing on hot hillsides, he wore only a thin shirt, khaki shorts, stout leggings, and tennis shoes. In one hand he carried a large knocked-down carton, and in the other his plant press and digging tool. Needless to say, he was an object of decided interest to and the subject of disparaging remarks by the hangers-on who frequent railroad stations, particularly in South America.

Late the following afternoon, he returned to Lima laden with spoils. The carton, now expanded, was full of cacti, and in addition he had a large press full of drying plants. The Prince theoretically solved his transportation problem by tying the press on top of the carton and carrying the combination on his stomach, his arms encircling the carton. By this arrangement he was just able to peep over the top of the load, and under this considerable handicap he began to steer his way toward an exit through the crowd. He was really quite an extraordinary sight and merited all the attention he attracted.

The Prince was a most accomplished plant collector, and where cacti were involved he had few equals. This first foray among the Peruvian ones demonstrated the extent to which his knowledge of cacti made it possible for him to collect only those species which were new or little known and to pass by the more familiar ones. The carton, full to overflowing, contained small living specimens of a large number of different cactus species. To have found such a varied assortment in less than a full collecting day, he must have covered a great deal of territory. I did not inquire how or where he spent the night or provided himself with food. He had probably forgotten the latter, to him an unimportant detail. In succeeding months I discovered that when the collecting was rich nothing else mattered to him—food and sleep least of all. He could do a punishing day's collecting and then stay up most of the night to write notes on the plants he had taken. The next morning he would be as lively as a cricket and full of enthusiasm for the day's work. For a full week he could maintain this punishing schedule and never seem to tire.

The day after the Prince dug them from the rocky foothills of the Andes, the cacti went to California by air express. All soil was carefully brushed off their roots; they were individually wrapped in newspapers and packed in a light carton. Like all the plant material we have sent home from South America (except seeds and dried and pressed plant specimens, which are not subject to inspection), this shipment of cacti carried our United States Department of Agriculture importation permit number and was addressed to the Bureau of Plant Quarantine in San Francisco. When it arrived, the cacti were unpacked, carefully examined for injurious insects and other pests, and, if necessary, fumigated before being sent on to the Botanical Garden in Berkeley. We have always received fine coöperation from the Plant Quarantine Service. They give special attention to perishable material and in other ways assist the rapid clearing of our importations. On our part, we try to send back only healthy, clean plants, and I think that our record in this regard is at least average.

Everyone, nowadays, takes for granted the large contributions to the success of our high-geared existence that rapid air transportation of human and other freight has made. It certainly meets one of the pressing problems of the plant hunter who works in far-off lands— to transfer in the shortest possible time the seeds, bulbs, roots, or cuttings from their native habitats in which he has collected them to the distant foreign soil in which he wants to grow them. Of course, if you have plenty of time and conditions in general are right and convenient, then you can collect the seed or bulbs at just the correct season, ripen them thoroughly, dry them for the proper length of time, and, finally, ship them home by parcel post. Most of them will survive the long journey and, on arrival, be in condition to grow successfully. In South America, however, we usually moved pretty fast from one collecting area to another. This meant that we had to collect the plants and their seeds, or other propagative parts, in the condition in which they happened to be at the moment we came across them. Sometimes they were thoroughly ripe or mature, and sometimes they were not. Sometimes there were woody plants we wanted to grow in California but not even half-ripe seeds could be found. This meant the taking of cuttings and getting them home to be rooted within two weeks, or less if possible. Also, we rarely had time to dry or ripen the seeds and bulbs artificially. Blessed be the airplane.

While the westernmost side valleys of the Río Rimac are easily accessible from the paved highway that leads from Lima to the Andean roof of the Peruvian world, during most of the year they yield only meager collections to the plant hunter. In the months of March and April, however, the returning rains awaken leaf and flower so that even cactus-dotted desert slopes break into bloom. One of the valleys we found particularly attractive was that of the major tributary, Río Santa Eulalia. In the narrow, deep-green area of the cultivated and irrigated portion of the valley floor, eucalyptus, willow, poplar, alder, and "pepper trees" grew thriftily. About habitations and along fence rows were shrubs and herbs. The contrast between these green and blossoming bottom-lands and the stony mountainsides two to three thousand feet above them was sharp, and the line of transition abrupt.

We have spent many hours working over those steep, rocky slopes in the Santa Eulalia Valley. Each time, the car is turned off the road at the same point and parked beside an Inca wall which runs along the bottom of the hillside and forms the support for a wide terrace. On it a monstrous cactus, *Trichocereus peruvianus*, grows abundantly, along with a number of its lesser relatives. It is colored a dark blue-green between the prominent ridges that parallel its squat, bulky body, and its spines are long, strong, and needle-sharp. From three to a dozen of the four- to six-foot columns grow together. Many of them are a foot in diameter. Their unusual girth and dark color make an impression of size and power that I have never felt among the more slender but far taller cerii so common on coastal ranges and Andean foothills in Peru and Chile. All about are the more delicate, gray-spined wands of *Espostoa melanostele*, the *lana vegetal* cactus, with its brown, woolly cortex breaking through the prickly surface in long stripes. Below these taller relatives the semicylindrical, greenish-brown *Melocactus peruvianus* grows in some quantity, with round bonnets of reddish hairs and soft spines perched atop. In each of these hairy tufts bloom a dozen or more little, brilliantly pink, urn-shaped flowers; sometimes the scarlet, pear-shaped seed pods have succeeded the flowers. When the digging tool is driven into the hard soil below these engaging barrel cacti, they come out with a tassel of roots attached. Grasped by this soft tassel, the sphere can be lifted off the ground and transferred to the collecting carton without danger of skin puncturing by Melocactus's short but numerous spines. There are other and still lowlier cacti—and especially one that looks like a series of short strings of small, fat, gray-green, hairy sausages, all radiating from a common center. If you attempt to dig it up, most of the sausage strings promptly fall to pieces. Every sausage that arrived in good condition at the Botanical Garden in Berkeley took root.

Above this cactus belt the steep mountainsides prove hard to climb. There are too many big boulders, and the smaller ones are too loosely packed for easy going. Now and then small depressions and flatter areas hold accumulations of soil. In and about them grows a thin but rather varied herbaceous vegetation. Each of these miniature flower gardens includes a plant or two of the brilliant *Onoseris*, which decorates vividly many a hillside in the valley of the Rimac. A low, spreading composite, it bears large, bright discs colored pinkish-magenta around the margin and dark-yellow in the center, and grows happily and flowers profusely in an almost dry soil. It is a most friendly, cheerful plant.

Sometimes one of the big cacti extends its altitudinal range far up the mountainside and then, clustering around its base, a few delicate plants that could not endure full exposure enjoy its shade and gain some protection from the drying winds. Once I found a sizable golden-backed fern tucked tightly between the roots of the heavy, blue-green columns where a spore had germinated to grow into a mature fern plant.

On one late-season afternoon that we spent in the Santa Eulalia Valley something new had been added to the barren mountainside. The gay flowers of *Onoseris* had passed their prime, and we busied ourselves collecting the seeds they were maturing and those of a number of less attractive plants. We climbed higher through the rocks, and soon the breeze which near the close of day blows gently up the valleys of Andean foothills stirred the drying vegetation and brought a breath of coolness. With it came a spicy fragrance reminiscent of an old-fashioned garden full of *Dianthus*. Although we knew that it could not be growing there, we searched the rocky surfaces for something that might look like a garden pink. The pleasant odor came and went and was hard to follow toward its source. Finally, on the far side of the ridge, we found scattered groups of a composite from whose yellow flowers the *Dianthus*-like fragrance was exhaled. It was not a very attractive plant, a little like a straggling, bushy *Coreopsis*, but we took the few seeds that had ripened, in the hope that from this species some fragrance might be bred into its more ornamental but odorless relatives that we grow in gardens.

Near the stark but now fragrant mountainside two or three low, reed-thatched huts had been built beside a diminutive, rapid-flowing stream of doubtful-looking water. Its course had become a strip of green lushness, six feet wide and colorful with more or less familiar herbs. Heliotrope had first preëmpted such stores of moisture as the little brook could give to the parched soil through which it meandered, and the odor of sachet from the dense, dark-purple flower spikes floated everywhere above the narrow meadow. Through the trailing heliotrope, Salvias threw up slender stalks set with deep-blue flowers; four-o'clocks, in quantity, grew strong but bloomed scantily; and a scarlet-flowered mint curled in and out, up and around, its less recumbent neighbors. Along the margin of the green streambank some of the species that endured the bleak aridity of the mountainside had moved down, and were responding to the influence of a moister soil by becoming something far greater in bulk and, therefore, almost unfamiliar. *Fourcroya occidentalis*, first collected near by and sent to Europe for naming many years ago, had grown prodigiously and could well have been mistaken for a species distinct from its sisters of the wastelands. We walked upstream along another Inca terrace, and then collected down toward the streamside habitations. There, on the stony banks, the four-o'clocks had gone on the rampage and dominated the otherwise increasingly sparse vegetation. The only unusual plant we found was a single specimen of a shrubby *Abutilon* that grew in the ruins of an ancient terrace. Its flowers were noteworthy, because the petals were reflexed and thus simulated a giant-flowered cyclamen. Lower down the valley, a species of *Clematis* was common. It trailed across rocky slopes and, in moister places, accumulated in masses and fountained up with hanging sprays of delicate green branches that were covered with hairy fruit-balls. On driest valley walls bromeliads grew in quantity. Their spiky leaves and tall, slender flower stalks relieved the monotony of the foothill landscape, but at the same time intensified its desert aspect.

5

DESERTS TO SNOW FIELDS

U NTIL RELATIVELY RECENTLY, most tourists up and down the west coast of South America saw only coastal Peru and, in particular, Lima and its immediate environs. Nowadays, more and more visitors make the journey eastward into the Andes on that amazing railway which runs from Lima almost straight up to the highest altitude a standard-gauge train has yet been called upon to negotiate. In one hundred miles the passenger is transported from approximately sea level to an altitude of over fifteen thousand feet; the highest point on the line is almost sixteen thousand feet. Expedition members many times made this increasingly popular journey from deserts to snow fields and back, sometimes on the railway and sometimes by automobile. The going up was always breath-taking, literally and also in terms of the magnificent scenery which borders the track or the highway at altitudes above ten thousand feet. The coming down was always a bit tame, but flavored with anticipation of the fleshpots that await the half-starved Andean sojourner in Pizarro's ancient capital. However, initial enjoyment of them is often decreased by the onset of a cold that prefers to settle in the head and ears. This affliction is, apparently, produced by the rapid descent from high altitudes to sea level and exchange of the cold, dry air of the Andes for the warm, humid atmosphere of the seacoast. If you meet a friend on a Lima corner and he cups an ear at you, it is good evidence that he is just down from the highlands.

The journey by rail from Lima into the Andes is made over the Central Railway of Peru. There is also a southern line, which, too, begins at sea level and reaches an altitude above that of Mount Whitney on its way to Lake Titicaca, with a branch to Cuzco. The "Southern"

78

must have been a considerably easier railway to build than the "Central," but it also goes up high enough and fast enough to produce unfavorable symptoms in quite a few passengers.

The highest point on the "Central" is a tunnel almost four thousand feet long; once out of it, you have crossed the continental divide and are east of the great cordillera and ready for the drop down to Huancayo at about ten thousand, seven hundred feet. When in 1869 the survey of the projected line over the Andes was made, the engineering problems involved appeared to be insurmountable, but they were ultimately solved by the construction of forty-one bridges, sixty-one tunnels, and so many zigzags and switchbacks that you soon get tired of determining whether the engine is pulling you forward or pushing you backward. Concerning the gradient, the *average* rise per minute used to be about thirty feet; perhaps the train now makes a faster trip to the summit.

This rather fantastic piece of railroad construction was the brain child of Henry ("Honest Harry") Meiggs, who began originally as a contractor in New York. With no other assests than a shipload of lumber that he had brought around the Horn, he arrived in San Francisco in 1849. He gambled on a profit but hardly expected the twenty-times-one he got for his lumber. In less than a year "Meiggs' Wharf" and his near-by sawmill were crowded with the logs cut by his men in the Mendocino forests and rafted down to the city. Later, there were charges of forgery of city warrants on a grand scale. Before the crash, Meiggs was far away. Ultimately came rumors that he was in Peru and that he was in charge of railway building and other operations upon which the then dictator was spending Peru's accumulated wealth.

Ninety years ago there could have been few precedents in railway engineering to guide Meiggs when he projected a route over the Andes from sea level. Locally, what he proposed appeared at the time entirely preposterous; when sufficiently provoked by his critics he is said to have sworn to "hang the line from balloons" if necessary. Today, as you travel over his dream come true, it is obvious that Meiggs must have been a man of vast imagination with engineering competence to match it. Before his death, the line had been extended to between twelve and thirteen thousand feet and the major construction problems were solved.

The profits accruing to Meiggs from his years and activities in Peru must have been very considerable. He is said to have paid, with interest, the obligations he had left behind in San Francisco and, in an effort to reinstate himself, to have contributed large sums to charitable institutions there. As a result he could have returned to California without official penalty, but he refused to do so on the ground that in the popular mind his reputation had been permanently impaired.

Many of our collecting trips in central Peru took us from coast to cordillera up the Rimac Valley, usually on the highway but sometimes by rail. Either way we found, at the proper season, a considerable variety of charming plants in flower; there were others less attractive but more significant botanically. Among the former I remember a vetch-leaved *Mutisia* sprawling over low bushes and, once, on the bank of the river, making a variegated pyramid of red and green where it had taken over the skeleton of a massive columnar cactus killed by flood waters. The bright flowers of many composites, among them *Heliopsis buphthalmoides*, were always conspicuous. This species shows a strange distribution, since it is known from nowhere else except Costa Rica, on the other side of the equator. A striking and curious shrub or small tree was a species of *Colignonia*. Its inflorescences are inconspicuous, but below them are modified leaves that simulate a flower and thus reminded us of a "white-flowered" *Poinsettia*. The Calceolarias, a number of different species, were abundant and sometimes colonized the shadier sides of steep quebradas, turning them into fields of gold. Along with these native Peruvian plants was the yellow mustard, a ubiquitous foreigner that is rapidly taking possession of favorable climatic zones in the Peruvian Andes. In some places it has already become so well established that the nonbotanical observer classifies it with the native vegetation. Sometimes, Fuchsias appeared in favored niches on the ever more precipitous slopes of the Andes' lower shoulders. There was one species we found upon which I shall never look without a qualm. We not only found it but succeeded in bringing it home alive. However, the initial steps in that achievement might well have started one of us home dead.

They occurred while we were collecting between ten and thirteen thousand feet, along that fine piece of highway engineering that makes it possible for an automobile to go east from Lima almost as straight up into the Andes as does the Central Peruvian Railway—from deserts to snow fields. We left the capital very early in the morning and had driven far up this highway before we undertook serious collecting. As the altitude increased, the highway and the railroad began to fol-

low more closely the steep and winding course of the Rimac. Above
the mountain valley in which lies the sleepy little town of San Mateo,
the river ran tumultuously in a deep and ugly gorge. Just overhead the
snowy peaks rose to more than fifteen thousand feet, but were unseen
because the high cliffs that wall the river piled up too steeply. From
the melting snows above, small torrents flowed noisily down every
depression in the cliffs. Along the rivulets, and in the moist hanging
meadows they create, we found many valuable plants.

Our program always consisted in dropping off a collector and driving on up the highway to a spot where there was room enough to
park the car, either against the cliffs or on the edge looking down a
hundred feet or more to the roaring river. From there a second collector started to work forward along the highway. When the one left
behind had collected up to the parking place, the car started on and,
depending upon collecting conditions, either passed the second collector or picked him up and left the first one behind again.

There were a few things worth collecting beside the highway, but
mostly we had to climb for the ones we wanted. They grew in crevices,
on narrow ledges, or over rocky outcrops, far above our heads, and
you had to find a rock slide or a little ravine in which to work your way
up the steep cliff walls. When you came to a ledge you collected along
on either side, as far as it was possible to go. Then you struggled up
again and out along another ledge. The going up was only a hard
scramble, slightly damaging to toes and knees, but the coming down
was not so good. It was like descending the steepest and roughest flight
of steps. With one arm, and often both arms, full of plants, you had
to lean as far back as possible and, at each step, drive your heels into
the gravel and loose rock. When there were only big boulders, you
bent almost double to maintain equilibrium as you jumped down from
one rock surface to the next.

I happened to be the one left behind when the automobile reached
the most amazing section of the highway we saw that day. Both it
and the railway line go through some of their worst contortions at
this point—corkscrew turns for the former, switchbacks for the latter.
The gorge of the Rimac is very narrow, continually winds in and out
between outjutting cliffs, and rises so rapidly that the gradient is close
to four per cent along the track, and worse in the sharpest turns of
the highways. On both walls of the deep ravine, parallel ledges, sometimes cut out of the living rock, carry the road and the railway. Bridges

have a habit of disappearing into tunnels, and tunnels turn into bridges. The whole thing becomes positively fabulous when you see the river itself drop out of sight into a tunnel, so that the railroad may gain altitude more easily by occupying what was, originally, the river bed.

This part of the gorge is called "Infiernillo," and constitutes a "Little Hell" entirely different from but just as real as the stretch of coastal desert highway similarly designated and described in an earlier chapter. In the Andean one, everything is at right angles to everything else, but mostly straight up and down, and overwhelmingly rough, barren, and desolate. The flood of the Rimac fills it with deafening noise. A continuous and menacing rumble rises from the boulders that are being ground together in the deep bed of the river. It provides a deep-throated undertone for the high-pitched roar of the white, racing surface water. Echoing back and forth from one high rock wall to the opposite one, the din is prodigious, and it acquires an eerie quality as powerful, but variable, downward drafts of air suddenly increase and then decrease the intensity of the sound.

Collecting slowly up the highway through Infiernillo, I tried to project myself back four hundred years to the days when Pizarro's mailed horsemen were riding up the narrow footpaths that the Incas had built through the Andes. There must have been more than one passage like Infiernillo, or worse, which only the compelling lust for gold could have induced them to attempt. Some of these ancient trails are still being used, and if, in Pizarro's time, they were as hair-raising as their remnants are today, the nervous systems of the conquistadors must have been shattered long before they captured the mountain capital of the Inca Empire. As elsewhere in mountainous terrain, trails in the Peruvian highlands follow the sides of river valleys. Every now and then a vertical cliff shoulders its way out to the river's edge, and then the trail is carried around it on wooden platforms built against the rock wall. Too often these narrow shelves are in need of repair, and the traveler picks his way over them gingerly and in prayerful mood. Much of the flooring is loose underfoot; sometimes part of it is entirely wanting. These gaps, some wide enough to demand a jump, frame unpleasant vistas of fast-flowing rivers, rough with great boulders, or of steep mountainsides, strewn with sharp rocks far, far below. On these rickety sidewalks I lost all shame and hugged the rock walls or touched them furtively with my hand, in the hope of gaining a sense of security that I knew would be false. At the time the danger to life and limb seemed very real, and in retrospect it appears even more so; but I suppose that John Muir was right when he said that "Few places in the world are more dangerous than home."

Standing on the highway bridge in Little Hell, I let my eye range over the cliffsides for evidence of interesting vegetation. I had a good view up and down the gorge from the lower edge of the bridge, but only one spot looked promising. There, a hundred feet above the far end of the bridge and two hundred yards downstream, I saw a large V-shaped crevice, the lower end of which was covered with a green tangle. It appeared to consist of only one kind of plant, with bright green leaves, and a few dots of color that meant flowers. Since the broad end of the crevice ended in an almost perpendicular cliff, one hundred and fifty feet above the river, I saw no chance of climbing directly up to get a closer look at the plant. However, just above the crevice, a ledge on the cliff wall ran uninterruptedly from the point I wanted to reach almost to the edge of a broad shelf of rock not far above my head.

By climbing the shaky handrail of the bridge and balancing on it, I gained enough height to shove my elbows over the rock shelf and, finally, to drag myself up onto it. Then it was easy to crawl over to the narrow ledge. Once there, the going was not difficult except that, now and then, there was a particularly rough or narrow spot. It was beginning to be somewhat late in the afternoon, and the flow of the river was increasing. Just below, an immense boulder had fallen halfway across the river's bed. The Rimac struck it with smashing blows and spouted high against its shoulder. This never-ceasing conflict filled the bottom of the gorge with spray that rose to the level of my ledge as a gentle, refreshing mist.

Slowly approaching the crevice, I saw that the plant I sought was a fine *Fuchsia*. It grew thick and lush, and completely covered the lower end of the V-shaped crack. I cannot understand why the rampant luxuriance of its growth did not immediately sound a warning note somewhere in my consciousness. Probably I was too intent upon reaching my objective, which was now so close at hand, or perhaps fatigue had dulled the edge of caution that must be kept keen when one is collecting in rough and unfamiliar territory. At any rate, without hesitation I lowered myself into the narrow, upper end of the crevice and, holding on to its edge, began to slide down toward the *Fuchsia*. When I reached it I let go and clambered out across the deeply matted tangle of dead and living stems and branches. There were a number of flowering shoots, and I reached out my hand to take one of them. I kept reaching out and reaching out, farther and farther, and suddenly it dawned upon me, first, that the flowers were actually moving away from my hand, and, second, that the whole mass of vegetation on which I was standing was beginning to slide over the lower end of the crevice.

Immediately I began to stamp my feet down through the latticelike plant surface in an effort to settle them in the rock or gravel beneath. Instead, however, of finding a more or less firm bottom, I splashed into thin, muddy rubble in which my feet began to sink. Some instinct, stirred perhaps by the sound that the rocky mud was making as it began to splash over the precipice, warned me not to flounder but to throw myself, full length, on the surface of the brush, and to crawl across it to the safety of the edge of the crevice. This I finally accomplished, and then pulled myself over the edge, and over onto the steep cliffside. Already more than half the heavy, straggling *Fuchsia* had slipped to the margin of the precipice, and the brittle stems were beginning to crack and splinter and drop large sections of the plant down into the river, far below.

Now I could see what had happened. The lower end of the crevice was a very shallow basin, in which water had collected from slow but continuous rock seepage. Probably this seepage began at the upper end of the crevice and followed along its solid rock bottom. Certainly there had been no hint of water at the upper end, when I had first entered the big crack and begun to walk over the top of its deep accumulation of loose gravel. Of course, the *Fuchsia* thoroughly appreciated the excess moisture, and had responded by growing so vigorously that it completely covered the lower end of the crevice. In the loose, wet soil, the roots could not anchor the plant firmly, and probably in a few more years its increasing weight and bulk would have toppled it over the edge. In other words, disaster was certain to follow additional weight, and this I had supplied.

After a little I recovered my breath, and, what was more important, my nerve, and again went down into the crevice to get what I could from that part of the *Fuchsia* that had not already gone over the edge and been torn to pieces and carried away by the river. Part of the time I held on with one hand to the rocks that stuck out from the crevice wall and, reaching out, dragged toward me some of the larger stems that bore flowering shoots. The flowers were four-inch-long tubes of glistening dark-maroon that ended in a frill of short, greenish-white, triangular lobes, and were borne in loose sprays of eight to twelve flowers each. The leaves were light-green, almost circular, with fretted edges, and very large for a *Fuchsia*. None of the stems I could reach showed even half-mature fruits; indeed, it was probably too early in the season to expect anything but buds and flowers. Since there was no seed, the only possibility of reproducing this fine species at home was by cuttings, and so I broke off a dozen pieces of stem of various ages and tied them into a little bundle. In addition, I took a few flowering shoots to go into my plant press, which had been hidden near the bridge.

Before starting back I buttoned the bundle of cuttings and the flowers into my shirt, because I suspected that I would need both hands free during the descent along the ledge. This turned out to be the case. The recent near-disaster in the crevice must have overstimulated my imagination, for the ledge looked much narrower than it had on the way up. Once you become worried and overcautious in rock climbing your judgment is likely to become so impaired that crawling on hands and knees seems to be the only safe thing to do. I did not get quite to that stage, however.

Our collecting in, above, and below Infiernillo was very profitable that day, and we returned to Lima heavily laden with plants. Early the next morning I wrapped the cuttings of the crevice *Fuchsia* in oiled paper and packed them in a reduced shoe box. By air express they reached San Francisco in eight days, and on the following day were placed in the rooting bench in the Botanical Garden.

In the Rimac Valley the coastal desert ends at an altitude of about eight hundred feet. Above, some rain may fall, but apart from cacti no appreciable amount of native vegetation is to be seen until the valley floor has risen another three thousand feet. There, the increasing vegetation includes certain sizable shrubs that attract the attention even of the casual observer. They are given a wide berth by the natives, and should be admired at a distance by everyone except the botanist who may find himself required to give them his close attention. We knew them as species of *Jatropha*, a genus belonging to the Euphorbiaceae, or Spurge family. There are a number of Jatrophas in Peru. We collected one of them in the Lachay lomas. It wound its thick, smooth, gray stems over the sand and rocks in an unpleasantly reptilian fashion. In the lower part of the Mantaro canyon two erect species were common. They are provided with vicious thorns, and horses as well as men have learned to recognize them and to keep their distance. Not all the Peruvian species are spiny, but, since they are euphorbs, their juices as well as their spines must be held under suspicion of causing skin irritations, sometimes serious ones.

In the valley of the Rimac, and elsewhere, species of *Jatropha* are referred to in the vernacular as *huanarpo,* and, more specifically as *huanarpo macho* and *huanarpo hembra.* Apparently, the former designation refers to a red-flowered, and the latter to a white-flowered, unarmed species. Today, and perhaps for many centuries, huanarpo has been alleged to possess aphrodisiac properties, and the words *macho* and *hembra,* or their genders, serve to indicate the sex for which each is appropriate. More than once, in widely separated areas, we were asked by smirking natives whether we had found "our huanarpo." On one occasion, in an Andean market town, a peon, upon learning that we were plant collectors, said with a wink that he knew where we could find some huanarpo, and this brought guffaws of laughter from a crowd of hangers-on. A merchant in Chincheros was positive that a mere prick from a thorn induced the wildest impulses. In addition, he could himself vouch for the fact that when you inhale the smoke from burning brush in which stems of huanarpo are included a highly disturbing reaction is instantly obtained. He also said that when groups of young people are picnicking it is considered a vulgar joke to bring in huanarpo and toss it on the campfire.

In scientific circles and in the popular mind, huanarpo, at one time was thought to be responsible for the *verruga* disease. This malady first attracted attention in the 'seventies of the last century, when a highly fatal epidemic appeared among the workmen who were constructing the present railway from Lima up into the Andes. The original terminus of the railway was Oroya. During the several years of railway building, there was said to have been a total of seven thousand deaths from all causes among the road crews, the majority due to what was then called "Oroya fever."

The disease has two clinical aspects. One, called *verruga peruana,* or simply verruga (Spanish for "wart"), is relatively benign. It is characterized by an eruption of nodules which vary in size from pin points to hazelnuts and usually cover the extremities and the face, although any part of the body may be affected. Heavy with blood and easily ruptured, the nodules give the patient a loathsome appearance. After several weeks or months they heal spontaneously. The other form is a severe anemia, often accompanied by high fever. The workmen who contracted it did not respond to treatments useful in other anemias and usually died. If the patient survived the anemia, he often still had to endure the eruptions.

The epidemic along the new railway was suspected of being medically related to an eruptive disease long known to be prevalent in middle altitudes in the Rimac Valley and elsewhere in the Andean foothills. In 1885, Daniel A. Carrión, a medical student, inoculated himself from the nodule of a patient afflicted with the eruptive phase, and died with symptoms of the anemia that had killed so many of the railway men. In other words, he established the twofold character of the disease. Technically, it should be called "Carrión's disease," but in popular parlance both forms are referred to collectively as "verruga." Beginning in 1926, the work of Noguchi and his associates furnished bacteriological proof of the unity of the disease by cultivation of the bacterium (*Bartonella bacilliformis*) from both the eruptive and the usually fatal form. Sometime later it was proved that this bacterium was present in certain wild sand-flies occurring in the areas where verruga was being contracted.

It now seems clear that in Peru verruga can be contracted only between 2,500 and 9,500 feet, particularly in Andean foothill valleys. It is also known from restricted areas in Ecuador and Columbia. The insect involved, one of the Diptera, looks like an exceedingly minute edition of the common mosquito. It is a *Phlebotomus,* and at least three species occur in Peruvian verruga terrain, but only one of them, *verrucarum,* is a proved vector of infection. It can readily pass through window screening or netting and, until DDT, the primitively housed mountain people had no protection against the tiny blood-seekers with their infected proboscises. They attack man ruthlessly, and a foothill family may suffer a nightly—they apparently operate only after sundown—average per person of up to fifty bites the year around. *Phlebotomi* are exceedingly sensitive to DDT, and thorough spraying of floors and walls will free a dwelling for some months. So far as the disease itself is concerned, antibiotics have greatly reduced mortality. The "mycins" are particularly effective in the eruptive phase. Nevertheless, you can be very sure that on our most recent expedition, as always in the past, we closed the car windows tight when, after dark, we came through the verruga zone on our return to Lima from the highlands.

Beyond Infiernillo, the traveler by highway or by rail enters the Andean fastnesses. The limit of shrub vegetation occurs at about twelve thousand feet. Above that altitude wood is at a premium and the huts of the alpine shepherds are built of turfs. These blocks of sod, cut from the high, barren plateaus, serve also for fuel. Sometimes it is hard to decide where the banked-up layers of fuel end and the hut itself begins. The sod contains a high proportion of organic material, so that when once alight it makes a fair substitute for firewood; except that the amount of acrid smoke it emits is out of all proportion to the amount of heat it gives. The hardy mountain people, who barely succeed in keeping body and soul together in the bleak punas of the central Peruvian Andes, make nothing of a little smoke; it does not even constitute a minor aggravation. For effective cooking or baking, however, something hotter than a sod fire is necessary, and they use the resinous *tola* heath, *Lepidophyllum quadrangulare*, which burns readily, even when green, and produces a hot fire. Bundles of this plant accumulate in great heaps near railway stations at elevations below the upper limit of shrub vegetation, waiting to be shipped up into the shrubless puna country.

The vegetation of those highland plateaus is limited in number of species. Thousands of square miles are covered with the coarse tufts of *Stipa ichu*, which derives its specific designation from the ancient Inca name for this alpine grass. The tufts, which grow at rather close intervals, are often as much as three feet in height and about a foot in diameter. When actively growing and green, and also when dry and hard, the ichu is grazed by herds of llamas and alpacas. A number of species of dwarf composites, a few gentians, valerians, madders, and even lupines and violas hide in the ichu and, in its protection, carry through successfully their brief alpine life-cycle.

On the broad plains beyond the first Andean crest, glacial lakes occur, and in them grow water plants which are, perhaps, responsible for the large frog population and, thus, for the trade in frog's legs that goes on between passengers and natives at railway stations in that part of the highlands. On the alpine meadows we sometimes saw an abundance of the cosmopolitan mushroom, *Agaricus campestris*, but had no evidence that it was eaten by the mountaineers. Various waterfowl visit these alpine lakes, and colonies of white herons make a charming picture as they methodically fish the margins of the blue expanses.

The puna people devote themselves principally to grazing but also grow a few meager crops. Most important is the potato, cultivation of which continues up to fourteen thousand feet. Usually the tubers of these high-altitude varieties do not correspond to our potatoes in bulk, color, or taste. Decidedly on the small side, and often strongly colored, many of them have an agreeable nutty flavor. Along with potatoes, *ocas* (*Oxalis tuberosa*) are commonly grown, and they do well even at extreme altitudes. In less exposed areas on the puna certain varieties of beans are grown with some success.

We have often collected on the puna and along the margins of the snow fields, on both sides of the highway that crosses the center of the Peruvian Andes and traverses the valleys and high plateaus south toward Cuzco and east toward the jungle. Often the mountain city of Huancayo was collecting headquarters. It is rather frequently visited by tourists who have a day or two to get some view of the Andes and their peoples. Its principal attraction is the Sunday market, which is one of the most important and colorful of all Andean markets. It is said to attract the largest number of different clans of highland Indians, who bring their distinctive wares for sale to the tourist. There he can buy the finest of white alpaca rugs or blankets. The one I brought home was to be selected from hundreds that a local expert kindly agreed to examine as they came into the Huancayo market. Finally it arrived in Lima and proved to be worth waiting for, because all the different fleeces that made up the five-by-seven-foot product were perfectly matched in texture and uniformly white.

The market is held on Huancayo's broad main thoroughfare, said to be a segment of one of the major Inca highways. On a good Sunday, with fifteen thousand people milling up and down, the boast that this is the largest outdoor market in the world seems conservative. The quantities of vegetables, fruits, cereals, and livestock on display give it the atmosphere of an old-time county fair at home. Because this is the garden spot of the Andes, where agriculture and its products are of a better quality than elsewhere, the appearance and character of the commodities on sale are superlative by contrast with other Andean markets. Thus, for example, the tanner has the finest hides to deliver to the artist in leather, who fashions a variety of ornate sandals, saddlebags, and smaller articles. A saddle, that mark of aristocracy in the highlands, becomes in his hands a work of art, ornamented with colored leathers and chased silver. One tourist from our Western cow country had acquired a superbridle that pleased him so immensely that he did not see how he could wait to get back to the States to display it to his fellow "dudes."

The abundant supplies of sheep, llama, and alpaca wool make for a gorgeous display of ponchos, blankets, and other woven goods. Would that the crude effects produced from German aniline dyes had never come to the Andes to replace the soft pastel shades obtained from juices of madder, barberry, walnut, and the other long-forgotten vegetable resources of the ancient dye artists. The vendor of dyes piles his varicolored powders in neat little cones on his table. He uses a crude homemade balance to weigh out five centavos' or ten centavos' worth. The *serranas* find it hard to pass up such an enticing array of intense shades. They linger beside the table and select, not what will harmonize, but rather what will be most arresting.

Near the dye merchant's is the apothecary's table. There you may examine an incredibly varied collection of dried leaves, roots, fruits, seeds, fungi, as well as dried lizards, toads, snakes, animal entrails, insects, and, in largest quantity, a series of objects of unfamiliar, and probably best undisclosed, origin. All the drugs have Quechua names, and the vendor is prepared, at the slightest encouragement, to reel off a list of those diseases and misfortunes that each of his wares will cure or ameliorate.

Tourists usually buy elaborately carved gourds, one of the specialties of the Huancayo Indians. Gay little plaster figurines, which look almost as though they had been imported from Italy, also have an attraction for the visitor, but by the time they reach Lima heads and legs often require the glue pot. For the discriminating foreigner, the products of the silversmiths should have the greatest appeal. His purse will be considerably lighter when he leaves these descendants of an ancient and relatively honest guild, but his *recuerdos* of Huancayo will be a good investment, of which he will never tire.

The *tiendas* and more ambitious stores that line the highway project their stocks of goods out over the sidewalk and onto the pavement. Nevertheless, they find it hard to compete with the appealing atmosphere of the truly out-of-door markets. Therefore, some of the shopkeepers operate loudspeakers, through which announcements are made in the Quechua tongue of alluring bargains on sale within. Between these announcements a program of "canned" music roars out, and knots of *serranos* gather around with awe and wonder on their faces.

Lying at an altitude of almost eleven thousand feet, in a somewhat protected location in the valley of the Río Mantaro, Huancayo is a sunny, temperate oasis within the battlements of the Andes. In the center of a rich farming country, its population has a somewhat opulent appearance; something that is rare in the highlands of Peru. Round about are groves of eucalyptus trees. The hillsides show the effects of two centuries of overgrazing and overcropping in eroded areas that are beginning to claim much of the formerly extensive stretches of cultivated land. The Huancayo region is old, geologically speaking. It differs from most Andean terrain in having remained stable, with no uplift of the land blocks for long periods of time, and so the hills are rounded and the valleys filled in. Its horizons are undulating and soft, rather than saw-toothed and grim.

One of the most successful forays from Huancayo into the snowy passes was made by Harvey at a season when the alpine vegetation was at the height of its flowering. He needed temporary collecting headquarters nearer the mountains, and had letters of introduction to Don López Alizega, who owned the Hacienda Acopalca and several thousand head of sheep. There, on the margin of the steep mountainsides, Harvey was hospitably received and his work facilitated. Once out of the valley over which the hacienda sprawled, the altitude increased rapidly and the snow was not far above. Along the edge of the extensive snow fields, and on the banks of cold rivulets that issued from them, he found the most extreme of alpine types of vegetation. Mostly the soil was heavy with moisture, but the herbs did not respond to maximum supplies of water, as do the plants of lower altitudes, by growing lush and rank; rather, they hugged the ground and aggregated themselves into low mounds or thick carpets, taking care not to expose more surface than was necessary to the chill and rarefied air and to the intense insolation of the high altitudes. Genera which at lower altitudes elongated their axes to form sizable herbs, shrubs, or small trees were, nearer the snow line, represented by rosette plants in which the axis had been completely telescoped. On the near-by rocky, arid ridges, in full exposure, were alpine cacti—particularly *Opuntia floccosa*, which formed white, cushionlike masses. At a distance they simulated piles of wool, which could have been sheared from the many sheep cropping the low vegetation on the cold, wet mountainsides.

Harvey's bag from the squashy meadows, their drier margins, and the stony ridges contained a greater variety of plants than he had anticipated. Among others, there were dwarf members of the geranium family, three-inch-high yellow gentians and two or three really minute ones, some of the same valerians and Violas that had been collected in the ichu-carpeted punas, and a species of *Werneria* whose yellow, dandelionlike flowers were, as he said, "kept down so close to the soil line that one could imagine that they were trying to escape the lawn mower."

Above him, as he worked from one collecting ground to another, the zigzags of a dim trail across the face of the rocky cliffs led up into a lofty pass and, still higher, into small alpine valleys. An inconsiderable traffic wandered up and down this trail. Once he saw an enterprising local merchant urging on a string of burros whose panniers dripped with the melt of ice chunks cut from the glaciers, miles behind the pass. In Huancayo he would obtain ten cents a load from what was left in the panniers after the burning alpine sun and the furnaces within the transportation had taken their toll.

At the beginning of one Andean winter I asked Harvey and Bob to arm themselves with tripod and cameras and make an excursion up into the land of snow and ice to capture on Kodachrome something of the landscape of the higher Peruvian altitudes. Lima was delightfully warm, dry, and sunny on the morning that I saw them off at the railway station. In a few hours their train had gophered through tunnels, climbed the steep walls of the Andean barrier like a mountain sheep, and finally deposited them at Ticlio station, near the top of the pass, to face a roaring alpine blizzard. They had made arrangements to stay in a mining camp at Moracocho, ten miles away. In the forbidding climate of the plains and valleys just beneath the highest peaks, the Indian shepherds, inured to hardship, do not maintain habitations fit to protect the wayfarer against the days and nights of the highland winter. Indeed, in any season, the naturalist in the higher altitudes of Peru would fare badly were it not for the mining camps and their hospitality.

At Moracocho a warm welcome awaited them. They were taken in charge by one of the North American mining engineers, and spent an unforgettable evening before his fireplace, in which discarded mine timbers burned with a roar that competed effectively with the muffled whine of the blizzard. Finally, decency demanded that good night's should be said. They bundled up and, once out of doors, had difficulty in steering a safe course toward the dormitory. In it they had anticipated a night sleepless with the penetrating cold. Imagine, therefore, their surprise upon discovering that the turn of a switch brought into action an electric stove geared to defy the climate.

What was left of the alpine afternoon, following their arrival at the mining camp, had been too cloudy and snowy for pictures. The early morning of the next day, however, was almost clear and the light good. Shafts of bright sunshine flooded the white peaks and vertical mountain walls, to give unexpectedly fine studies in light and shade; but not for long. Soon the bitter winds were astir, bringing a drizzle of rain that was almost at the freezing point, that fogged lenses and found its way under turned-up coat collars. Imperceptibly the rain became sleet and the sleet became snow, and soon they were again facing an Andean blizzard. The white flakes began to pile in drifts, to flow down the long valleys, and to turn the lower slopes from brown to dirty gray with the light coating of new-fallen snow. Nevertheless, the motion pictures taken under these unfavorable and unpleasant conditions turned out well. They gave a striking picture of the stark crudity of Andean snow-line landscapes, and reproduced the onset of an alpine storm as it darkens the sky and creates increased contrasts between the background and the white peaks that spring up out of snow fields and glaciers.

Next day the rapid train ride down from the land of snow and ice gave Harvey and Bob the most impressive view of the zonation of vegetation that characterizes the brief journey from snow fields to deserts in central Peru. A little distance below the cold, wet, or snowy slopes of the highest plains there came a sudden transition to alpine aridity that supported only cacti. Then, since it was spring, they saw the middle Andean foothills green and flowering, even brilliant with drifts of yellow, lavender, and pink. Below, a slow transition displayed the lower Andean foothill equivalent of the coastal desert, with its rock-strewn gray, tan, or brown mountainsides which, rarely, swept up to a light-green crest—a severe landscape and one that was not relieved by its scattered forests of columnar cacti. Sometimes the deserts are drier, sometimes the snow fields are more extensive, but, from coast to cordillera and vice versa, there is always that fundamental contrast between deserts and snow fields.

6

EYEBROW OF THE JUNGLE

THE ANDEAN HEIGHTS, their utter wildness, their vast and silent alpine plateaus, their sheer descents into the Amazonian jungle, their mountain folk and the malignant spirits which for them haunt the high altitudes, create something which ever beckons anew. Within them there are glorious moments to live; there the air is freer and strangely inspiring; there one can learn some of the elsewhere forgotten lore of ancient peoples; there plants and animals as well as air, sky, and thoughts differ from anything we know here below. There we learn to conquer fear and suffering and satisfy our scientific curiosity in a vast kingdom of alluring adventure." Thus, in his own words, my friend and long-time plant collector, Felix Woytkowski explains in considerable part why, again and again, he has journeyed for many weeks on end along and over the Andean backbone of Peru, journeys which have often extended downward into the equally inhospitable lowlands.

Today the airplane will take you into or over the Andes. If, however, you are a hardier traveler, intent upon an intimate contact with the Peruvian scene, you can travel by car or bus over highways and roads that run up from the coastal strip over the often frigid and largely barren Andean plateaus, or punas, and down the eastern flank of the highlands into the low tropical rain forest or jungle. Through these lowlands, known as the *montaña*, pour some of the ultimate sources of the Atlantic-bound Amazonian river system.

On the often precipitous descents into the jungle, the trans-Andean voyager by road comes rather suddenly upon the botanically famous *ceja de la montaña* or "eyebrow of the jungle." Like the Peruvian coastal lomas, described earlier, it is a fogbegotten, dripping, otherworldly land where swirling, drifting cloud masses signal the advance upward of tropical air from the hot, moist lowlands to the increasing chill of higher elevations. All the way from Ecuador to southern Peru and Bolivia, *cejas* occur, with their extent determined and their character influenced by altitude, the abruptness of Andean descents eastward, and the quantity of upward-flowing humidity. In the most spectacular and typical cejas below major passes through the cordillera, mist, fog, and rain are rarely absent. As a result, the floor of the characteristically low forest is a mattress of epiphytes—mainly mosses, ferns, and lichens—along with delicate seed plants, many of the species not elsewhere to be seen. Not only does this living mattress enshroud soil, fallen tree trunks, and rocky outcroppings; it also flows up the forest trees to festoon lower branches to which cling orchids, bromeliads, and filmy ferns in great variety; in open spaces shrubby members of the Heath and Madder families are glowing masses of color in their flowering season. Unhappily, most ceja species, many of them beautiful and otherwise desirable as garden subjects, can be grown successfully in temperate climates only under special greenhouse conditions.

During our numerous periods of plant collecting in Peru, one or another of us saw something of the more accessible and thus botanically better-known Carpis and Gaza cejas which lie near the highway from Lima to Tingo María and on to Pucalpa. As will appear in a moment, Felix worked in almost unknown "eyebrows" elsewhere in the Central Andean region. In southern Peru, first César and later Roy collected in equally unknown ones in eastern Depto.* Puno, where the high plateaus are dissected by river valleys that soon become tropical as they fall fast to the Río Madre de Dios, an important tributary of the Amazon. In total botanical composition the two ceja areas, central and south Andean, are remarkably similar. However, we found quite unexpected seasonal distinctions in the flowering of ceja species. For example, of some two hundred in flower in the Puno ceja during May and November there were only a half dozen blooming in both of the two months. This suggests that you must think twice before describing the composition of even a tropical or near-tropical vegetation after observations made at one season only.

* In Peru, a *departamento* is a major political subdivision within which are a number of lesser subdivisions, the *provincias*. In some other South American republics (Chile and Argentina, for example), the designations are reversed, a *provincia* being made up of *departamentos*.

This chapter begins with a quotation from a report by Felix about one of the plant-collecting expeditions he has made for me during the past fifteen years. Felix came to Peru from Poland in the early 1930's. For many years he devoted himself exclusively to collecting insects for museums and private enthusiasts. He has added immeasurably to knowledge of the entomology of Peru. Probably no one concerned with natural history has as wide a familiarity with the Peruvian hinterland. Since botany and entomology have obvious interrelations, I felt confident that Felix could successfully combine plant and insect collecting. Of recent years he has emphasized the former and become a source of Peruvian species for amateur and professional orchid collections. He is fluent to competent in a considerable number of languages and likes to speak and write English. The numerous quotations from his reports which follow indicate the large store of adjectives he has available to express his reactions to a variety of scenes and occasions.

He once went for me to the quite remote ceja regions in the Depto. Junín. Leaving the main highway at Tarma, the narrow mountain road plunges down along the sides of almost vertical canyons toward San Ramón at the rate of 1,500 feet an hour. Along with some twenty countrypeople going to roadside farms and villages, Felix and his helper rode the open platform of the truck otherwise occupied by hens, pigs, and miscellaneous baggage. Like the Prince in an earlier chapter, he found his situation "the most healthy and enlightening method of getting acquainted with the countryside." He felt "like a sailor during a storm as the truck swerves, jolts, and absorbs constantly the shocks of hidden holes, abrupt breaks, and the products of certain unfathomable whims of the driver. This fine feeling of sailorship is enhanced by one's unshakable conviction that at any moment we may all sail out to meet the bracing air on the way down into the rocky depths below. This predeath anticipation is your faithful companion whenever you travel by truck in Peru over the Sierra and down into the montaña."

Just as they swung around one of the sharp curves, a six-foot mound of earth and rubble crossed the road. It served to anchor the beams of a temporary bridge thrown across a small but deep canyon. As the truck slowly surmounted this obstacle, the driver remarked that on the previous day the truck of a friend had come upon it too fast and toppled off the bridge. Looking downward as they inched across it, narrow and shaky, they expected to see evidence of the catastrophe, but, "the solicitous engineer in charge of this road section had done a quick and admirable job of removing the wrecked truck and the eleven passengers' corpses. The bottom of the abyss looked free from guilt, peaceful and horribly clean where a small but torrential stream fed by a crystalline, icy cascade crashed against a colossal, rounded, polished boulder upon which the truck had been squashed and its passengers mashed into something unrecognizable; well, the spot was not too bad for one's eventual death—quick and painless."

In four hours' travel down from the cold, barren Andean highlands they entered the Amazonian rain forest. After the first hour's descent the mountainsides showed forested tracts; after ten miles more, at Utcuyacu, the forests stretched up overhead to the highest ridges, with mists and clouds blowing across them. No one had ever attempted to botanize the numberless valleys, the incredibly deep, narrow canyons and precipitous ravines that Felix saw about him. He recognized bits of grass-steppe on rocky surfaces toward the summits and, lower down, bare outcrops and stony fields on sharp contours; otherwise the panorama was one continuous green world. Later on, he found that near Utcuyacu the "eyebrow of the jungle" vegetation and that of the true montaña, or jungle, met and intermingled.

During the journey by truck he fell into conversation with the new owner of an old Utcuyacu hacienda, who offered hospitality to him and his helper. The hacienda buildings stood on small strips of almost level land at the foot of a high, steep-shouldered mountain. These strips were margined by ancient stone walls which attempted to retain the constantly eroding soil and impede the descent of the crumbling mountain slopes above. On three sides of the main buildings, a mixture of jungle and ceja formed an almost solid wall of vegetation. In cutting it the *hacendado* had expended months of hard labor to discover that within were coffee shrubs and orange and avocado trees planted many years before. To Felix's delight, the ancient orange trees were a mass of cobwebs, from which he took a nice collection of spiders, most of which were new to him. Lack of pruning and heavy incrustations of lichens and mosses were responsible for an almost complete absence of fruit.

After a survey of both faces of the valley in which the hacienda lay, Felix decided upon a series of explorations over them to the highlands above. He wanted to collect the upward-zoned vegetation—first, low ceja forest alternating with layers of brushland; then, transitions from higher forest to grass-steppe; and, finally, broadening streaks of boulder-strewn terrain. Ravines ran upward as far as one or another of these rather sharply defined vegetation zones. He and his helper, a powerfully built Indian youth native to the North Peruvian Andes, began the ascent of one of the apparently most up-reaching ravines. Then they tried another and still another. Each one, sooner or later, was blocked by sheer rock walls hidden from below by the dense vegetation. Less was in flower at these lower elevations than Felix had anticipated; most common was an orchid and once, only once, he came upon another, a "truly gorgeous one," with big, long spikes of lavender flowers. The first proved to be an *Oncidium* and the second an *Epidendrum*.

Finally they tried a somewhat broader ravine down which a little stream tumbled over broken white boulders. After a few hundred yards of difficult climbing in and along the water, an almost vertical rock wall confronted them. This time, having provided himself with a rope, Felix sent his helper to tear his way through the thickets bordering the stream and lower the rope to him from an overhanging ledge. Reunited above, the helper was for a rest but Felix insisted upon pushing on. Then came the sad discovery that plant press and insect-collecting kit had been forgotten. Down below at the base of the cliff they could see them and there they stayed; neither one would make the round trip on the rope or through the thickets. Thereafter, what was collected went into Felix's rucksack.

The possibility of further upward advance was not encouraging, but they persisted. Felix was aiming at what from a distance appeared to be relatively open brushland. It proved to be something far different, an almost impenetrable complex, often six feet high, of strong rough grasses, low dense shrubs, and small twisted trees. Once in it, they could see only a yard or two ahead. Although penetration of this maze seemed to provide the only route upward, it was clear that another had to be found. The nearest tall trees rose somewhat to the left. They tried to work around the barrier toward them. Suddenly Felix realized that his helper was losing his nerve; as he describes it, "his looks cried fear and distrust." When they finally succeeded in finding the tall forest, the sun was pointing to about two o'clock and Felix knew that they must soon begin their return downward to the hacienda.

The tall forest presented, in Felix's words, "a marvelous variety of vegetation pictures." It faced full north and, although only a few hundred yards from the grass-steppe maze, contained scarcely a single one of the species that he had seen there. In contrast, and truly astoundingly, a unique microclimate high up on the mountainside had created an environment permitting the development of an almost typical ceja-jungle vegetation. In particular, there were species of genera familiar to us as foliage plants for the house—*Monstera, Anthurium, Philodendron, Diffenbachia, Xanthosoma*. Growing among them were Fuchsias and, everywhere, lush mosses and ferns.

"How could I forsake this little wonderland to speed the return journey?" writes Felix, and apparently he did not, for a while at least. At every step something new appeared: the big, golden "pocketbooks" of a prostrate *Calceolaria*; a vivid blue *Commelina*, near relative of *Tradescantia*; and orchids crowding each other upon the rotting trunks of fallen trees. A standing trunk on the margin of an "absurdly steep slope bore an incredible plant garden," says Felix. "Low and taller species thoroughly covered its lower bark, and coming nearer I thought I saw, higher up, the 'lady-slipper' flowers of a large orchid; my helper began to cut into the eight-inch-thick trunk with his machete, but the wood was very hard, the ground wet, oily, and steep, and my patience precarious. When it fell I saw the day's first truly valuable find—a colony in full flower of the orchid I had seen. It was a *Phragmipedium* with big, pouched slippers, the side petals ending in foot-long, brownish-red appendages. Moments later I saw another orchid, new to me, showing a white lip lined and spotted with brilliant purple; at the bases of sepals and side petals there were white blotches covered with a purple pattern. I packed my finds in the rucksack and contentedly started the homeward journey."

The getting-down to the bottom of the ravine which they had ascended became each moment a more discouraging problem. Sliding, slipping, slowing too rapid descent by grasping at passing tree trunks and shrubs, they at last reached the stream. Working down its stony, staircase-like bed, through pools and over little cascades, was relatively easy. Without warning, the Indian, who had been leading the way, stopped abruptly. "Overtaking him," writes Felix, "I looked down onto a cataract rushing almost vertically over great boulders to a pool thirty feet below. On either side the sheer rock walls came close together. After a moment, we turned back upward to search for some way around this obstacle. Soon we came to steep, forested, and brush-covered slopes where bush knives were required to advance at all. Then great rocks, like a veritable forest of stone, barred our way. We twisted through them and then faced a horrible thicket of Chusqueas, near-bamboos, with leaves that cut like razors. We tried from a different angle to return to the stream, but this new direction proved impossible. We followed the paths of animals, but they led nowhere. I then knew that we must spend the night on the mountainside. By this time my Indian companion, fear-stricken and exhausted, had begun to acquire the aspect of a beast of the wild; all inhibitions and the thin veneer of a civilized being began to disappear; his eyes bulged and in them was the indefinable look of a fox caught in the snare. It is interesting that this look of agonized terror is different among wild animals—in the eyes of a doe there is sadness and tears.

"It was getting cold, and a drizzling rain soon began. We climbed a little higher to where I remembered a small, vegetation-free glade below a thick-spreading tree. I told the Indian to gather twigs and wood for a fire; when he had done so I found that he knew how to light a fire only in a stove, not in the forest. I made him a lecture about being brave, resourceful, and at home in the forest, relating gay episodes from a Peruvian hunter's life, how the jungle hunter lived, etc., etc., but all to no avail; he was frightened beyond his control. The icy rain augmented, sharp as a needle spray, and soaked us to the skin, to the bones. My sad companion shivered beside the smoldering fire and tried to squeeze his body into the soft, saturated humus soil in the hope of getting a little warmth from below so that he might sleep. Keeping him up and awake was a problem; I feared pneumonia because these mountain people are strangely delicate and readily contract serious diseases."

From daybreak until early afternoon they started by a half-dozen different routes to find the canyon bottom. Each one was thoroughly unsuccessful. Felix asked the Indian for a suggestion. His response was typical—"rest, sleep, and wait for another day." Thereupon, Felix came to a decision. They would forget the ravine and start straight down the continuously steep, partly forested, partly brush-covered, partly rocky mountainside. He knew what it would mean. Without any assurance of what lay in wait for them at any point, it meant slipping, sliding, jumping, roping, and cutting for hours. At dusk, badly battered and very lame, they reached the hacienda.

During succeeding days the collecting near Utcuyacu in the "eyebrow of the jungle" continued to be not much less difficult, for they could find no established paths through the low forests into higher country. To the northeast there was another old hacienda, "San

Nicolás," to which the owner came periodically to harvest a scanty corn crop or to pick such few oranges and avocados as his long-neglected plantation yielded. Near by, along a boggy trail, Felix found many plants in bloom, some unfamiliar: a huge species with most attractive *Gloxinia*-like flowers; a fire-red *Aphelandra;* Fuchsias in abundance; a pretty *Oxalis;* two different tropical morning-glories; a diminutive tree—apparently a member of the Madder family—completely covered with flowers; and, everywhere, winding through and over the trees, a variety of vines of which the most spectacular were a fine blue *Cobaea* and a bright orange-flowered *Bomarea.*

Local information suggested that some distance down the road below Utcuyacu the high margins of another valley might be more accessible. Remarkably enough, this information proved to be correct and they found excellent collecting around a long-abandoned *chacra*, or farm, recently taken over by an active and enterprising newcomer. Disappointed in the productiveness of the soil, he had become a lumberman. On high forested mountainsides near by, one of the South American conifers, *Podocarpus utilior*, called "uncumanu" by the *Indios*, grew abundantly. For some time the new owner had been felling all readily accessible trees by axe and sawing them into planks by hand. The demand for these proved sufficient to cover the cost of importing food and to pay the wages of such few, reluctant laborers as the region provided.

The lumbering operations had required the clearing of numerous paths from the *chacra* upward into the highlands, and along these Felix and his Indian ranged far and wide in search of plants and insects. Of the latter, the wood-boring and wood-devouring were especially numerous because many small, succulent saplings had been crushed onto the moist forest floor when the heavy trees came down. Each day Felix visited the most recently timbered plots, and sometimes he collected at night with lights. In addition to the wood destroyers, he caught hunting insects that preyed upon them and the tropical butterflies as they drank the sweet exudates from bruised bark.

One day they climbed along the forest paths northward from the chacra and around two hills, crossed a little quebrada, and worked their way up to the flat top of a hillock, actually a slender spur of the mountain that rose steeply overhead. The little plateau was very narrow and on three sides fell away abruptly in talus slopes. Both it and the upper levels of talus were thickly covered with a slender-leaved fern that in spots grew over six feet high. The scattered trees were small and misshapen; here and there between them great clumps of two other, coarse-leaved ferns overtopped most of the ground cover.

Attached to the branches of the low trees and hiding their gnarled bases, mounded over piles of broken rock, and competing with the ferns where they grew lowest were orchids, more orchids, orchids everywhere. This bit of a hilltop, one hundred yards long, ten yards wide at one end and two at the other, was, in Felix's words, "a true wonderland of orchids, with the most striking and beautiful of the more than fifteen species growing in such profusion that I thought I was a visitor at a flower show—of course, the artistry of arrangement was superior to anything the human hand and brain can improvise." He goes on to say, "Imagine, please, four or five sizable plants all around the base of a small tree and more on its lower branches, each with two to three spikes of gorgeous white, purple, and brown *Cattleya*-like flowers drooping over mosses and decorated by ferns; each flower was three inches or more across and there were up to fifteen flowers on a single spike—beautiful as beauty may be beautiful."

The floor of his "orchid wonderland" was damp humus, unbelievably deep, the product, over many centuries perhaps, of decaying fern fronds. Where this rich organic material was deepest, two or three tall orchid species formed dense thickets. One was especially noteworthy, with long leaves clasping a tall stem which bore from ten to fifteen large flowers, cream-red with a white center, and with a fragrance which drifted back and forth over all the hilltop. Other species were peculiar to the twisted tree-branches where, as Felix writes, "their generous clumps were posed like artificial bouquets and always chose ostentatious positions so that their abundant small white flowers, disposed in ringlets round the stems, would be noticed at first glance."

Many of the orchids surrounding him were unfamiliar and he could not place them generically; when later on they were submitted to specialists in the family Orchidaceae, some proved to be previously unknown botanically and others still remain unnamed. In addition to those he could not place were species of genera he recognized: Stanhopeas, Epidendrums, Anguloas, Trichopilias, Angulcastes, Gongoras, and Lycastes in profusion. To cap the climax there were groups of a number of different heathers and other low shrubs on the upper talus slopes, all flowering in a variety of strong colors. In a total of many months over a period of many years Felix had never seen anything approaching the beauty and importance botanically of this "orchid hill" he had discovered.

His botanical and entomological success in the Utcuyacu ceja-montaña area encouraged Felix to attempt an additional collecting journey to the crest and, hopefully, over one of the mountain ranges that stretched one behind another into the misty distance. He decided upon one that always showed on its upper levels a heavy blanket of cloud; this would mean a great stretch of cloud forest, most typical of cejas. It was miles away and on its green flank from top to bottom he could see distinctly, here more and there less, a silvery streak which he knew must represent a considerable cascading stream dropping almost sheer for hundreds of feet, perhaps a thousand. No one could tell him anything about its origin or its fate; for years everyone had seen it, but no one had even thought of trying to find a way to it. Such is the reaction of the dwellers in the Peruvian hinterland concerning any natural object of interest or mystery which is not immediately at hand—"Sufficient unto the day is the evil thereof."

For a good reason there was considerable local information about another stream, the Agua Dulce, that was actively continuing the excavation of a deep, narrow canyon on a nearer mountainside. It was claimed that a path led up through the torrent-encasing ravine to the summit of the ridge, although from below the density of the fog forest obliterated the course of the upper fourth of the deep depression. Then followed the reason for local knowledge of the Agua Dulce. After close questioning and much evasion, it was admitted that just beyond the crest and on the far slope of the mountain down which the stream poured there was the site of an old Spanish gold mine near a large lake—that is, there was a smell of treasure in the air.

Almost needless to say, the search for treasure—earthbound minerals or, sometimes, pirates' loot—has consumed the endless toil of thousands upon thousands belonging to ancient as well as modern races of men. In few parts of the world did the lust for gold lead men to more remote, more inaccessible regions than those originally prospected by the peoples, today almost completely unknown, who ruled the Andes over many centuries before the Incas succeeded to their domination, all the way from Ecuador to Argentina.

Pizarro's conquistadors early saw abundant evidence that there was gold beneath the breathlessly high Andean plateaus or in the foothills stretching both westward to the Pacific and eastward into the Amazonian rain forest. They saw the golden plaques on the walls of Inca palaces, the amazingly lifelike representations of plants and animals in beaten gold that adorned their gardens, the stores of golden ornaments within the coastal pyramids. These and many other irreplaceable evidences of one of the refinements of Inca culture were gathered up to be melted down into bullion for shipment to Spain. Then began the hunt for hidden treasure they felt certain had been sequestered when the conquered race began its long and largely ineffectual struggle to preserve from their ruthless conquerors some remnants of past glory. Torture revealed some of the hiding places, and more torture the location of the mines from which had come the precious material for the Inca goldsmiths.

From time to time evidences of Spanish mining operations in the Andes are being found. Some appear to have been considerable, products of the labor of great numbers of enslaved Indians driven relentlessly to work, ever more extensively, the rich veins of gold. These sites are often so completely isolated, at such extreme altitudes, or so deeply buried in the jungle that it is difficult to imagine how the Spaniards could have reached them, how they could have managed to support life at them, or how they could have transported the products of their mining to their far-off coastal headquarters—perhaps as good an illustration as any of how sharp is the spur of treasure-trove.

I have no doubt that there is still hidden Inca gold to be found in the Peruvian Andes. Certainly the modern *serranos*, the mountain men, believe so. They look with mingled interest and suspicion upon every stranger who leaves the beaten track in the highlands. The motives of the plant hunter are particularly suspect. He walks along slowly and purposefully examining the ground around him as though following a scent. He works his way into places unlikely to attract the average tourist. He stops every so often and picks up something which he examines with care before depositing it in some sort of receptacle. All this the Indian watching from a distance takes in; it convinces him that here, again, is a searcher for hidden Inca treasure. Two or three times in areas which seemed to me most unlikely to attract the treasure hunter I could not escape the conviction that someone was watching me. Once I turned quickly enough to get the impression that something had moved fast out of sight behind a big boulder. I am certain that after I disappeared the watcher took up where I had left off, in the certainty that I had been, unsuccessfully, following a lead.

Felix wondered how any trail could actually follow upward the course of the Agua Dulce. The stream was a raging torrent, and its course had often been subject to alteration when tropical rains provoked rockslides which tore away and dropped masses of the forested canyonsides. More than once at night, in his near-by hut, he had been awakened by the roar of falling water that shook the ground like an earthquake and threatened the primitive log bridge on which the main road crossed the stream. The trail had been constructed years before by someone far more ambitious and persistent than any of the current inhabitants of the region. When Felix actually started to climb, he soon found that the trail kept well away from the stream side and progressed upward in zigzag fashion over the contours of the mountainside.

At the beginning the steep ascent passed through an open, tall forest. Soon it crossed a partially denuded slope strewn with heavy rocks left behind by an extensive slide. Then the zigzags began to be set at much sharper angles and to traverse precipitous, grassy slopes. Thinly scattered across them were little, old, misshapen trees inclined at crazy angles. Over the sometimes nearly horizontal trunks there were colonies of mosses, low ferns, and bromeliads (members of the Pineapple family) that extended in clumps of irregular shape along almost vertical branches—the whole producing a sort of hobgoblin effect. The only worth-while plant was an orchid, a species of *Masdevallia*, with long, tenuous stalks which circled the tree trunks to thrust up their creamy-red flowers, quite incongruously, among the fern fronds. Another find was, again, an orchid which Felix did not recognize. Its firm, straight stems were topped, in pairs, with flowers that combined dark-red and orange and carried bright-yellow appendages that shimmered in the sunlight when the mountain breezes lifted them.

Above, the thin, grotesque forest ended as abruptly as it had begun and was replaced by the true grass-steppe. Over it a strongly growing grass, a species of *Ichnanthus*, was dominant. At the trailside were thickets of a tall, white-flowered *Eupatorium* mingled with a species of *Cuphea*, a sticky but otherwise charming *Desmodium*, and, best of all, a deep wine-red *Lantana*. Farther on were dense aggregations of a species of *Seemania* with many showy, pendulous, red flowers disposed on tall, stout, red-purple stems. It was quite in contrast with the same or a closely related species growing at lower altitudes—Felix had now reached an elevation of nearly seven thousand feet—which was much less vigorous, with pale-reddish flowers. Felix remarks that "the flowers of the alpine race looked like the faces of *indios* who live on the desolate Andean plateaus or punas, sunburnt and windbeaten, whereas the flowers in the valleys below looked anemic, soft, and pale."

Soon the trail began to present dangerous problems and there were instantaneous decisions to be made. The zigzags worked up across the scree-covered face of a ridge not much below what appeared to be the summit. Their inclination approached eighty degrees and, particularly at their acute angles, whole sections had been pushed out and down by rockslides. At those points, what had for some time become the mere semblance of a trail was replaced by loose rock and small boulders. On such a steep slope and on such a surface the wrong step starts a slide and can bring down an avalanche of rock from above. In another chapter is the story of what happened when I took the wrong step on a somewhat similar mountainside in the Central Chilean cordillera far to the south. More experienced in rock climbing than I was, Felix avoided loose rock and scrambled from one intact portion of a zigzag to a similar portion on the next higher level. He persisted in this exhausting toil because he was determined to see another, and perhaps new, vegetation zone that he felt certain would begin above the scree slope.

He was right, but was somewhat surprised to find himself again in the grass steppe. It was, however, marginal with stony plots where many plants he had not seen below were growing. Some were familiar, some not. Among his old friends were species of *Calea* and *Befaria*, the latter particularly attractive with their abundance of showy, pink-and-white flowers. Both were small shrubs, members of the *Ericaceae*, or Heather family; he calls *Befaria* the "South American Rhododendron." A *Vallea* he speaks of as "an old tree friend exhibiting its artificially delicate, frail flowers in a beautiful shade of red." More conspicuous was a *Tibouchina*, a rather common ornament of California gardens, which bore its deep-purple disks high above the grasses and smaller shrubs. Less familiar were decidedly handsome plants, vigorous but not woody, covered with deep vermilion flowers; these proved to be a species of *Hepiella*. A goodly number of humbler plants grew partially concealed between the heavy grass-clumps or under the fronds of strong-growing ferns. On rocky flats he found orchids, the most abundant an attractive species of *Epidendrum*. Altogether, this diminutive alpine garden was not only a variegated pattern of color and form but was also unexpectedly rich botanically. Felix felt that the extreme effort involved in conquering the scree slope just below had paid satisfactory dividends.

From the alpine garden upward, there was little difficulty in moving forward rapidly. Soon he entered a low, rather open forest growing on small benches and flats alongside the trail. On them he found his collecting limited, for after a few hundred feet each forested tract came to an end in a wall of rock or an abrupt declivity. Orchids were numerous. Unique in growth habit was one that formed mounds almost three feet in diameter, spreading out into hundreds of short ramifications. Everywhere on tree branches was another orchid, an *Epidendrum,* eye-catching because of the dark-purple of its stem bases, On the ground below, he found diminutive orchids with white, bell-shaped flowers reminiscent of our "snowdrops." There were other orchids, too, one of them with pale-brown flowers. Apart from the orchids, most of which were blooming, there were many other sorts of plants which were out of flower, and he says, "Surely there are here plenty of rare species, but to herborize them properly one should camp for a whole year; then he would catch the flowers of all of them." If you care to read through our Andean notebooks you will come across similar proposals when, from the equator south to Patagonia, and all too often, we have found ourselves in the right place at the wrong season.

The Andean zone represented on the last two thousand feet which Felix had climbed makes a strong appeal to him: ". . . it is beautiful, healthy, and attractive; there is little tropical about it save the botanical names of the plant families that inhabit it, save the tribes of large black monkeys, save some of the insect species; this is the moderate-climate land where the curse attached to everything tropical cannot reach; but this fine zone is so hard to reach that it is almost useless and un-inhabited."

Climbing again toward the crest, the transition from one vegetation zone to another was the most abrupt of the entire ascent. Almost without warning, he came face to face with the wall of the fog forest. From Utcuyacu, far below, he had watched the constant flow of mists and clouds backward and forward across the mountaintop, but he could not have imagined that the margin of the forest they created would be so sharply defined. He thus describes the abrupt transition: "As my foot behind rested upon the dry soil of the grass steppe, the other one began to tread the dark, muddy soil of the rain forest; the pleasant dry and bracing air of my favorite Andean zone came to an end and then began the cool and acid puffs of rotting, humic ground." Again it proved to be the wrong season for collecting; he could find almost nothing in flower. Of most interest was a new and strange ground-orchid bearing peculiarly formed, pale mauve flowers.

On the far edge of the fog forest someone had attempted to clear a few acres along the steep slopes in order to grow corn. Immense effort must have been required to cut the dense stand of trees and burn the fallen trunks and branches. Some, especially massive or the wood of which was iron-hard, had been left standing. But, unfortunately, the farmer had failed to reckon with the exuberant vegetation of the forest, which almost before he had harvested his first crop began to reoccupy every square foot of his cornfield. The dominant among the invaders was a species of *Bocconia*, belonging to the Poppy family. Thousands upon thousands luxuriated in the added light and loosened soil that the farmer's clearing and cultivating had offered them.

This type of swift invasion of land prepared for cultivation is characteristic of tropical regions. It has been one of the major problems that serve to discourage all but those whose individual initiative and persistence or favorable financial situation is sufficient to wage perpetual warfare upon the invaders. In Peru, and doubtless elsewhere, uninitiated city dwellers or immigrants from afar have been encouraged to farm in the jungle. Sometimes the encouragement comes from governmental agencies assigned to the exploitation of undeveloped tropical portions of their countries; perhaps more often it comes from land speculators with something to unload. In either case the result is usually increasing discouragement and ultimate disaster. Fortunately, the successful use of chemical destroyers of weeds and larger plants, increased knowledge of crops best adapted to jungle agriculture, and greater availability of technical assistance are meeting many of the problems peculiar to the farmer in the tropics. Similarly, the important advances in combating tropical diseases is going far toward eliminating the health hazards he has hitherto faced.

The trail that Felix had all along been following seemed to end at the beginning of the abortive cornfield, and he did not try to pick it up on the other side. The return journey down the mountainside was relatively easy because he could anticipate and avoid most of the rough going he met on the ascent. Just the same, as I well know, the descent of steep, broken terrain cannot help but be remarkably muscle-stretching—certain of these muscles proving to reside in unexpectedly important portions of your articulation.

The products of Felix's Utcuyacu–Agua Dulce collecting were numerous and were botanically significant because they added considerably to knowledge of the character and distribution of the types of plants that grow in the "eyebrow of the jungle" and the sharply delimited vegetation zones adjacent to it. In addition, he discovered a number of species, particularly among the orchids, which had never before been known scientifically. As we shall see in another chapter, he has had other successes when elsewhere in Peru he has collected for me in ceja or montaña.

7

THE MONTAÑA

In his *Exploring for Plants*, David Fairchild contends that, "Never to have seen anything but the temperate zone is to have lived on the fringe of the world." And he documents his contention as follows: "Between the Tropic of Capricorn and the Tropic of Cancer live the majority of all the plant species, the vast majority of the insects, most of the strange and dangerous and exciting quadrupeds, all of the great and most of the poisonous snakes and large lizards, most of the brilliantly colored sea fishes, and the most gorgeously plumaged of birds." And he concludes with the remark: "Not to struggle and economize and somehow see the tropics puts you, in my opinion, in the class with the boys who could never scrape together enough pennies to go to the circus. They never wanted to badly enough, that's all." I agree, except that other than purely financial considerations may sometimes deter the prospective traveler from pointing toward the tropics. The popular imagination is quite concerned about those same "strange and dangerous and exciting quadrupeds," about the anacondas, bushmasters, and other large or poisonous snakes, about insects in quantity, unfamiliar diseases, and humanity in a primitive and therefore, presumably, a decidedly unwashed condition.

For dwellers in temperate climates the vegetation of the tropics has a great appeal. It reflects the atmosphere of a part of the world with which they are totally unfamiliar, makes an impression of unreality, and has a quality of mystery. I have spent many hours in the tropical houses of a number of the world's largest botanical gardens. Some of those hours were devoted to watching the reaction of the public, which is always attracted by greenhouses, to the palms, aroids, lianas, orchids, and other tropical plants that usually are so cleverly displayed as to give some picture of the equatorial rain forest. Just within the greenhouse door, voices tended to become hushed, comments were fewer, children's romping feet acquired a soberer pace, and the slowly circulating stream of visitors watched, half fearfully, the man-made panorama of an almost otherworldly vegetation. But, at that, they have no conception of how much more impressive the tropical rain forest itself can be.

Our expedition members saw segments of the tropical rain forests in Peru and Colombia and came across many of the types of living organisms to which the quotation from David Fairchild refers. The following account, detailed by Harvey and Bob, of one of our earliest contacts with the Peruvian jungle gives some picture of its landscapes, life, and vegetation.

By train from Lima they crossed the Andes to Cerro de Pasco, that famous copper-mining center up in the clouds, where so many young North American mining engineers have served a part of their apprenticeship. Cerro de Pasco is at an elevation a little over fourteen thousand feet. Thence, a highway leads into the montaña of Huánuco Province. On it you coast down the slopes of the inner range of the Andes to one thousand feet and less, where you can breathe freely in honest-weight air and lose that feeling of being cold with no place in which to get warm. When a Peruvian uses the word "montaña," the uninitiated interpret it as meaning "mountains," whereas actually it refers to the quarter-million square miles of forested lowlands flowing eastward from the feet of the inner Andean ranges and constituting a portion of the vast Amazonian rain forest.

For the two botanists accustomed to altitudes near sea level, the night at Cerro de Pasco was not restful; it was, indeed, scarcely endurable. With enough covers to keep warm, the weight impedes the double-quick breathing that is necessary in the rarified air to supply sufficient oxygen. Periodically, you awake to gasp for extra breath. Talk about "having a heart"—there is no possibility of your forgetting that you have one. To boost the circulation, it pounds away at an alarming accelerated rate, with now and then a few extra-fast quarter beats thrown in.

In that high country the copper skins of the Indians acquire a bluish cast that makes them look more than half frozen. Actually, of course, they are thoroughly accustomed to the cold, often very thin air, and sicken when transferred to the coastal lands. The women wear their numerous homespun woolen skirts clear down to the mud. Each successive layer is put on outside the others. No one knows how many skirts they wear. But their feet have no protection except the mud that clings to them in quantity. These mountainfolk love their freedom, as far as feet are concerned; you could as well try to lasso a wild mustang and break him to harness as attempt to put shoes on them.

Like the Indians farther south in the Andes, those of Cerro de Pasco are sprightly and travel in high gear, quite in contrast to their coastal relatives who never get out of compound low. The women usually glide along at something between a fast walk and a slow trot. Their great accumulation of long skirts conceals leg movements and they look as though they were coasting on roller skates.

After an uncomfortable night in Cerro de Pasco, Harvey and Bob hired a car and started downhill for Huánuco and the montaña. The road descended rapidly along the clear headwaters of the Río Huallaga, a stream which, farther north on its way to the Amazon, becomes a wide, muddy flood. At its source near Cerro de Pasco, the Huallaga lies only two hundred and fifty miles from the Pacific, across the Andean ramparts, but its waters must prepare for a journey of almost three thousand miles before they reach the Atlantic.

Their driver gave the impression of setting a pace to match that of the churning, white mountain torrent. Following the lighthearted custom of mountain drivers in Peru, he shut off the engine, disengaged the clutch, and coasted much too rapidly around the sharp curves. Frequent admonitions to take it slower, so that the botanists might size up the vegetation along the roadsides as well as save their necks, were graciously heeded—but only for a minute or two each time.

I have always had great respect for the faith of Peruvian chofers. However, faith without works is dead, and many of their cars need much better works, especially brakes. While there can be no objection to the custom of taking the cars to the priest to be blessed, they should at the same time be taken to the garage to be checked over. Ordinarily, the cars are driven as long as they will function. When they break down on the road most of the drivers do not know how to make effective repairs.

Along the first of the descent Harvey and Bob saw the meeting of plants from the high puna country and some of the more hardy ones which came up from the montaña. The "old man cactus" made those same patches of cottony white so commonly seen on the cold plateaus above. Where sheep were grazing these patches suggested that a shearer had left piles of wool on the mountainside. Columnar species became more and more common down the valley. Soon the dry slopes of the hills were forested with them and with Aloes and Fourcroyas. One of the Peruvian cacti, the lana vegetal, is so called because from it is obtained a brown wool-like fiber used extensively in the Andes for stuffing mattresses and pillows. Perhaps a bed of cactus does not sound very inviting, but it is not nearly so bad as it sounds. When the stems of lana vegetal become mature and dry, the outer spiny layer is loosened and under it appears a fibrous cortex that surrounds the central woody core. This cortex is transformed into a fluffy mass of woolly material which simulates a dry cattail head. It has a kinky quality and feels much like wool but is too smooth to be spun into thread. As a filler for mattresses and pillows it does not pack into a solid lump as does the cotton commonly used in Peru for this purpose.

The Fourcroyas are numerous here and at a distance resemble Aloes. Their swordlike leaves are cut at maturity and then soaked in water until the softened tissues disintegrate by decay. Later, the tough woody fibers are washed free from the softer tissues and hung up to dry. At first they show a greenish tinge but soon bleach to a near-white. The fiber serves principally for the manufacture of rope and twine but is also used in mats and sandals. The often rather remarkable suspension bridges flung across Andean gorges have from time immemorial been fashioned in part from it. In Inca days these bridges were hung on gigantic fiber cables. Today the cables have mostly been replaced by heavy wire and only the planks and guard rails are held in place by *Fourcroya* twine.

As the car still further descended the Huallaga Valley the city of Huánuco came into view. Near-by hillsides were dry and almost bare of vegetation, but the valley floor was green with herbs, trees, and shrubs, which became dense along the river itself. Characteristic trees were Humboldt's willow, *Acacia*, the widely distributed *Acnistus*, *Eucalyptus*, and *Schinus molle*, this last better called the "Andean" rather than the "California" pepper tree, because of its Peruvian nativity and wide distribution throughout Andean valleys and down the western river channels to the coast. An introduction that has succeeded remarkably well in the Andes is the Eucalyptus. Indeed, most of the drier regions of Peru may be said to have been pretty generally "eucalyptized," to borrow a term from David Fairchild. One looks over many a mountain valley to see old groves that give the impression that they have always been an integral part of the landscape. You sometimes wonder how such a valley might have looked before the days when the padres brought Eucalyptus to the New World.

The city of Huánuco is the meeting place not only of the vegetations but also of the peoples of sierra and montaña and their commerce. Trucks and passengers pause at this halfway point. There, goods are unloaded and distribution to the interior begins. It is a cheerful place. At an elevation of a little over six thousand feet, the climate is halfway between the forbidding cold of the Andes and the steaming heat of the tropical rain forest. The middle of the day is hot; streets are deserted; and the tiendas are not only closed, but locked and double-locked—the final guard consisting of an iron bar which is secured by rusty padlocks so enormous and so antiquated in structure that they appear to date from the days of the conquistadors. Not until almost six o'clock does the town really begin to live. From that hour until midnight it is gay and noisy, as townsfolk and peons from the countryside promenade in the streets and congregate in the inevitable plaza.

Unfortunately for Huánuco, as also for many other cities in South America, the old-time municipal plaza band, which was bad enough but stopped now and then for breath, had been replaced by a centrally located loud-speaker—overloud and without any oxygen requirement. The city fathers agreed with the citizens, who were certain that if a little music was good more was better, and so they turned the dial as far as it would go to the noisy side and left it there in perpetuity. But the crowd was cheerful, and it was good to hear laughter again after the stolid silences of the Andes.

The days in Huánuco were usually sunny, with some fleecy cumulus clouds rising from the mountain walls flanking the river valley. The higher ridges were white with limestone outcrops. The red soil glowed through a scant vegetation of shrubs and cacti. Well up from the valley floor, a few farms stood out boldly green. Beyond the city, the broad valley bottom was filled with cultivated fields, principally of sugar cane. Looking northward, the view faded into a purple haze overhanging the jungle. The city itself was full of color. The walls of the adobe and stucco houses were calcimined in shades of pink and blue and purple and were attractive in their very lack of color harmony. The mountainsides farther down the valley often approach forty-five degrees of slope and are, therefore, very dry. When rain fell it ran off these slopes as from a roof; there was little opportunity for conservation of water in the soil except where certain natural pockets caught and held it, supporting green islands of the pepper tree, willow, *Baccharis*, and native and introduced grasses and other herbs. A ribbon of such vegetation made a conspicuous contour line where unusual enterprise had constructed an irrigation ditch to carry water to plantations around a turn of the valley.

A little more than one hundred and fifty years ago, the Spanish botanists Hipólito Ruiz and José Pavón discovered *Nicotiana tomentosa*, the giant "tree tobacco" of Peru, which was described in the first chapter. The years that Ruiz and Pavón spent in Peru and Chile gave the world its first comprehensive knowledge of the plant wealth of the west coast of South America. On one of their exceedingly arduous and hazardous expeditions into and over the Peruvian Andes they made collections in the neighborhood of Huánuco. Some distance to the east they found the tree *Nicotiana*, and I wanted seed from plants which I hoped would still be growing in that "type locality." So Harvey and Bob on their journey into the montaña were instructed to keep a careful eye out for *Nicotiana tomentosa*. Unfortunately, nothing resembling this interesting plant was found there.

After several days of botanizing up and down the Huánuco Valley they entrusted themselves and their equipment to a truck en route down into the montaña. Their road soon left the valley, climbed over a nine-thousand-foot ridge, and then followed the Chinchao, a tributary stream which unites with the Río Huallaga before it reaches Tingo María. Tingo was to be their ultimate collecting headquarters in the montaña.

The highway was a marvel of engineering. In many places it hung so precariously on the sides of tall, sheer cliffs that it was hard to understand how such a shelf could have been blasted out of the solid rock faces. There were many sheer drops of hundreds of feet. It was rather terrifying, but not much more so than some of the other Andean highways that we all traversed many times. In somewhat less than five hours the truck arrived at Puente Durand, a small settlement consisting of a few thatched cabins, on the banks of the Río Chinchao. Here they stopped for two days. The region round about proved to be so rich, botanically, that they collected at Puente Durand again on the return journey.

In those days the reason for existence of this settlement was a suspension bridge wide enough for horses over the clear, rushing waters of the Chinchao. It was built originally by a Dr. Durand in order to bring to the highway the *coca* from his hacienda, located in the jungle some distance westward. Transportation was by horse or burro, or by Indian carriers. In early days, before the highway was extended down into the montaña, it was customary for Indians to carry the heavy bales of coca all the way to Huánuco, over steep mountain trails. Each bale weighed about one hundred and twenty-five pounds, and a wiry little Indian could carry one of these all day long on his back, supported by a modified tumpline over the shoulders. Now the coca was simply deposited in a warehouse near the highway to await a truck. Some of it went to Europe and the United States for the manufacture of cocaine. The plant is *Erythroxylon coca*, a shrub that grows wild in the Peruvian jungle and has also been in aboriginal cultivation from Inca days, if not earlier. The leaves, which look somewhat like those of the laurel, are gathered from the plants, dried, and then compressed in large burlap sacks.

The Peruvian Indians have inherited the cocaine habit from their pre-Columbian ancestors. Bringing relief from fatigue and hunger, cocaine makes the Peruvian highlander capable of almost unbelievable feats of endurance. For days at a time he will carry heavy loads for long distances at high altitudes. At a steady and remarkably fast walk he climbs in and out of deep gorges on trails that an unburdened "gringo" has difficulty in negotiating at a far slower pace. The active narcotic principle is not readily released from the leaves, even when they are chewed, unless an alkaline substance is added. Therefore, the coca addict always carries a supply of moistened lime paste—in a small gourd or leather bag—and some of the lime goes into his mouth on the coca quid. It is said that a special kind of limestone is required for the burning of the lime oxide he uses, but just what its specific quality may be no one seems to know. In some parts of Peru, particularly in the Cuzco district, potassium obtained from plant ash is used in place of lime. The Indians are reported to have individual preferences for certain plants that are burned to provide this ash. Popular among these is *quinoa* (*Chenopodium quinoa*). The ashed petioles of particular species of palms are also esteemed. As can readily be imagined, the presence of raw lime on the lining of the mouth is hard on those tissues.

Rose-colored bracts of Delechampias brighten borders of Inca trails.

Mosses, ferns, and seed plants festoon dwarf trees on the "meadows on the desert."

On north Peruvian coastal deserts resistant *Distichlis* temporarily binds the sand.

Stranded desert travelers spelled out "Little Hell" with Tillandsias.

Ruins of one of the Inca cities on the dry Peruvian coast. Cajamarquilla near Lima.

Paul and Bill discovered this new Peruvian cactus (genus *Browningia*) near the Marañón.

I was not surprised to read in a Lima newspaper that incidence of mouth cancer is exceedingly high among the mountain people.

To prepare a quid of coca is simple. According to one technique, several leaves are folded together, popped into the mouth, and adjusted between gum and cheek. Then, with a little stick that is carried in the gourd or bag, a bit of lime or potash is smeared over the leaves. The quid is not actively chewed, as is the tobacco masticated by more "civilized" races, but is only occasionally compressed to hasten the flow of the narcotic from the cells of the leaf. It seems surprising that the use of coca does not produce unpleasant aftereffects, a hangover of some kind, but there is no apparent evidence that it does. However, Indians who take cocaine to excess have a rather greenish cast of countenance and are said to age rapidly. This must mean very rapidly, because old age, as we think of it, is rarely attained in the Andes, where life is hard and even the most elementary principles of hygiene are unknown. In the Peruvian highlands the cocaine habit appears to be more or less universal, among men at least, and often to begin at an early age.

The few cabins or shacks at Puente Durand were built so close to the roadside that each day the passing trucks threatened to knock them down. It had been difficult enough to grade sufficient space for a road, let alone space for houses, because the valley of the Río Chinchao is very narrow at this point and the road is built against the mountainside one hundred and fifty feet above the racing water. The *casa* of Harvey and Bob's host stood, however, on a bit of level land just below the highway. The *patrón* and his señora made their paying guests feel genuinely welcome.

On the first evening, supper was served on a screened porch that looked westward over the valley to a wall of dark-green jungle foliage. Rising almost directly below was the continuous roar of the river. Silhouetted against the evening sky was a single tall, slender *Bursera* tree. Its upper branches were hung with twenty or more birds' nests that in shape resembled those of the oriole but were more than three feet long. Swaying in the wind, they seemed about to fall at any moment. Dark-colored birds with long yellow tails entered and left the nests through small openings on one side.

A large earthenware jar of fermenting wheat *chicha* stood under the dining table. Some of this native beer was decanted for the botanists although the host, Señor Valverde, said that it had not yet become quite mature. Nevertheless, it was extremely good. In its manufacture the corn or wheat is first germinated, and when the sprouts are about an inch long the seedlings are thoroughly dried and then ground to a powder; water is added to this powder, and fermentation is allowed to take place. The Indians often employ a different technique, especially as far as the grinding is concerned. Señor Valverde ground his dry wheat sprouts in a small hand-mill. The Indians are likely to grind their corn between their teeth. Every now and then in the back country one comes across a minute settlement with a group of Indian women sitting about a large jar or wooden, boat-shaped bowl into which they periodically eject the masticated grain. Although one knows that the chicha fermented from such an unsightly mess probably contains a germicidal proportion of alcohol, it is sometimes hard to forget the method of production. It is, however, far wiser to take a chance on Indian chicha than on most Andean water.

After dinner Harvey and Bob began to wonder just what sleeping arrangements were going to be made. The house appeared to be hardly large enough to accommodate their host and his wife and little daughter. Soon, however, a candle was lighted and placed inside a tin-can candlestick, and their host asked them to follow him. With bedrolls on their shoulders they crossed the suspension bridge. As they left the shore and approached the center of the swaying, rocking bridge, the river underfoot was talking, first in deep, throaty gurgles and then in quick, gasping roars. Set well up on the other riverbank under the wall of jungle was a small thatched hut. It contained three dirt-floored rooms —the larger, middle one was well stocked with chickens, the one to the right was a general storeroom, and that to the left was occupied by two setting hens. With considerable protest these two were forced to desert their nests and were finally secured in the storeroom. Two dirty wooden platforms stood on either side of the henhouse annex. In the uncertain candlelight most of the feathers and some of the other debris was removed, and Harvey and Bob rolled out their sleeping bags on the platforms.

They had forgotten to leave a call with Señor Valverde but the roosters next door attended effectively to awakening them at dawn. Harvey's diary says: "Thereupon the Peruvian jungle was treated to a Wyoming cowboy's estimate of roosters in general and our next-door neighbors in particular. It was really a rather fine bit of language for such an early hour in the morning. We fooled the roosters by refusing to get up. When we finally did, and looked out the door, there was a grove of papaya trees growing all around the cabin, and some of them were heavy with ripe fruit. That gave us an idea of what we wanted for breakfast—hen and papaya fruit—and we got both."

That day they collected along the Río Chinchao and up a stream that flowed into it from the west. The dim trail through the rain forest was overhung with small tree-ferns, and underfoot were many Adiantums and other smaller fern species. The endlessness of the green vistas was immensely impressive. For thousands of square miles to the north and east this green sea billowed and surged, almost without interruption, a part of the vast expanse of Amazonian wilderness.

They found a species of *Renealmia*, a member of the Ginger family, which one of the government officials in Lima had asked them to collect in order that it might be accurately named by experts in the United States. He was concerned with this plant because of the oil that its underground stems contained. The plants resembled the ginger of commerce and the peons called it *achira*. Like so many local names for plants everywhere in the world, this one was not specific; the same name was applied by the same peons to a white-flowered *Canna* which resembles the *Renealmia*.

The most exciting find was a splendid *Eucharis*, a member of the Amaryllis family, much larger than the species that is commonly offered in the trade. The leaves were two feet long; the flowers four inches and more in diameter, white in color, and shading to a delicate green in the throat. It grew in a dense mass, hundreds of great plants. At a distance the luminous, almost phosphorescently white flowers, like great plaques, seemed to float in the virescent light that rose from the jungle floor and was reflected from the dense background of leafy vegetation. A peon was sent back to Puente Durand for a grub hoe and a coca sack. Then they dug a hundred bulbs. That night these bulbs started by truck for Lima, to begin their long journey to California.

In addition to this *Eucharis* there was a wealth of species of many families, almost all of them unfamiliar. A large terrestrial orchid was plentiful. Its purple flowers, marked with sulphur-yellow, measured two inches across. They found a single plant of *Phragmipedium boissierianum*—quite a name for an unoffending and very handsome green-flowered orchid. Its giant "ladyslippers" looked to be far too heavy for the delicate hairy stems which supported them. Where the jungle was somewhat less dense there were a few plants of a red-flowered amaryllid, apparently a *Hippeastrum*.

Above the tributary of the Río Chinchao which they were exploring, the mountainsides were steep and high. Here and there they saw small cultivated fields which stood out like murals against a background of forest green. There the ancient witticism about the farmer falling out of his farm could be taken literally. In most of these cultivations coca was being grown along with potatoes, beans, and upland rice. There were some plantations of bananas and plantains, but these plants do better at lower altitudes. Papayas were omnipresent, some in cultivation but most of them gone native. Also cultivated was a sister species (*Carica candamarcensis*), not much larger than a good-sized shrub and bearing attractive small golden fruits. But the fruit was not so good as it looked. They also saw trees of the custard apple and the avocado— *chirimoyas* and *paltas*.

West of Puente Durand lay the region called Gaza, apparently a corruption of the Quechua word *ccasa*, meaning "cold." This region had an elevation much like that of the Carpis ridge and afforded another good example of the *ceja de la montaña*. They collected there later, on an expedition which Bob's diary refers to as an attempt "to pluck the eyebrow." Quoting it further: "The Indian *arrieros* were up at daybreak, actually before the roosters got thoroughly into their morning broadcast. They brewed their coffee over an open fire near the cabin and fed their animals, while we, hoping for a very early start, hurriedly downed our breakfast at Señor Valverde's. It was eight o'clock, however, before the *bestias* were ready. One had escaped during the night, saddle and all, and had apparently returned to a hacienda in the mountains. There was one horse with a saddle. It was larger than the other horses and mules, so Harvey mounted him along with our raincoats, cameras, and packages of luncheon. I acquired a small animal with a heavy, padded packsaddle and no stirrups. It was a case of straddle, not sit. We had asked for a *bestia de carga* to carry our field presses. Instead, we got a husky little coca-chewing Indian. Our protests were answered by the statement that a mule would cost two sols, whereas the Indian would carry as much for one sol. But at the end of the day we gave him three in an effort to ease our consciences rather than pay him for work which had proved to be much less strenuous than carrying the bale of coca which he was accustomed to tote.

"For a couple of miles our trail led north along the mountainsides west of the Río Chinchao and then turned west up a deep valley. It was a beautiful, fresh, clear morning and as we climbed higher the jungle panorama began to unfold. Above the immense stretch of green forests the deep-blue sky was dotted with fluffy white clouds, like piles of cotton on a calm azure sea. In this land of dense vegetation, one rarely gets such views. Before long we overtook three peons carrying heavy back-loads and escorting a young and rather striking-looking maiden who was riding a horse. Somehow, I had the feeling that she was a bride. Her serious dusky face bore a half-frightened look as she peered from under a heavy grass-green mantilla. Perhaps it was my imagination, but to me she looked as though she had just been dragged away from her home.

"As the horses slowly made their way up the valley, we came upon a rushing stream. Its sound brought back visions of a Big Horn Mountain cascade full of trout—and then the heavy jungle trees and the great ferns choking the streambanks brought me back to the Peruvian reality. After picking our way across its boulder-strewn bed we began again the zigzag ascents. For two hours the trail ran through extremely dense forests. It was the world's roughest and steepest, not to mention muddiest, trail. I might have felt more compassion for our laboring peon if I had not been so busily engaged in keeping my mule enthusiastic about going uphill. No matter what was the condition of the trail, my animal dozed, and if I had stopped abusing him for an instant he would have gone sound asleep. Furthermore, even to stay on the none-too-comfortable packsaddle with no support for my feet was a bit of a problem, and on the steep ascents I continually tended to slide backward. After a while I began to fear that my knees would lose their grip. In fact, I more than once considered walking a bit, even at the risk of losing caste in the eyes of our native companions."

Typical of the foggy "eyebrow of the jungle"—decribed in greater detail in the preceding chapter—the Gaza ridges were incredibly rich in plant species. Mosses and lichens mantled the trunks of the tall jungle trees. Under the dank underbrush, club mosses and ferns covered the soft, deep soil. Begonias were abundant, some of them low herbaceous species, others great shrubby growths, and the jungle was bright with their flowers. On every side *Calceolaria* made splotches of golden yellow. The trail and every open space was overhung with the brilliant, bell-like flowers of a number of *Fuchsia* species. Always, the plant hunter's "take" from the *ceja de la montaña* is limited only by the size of his plant presses.

Below Puente Durand the highway to Tingo María continued northeast, followed the Chinchao through narrow gorges to its confluence with the Huallaga, and then turned north to follow the course of this important waterway. Tingo María was becoming a boom town when Harvey and Bob saw it a good many years ago. A very busy sawmill was ripping out rough boards for wooden houses that were to replace the cooler, bamboo-walled dwellings which jungle residents for generations had found to be entirely adequate for their needs. Shiny new galvanized iron was being trucked in to make hideous this formerly thatch-roofed settlement. A considerable structure housed the headquarters of the road gangs who were pushing the highway eastward against fearful odds toward Pucalpa, far over to the east on the Ucayali River, a Peruvian gateway to the Amazonian river system.

To put a modern highway through the tropical rain forest over the backbone of rock which separates the valleys of the Huallaga and Ucayali required much imagination and even more intestinal fortitude. When completed, and long since it has been, the Peruvians visioned west coast freight accumulating in Lima and eastward along the highway, the loading of this freight on an endless stream of trucks headed over the Andes for Pucalpa, and then its transport by water to Iquitos, where it would be reloaded for the last time into freighters and carried almost twenty-five hundred miles down the Amazon to the Atlantic and thence to the Seven Seas. In the opposite direction they saw, someday, all the goods that Peru imports from Europe being shipped by water directly to the end of this new highway. In other words, when the highway reached Pucalpa, then the center as well as the coast of Peru would possess a shorter, direct water connection with European markets. The resulting saving of time and money in the case of both export and import trade would be large. It was a project to fire the imagination.

In those days the highway had pierced the jungle to a distance thirty miles east of Tingo María. This remarkable accomplishment was a tribute to the energy and enterprise of the government and the ability and enthusiasm of its young engineers. Even to run a preliminary survey across an almost impenetrable jungle appeared to be a superhuman undertaking. One of the surveyors was lost in the rain forest for eight days, even though he had all his instruments with him. If you don't believe this story, try to imagine yourself in a deep, perpetual twilight created high above by a canopy of tropical foliage in which every leaf fights for a place in the sun; where tangled lianas hang in huge, twisted masses from the branches overhead to obscure more than a limited view; where dark, smooth, strangling stems of climbing figs circle the giant tree-trunks like serpents; where rain seems always to be falling on the green roof of your world and penetrating it in streams that turn the jungle floor into such a slimy morass that the forest trees must send out farflung basal buttresses in order to assure a firm anchorage in that ages-old accumulation of vegetable decay of which the jungle soil is made. Only bold, hardy men conquer the jungle. When they have overpowered it, the fight to maintain the victory at once begins.

Aside from too much rain, Tingo was a rather agreeable place in which to live. A few hardier trippers, most of them from Lima, were already experimenting with a jungle holiday. The government was building for their accommodation a tourist hotel several miles south of Tingo. It was to be an elegant affair. The bathrooms had already been tiled, and the last word in plumbing and fixtures was being installed. The contrast with native facilities was extreme. Old jungle dwellers had laughed derisively at a German settler when they saw him building a bamboo-thatch outhouse. Why, said they, should one limit himself spatially in this manner, when God has given his people the freedom of all the out-of-doors?

The hotel, then just beginning to take form, ultimately became a member of the present-day chain of tourist establishments built by the government and operated by the Compañía Hotelera del Peru. This chain includes the larger cities except Lima, which is well supplied with entirely modern hostelries, and, by contrast with the quite impossible local inns we had to endure on our earlier forays into the Peruvian countryside, its hotels are havens of refuge. Those I know best, and particularly one of the newest, in Cuzco, are well designed for comfort, quite charmingly decorated and furnished, and rather efficiently staffed.

The botanists made the decidedly primitive Gran Hotel del Aguila their headquarters. The main structure and its various annexes were constructed of bamboo, with a roof of palm thatch. The floors were made of planks raised on stilts some three feet above the marshy ground. The dining room was a large open porch where the elite loafers of the town gathered in the afternoons and stayed until late at night to exchange cheap talk and expensive drink, and to enjoy the free and very loud radio rendition of Spanish songs from the Lima station and swing music from Schenectady. In one of the annexes the *botánicos* had their bunks and kept at plant drying night and day. The air was always humid and the drying was slow; therefore they had to employ artificial heat supplied by their gasoline pressure lanterns. Felt driers were replaced by heavy corrugated paper ones, and the presses were hung over the lanterns. Warm air passed upward through the tubules of the "corrugateds" and the wet specimens then dried quite rapidly. They were at once bundled, wrapped in oilcloth, and shipped as soon as possible by truck to us at base headquarters in Lima. There we unpacked the specimens, took care of any additional drying that seemed necessary, and started off a shipment for California.

Drying pressed specimens with artificial heat is not a new idea, and for many years we have used this technique successfully in many parts of South America. Modern gasoline lanterns are exceedingly effective mechanisms for creating quick heat and they are readily portable. If the gasoline in out-of-the-way places in the Andes had been as good as the lanterns, less profanity would have been used by expedition members. When there is water or other impurities in the gasoline these pressure lanterns can become as temperamental as an automobile engine fed with bad fuel. The lanterns are perfectly safe but they are not entirely foolproof. One night in Tingo, Harvey awoke to find that one of them had burned out. Half asleep, he got up, fumbled around for the five-gallon gasoline can, and began refilling. Unfortunately the metal was still hot and things immediately began to happen. Flames first shot up from the lantern and then from the can, and for a moment it looked as though the Gran Hotel del Aguila would go up in smoke. But the fire was quickly smothered. When the lantern had cooled Harvey refilled it, and the plant drying proceeded without further interruption. Walter and Alan had the hardest luck with lantern heat, and from Peru to Patagonia they left behind them a trail of burned "corrugateds" and charred plant specimens. They even succeeded in destroying part of a nice garden and burned up a shack or two in Patagonia.

Tingo María, nine degrees south of the equator, and at an elevation of something like three thousand feet, is still not actually in the true jungle. The vegetation is, therefore, not of the extremely tropical, rain-forest type which appears in its full luxuriance along the Amazon in Brazil. Afternoons are generally rainy, but the mornings give opportunity to collect plants up and down the Río Huallaga and along

the highway north or south. Contrary to common impression, the tropical rain forest is an almost tiresomely monotonous green. Near Tingo
the forest floor shows only lichens, mosses, ferns, and those types of
shrubs and herbs that can exist where there is a minimum of light.
There are Arums, Marantas, Calatheas, wild peppers, and some showy-
flowered members of the Madder family. Here and there a shower of
bright petals or a few showy corolla tubes lie on the ground. Then you
gaze upward in the hope of determining which of the entangled tree-
tops or lianas shed those tantalizing bits of evidence that the roof of
the jungle is in flower. Where streams, trails, roads, or clearings create
openings in the dense montaña, the collecting is better. Along such
forest margins, small species of bamboo, "Panama hat" palms, tree ferns,
the ginger, and other attractive plants disport themselves. Conspicuous are the red and yellow bracts of the great banana-leaved Heliconias,
the macaws of the plant world.

The river was the center of Tingo's life. On its banks community
bathing, gossipy washing of clothes, fishing, and general loitering were
always in evidence. There might be a *balsa*, or raft, under construction. Logs for rafts were preferably cut from the balsa tree, *Ochroma*,
locally called *topa*. With much less than the weight of cork, balsa
is the lightest of woods. Because of the great demand for these logs,
there can be relatively few large *Ochroma* trees left in the forests near
Tingo María. The lightest wood comes from the low-lying, truly
jungle country, where the trees grow very rapidly and may attain a
diameter of eighteen inches in five years.

Ochroma is a relative of both the cotton plant and the tree which
yields kapok. Its fruit is a large pod about six inches in length. When
its segments break open, a brown cottony mass of down is exposed and
the pod comes to look like a rabbit's foot. In fact, the first species
named from Central America was called *Ochroma lagopus*, the "rabbit-
foot *Ochroma*." The down is used in making pillows and mattresses.
All seeds must be removed, or the mice that relish them will burrow into
pillow and mattress, something not conducive to restful sleep.

In constructing a balsa, strands of tough bark are used to lash the
logs to one another and to strong cross-timbers placed fore and aft.
A raised platform occupies the middle of the raft. On it cargo and
passengers may keep relatively dry when the balsa shoots the rapids of
the lower Huallaga. The rivermen who pole these rafts are experts
and know the river well. When they have delivered a raft at the end

of their special stretch of river, they return overland and await an opportunity to take down another raft. Much of the local river traffic
is carried in dugouts of various sizes, some of immense proportions.
The Huallaga is always a reddish-yellow flood laden with tree trunks,
brushwood, and acres of soil starting its transcontinental journey to
help build the delta of the Amazon out into the Atlantic.

They made a number of collecting trips in the jungle across the
river. One of them Bob describes as follows: "Señor Aguila, who owns
our hotel, promised to take us bright and early to the chacra, or small
farm, of one of his relatives who lives on the opposite bank of the
Huallaga. We walked to the river beyond the new government hotel
and shouted at the tops of our voices to attract the attention of some
peons on the opposite riverbank. Aguila ordered a dugout which, after
bailing it dry, two men brought across to us. It was about twenty feet
long. We all piled in and poled upstream for a while. Then we swung
into the current, the two native rivermen paddling like mad with their
short, hand-carved paddles. Despite their best efforts, we went downstream one hundred yards in crossing about half that distance and then
poled back upstream to the landing. Near by, on land recently cleared
of jungle growth, corn and bananas were planted. Aguila's relatives
had built a few crude huts and set up housekeeping, surrounded by
much filth. After getting his gun and cartridges, the man of the family,
a young, clean-looking chap, joined our expedition. We struggled
over all manner of logs and tree trunks on the margin of the clearing
and then, on a very faint trail, plunged headlong into virgin rain
forest. The hunter soon outdistanced us and we saw no more of him.
Once we heard his gun far away, and often he and Aguila whistled
back and forth through the verdant jungle gloom.

"It was a flat, low area with many tall, large-trunked trees, the tops
so overgrown with vines that we rarely caught a glimpse of the sunny
blue skies above. Yes, it was a clear day at last. The lower-story vegetation was not so dense as we had found it elsewhere in the jungle, and
we were able to wander about at will. We did so until to me all directions were the same and I had not the slightest idea from which one
we had come. This geographical uncertainty was accentuated when we
stumbled upon a river which proved to be the Monzon and to be running in exactly the opposite direction from the one which I was prepared to have it take. Most of the time we were up to our necks in
ferns and huge-leaved Arums, but collecting was poor because few

things flower in such gloomy, sunless depths. The tangled masses of vines and orchids which appeared on the upper parts of every tree were very enticing, but climbing to them was impossible.

"Aguila disappeared suddenly and I began to think that he had brought us out with intent to lose us. Finally he reappeared, but from a totally unexpected direction. When we started back to the river he led off at right angles to the direction I would have taken. Of course he proved to be right. Upon arriving at the chacra it was too late to return to Tingo for lunch and so we sat down on the ground around an open fire in front of the cabin and prepared to sample an authentic native repast. It consisted of four baked bananas for each person. The ripe fruits were laid on the coals and left there until the skins were thoroughly charred, then peeled and passed around. They were very good, even if a bit scorched in spots. All during the meal I had my eye on a big bowl of nasty yellow-brown paste and kept praying that the, family's hospitality would not include this mess. It proved to be fresh banana pulp, which ferments when allowed to stand for two or three days. Mixed with water it makes quite a drink, called *chicha de plátano*. I was very jittery when the rather filthy housewife unceremoniously reached into the revolting, sticky mass and took out a goodly handful. She shook it off into a smaller bowl, added a little river-water, mixed the combination with two dirty paws (they came out cleaner), threw out the larger pieces, and then handed it to me to drink. I couldn't very well refuse and so I sunk my face in the bowl and found it didn't taste nearly as bad as it looked. In fact, it was really quite refreshing. Meanwhile, Harvey had been doing his best to look preoccupied and remote, but I wasn't going to let him get away with anything like that and handed him what was left in the bowl."

Through a newly made friend in Tingo María, Harvey and Bob received an invitation to spend a few days at the Hacienda Shapajilla, about ten miles to the east along the extension of the jungle highway. Don José, the hacendado, and his good-looking señora gave them a hearty welcome and put them up in a bamboo-thatch storehouse near the ranch house. It was a rather large hacienda, on which sixty peons were regularly employed. They received a minute daily wage in addition to their food, most of which was rice, yuca, corn, and tropical fruits in great variety, all produced on the hacienda. Fish they took from the river, and game, principally peccary, from the forest. What they caught or killed was supposed to be reported to Don José, who was then at liberty to take for his family's use as much as he desired.

Some cotton was grown, but the climate was too wet for much success with it. The principal money crop was *barbasco*. The word refers to the roots of the cube tree, *Lonchocarpus nicou*, a member of the Pea family, and to the milky juice obtained from the pulped roots. For many centuries barbasco has been used by the jungle folk as an effective fish poison. When the peons at the Hacienda Shapajilla wanted a really big haul of fish, they "barbascoed" them. First, a bamboo wicker dam was constructed across the Río Supte. Then, several men went upstream about a half mile and a second party about a half mile farther, each carrying a bundle of barbasco. Between stones they pounded the roots to a juicy pulp and tossed it into the stream. An alkaloid in the juice immediately began to diffuse in the water. It had an asphyxiating effect on any fish in the neighborhood, so that by the time they reached the bamboo barricade they were quite stupefied and floated belly-up. A jolly group of nude peons thereupon waded into the water and tossed the catch ashore. The fish that were not to be eaten immediately were split in half and put in the sun to dry. When there was little sunshine the product tended to become rather unpleasantly "high."

The active principle in barbasco—or cube, as it is also called—is rotenone. It is poisonous only to cold-blooded organisms, or at least is not poisonous to mammals, and so there is no danger in eating a "barbascoed" fish. Rotenone acts upon insects as it does upon fish and has become an important constituent of many insecticides. When you get out the little spray gun and fill the room with a rather smelly mist, the effectiveness of your activities is likely to depend in part upon the presence in the spray mixture of a trace of rotenone. The same is true of many plant sprays.

On All Saints' Day Don José took the family and guests to Pumahuasi in his ancient sports roadster. Near by, Harvey and Bob found good collecting in newly made clearings where the flora of the jungle floor, partially freed from undergrowth, was easy to get at.

The local drunkery was the busiest place on the village Main Street. There, so many of the road workers had accumulated that its bamboo walls bulged dangerously. An itinerant orchestra with fiddle, banjo, and *harpa* dispensed doleful music, and there were many unsuccessful attempts to organize community singing. The rest of the citizens celebrated the holiday along the riverbank, where they were fishing, wash-

ing clothes, drinking chicha, poling dugouts up and down, swimming
—everyone, even tiny youngsters, as much at home in the water as
on the land—and dynamiting fish.

The latter was forbidden by a national statute, but the montaña
knows little of man-made laws. Highway construction had stimulated
this method of acquiring fish, since apparently it was impossible to
prevent pilferage from the road workers' supply of dynamite and
blasting caps. The charge had to explode almost as soon as it hit the
water; otherwise the fish would scatter at the first disturbance of their
native element. Such close timing led to many gruesome accidents.

Here and there along the banks of the Supte and the Huallaga, a
tall, woody grass, *Gynerium sagittatum*, formed pure stands. The
straight, smooth stems, light in weight, are the standard material for
making arrows, as the species name implies. To one end of the four-
or five-foot lengths is fastened a foot or two of hard black palmwood,
carved its entire length into sharp points and recurved barbs. The
other end is feathered in more or less conventional fashion. For bows,
the same palmwood is used. The Indians hunt both fish and game with
these bows and arrows. The fish are shot from the riverbank, and the
hunter dives in to recover the arrow and the fish that it has impaled.
It is strictly a sporting proposition as well as being a far more picturesque technique than bombing with dynamite.

The bow-and-arrow palm was known as *shapaja*, and its abundance
in Don José's hacienda gave the name "Shapajilla" to his establishment.
From it also were cut the long fronds used in the standard type of
montaña thatch. While plant hunting one morning near the hacienda,
Harvey and Bob came upon two Indians. With machetes they were
hacking to pieces the decaying trunk of a shapaja. Great, soft white
grubs, often two inches long, the larvae of a large black beetle, had
honeycombed the softened palm tissues, and the machetes exposed
them in large numbers. A kettle standing near by contained a mass of
the writhing, wriggling larvae, and the Indians said that as soon as
enough had been accumulated, there was going to be a fine big "grub
fry." These larvae are looked upon as one of the great delicacies of the
montaña. The two Indians considered themselves very lucky to find
such an abundant supply in a single palm trunk. In their grub collection
a few of the adult beetles had been included. Their addition is said to
add character to a grub fry by providing something crunchy to bite
on while the soft, rich larvae melt in the mouth.

Fully to appreciate the Peruvian tropics a visitor should have some knowledge of entomology. The only seriously disagreeable insects are the hymenopters, which become more than resentful when, strictly by accident, you disturb their nests. In addition there are little black flies with a bite that raises a small blood blister. Minute red spiders, *beta colorada*, akin to the chiggers of the southern and some other sections of the United States, can make life a burden unless early discouraged by judicious use of sulphur. Nighttime in the montaña is always gay with clouds of fireflies. The common species is provided with two green headlights continuously illuminated and an abdominal white light which flashes intermittently and constitutes a sort of "landing light." You can't help looking for a red tail-light, but probably that's expecting too much. The bombardier beetles are always an object of curiosity. On open ground their little burrows can be excavated and the inhabitants made to deliver several charges of a nitrous substance in quite up-to-the-minute chemical warfare fashion. Leaf-cutter ants are everywhere, beating down their trails on the jungle floor as they hasten home with neatly excised pieces of green leaf. Often their burdens are larger than themselves. The total quantity of leaf accumulation in the underground ant galleries must be enormous. On these leafy stores they cultivate fungus gardens to supply food for their armies of hungry workers.

On the return trip to Cerro de Pasco and thence to Lima, Harvey and Bob stopped off several days in the Carpis "eyebrow of the jungle" through which they had ridden during the journey to Tingo María. For lack of better accommodations in the rain forest, they were forced to put up at an Indian shack occupied by a mother and her grown son and daughter, all of whom made it abundantly clear that the botánicos were not at all welcome. Indeed, such shelter as the bamboo thatched *casita* provided had practically to be commandeered. When their scanty supply of tinned food bought in Tingo María began to run low, the grudging hostess could supply nothing but hominy. She finally managed to find a few eggs but absolutely refused to provide a chicken. At each renewed demand she dolefully repeated, "*No hay, señor*," although there was more than one fowl wandering about the shack. In desperation they offered what in the Montaña constituted a small fortune, but all they got was, "*No hay, señor*." When an Andean Indian will not sell, he will not sell.

8

WHERE THE AMAZON BEGINS

In the shadow of Andean snow fields and glaciers, near the southeastern corner of Peru, begin some of the first trickles of what are to become important among the two hundred tributaries of the Amazon, that mightiest maze of continental waterways in the world. Some say that the headwaters of the Marañón, north of Cerro de Pasco in Central Peru, must be called the beginning of the Amazon. Others urge the claim of the Ucayali to be the true source of the main river. To form the Alto Ucayali, the Apurímac and Urubamba rivers meet at a point where the innermost of the Andean ranges look eastward over the beginnings of the boundless Amazonian hinterland. Flowing into the Urubamba are the Paucartambo and the Mishagua, and near the latter's source a branch of the Madre de Dios has its beginning, a beginning that ends in the Madeira, one of the longest major tributaries of the Amazon. In the center of these ultimate ramifications of the Amazon's fanlike fluvial system, which begins almost in sight of the Pacific and discharges into the Atlantic four thousand miles away, lies Cuzco, "City of the Sun," "Hub of the Universe," ancient capital of Tahuantinsuyo, the Empire of the Incas. In the city itself, and beside the headwaters of these Andean rivers, and on the precipitous cliffs thousands of feet above their sunless floods, stand so many Inca and pre-Inca fortresses, shrines, and settlements that the Cuzco area has been called the archaeological treasure house of South America.

Going to Peru without seeing Cuzco is, today, like going to Rome without seeing St. Peter's. Long before it became a tourist Mecca, we pried about the city's narrow, Inca-walled streets; bargained side by side with its citizens for the brilliantly hued Indian ponchos and scarves; searched out Spanish Colonial religious paintings which, in those days, could be bought for a song; and climbed Sacsahuaman's near-by hill to wonder at the cyclopean stonework of the ancient builders. Finally we tore ourselves away to begin plant collecting along the sources of the Amazon.

We had come to Cuzco by air from Lima to Arequipa and thence by train. This, my first air journey, was made in a Ford trimotor plane which certainly should date that journey. Something must have gone wrong with our plane, because we had an experience that could not have been in the rule book.

An hour or two out of Lima, and, literally as well as figuratively, out of a clear sky, the airplane nosed sharply down through dense, low fog and landed lightly on the broad, hard-packed ocean beach. Nothing was in sight except a big truck full of gasoline cans. It pulled up beside us almost as soon as we had stopped rolling along the sand. So far as I know, the passengers were not asked to leave the airplane, but most of us did leave, even the singularly terrified señorita who from the moment the wheels left the ground at Lima airport had never taken her eyes off her lap and the beads that she was counting there.

The wind blowing up the beach was terrific. Only by putting his shoulder to the blast and spreading his legs wide apart was the pilot able to maintain his position on the wings while he attempted to pour canned gasoline, through a much-too-diminutive funnel, into the fuel reservoir beneath his feet. Of course, the wind snatched away a goodly share of what he was pouring, and soon the fuselage and the open door through which we had descended became enveloped in a cloud of gasoline vapor. The passengers drew back to a respectful distance and stood watching what appeared to be a futile effort at refueling.

At this juncture one of our fellow passengers appeared in the door, a young man who had been airsick and sufficiently affected by the altitude to require an oxygen bottle. The steward probably assumed that this passenger would be glad to rest during our emergency stop and so had hesitated to disturb him. At any rate, there he stood in the door, and, as we watched, put his hand in one pocket and pulled out a cigarette; from the other pocket he produced a box of matches. The cigarette had reached his mouth and the match was ready to be struck when, with one voice, we shouted a warning. At the same instant the steward appeared on the dead run and knocked down the matchbox —just in time. At the end of this pantomime another cloud of gasoline enshrouded the plane, and the young man hurried inside again. Somehow I began to feel that air travel on the Peruvian coast was a rather too informal sort of affair. It was, therefore, with considerable trepidation that I got aboard again when the refueling was finally finished.

Safely landed in Arequipa at two-thirty in the afternoon, we proceeded directly to Quinta Bates and into the waiting arms of Tía Bates, for many years the "Hostess of the Andes" and beloved friend and counselor of Indian and foreigner alike. Her guest book read like a roster of most of the world's great and near-great.

At nine that evening our train left Arequipa for Cuzco. We had no more than squeezed into our minute compartment on the *coche dormitorio* and finally managed to dispose ourselves on the narrow berths when I felt a dull headache begin, with intermittent flashes of biting pain. The train was rocking and swaying and laboring with that unmistakable vibration which means that a heavy grade is being negotiated. How heavy it was I did not at the time realize, but actually the altitude increases within a few hours east of Arequipa from eighty-five hundred feet to close to fourteen thousand. At each upward foot of altitude the pain in the back of my neck increased until no further increase was possible, and then I partially lost consciousness. What I was suffering was a rather severe case of *soroche*, or mountain sickness, which, however, has a number of variations, all decidedly unpleasant and one of them now and then fatal, as we learned some years later when we witnessed in Cuzco the death from heart failure of an elderly New England woman who had been vacationing along the west coast.

We got off the train in Cuzco late in the afternoon and found ourselves at the door of the railway hotel, the best that, in those days, Cuzco had to offer. I was feeling too low, after my bout with siroche, to take an interest in anything but bed. Ordinarily, Cuzco's altitude of 11,800 feet should not have made me as acutely conscious of heart sounds as I was that night. All I needed, however, was twelve hours in a horizontal position, because in the morning the altitudinal adjustment had been made and once more everything looked bright and cheerful. In the succeeding weeks of hard collecting, sometimes at altitudes above fourteen thousand feet, I felt no inconvenience, and even an exhilaration.

That first morning in Cuzco we dressed near the windows in order to watch the Indians who were crossing the rough, cobbled, plazalike area behind the hotel. This was our initial glimpse of the bright and rather charming native costumes that were universally worn, and that represented the chief touch of attractiveness in the decidedly primitive, and somewhat unclean, ensemble of life in the Peruvian Andes. I had supposed that the mountainfolk would be short, barrel-chested, and, in general, pretty powerfully built in order to meet the physiological demands that high altitudes impose. These first Indians we saw were, however, rather slender people and not below the average height of the Peruvians in coastal cities. They were jogging along in single file, on their way home from sojourns in the ancient capital of their forebears toward those minute collections of meager farmsteads that dot the high plateaus and mountain valleys of the Cuzco region.

In one group we saw two women, one of whom carried a baby almost completely concealed in the capacious shawl thrown over its mother's shoulders. It must have been a heavy baby because, although her step was light, the woman was leaning forward as she trotted along. The other woman was last in line. As we watched through our window, we saw her stop suddenly. With anxiety in face, pose, and every movement, she fumblingly examined a small pouch that hung at her waist. Then she turned around and, half stooping, slowly retraced her steps, searching the ground meanwhile. Now and again she paused, bent down, and picked up some object that was invisible to us. Although they glanced at her over their shoulders, the other Indians went straight on, and long before she passed beyond our line of vision they had disappeared in the opposite direction. We felt like spectators at a play who are permitted to see only the setting, and not the development, of a simple human drama.

The incident of the Cuzco Indian woman and her mysterious searchings would have been forgotten had she not reappeared half an hour later, when I stood at the hotel entrance talking to the manager. With her mincing, half-running, half-walking gait, she was again on her way across the rough roadway. At my request the manager asked—in that guttural, clicking, bastard Spanish-Quechua tongue so common in the highlands—what she had lost. She stopped with a surprised, doubtful, and slightly furtive look in her eyes and, after some urging, reluctantly opened a small, dirty hand and exhibited a dozen or two parched kernels of the large Cuzco corn. The manager explained that this corn probably represented all that she would have to eat during the long journey on foot that was ahead of her. Then I understood why she had been so worried when she discovered that, through a hole in a pouch, most of the corn had disappeared. All she could do was follow back along her path in the hope of picking up as many of the lost kernels as could be found.

The *serrana's* feet were bare, soiled, and leathery, but small and beautifully formed, as are those of most of the mountain people. She was pregnant, but not very obviously so. Her broad hips carried a succession of knee-length skirts—the outer one, made of rough, heavy, dark-blue woolen material, flared out at a wide angle. Over the skirts she wore a large apron dyed a brilliant magenta, a color that is popular among Peruvian Indian women. A long, narrow jacket, of navy blue and cut in a stiff, semimilitary fashion, high-shouldered, and decorated along the seams with narrow, bright-red braid, might, at one time, have covered the entire nakedness beneath but did not do so now. A large ragged shawl, of yellow wool striped with red, hung over her shoulders and down her back, and was held at the neck with a big brass breast-pin. She was, obviously, a young woman, and her face was still round and full but seamed and worn with toil and privation and with exposure to the severity of Andean climates. When she smiled—the self-conscious, half-grinning smile of the Peruvian Indian—we saw that her teeth were worn more than halfway down to the gums but otherwise seemed sound enough. Hard parched corn, and especially the dirt and grit that is likely to adhere to it, is wearing on the teeth.

The most remarkable part of the Indian woman's costume was her hat. It was half a flattened sphere, the framework made of reeds or straw over which blue cloth had been stretched. On the cloth that covered the flat top there were crossing bands of what had once been silver braid. A depression in the center of the curved surface accommodated a little of the wearer's head. The whole contraption was a foot and a half in diameter, and, according to the approved mode in the Andes, she wore it tilted forward over her eyes.

We rejoiced in being the only visible transient foreigners during those long-ago October weeks. I knew, however, that the handwriting was on the wall when a local Main Streeter remarked, with pride and in his best English, "On this precise day the Cuzco Tourist Association is borned." Thereupon I learned that the fame and efficiency of Californians, Inc., had gone almost to the ends of the earth, because, in remote Cuzco, my friend asked me to send him all their literature in order that he might demonstrate to his associates in the day-old tourist organization how to spread the wily net of anticipation and devise the guileful invitation.

In those days, Cuzco, the ancient Inca capital, still reflected a mingling and blending of the flavor of Inca times, the romantic glamour of the conquistadors, and the current life of the Andes. We used to hunt for an inconspicuous spot near a populous one and stand there trying to sort out the crowding impressions of life and work in one of America's oldest human settlements. Often, watching their descendants, we tried to induce imagination to repopulate Cuzco's plazas and narrow, winding streets with the people of the past—to conjure up the cortege of an Inca noble as it entered a smooth-walled stone doorway that his ancestors had built and that still stood on a modern Cuzco street-corner; or, again, to make believe that we heard the pounding hoofs of Pizarro's mail-clad cavalry as, with fierce shouts, they rode down the defenders of ancient Cuzco in its narrow, twisting lanes.

Late one afternoon we took our stand near a corner of the Plaza de Armas to watch the rosy sunset light climb the towers of the Cathedral. We must have been daydreaming of Spanish Colonial times and of all the things, righteous and unrighteous, that had been done in the name of God and in favor of his earthly representatives in that very plaza— because, without warning and with the same impulse, we turned to each other in speechless amazement. Throaty trumpets were sounding a strange fanfare, the hoofs of many horses rang out quick and sharp and clear, and we heard the clash and clang of metal harness. Could all our wishing and daydreaming have actually returned those long-gone days? Could the conquistadors, just for us, be riding again, back from a raid on the scattered remnants of the Incas' armies?

The volume of sound rapidly increased. Then round the corner, from one of Cuzco's steepest, narrowest, rockiest streets and into the plaza at our side, rode a mounted detachment of the Peruvian army's mountain troops. We were so sensitized, so receptive to impression, that the reality was almost as unreal as the fleeting vision had been. The cavalcade approached us at a fast trot. First came the buglers, their heads thrown back to give more amplitude to their high-pitched notes, then an officer riding alone, then troopers, two and two, with shining sabers and steel helmets, then mules, with quick, dainty hoofs, carrying segments of mountain howitzers strapped on their backs, and finally more troopers. In an instant the quiet, deserted plaza was full of echoing sound and rapid, glinting movement.

There are other bygone Cuzco memories—the second-hand market in the Plaza San Francisco, for example. During our walks about the old city we often chanced to pass through this plaza. It had always been deserted, except for llamas in groups of four or five, and dark-clad, mantilla-draped figures on the broad steps of the church that faced one side of the plaza's coarse pavement. The llamas were standing near the doors of saloons that, along with other one-story buildings, lined the remaining three sides of the plaza. Early in the morning they had carried loads of farm produce along some of the many rough trails that begin far away in the mountainous countryside and, from all directions, converge on the city of Cuzco. Now, freed from their burdens, they waited a little impatiently while their masters were fortifying themselves over against the long homeward journey.

On this particular afternoon, however, we found the Plaza San Francisco crowded and noisy. Along the high sidewalks that ran in front of saloons and shops, llamas were standing two or three deep. Townsfolk and Indians came and went through the mouths of streets that emptied into the plaza, and the large open space itself was full of people. It was obviously a market, but a different sort of highland market from any we had ever seen before.

In parallel lines on the pavement was displayed a most amazing collection of disreputable merchandise. It was not a second-hand, it was a third- or fourth-hand market. Junk of every description was neatly arranged and displayed, or, in other cases, heaped together in piles of confusion. The owner of each collection, almost always a woman, sat cross-legged or on her heels behind her stock in trade. Offered for sale were hundreds, perhaps thousands, of bent, rusty nails of all sizes and types, old screws which long since had lost their virtue, brassy and damaged safety pins, nuts and bolts that would never again be joined together, and many more such things. Near by lay the characteristically minute electric light bulbs of Peru, no one of which would ever burn again; cracked and broken chinaware; bedraggled fripperies of silk and lace; bits of worn tire casings. There were, in addition, piles of miscellaneous rubbish, mostly plumbing fixtures and metal fittings, so dissected and so damaged that their original form and function could scarcely be imagined.

That there were people who could be induced to buy such practically worthless and almost useless articles was difficult to believe. Being sold they were, however, and some of the buyers were almost as dilapidated as their purchases. Obviously poor of pocket, both vendors and purchasers were by no means poor in spirit. Ancient, doddery crones and shuffling grandfathers, wearing the most inconceivably ragged clothes, were bargaining for a bit of this or that with extremely animated voice and rapid gestures. The condition of their costumes was good evidence of the permanent quality of homespun, because the heavy woolen ponchos and skirts they wore seemed to consist more of holes than of fabric.

It was more than twenty years since I had been in Cuzco when I saw it again, with Betty, a year ago. It was not on our itinerary, but the kind proposal of the faculty of the venerable University of Cuzco —established by Royal Decree in 1692—to present me with an honorary Doctor of Science degree took us to the ancient Inca capital. Today almost everyone traveling to Cuzco flies there. The trip is quick and comfortable but some people do not enjoy compensating for high-altitude shortage of oxygen by sucking it from a tube.

The current Cuzco scene leaves me cold. All the vestiges of Inca stonework I had admired years before are still there; a few of the same Indian porters still struggle across the plazas and up steep, cobbled streets with their ponderous back-loads. But gone are the throngs of South Andean Indians in their colorful if dirty and ragged costumes; only now and then did we see a flat-hatted and flaring-skirted *serrana* looking quite out of place among conventionally clothed passers-by. Gone are the disdainful llamas with their beribboned ears and intriguing cargoes, marching in single file on their way to the market places or parked before groggeries, which formerly were one of the most picturesque elements of the Cuzco street scene. Long since they have been replaced by buses that carry the mountainfolk and their baggage back and forth to market. Added to the buses are trucks and cars constantly on the go around the plazas and along winding streets scarcely wide enough to give them passage and creating traffic problems which have been met in part by—ye Gods!—stop-and-go traffic lights at principal intersections. It is all too much of a contrast for me; too much of what Cuzco was and should have continued to be has obviously gone forever.

I will never succeed in thoroughly adjusting myself to the geographic, vegetational, and archaeological complex that lies to the north and east of Cuzco. Many years ago, as a schoolboy in Geneva, with my red-lined, brass-buttoned reefer and hairy, book-filled knapsack, and more than once since then, I have lingered on the Pont du Mont Blanc and watched the Rhone slip quietly out of Lac Leman and break against the Île Jean Jacques Rousseau as it gathered power for the long, winding journey through busy cities and beside terraced vineyards, to Avignon and onward into the Mediterranean. Without following its course, I had no difficulty in visualizing the landscapes it would see, the kinds of people it would watch, and the sorts of vegetation it would water—the European type of countryside. When, however, I stood beside the Andean sources of the Amazon, nothing was familiar, neither the land of their birth nor the wilderness they were to traverse. On their mission to the opposite edge of the continent these violent young rivers bathe the margins of mile upon mile of tropical rain forest, deposit the granitic sand of the Andes on the Amazonian plains, and wash the pigmented jungle soil down into the vent of the continental flood, where the waters draining three million square miles of mountain and plain become a single stream. Experience provided no background, and only imagination could depict the complex of tall, close-growing, perhaps beautiful—sometimes, dangerously beautiful—jungle trees, interwoven lianas that they support, streamers of lowly, flowerless plants hanging from their branches, the flourishing understory of the forests, and, below, the rank growths on the soil from which these forests spring. These tumultuous waters were to journey through unreality, seeing landscapes, vegetations, and peoples all new to my experience.

There has, however, always been enough unreality in the territories surrounding the one-time Inca capital to occupy my mind, and, in particular, unreality in those snow-crested, deep-walled gorges, rich in unaccustomed vegetation, which the Amazon's beginnings have helped to chisel out between the miles-high ranges. At one time or another, many members of our six expeditions collected along them— the Urubamba, the Apurímac, the Paucartambo, the Madre de Dios— and through the country between them and our Cuzco headquarters.

One of the plants I hoped to find in South America and have an opportunity to study in its native land was *Nicotiana tomentosa*, the "tree tobacco" of Andean Peru. In the first chapter we met this striking species growing in the Botanical Garden, on the day I was introduced to *Nicotiana*. Its remarkable height and bulk, and something exotically lush about its general appearance, were impressive. From that day forth I tried unsuccessfully in imagination to picture it in its

Andean environment. How could this soft-tissued near-tobacco, which blackened and died when a few degrees of frost descended upon a California garden, withstand the rigors of those highlands in the neighborhood of Cuzco of which it was reported to be a native? Before we went into them, all that I knew about those highlands was that the city itself lay at an altitude of almost twelve thousand feet and near it the map showed lofty mountain ranges culminating in twenty-thousand-foot Mount Salcantay and in other peaks as high or higher. What was that tender "tree tobacco" doing in such company? We had been in Cuzco only a day or two before this riddle was solved.

The Peruvian government owns some short railway lines and one of them runs from Cuzco through the "Grand Canyon" of the Río Urubamba, and past Machu Picchu, the outstanding tourist attraction of Peru. It climbs out of the valley in which the city lies, runs across exposed plateaus rimmed on the horizon with a succession of mighty, snow-covered peaks, and then starts downward toward the Urubamba. In those early days of tourist travel in the Cuzco area you rode in an *autocarril*,—an open, motor-driven hybrid between a streetcar and a station wagon. It was bitter cold just after sunrise when the "train" left Cuzco, and even colder on the return journey after dark. The hotel thoughtfully provided heavy blankets for its guests who were taking the autocarril but these did not help very much.

After the initial ascent, the line began to descend on a cliffside shelf blasted out of the mountainside. We had no more than reached the shelf when an Indian and his two burros appeared on the track at some distance ahead. There was no room for passing toward the cliff, and scarcely space enough on the outer edge, so the Indian decided to keep ahead of us. This was a challenge to our driver. He had turned off the gas at the start of the downgrade and was saving his brakes as much as possible by using the compression of the engine. Now, however, it became a question of speed and not of brakes or compression, and certainly not of compassion for the Indian. In a moment or two the careening autocarril was on the heels of the trotting burros and their hurrying master, and our driver began to enjoy himself immensely.

The wiry little animals developed a remarkably fast gait, so fast indeed that soon the Indian gave up and found a spot where we could pass him. Then, without any warning, brakes and compression went on, we nearly broke our necks against the seats in front, and the autocarril almost stopped. The driver's neck and ears showed embarrassment as we got out on the running board to see what was going on ahead. There, one of the burros was exhibiting strong evidences of irritation and an intention to do all that his small hind hoofs could to flatten the front of the autocarril. He would trot a few steps, stop, teeter back and forth for an instant, and then let fly a lightning kick. It was a comical sight, because he never let the car approach near enough so that his kicks could possibly reach it. Finally, the driver stopped and the little burro slowly disappeared around the curve, still kicking. He and his mate must have found a place to leave the track, because we saw no more of them. I fear that we gave no thought to their owner, who must have lost many hours in searching for what were undoubtedly the most valuable of his possessions.

Extensive panoramas came into view as the track swung out around rocky promontories. To the east, one blue range after another rolled higher and higher. To the north and west, snow-covered peaks just showed above the eight-to-twelve-thousand-foot walls of the Urubamba's deep, narrow gorge. At intervals you looked down into it and caught a hint of the amazing zonation of vegetation on its precipitous sides. Even at a distance I could see that, beginning with barren terrain at higher elevations, each thousand-foot decrease in height correspondingly increased the covering of green on the mountainsides until, near and in the bottom of the canyon, the vegetation was luxuriant. The character as well as the amount of the vegetation changed successively with the differences in altitude. Thus, the river margins were to some extent forested, and within depressions on more gradually sloping canyon walls trees and large shrubs extended upward for some thousands of feet. Above, and on exposed areas where the cliffs rose almost from the water's edge, the vegetation was thinner and largely herbaceous.

Once I saw the depth of the Urubamba gorge, the answer to my question about *Nicotiana tomentosa* and its occurrence in the Cuzco region was forthcoming. However lofty Cuzco and the summits of near-by mountain ranges might be, the headwaters of the Urubamba were running at between seven and eight thousand feet and, a little farther downstream, at six thousand feet and below. Within fifteen degrees south of the equator such altitudes mean heat and moisture and, ultimately, the jungle. It was obvious, therefore, that somewhere along the semitropical river valley *Nicotiana tomentosa* could readily find a congenial environment. The only point that remained to be determined was in which of the vegetational zones lying in horizontal bands on the steep, sometimes almost vertical, mountainsides would it be found to occur most characteristically. In other words, I still had to find it.

The track soon reached the upper end of the canyon and thereafter followed along the course of the river, sometimes on its very banks in places where the cliffs pushed outward toward the water's edge. In one such spot a section of the almost overhanging canyon wall had slipped, and rocks, brush, and other debris covered the rails. A gang of men was engaged, rather lackadaisically, in clearing the track. While the autocarril waited for them to finish the job I climbed around the slide and started down the track to do a bit of collecting. As I walked along I began to look more and more critically at some of the large, treelike shrubs growing on the near-by riverbank. They had an increasingly familiar look, and the next moment I realized that I had found *Nicotiana tomentosa*.

It was very satisfying to see those monstrous near-tobaccos in their natural surroundings. Their variability in leaf shape, flower form, and flower color was surprising. At first, it looked as though there were no two plants anywhere nearly identical, and I settled down to record the evidence on paper and on film. Before I was through, the autocarril appeared and, aboard it once more, I cast lingering glances back to the little *tomentosa* forest and hoped it would not be the only one we would come across that day. I need not have been fearful on that score; all the way, from the point where we first found it to the Machu Picchu bridge and below, the landscape never lacked a "tree tobacco" or two rising above the increasingly dense shrub vegetation of the canyon floor.

We had hoped to climb up to Machu Picchu and down before nightfall. In those days the last station on the railway was still a mile or two above the bridge across the Urubamba where what was then nothing but a steep, rough trail to Machu Picchu began. That bridge over the racing, roaring white waters of the Urubamba! How can today's pampered travelers, crossing it in their autobuses to the road which now runs to Machu Picchu, conceive of what it was twenty-five years ago? When, with faltering steps, we inched across it, the bridge consisted of a series of round poles set lengthwise, with a sagging wire handrail along one side. In some spots the platform was only three poles wide. Now and then the wire lashings that united the poles had broken, with the result that a piece of the flooring was ready to spring up against your face or slap you on the back. Everywhere the white water of the Urubamba was visible between the poles, and in some places were gaps through which it seemed to reach up, eager to pluck you down into its depths. Underfoot, the manure deposited by many pack trains was thick and sometimes fresh and slippery. The whole structure swayed violently with the shifting weight of our passage and trembled continuously with the pounding of the racing river against the bridge supports.

We progressed bravely, if not rapidly, up to the point where a great boulder, near the center of the roaring flood, acted as midpier for the flimsy bridge. In Cuzco we had been told that, the week before, a surveyor, transit on shoulder, fell from the bridge just he as reached this halfway point and immediately disappeared in the raging, deep-flowing waters. As we approached the spot it was hard to drag our eyes away from the leaping water below and from the ripping tide of its flow against the tremendous boulders downstream. The surface of the river seemed to be so close and the bridge was so narrow that I felt surrounded by swiftly flowing water and found myself beginning to sway and stumble with giddiness. It occurred to me that a similar vertigo might have been responsible for the surveyor's fatal misstep.

Horses were supposed to be in readiness on the far side of the bridge to carry us up the two thousand feet of difficult trail to Machu Picchu. No horses were in sight. Near by, a group of Indians were assembling poles and lumber, presumably and hopefully, for bridge repair. They shook their heads stupidly when we tried to find out where the horses were that we had ordered. The lunch hour having already come and gone, we decided to satisfy what little the passage of the bridge had left of our appetites.

At this point the valley walls are precipitous and run up a thousand feet or more, almost from the water's edge. The midday sun had been pouring its heat into the narrow gorge, and we began to shed outer garments which early in the day had been all too thin. Finding a log near the margin of a small clearing the bridge menders had cut into the rain forest, we made a pretense of eating. The vegetation, climate, and insects reminded us again that seven thousand feet in this part of Peru means something decidedly tropical. Long before we had passed on the large remnant of our luncheon to the Indians by the bridge, winged and crawling pests were raising welts on all exposed, and on most unexposed, areas of skin.

We started up the trail and found it hard going in the melting heat, for we were much too heavily burdened with clothing and equipment. The hoofs of horses and burros had loosened the dirt and rubble underfoot, and it was easy to slide backward down, or sideways off, the narrow path. Then the sky became overcast, and we welcomed the consequent decrease in the intensity of the sun's burning rays. Soon, however, rain, which later we came to expect each afternoon in the depths of Andean valleys, began to descend, and immediately the trail turned into slippery mud. When the first drizzles rapidly became a heavy shower, we sought shelter beside the trail in a thicket of large-leaved shrubs. Various kinds of stingers and biters had apparently conceived the same idea. They waited beneath the leaves and welcomed us, some silently, some buzzingly. Months later we were told that poisonous snakes, including the deadly bushmaster, frequented precisely the sort of trailside brush into which the rain had driven us.

As we crouched under our imperfect protection from the steady downpour and peered out toward the trail, a succession of little boys passed by. Their bare feet made soft, sucking sounds as they dragged them from the mud. Their faces were thin, their clothes ragged and muddy, and their bare legs gruesome with fresh, raw sores and the pitted scars of earlier ones.

There have been many descriptions of Machu Picchu, the "City of a Thousand Steps." You read of its terraces and aqueducts, of its mansions and palaces and temples, needing only roofs of thatch to make them what they were many, many hundreds of years ago when the dwellers in impregnable Machu Picchu looked down two thousand feet to the Urubamba, a thin white ribbon racing through the bottom of its green-walled gorge. Much has been written of the art of the Inca stonemasons who, without benefit of level, square, plumb bob, or mortar, built the Torreón—that beautiful, curvilinear, fortified tower—or laid those matched and perfectly fitted blocks to make walls and steps and windows the like of which can be seen nowhere else in the world. Neither the written word nor the sensitized film can, however, do justice to the far-flung panoramas that surround this jungle-bordered city of stone. No other remnant of the pre-Columbian civilizations of the Andes commands wider horizons, such a world of blue-green mountain ranges, mist-hung crags, and white-mantled peaks.

Machu Picchu holds a story, hidden perhaps for all time. When and why was it built? Against whom was it so effectively fortified? Was it a city of refuge, the last Inca capital, or a holy place? And why, unless abandoned to the engulfing jungle long before they came, did not the conquistadors discover it and add its destruction to that which they wreaked on other remnants of pre-Columbian civilizations?

The ruins of Machu Picchu once provoked a prediction of what lay beyond for those who, in the recent past, were responsible for worldwide conflict. It should also apply to those who may become responsible in, alas, the not too distant future, for an even greater holocaust. I have taken it from a newspaper clipping someone gave me in the early 1940's and it goes, in substance, as follows:

"The mystery of Machu Picchu grows with each successive authority who writes of it. One thing, at least, is certain. Machu Picchu is a totalitarian ruin. The Inca state was a completely totalitarian state. The Inca himself was a dictator—judge, emperor, god. He personally owned every citizen and every product the people of his vast empire produced. He prescribed, through deputies, every detail of life and action. Freedom was unknown, undreamed. Today, Machu Picchu is a ruin barely to be held, by constant effort, from the fangs of the jungle. There is much to admire in the culture of the Incas but their system was utterly false to eternal human values. Let other dictators, in the still watches of the night, ponder the story of Machu Picchu."

Be that as it may, there are few of those who have seen Machu Picchu who will not agree that "in the sublimity of its surroundings, the marvel of its site, the character and the mystery of its construction, the Western Hemisphere holds nothing comparable."

Twenty-five years ago Machu Picchu was relatively unknown to tourists. Indeed, my first visit was only incidental to plant collecting in the Urubamba Valley far below it. Today, by contrast, a stopover in Peru more or less automatically includes Machu Picchu via Cuzco, and tourist agencies urge this "side trip" upon prospective members of their tours to the South American west coast. Our recent contact with numerous "three-weeks-by-air-around-South America" trippers indicates that the usual three-day allowance for Lima–Cuzco (Machu Picchu)–Lima is too abbreviated. For many, perhaps most, foreigners, at least one full day and a night should be available to recover from the sudden elevation from sea level at Lima to 11,500 feet plus at Cuzco.

We allowed ourselves five days, including the two flights, and spent thirty-six hours in bed surrounded by hot-water bottles—the heights around Cuzco were white with snow one morning—or in a state of suspended animation in the hotel lobby. As before, a severe pain at the back of the neck and considerable nausea were the symptoms of soroche. In our case, they were reduced by Coramine. A Lima doctor had suggested it in pastille form to be dissolved in the mouth but we found the liquid far more effective. I venture to suggest that, unless your doctor at home says "no," a little bottle of Coramine will probably make your sojourns at high altitudes more comfortable.

For me the contrast between Cuzco, old and new, was surpassed by the contrast between my experiences going to and from and at Machu Picchu over twenty years ago and last year—the former have been touched upon earlier in this chapter. Today you ride in a railway car, powered by motor, which accommodates in comfort a considerable number of tourists and a sprinkling of countryfolk. There are, of course, the same switchbacks required to top the high hills rimming Cuzco and the same rapid descent to a broad valley before entering the deep depression through which the Urubamba flows down into the tropical rain forest.

As we crossed the broad valley, our Peruvian tour conductor, who had our sympathy during his struggles with English grammar, called attention to how appropriate it would be as a landing field for jet "clippers" and intimated that in the very near future the necessary runways would materialize. Then, said he, the Cuzco–Machu Picchu tourist trade would really boom, for the airlines would fly visitors nonstop from the big cities of the United States and Europe to this best-known South American tourist attraction. He even hinted that cheap, weekend round trips were contemplated. During this recital we heard scornful snorts coming from a Peruvian seatmate. He pointed to the soggy, often marshy, soil of the broad valley and estimated that it would be a long time after the necessary drainage operations were undertaken before the area could become anything but what it then was, a lush pastureland. However, something must and doubtless will soon be done to improve the Cuzco landing field. When last year we took off on the return flight to Lima, the motors had to be raced terrifically before the chocks were pulled away so that we could take a fast jump off the relatively short runway and gain sufficient altitude to get safely out of the pocketed Cuzco Valley.

When, soon, the train gathered speed and hurried down into and along the narrowing canyon of the Urubamba, almost everything proved to be as it had been so many years before. The sun touched only the top third of the vast upward sweeps of the mountainsides, which showed the same sharp zonation of vegetation and the same extensive outcrops of orange-red rock. On the riverbank there were the same well-preserved abutments of an Inca bridge and on a bit of level land the same ruined houses, with their sharply peaked end-walls, that had —perhaps five hundred, perhaps very many more years ago—been a part of an Inca communal farm; and, farther down, close to the water, there were the same thickets of *Nicotiana tomentosa*, the "tree tobacco of the Andes," the discovery of which on its native heath had highlighted my first ride to Machu Picchu.

On the other hand, from the moment we left the train at the bridge over the Urubamba until we came down to it for the return to Cuzco, many things were different, very different. Replacing a rough, slippery trail, two-thirds washed out where the many short zigzags were steepest and replete with unnerving vistas straight down a thousand or more feet to the white water of the Urubamba, there is today a reasonably wide automobile road of long zigzags that climbs the two thousand feet to Machu Picchu on reasonable grades. From above, the road looks like a thin white snake twisting its way up over the dark-green, almost vertical slope. The twists represent the points where each zig becomes a zag. Although you can see that each one is properly banked with rock and rubble, there are a few seconds each time when you cannot help wondering whether the bus can possibly double back so abruptly.

Because of these exceedingly sharp twists, the buses are diminutive. But, surely, they do not need to be so rattletrap. Ours—and the others looked to be no different—groaned and creaked and shook as if about ready to fall to pieces. Betty and I sat on the narrow front seat at the right of the driver and close beside the door. On the first jolting, upward pull it swung wide open and we leaned left until the next jolt jerked it back again. Then we saw that the door catch was broken off and replaced with a bit of wire. However, the motor behaved nobly, with only a few splutters and chokes on the steepest grades, and the engine always managed to boil just as we approached a spring bubbling up beside the road. At a word from the driver, his assistant climbed over us and through the door. He hung there until just before the water-stop, then dropped to the road and jammed blocks under the rear wheels. Some of our more timorous fellow passengers apparently found the bus trip up, and more so the rather rapid descent, somewhat distressing; at any rate, their frame of mind seemed to be quite introspective and they managed only the most fleeting glances down the almost vertical slopes below or at the splendid panoramas that burst upon us at openings in the forested road margin.

The original trail gave you no foresight of Machu Picchu. You had dragged yourself up through the last hundred feet of trees and high, dense brush when, without warning, you were in the open and at the lowest level of the rock-bound city. You looked, wiped the sweat out of your eyes, and looked again. Yes, there it actually was, so almost unbelievable, so far beyond expectation, so seemingly out of place and yet so perfectly in place, spread out on its thin saddle between the steep flanks of Machu Picchu on one side and Huayna Picchu on the other. Although almost completely obscured by jungle growth when in 1911 he discovered it by much the same route, you do not need much imagination to picture Hiram Bingham's amazement and joy at what he saw before him. In his *Lost City of the Incas* he describes his long search in the South Peruvian Andes through almost inaccessible valleys and on the mountainsides above them for what may have been the last capital of the Inca Empire. It had been vaguely referred to in Indian legends and by the Spanish chroniclers, but until he found Machu Picchu there was no evidence that a completely unique and unbelievably well-preserved monument to the life and cultures of pre-Columbian days in the Andes was still in existence.

From the bus, also, you get no hint of what Machu Picchu is, for instead of bringing you to the top of the trail, in the midst of the walls, steps, temples, and terraces, the road ends at the Albergue Machu Picchu—a pleasant-enough little inn, quite simply and conventionally designed, where the one-day trippers eat a remarkably good luncheon. The English menu read: "onions soup, spaghetti with tomatoes sauce, roast veal with potatoes purée, natural orange, tea or coffee." A year ago the inn could accommodate only a very few overnight guests, but we were told that it was soon to be enlarged. In clear weather the sunset and, especially, the sunrise panoramas are said to be "out of this world," as we could well believe. With the rapidly increasing tourist enthusiasm about it—"Oh, *didn't* you go to Machu Picchu?"—some establishment for rest and refreshment is essential, but a clever architect,

Llamas: Andean burden bearers, source of wool, and, finally, meat supply.

Not aigrettes but llamas, near camels of the Andes, carrying fodder.

Cube (barbasco) roots, yielding fish poison and insecticide rotenone.

Indians of the Peruvian jungle: arrowheads and bows of palm wood.

Sugar cane goes to the gin mill and returns as a jug of aguardiente.

We found many new or little-known Peruvian orchids:

Lycaste dyeriana.
Acineta densa.

Coryanthes leucocorys.
Maxillaria rufescens.

and there are plenty of them in Peru, could have produced a structure quite in keeping with the spirit of Machu Picchu. Indeed, I do not doubt that there were enough odds and ends of Inca stone not required for the restorations in progress to have built with them at least the front surface of a modest building and thus to have created a proper introduction to the "City of a Thousand Steps" just around a corner of the mountain.

Because of a siroche hangover I had all that I could do to follow our guide-lecturer up and down the first tiers of those "thousand" steps. (Paul and Bill, a few weeks earlier, had "done" Machu Picchu much more thoroughly than most visitors, climbed the precipitous sides of the two peaks that form the extremities of the knife edge on which Machu Picchu stands, taken many hundreds of pictures, and still had energy left for much plant collecting during their overnight stay.)

Our guide continued to herd his sightseeing party rapidly up and down and here and there, commenting authoritatively on the actually presumed significance of each sector of the stone city. He was quite astonished that Betty and I preferred to forego his lecture and spend the remainder of the tour by ourselves in the Sacred Plaza at the foot of the steps leading to the famous *intihuatana*, or sundial, the apex of Machu Picchu. About us were remarkable illustrations of the ultimate refinements of Inca stonework—the smooth, white granite ashlars perfectly matched and as perfectly fitted, one to another. It was a pleasant day, and we were tired and glad to rest on the massive, peculiarly shaped block of stone which could have been a sacrificial altar —the ancient Peruvians indulged in human sacrifice—and to study, across the plaza, a marvelously proportioned three-sided structure rising above a broad stone bench on which it is supposed that the mummies of departed Incas were exposed to the Sun God, ruling divinity. There was also the wall with its three "picture windows" which in legend are linked with the beginnings of the Inca regime. These, and all the other accomplishments of the Machu Picchu stonemasons, evidence what can be accomplished with nothing but stone hammers and bronze axes, chisels, and crowbars, plus forced labor and no time limit. Later, we walked over to the low wall that bounds one edge of the plaza and, spellbound, gazed down the almost perpendicular, forested mountainside that represents the other flank of the Machu Picchu saddle to the threadlike Urubamba two thousand feet below, where its course turns back upon itself around the base of Huayna Picchu's vertical-sided peak. We watched the lofty green ranges across the gorge fade into the cloudy horizon; on the left they culminate in the twin immensities of Salcantay and Soray, one reaching skyward a little more and the other a little less than twenty thousand feet. We probably did not see some of the things that most of our tour companions saw, and we certainly did not take as many Kodachromes, but we like to think that we absorbed and carried away a little more than they of that atmosphere of mystery and otherworldliness which permeates Machu Picchu.

Quite a few things about Machu Picchu itself were different. What I noticed particularly was the success with which the constant attempt of the near-jungle vegetation to take over had been thwarted. When I first saw Machu Picchu, only the most spectacular sections of the stone city had been partly freed from obscuring trees, shrubs, vines, and other plants. A year ago the biennial clean-up had just been completed and there was very little growing on the marvelous walls or on the plazas, courtyards, and staircases. More than this, you could examine interesting outlying subdivisions which before had scarcely been visible through the dense vegetation within and over them. A certain amount of restoration has been done and, on the whole, well done. The force of the 1950 earthquake, which did so much damage in Cuzco, was strongly felt at Machu Picchu. It threw down the tops of some of the late-Inca walls and loosened, here and there, the far more perfectly fitted early-Inca stonework—perhaps the much more severe *terremoto* of just three hundred years before was also partly responsible. The great bank of near-by *andenes*, or terraces, on which the ancient inhabitants produced their corn, potatoes, and peppers, also suffered, and restorations were in progress there, together with more extensive clearing than before.

Another mystery has been added to that of Machu Picchu. South of it, and almost three thousand feet higher on the walls of the Urubamba canyon, the ruins of two sizable cities have been found. By narrow, paved trails and flights of stone steps built on narrow saddles and across precipitous slopes, these settlements are connected with Machu Picchu. Although they do not contain such architectural achievements as it does, much of their stonework is equally good, and their terraced construction, paths, and stairways and systems of water supply and drainage correspond to those of Machu Picchu and date both groups of ruins within the same period of Inca culture.

Over the years we have made many collections in and about Machu Picchu. Some of the plants we found suggest that the Incas might have grown them as ornamentals. Certainly there appeared to be an unusually large number of showy species in, or close to, the ruins. For example, a splendid red orchid, a *Maxillaria,* was common in the terraces and on bits of open ground between the buildings. Again, there were handsome species of *Oxalis* and a succulent that looked like *Sedum* growing in crevices of the smooth and close-set walls. Finally, almost in the streets of the ruined city, we found *Calceolaria tomentosa,* the giant "slipperwort." We did not come across it elsewhere in the Andes, although it is known from other Andean areas. Probably the presence of so many plants of these and of other fine ornamentals in and around the "City of a Thousand Steps" was only coincidence, but it made a different impression.

In Berkeley the giant *Calceolaria* from the ancient city, like many other species from the Andes, prefers partial shade, even though in its native habitat it grows up through low brush to luxuriate in full sun. The dry air and generally reduced moisture conditions in California gardens, contrasting with the humidity of their native habitats, is doubtless responsible for the favorable reaction of many sun-loving Andean species to shaded, and therefore moister, situations in their foster home. This Machu Picchu *Calceolaria* has been a distinct novelty and has attracted much attention. With us it is a perennial, at least a limited one, and in one year grows to a height of ten to twelve feet. The leaves, often eighteen inches long and almost as wide in the blade, are borne in twos on opposite sides of a thick, woody stem, which they surround with clasping bases that unite to form a cup. The striking, bright-yellow flowers, often as big as small hens' eggs, hang on the periphery of tall pyramidal inflorescences that are produced from the ends of a series of stems. Each spring a ring of new shoots starts from the crown of the previous year's main axis, grows fast, and blooms in May and June (sometimes even earlier) and also later in the year. An outstanding plant in any company, it is particularly impressive when growing among the many other, relatively pygmy, Calceolarias that we brought back from South America.

Below the Machu Picchu bridge one enters a far more tropical region, with cultivations of sugar cane, coffee, tea, cacao, oranges, and bananas. The climate and vegetational contrasts that pass in review as one follows down the river northward are almost beyond belief. A relatively short distance separates the cold heights of Cuzco from the luxuriant tropics of the lower Urubamba Valley. In the hot, moist jungle—malaria-ridden and infested with unpleasant insects and dangerous serpents—the supreme Andean heights are almost overhead and openings in the forest show a lofty northern horizon rimmed with perpetual snow. Two worlds, as different as day is from night, stand side by side, a day's journey apart.

The Incas, from their high Andean capital and from their terraced settlements clinging to the barren walls above the upper reaches of the Amazon's beginnings, looked with longing eyes toward the lushness of the lower valleys. By conquest they attempted to include these semi-tropics and their dwellers in the "new order" in the Andes. This proposal was not too successful. The death-laden darts that the jungle men blew from the dense shelter of the rain forest, and such natural defenses as the fevers and poisonous plants and animals of their homeland, turned back successive invasions.

The chroniclers refer to the Amazonian tribes as fierce and warlike, but their descendants cannot be so classified. The Indians, who once or twice appeared out of the jungle, were as subdued as they were filthy and diseased. They bartered bows and arrows for trinkets and were sufficiently uncivilized and unenlightened not to demand a fee when we proposed to photograph them. Their lack of contact with the outside world was also evidenced by inability to speak a word of Spanish, or even Quechua, the lingua franca of the highlands. Therefore, barter had to be carried on in the primitive language of gesture and grimace.

For a somewhat intimate contact with the highland Indians of the Cuzco region which, years ago, was possible in Cuzco itself, the forty-mile excursion to Pisac is now required. This village is typical of those numerous ones hidden away in folds of the southern Andes of Peru. It lies at a considerably lower altitude than Cuzco on the banks of the Vilcanota, one of the streams that ultimately swells the flood of the Urubamba.

Sunday is market day in Pisac. To it come the Indians from neighboring communities to dispose of the products of their handicrafts and, more especially, to indulge in a round of gossip. Some one or more features of the picturesque and colorful costumes serve to identify the representatives of each of the different clans. Among the commodities for sale, particularly to tourists, are handwoven *illicllas* (shawls), *chullus* (stocking caps) and *clumpis* (belts). Mostly, the designs and color combinations are pleasing. The Indian vendors are decidedly conscious of the presence of foreigners, but their families pay no attention to them and congregate around the margins of the market plaza. There, unsavory smoke drifts about from little fires where unpleasant-looking food is being prepared, babies feed at the breast while their mothers eat, children relieve themselves, and subdued chattering in the guttural Quechua, native tongue of the Peruvian Andes, never ends.

Near Pisac the extent, character, and preservation of the Inca agricultural terraces, called *andenes,* is outstanding. In parallel steps they sweep all the way down a rounded and seamed mountainside, accentuating its contours and finally merging with the level valley floor; ordinarily, such a bank of *andenes* would end far above. On neighboring mountain slopes dark-green stripes show the courses of the *asecias* or conduits that the Incas built to bring water to the *andenes,* on the lowermost of which the Pisac folk grow today the same crops that their ancestors grew there centuries ago.

The principal church had been built to one side of the market-place plaza. It was thrown down by the latest earthquake but its chime of bells had been salvaged and hung on a temporary scaffold. Late in the morning the bells began to toll and many of the Indians started toward a chapel on the edge of the village. We followed, and stopped near the door. Within, the floor was tightly packed with kneeling worshipers. Gathered around the doorway stood the *alcaldecitos,* magistrates of Pisac and surrounding communes, in rather elaborate costumes, each holding his silver-mounted staff of office and carrying a large conch shell. There was a bit of byplay, during which some chicha-inspired frivolity was suppressed, and then, in solemn file, they all entered the chapel. Thereafter, at intervals, they sounded in unison a sustained and mournful note on their conch shells. It seemed to echo the isolation of that Andean valley, so far off the beaten track.

Above modern Pisac is the site of an ancient Inca city which, for me, to some extent exceeded Machu Picchu in providing a picture of pre-Columbian life in the Peruvian Andes. The two-mile climb up from Pisac's plaza was exceedingly steep, rough and fatiguing—today you ride a horse—but the exertion was well repaid. Before me were the ruins of a considerable city which had been quarried out of an almost perpendicular rock face. There were narrow flights of steps so steep that going up, and especially down, was almost a hand-over-hand affair, and I did not attempt to examine more than what had been built on lower levels. On one was the principal temple, constructed of most perfectly fashioned and polished blocks of stone. Undoubtedly, it had never been roofed, because within its walls was an intihuatana, one of the few sacred sundials the padres who accompanied the conquistadors had not demolished or damaged in their zeal to stamp out the sun worship of the Incas. No one seeing pre-Columbian Pisac can fail to appreciate what a prodigious amount of labor and time must have gone into its construction, or to imagine how wearisome must have been the up-and-down existence of its inhabitants.

There is much more that could be told about our plant hunting in that center of floristic contrasts and archaeological treasures where the Amazon begins. Suffice it to say that, over the years, the area has yielded us a rich and abundant harvest of new or little-known plant species and, in addition, never-to-be-forgotten pictures of superb alpine panoramas and of the ways of life of long-gone Andean civilizations. In that marvelous area there remain many more harvests waiting to repay those willing to climb the high passes and botanize the sharply delimited zones of vegetation that cling to the abrupt mountain slopes sweeping down from snow fields and alpine aridity to jungle-filled river bottoms, thousands of feet below. From now on their toil will, in part, be mitigated by the roads being torn out—by those steel behemoths that clear and level—to provide communication to and from hitherto unexploited mineral deposits deep in the Andean ranges.

9

INCA TRAILS

WHEN, IN pre-Columbian times, the Incas were establishing their "new order" in the Andes, the importance of good highways to facilitate troop movements and exchange of merchandise loomed large in their plans of conquest or in their proposals for exploiting a negotiated peace. Many remnants of their highway systems remain, to demonstrate that whatever the "new order" undertook to accomplish was effectively accomplished. In engineering, as well as in statecraft, it was highly efficient. Stone-paved trails and broader paths once extended along or parallel to the Andean ranges from Quito to Chile, with branches running east and west from the main north-and-south trunk line. In terms of present-day geography, one of the important Inca routes led westward from Cuzco to Abancay, thence over Andean summits to Andahuailas and on to Ayacucho and Huancayo. This highway was old when Pizarro rode along it, four hundred and more years ago. Our botanists traveled it in both directions; sometimes this cross-country collecting expedition was made in the dry season and on other occasions in the wet season. Thus, the Prince was able to go from railhead at Huancayo to Ayacucho by autobus, but from that point onward most of the journey to Cuzco had to be made on horseback or on foot. Some years later Harvey and Bob, starting from Cuzco, had to do far less riding and walking. Today the entire route of the old Inca trail has been made passable for automobiles, so that one can drive all the way from Lima, through Huancayo, to Cuzco, as did Paul and Bill last year.

Penetration of the Peruvian highlands by railroads and highways is soon followed by an unnatural extension of the distribution of some plant species across altitudinal and other natural barriers to equivalent vegetational zones far distant from their original, some times restricted, habitats. For example, *Nicotiana glutinosa* was once characteristic only of lower middle altitudes on the western front of the outermost Andean ranges. Years ago, with the completion of the railway eastward across the summit, and then southward, the minute seeds of this *Nicotiana* were carried in the crevices of crates or bales or hand baggage over the lofty pass and into the temperate climate of Huancayo. There, the seed fell into congenial soil and proceeded to establish a plant species never before a part of the vegetation of that portion of Peru. Later, again through man's intervention, the seeds traveled farther south, to a point where the highway and its traffic ended at the foot of another Andean range. As soon as the summit of this range and the country between it and Cuzco had become free for the automobile, *N. glutinosa* moved on almost to the gates of the "City of the Sun." In a few years the reports of today's students of plant distribution in the Andes may be something quite different from those brought back by earlier botanists who collected in the same territories.

For his journey from Ayacucho to Cuzco, the Prince hired a pack train. He and his native packers camped along the trail, wherever the collecting was rich. At the start, he made his own fire and cooked his own food. Soon, however, this proved to be too much trouble, and he joined the packers around their fire and dipped with them into the common pot. Then, after the meal was over, he brewed himself a cup of tea from his private stock, drank it out of his own tin cup, and thus maintained a certain aloofness and dignity in the eyes of his attendants. The account of his experiences and adventures during this overland journey was, unfortunately, lost in the wreck and burning of a local plane that was carrying the airmail from the mountains into Lima. His collections, sent by parcel post, reached California in good condition and contained much of value. Of special importance was a previously unknown species of *Nicotiana*, one of five new species of this genus we discovered in Peru. I named it *Nicotiana benavidesii*, in honor of the then president of the republic.

Harvey and Bob traveled much the same route as the Prince, but in the reverse direction, and at a season less desirable from the point of view of personal comfort but more desirable as far as the condition of the vegetation was concerned. February, in the central and southern Peruvian Andes, usually represents the height of the rainy season and, therefore, of the flowering season. Cuzco had been wet and cold, and their collecting sorties from that city provided them with a foretaste of what the roads might be like on their cross-country jaunt. The first lap of their journey took them by truck from Cuzco to Abancay. The distance to Abancay was announced by the driver to be approximately five hours. Thus, if the truck started on schedule at eight o'clock in the morning, they would disembark at Abancay in time for lunch. Actually, they got under way at nine-thirty in the morning, and arrived at ten-thirty at night.

The heavily laden truck climbed out of the Cuzco valley. It more or less followed a cobbled surface laid in Inca days, to be traveled by nothing heavier than the feet of relays of runners bringing seaside produce to the tables of the mountain-dwelling Inca nobles, by the light hoofs of llamas, or by the sandals of travelers or of sturdy porters transporting material not trusted on the backs of four-footed beasts of burden. At the beginning, this ancient roadway ran through high, open, partially cultivated terrain that was green with meadows and pepper trees, blue with lupine and *Salvia*, and yellow, in wide swathes or irregular patches, with *Grindelia boliviana* and shrubby growths of *Cassia latopetiolata*.

After crossing the high watershed between the Urubamba and Apurímac the road descended, much too dangerously, toward the valley bottom. The rains appeared to have done their worst on the modern additions to the ancient roadway, but there was still room for more deterioration, as Harvey and Bob discovered when heavy showers overtook them. With the rain came a dense fog that made the traversing of slippery shelves on steep mountainsides, a precarious undertaking. Two passengers, in relays, were called upon to walk a few yards ahead of the truck. It was their duty to take soundings in the deep mud, look for slips and slides, and act as guides. The road ahead was totally obscured by the fog, and the driver charted his course entirely by what he could see of the backs of his passenger guides.

Even before they reached the waters of the Apurímac, foaming and roaring in their deep bed, bad news came to meet them. A traveler, climbing on foot out of the valley, stopped the truck and insisted that the road had disappeared on the farther side of the gorge. Then a group of horsemen appeared. They advised the driver to turn back at once, because he would be unable to go forward more than a mile or two. The story grew and grew, and finally gave a sum total which suggested that the road had fallen into the Apurímac over such a long distance that at least a month would be required to repair it. The driver, however, decided to proceed, but in a disconsolate frame of mind. Some distance farther on, and now below the fog, they pulled up behind a truck that had been halted by a mountain of dirt, gravel, and boulders, under which the road had indeed disappeared. At this point the narrative is continued by Harvey:

"The passengers from the first-arrived truck were standing around, scratching their heads and gesticulating. The passengers on the newly arrived truck dismounted, scratched their heads, and gesticulated some more. One courageous soul cautiously made his way over the slide and reported that another truck was approaching from the opposite direction. Eventually, a heterogeneous crowd was assembled, distinctly jovial and even in festive mood. Everybody talked, everybody had a plan. Some wanted to turn back at once, before other slides should block all escape. Some wanted to pitch in and begin digging out— that is, they hoped others would feel constrained to do so. Some of the more highly geared thinkers conceived the notion of having the passengers cross the slide on foot, trade trucks, and each group proceed in its original and proper direction. The whole thing was quite democratic, and worked much as does any democracy in a crisis.

"There was a policeman in one of the parties. He had a beautiful uniform, and some gold braid. More than that, he was a smart man. He looked the situation over and recognized three elements: (1) a large group of people imbued with a definite objective; (2) an obstacle blocking realization of that objective; (3) sufficient motivation, if organized and directed, to make possible expenditure of considerable energy toward removing the obstacle. Thereupon, he threw back his cape, stuck out his jaw, and barked out dictatorial decrees. All shovels were at once requisitioned. Axes were set to fashioning pikes and poles for digging gravel and rolling boulders. The passengers were organized into shifts. You should have seen the dirt move. From our side of the slide, taunts were shouted to the passengers on the farther side, with the result that gravel and boulders were soon flying from all directions. Great shouts rang down the valley of the Apurímac each time a large mass of rock was pried loose and started on its thunderous race down the steep slope."

Harvey and Bob took off their coats and fell to work. However, it soon appeared that they were actually impeding progress, because

so many of the peons immediately stopped work to enjoy the strange
sight of gentlemen, foreign gentlemen at that, engaged in hard labor.
Then, in the hope of accelerating operations, Harvey set up a motion-
picture camera and made as if to record the proceedings. Now, one
might imagine that nobody would care to be recorded for the screen
gracefully leaning on a shovel while others were at work, but so it was.
Half the slide clearers immediately struck statuesque poses, of the tin-
type variety, nor could they be persuaded that Harvey wanted motion, and lots of it. Since the *norteamericanos* found nothing useful
to do at the scene of operations, they decided to accomplish something
botanical, and for two hours worked back and forth on the mountainsides beyond the slide and along the banks of the river. There,
they braved the first of many onslaughts of swarms of gnats and midges
that infest the length and breadth of the Apurímac.

After this first and most protracted halt there were other stops
for lesser road repairs. These frequent stoppages began to irk most
of the passengers. The botanists, however, were well pleased because
each halt gave opportunity for samplings of the roadside vegetation.
Gradually, the truck climbed out of the valley. After reaching a considerable elevation the road flattened out, and they wallowed across
high, treeless puna, where cold, drizzling rain fell at frequent intervals. This extensive alpine plateau ended abruptly where they began
the descent into the Limatambo valley. They looked down, deep in
this valley, to the town of the same name, cradled between wall-like
mountainsides. The air distance seemed inconsiderable, but when they
saw the many loops, curves, and switchbacks by which their road
wove its way downward, it was no surprise to find that all of twenty-
five miles separated them from Limatambo.

Just as they began the descent, darkness, with accompanying mists
and fog, enveloped them. Soon the vapors became so dense that the
headlights of the truck threw back blinding light into the driver's
eyes. There was nothing to do but turn off the headlights. Thereafter
the driver relied upon a sixth sense and the prayers that he continually
directed toward the image of Saint Christopher which looked down
upon him from above the windshield. For hours they slipped and
slithered down to Limatambo, and then on toward Abancay. When,
at last, and completely spent with the nervous strain of eleven hours
of rough and harrowing journey, they entered its plaza, all Abancay,
except its dogs, was asleep.

The city lay in the cultivated valley of the Marino River, a small stream that flowed past its outskirts and, some miles below, emptied into the larger Pachachaca. The hills above were green with grass and shrubs, and this green extended up the quebradas and back into the mountains, where forests filled the higher valleys. The climate was agreeable enough, with sunny days and rainy nights, on some of which the rain was torrential.

Near the road between Abancay and the bridge over the Pachachaca, the Prince had discovered *Nicotiana benavidesii*. This new species was distinctly limited in its distribution, for it occurred only in the "type locality" and westward in the valley of the Apurímac. It is a question why it does not grow in the valley of the Marino and upstream along the Pachachaca. Along the road they found masses of a giant *Equisetum*, the horsetail or scouring rush. Its tall, weak, green, canelike stalks reached twenty feet in height and leaned against small trees or upon one another.

Over the old stone walls about Abancay the nasturtium (*Tropaeolum majus*) was particularly at home, although its distribution is general in the Peruvian Andes. So charming and unique a plant must have made a strong appeal to the eyes of the early padres. Over two hundred and fifty years ago they sent its seeds to Europe, whence it spread widely and was favorably received wherever ornamentals grew. Less popular is a sister species, *Tropaeolum peregrinum*, sometimes called the canary-bird flower. A common climber in the lower slopes of the Andes on the Amazonian side, its dainty yellow blossoms, spurred with green hooks, and its small, lobed leaves add a touch of grace and charm to the roadside vegetation.

Growing through all the valleys near Abancay, the pepper trees were resplendent in an abundant crop of red berries. The berries were sold in the market place, not for decoration, as with us, but rather for the making of a particular variety of native beer called *chicha de molle*. The Andean Indian does not limit himself to maize as a source of chicha. As we have seen, he uses wheat and bananas as a base for fermentation, and even peanuts are often made into a milky chicha, said to be very nourishing.

In the Abancay market the red seeds of *Bixa orellana* also were a familiar commodity. As a source of dye for foods, particularly rice, the seeds of this tree are popular in many parts of Latin America. The dye is also used to color butter or oleomargarine, and the seeds have been shipped to the United States and to Europe for this purpose, as well as for dyeing confections and even cloth. The tree itself is attractive, particularly when its branches are hung with the orange-colored seed pods, reflexed to expose the red seeds within.

In the mountains some ten miles north of Abancay, and at an altitude of fifteen thousand feet, lies a glacier that is responsible for the presence of two near-by alpine lakes. After a stiff climb the botanists collected in the forest that filled the large quebrada extending southward from this glacier. Near the snow and ice the trees gave way to cold, desolate puna. Of special interest in the forest was the presence of *Podocarpus glomeratus.* Southward from Central America this genus takes the place of the pines, firs, and hemlocks of the Northern Hemisphere, and this substitution constitutes the most striking difference between the South American mountain forests and those of the north. *Podocarpus* is a relative of our conifers, and is often known as *piña*, although near Abancay the common name is *intimpa*. The leaves are not needle-like but rigid and thickened, and measure about a quarter of an inch in width. This species supplied most of the lumber and cabinet wood for Abancay and the vicinity.

The vegetation showed that the forest climate was moist the year round, because such epiphytes as orchids, peperomias, bromeliads, leafy liverworts, and mosses were present in quantity and in considerable variety. Among plants of other types in bloom, the yellow of a large-flowered *Calceolaria* supplemented the red of *Fuchsia boliviana* in adding a warm, gay note to the green of the forest. Here and there was an odd-looking plant with opposite leaves that made acute angles with the square green stem. It proved to be a *Sideroxylon*, and bears the specific name *herrerae* in honor of the late Dr. Fortunato Herrera, long the botanist of the University of Cuzco.

By contrast with the cool, wet *Podocarpus* forest, they found semi-tropical vegetation in a valley west of Abancay. Narrow and deep, the valley ran north and south, and received full sun at midday. Its walls were stony, with loose, gravelly soils. Bombax trees were the dominant species, growing in thin, parklike stands. Along washed-out gulleys they saw the large, tuberous storage roots of *Bombax*, dark-colored on the outside and of the consistency and color of a potato within. Scattered here and there were pepper trees, a shrubby *Ipomoea*, and thickets, as well as solitary plants, of *tuna* (*Opuntia*), some of which attained a height of fifteen feet. The fruits of the tuna, or prickly pear, are gathered in large quantities by the Abancay Indians, both for home consumption and to sell in the market place. Travelers in the hot valley depend upon these fleshy fruits to allay their thirst. *Jatropha,* also, was there in quantity, and *Dalechampia,* with its lurid bracts, climbed over the Opuntias and Bombax trees.

Where alluvium had accumulated in the valley or in its tributaries, there were crops of sugar cane, cotton, maize, beans, and potatoes. The introduced castor bean had taken almost complete possession of certain areas. Fields of sugar cane were particularly common, and their product was accommodated in a number of sugar mills, most of them, actually, rum mills. The "agrimony" poppy, always a striking plant with its silver foliage and yellow flowers, grew happily on the margins of cultivations. From Mexico to Chile only one other tropical American weed is more ubiquitous, and that is the milkweed, *Asclepias curassavica,* sometimes called "bloodflower."

After a botanically profitable sojourn in the Abancay area, the journey was resumed. Their route from Cuzco to Huancayo is full of ups and downs. There are four major downs: into the valleys of the Apurímac, Pachachaca, Pampas, and Mantaro. In each case the descent carried them to altitudes of approximately six thousand feet. Thence, they climbed to puna that lay at about twelve thousand feet. Down from that high, steppe type of grassland, where shepherds, mottled dark-purple by the biting cold of the wind and rain, tend their tiny fields of potatoes and herd their sheep or llamas; through shrubland; into brushland; into cultivated valleys; and then up through the reverse of this series of vegetational zones—this was the story all the way from their starting point to their destination.

The first stop west of Abancay was made in a shivering, unenterprising Indian town. To compensate a little for the dreary aspect of their community, and demonstrating a latent instinct for the beautiful, some of the inhabitants had planted the "passion vine" of the region around their habitations. Its flowers had dark-purple corollas, shaped like teacups, with light-colored stamens. This charming climber had been chosen from among a considerable repertoire of ornamentals that nature presented along the trail: blood-red *Bomarea, Vallea,* bluish-lavender *Eupatorium, Dalechampia,* blue *Salvia, Lippia, Buddleia, Escallonia,* and many others.

After more puna travel, the road dropped down into the valley of a smaller river, the Pincos. At the Hacienda Pincos, a sugar plantation on the river, Harvey and Bob enjoyed a delightful interlude in their up-and-down journey across the Andes. When they inquired about horses for Andahuailas, the next leg of their journey, the hacendado not only agreed to provide them with horses, but insisted that they put up at the hacienda for as long as they could stay. This invitation was gratefully accepted, not only because the clean, modern ranch house, and what they suspected would be most excellent provender, was a lure, but also because the first of the days set aside for the national carnival had arrived, and during those days travel, in the highlands at least, is difficult and unpleasant.

At the hacienda *Carnavales* was being vigorously celebrated by most of the eighty laborers. They knocked off work and enjoyed themselves by throwing flour and red paint at one another, dousing everyone with water, playing their flutes and snare drums, dancing in staggering fashion, and consuming all the alcohol in sight.

In the valley of the Pincos groves of oranges and large patches of sugar cane grow successfully. Below, the river drops rapidly through increasingly semitropical countryside and finally becomes a series of falls and cataracts that carries its waters into the true Amazonian jungle. At that time the entire sugar cane crop was devoted to the manufacture of *aguardiente*. Liquor merchants came from great distances and carried away their fluid purchases on pack animals. Sometimes the precious gut-rot was poured into large goatskin flasks; these were secured one on each side of a horse, whereupon the animal looked as though possessed of three bodies instead of one. The skins were reversed, so that the hairy side was bathed by the *aguardiente*. Under such conditions almost any other alcoholic beverage would lose caste and acquire a doubtful flavor. However, *aguardiente*, that powerful distillate of alcohol and fusel oil, is proof against even the stench of goat; or perhaps the fact that, once past the lips, it rapidly overcomes all the senses, including taste and smell, may explain a lack of prejudice against goatskin bottles.

When the days of carnival were over, Harvey and Bob were provided with good horses and a trusted peon guide for the trail to Andahuailas. At the beginning they passed through shrublands but, in two hours, came out on the rough grasses of the puna. Thence, westward to Andahuailas and at lower altitudes, they crossed grazing lands that stretched far away over rounded hilltops.

In Andahuailas a beautiful Spanish Colonial bridge crossed the river, like a jewel dropped beside the architectural crudities of an Andean town. Over this bridge all traffic to and from the south had to pass. The *botánicos* often stopped to watch a cross section of Andean life flowing over it—Indian women in their bright, ragged costumes, most of them with a baby between their shawl-covered shoulder blades (and another on the way), and men bearing immense bundles of grass, alfalfa, sticks, or almost any imaginable burden. One carried a half-grown sheep that poked its head contentedly out of a fold of his own-er's poncho and watched the passing scene. Every so often he looked down, with hauteur, upon other sheep and goats and pigs that were being driven along beneath him.

Pigsty and kitchen were synonymous in many of the homes. When a pig was fat enough to butcher, there was no looking forward to hams, bacon, sausages, or fresh loin of pork. Rather, the animal was killed and then a flock of neighbors, women and children, rolled it around in the mud and scraped away at it, in an effort to eliminate some of the bristles. Thereafter it was hacked into bits and jammed into a big kettle, under which all day a fire was coaxed to burn with odds and ends of sticks and twigs carried in from hedgerows or from the moun-tainside. In the evening the lard was poured into five-gallon gasoline cans, to be sold or exchanged for something which the family needed or, usually, for alcohol. The meat, fat and lean, was dispensed among the neighbors and eaten at once, or on the next day. Neighbors who came with their plates for a helping of *chicharrón* were expected to give back a plate of the same when they killed their pig. According to such a scheme for disposing of fresh meat no refrigeration is nec-essary.

The longest bit of their Andean journey took them northwestward, with two guides, from Andahuailas to Chincheros. During it they were in the saddle for twelve hours. Most of the trail was so deep in mud that at times they were forced to leave the beaten track and ride over the puna grasslands. On sloping ground the high meadows were soggy and treacherously slippery, especially for unshod horses. Huge erratic boulders, often as big as houses, were crazily strewn on level stretches, or hung precariously on the slopes. This boulderland had a bad reputation. In those days brigands were said to frequent it and levy toll on unprotected wayfarers who, after being stripped of their possessions, were murdered and their corpses hidden. The guides were constantly on the alert, and insisted on keeping the pack animals close to the saddle horses.

Near the end of the day, descending toward Chincheros, they looked down upon extensive plantings of maize. Near the town the hedgerows were ornate with the national flower of the republic, *Cantua buxifolia*, sometimes called the "magic tree of Peru." A great many years ago it was introduced into European and other gardens, and was once a favorite among shrubby ornamentals in places where it could be successfully grown. We have brought home selections of what appeared to be unusually good varieties of this *Cantua*, as well as of other species of that genus not so well known horticulturally.

The town proved to be a peaceful, friendly place, and might have been restful, had it not been for the extraordinarily large, and vocal, dog population. Droves of dogs greeted the horsemen when they arrived. Immediately a series of vicious dog fights was staged in the plaza, perhaps to express the excitement that pervaded the community upon the arrival of so many visitors. The *botánicos* were too tired after their grueling day in the saddle to be awakened by anything short of an earthquake or a bombardment. On subsequent nights, however, their sleep was continually disturbed by community baying and howling. Leaving Chincheros the trail made a quick descent to the Río Pampas. Soon they met the rapidly extending automobile highway. They exchanged horses for a truck, in which they were transported to a point where a car could be hired. After an all-night ride they entered the historic city of Ayacucho along with the first rays of the morning sun.

By automobile and train, with various stops for botanizing, they finally reached Huancayo, their destination. During this last lap they did their most important collecting, or at least the most exciting, in the alpine valleys of Yauli, about an hour by train from Huancavelica. Everything was fresh and green, and most of the vegetation was at the height of its spring blooming. The natural flower gardens spread before them were more extensive and attractive than any they saw during their many months of botanizing from coast to cordillera in Peru. Here were fields of *Cosmos*, *Siphocampylos*, *Zinnia*, *Helianthus*, *Calceolaria*, *Mutisia*, and *Bidens*, to mention only the more abundant genera that clothed the mountainsides with a variegated mantle.

During those weeks in February and March they made one of the most extensive surveys of the character and distribution of Andean plants that had ever before been attempted in the areas they explored. Although each night they had a roof, of sorts, over their heads, and even though they were transported by horse or in wheeled conveyances most of the miles they covered, there were many things that were fatiguing, disagreeable, uncomfortable, and even painful. On the other hand, there was much that was pleasant, a little that was comic, a great deal that would be a reward for any botanist, and, daily, an intimate contact with all the varied aspects of life in relatively little-known corners of the Peruvian Andes.

10

DESERTS AFLOAT

T RAVELERS BY SEA from Panama down the west coast of South America are mystified as well as perturbed by a sudden change from tropical airs to chill, foggy breezes. With little warning, blowing fog envelops the ship at a point about four degrees south of the equator or opposite Point Pariñas, the most westerly extension of our sister continent. This remarkable atmospheric shift occurs where the tropical waters are met by the mighty, one-hundred-mile-wide Humboldt Current. It bears not only cool waters but in addition a rich flora and fauna, everything from microscopic seaweeds to the wide-winged albatross. At the meeting place of the two zones of ocean temperature the marine organisms characteristic of both give up the ghost, and in a wide graveyard a feast is spread for sharks and other predatory denizens of the deep. This famous current of northward-flowing water establishes by its name an undying monument to the eager, tireless scientist, Alexander von Humboldt, who visited Peru in 1802.

As we have already discovered, the Humboldt Current provides western Peru with an air-conditioned climate, a cool and dry one. The average annual temperature at Lima is sixty-six degrees. By contrast, that of Bahia, at the same latitude but on the other side of the continent, is eighty degrees. The upwelling of cold water from the tremendous depths of the Pacific along the west coast has a part in the cooling and drying process. As humid air blows over the cold Humboldt Current it is chilled and condensed to form rain and fogs. The latter are often wafted inland to support "meadows on the desert," but rains rarely fall on the land because the rapidly warming air takes up moisture rather than discharges it.

In the months of January, February, and March a warm ocean current flows south along the coast from the equatorial regions. Since this current makes its appearance more or less during the Christmas season it is called El Niño, "the Christ child." Where the Humboldt Current deviates westward toward the Galapagos Islands, El Niño wedges itself in along the coast. As it moves southward it seems to deflect the Humboldt Current still farther out to sea. This landward intrusion of El Niño occurs each year, but only rarely does this warm current extend southward far enough to affect the climate of the coasts of northern and north central Peru. But when it does, then come torrential rains that flood the deserts.

One March, the Lima newspapers carried accounts of high water in the north. Roads had been washed out, bridges had gone down the rivers, mud houses were fast disintegrating, and each day the rains increased in violence. I had heard stories of the vegetation that clothed the desert in former rainy years—of head-high grasses, of the sandy, wind-swept dunes transformed into a rolling sea of green. It looked as though the arid coast of Peru, for once at least, was going to show us something quite exceptional in the way of vegetation. It was too good an opportunity to overlook, so I asked Harvey and Bob to head north again. Incidentally I wanted information about the tobacco varieties that were being grown commercially near Tumbes, at the coastal frontier of Peru and Ecuador.

North as far as Trujillo, across the coastal strip over which they had already traveled both on land and in the air, there was little change in the desert landscape that was so well known to them. They saw the same sandy wastes, the same green oases where diminishing rivers crossed the coastal plains to the sea, the same tan hills slowly rising to a misty, blue-green background. Past this previous farthest north Harvey and Bob began to look down from eight thousand feet upon "deserts afloat." Spread out below them was a wide, level plain, across which the first Andean foothills floated in a hazy distance more than seventy-five miles to the east. This was the Sechura Desert. Toward the coast, there were broad expanses of water. To the north the swollen, yellow Piura and Chira rivers spread their overflow into great, shallow, clear-blue lakes. Everywhere was a startling confusion of sands and waters.

Northward from Chiclayo, over a still arid portion of the desert, the picture gradually changed. Imperceptibly the monotonous yellow and brown plains began to become more and more stippled with dark dots. At first this stippling was light and then gradually it became deeper and almost continuous. Each stipple represented the position on the sands of a shrub or small tree. Most of them were *algarroba* (*Prosopis*), but some were *Acacia* and *Capparis*. If a brief rainy season occurs they bring forth leaves; otherwise they wait until a year when there is sufficient moisture to produce foliage. The roots strike deep, as much as twenty-five feet, until they make contact with the water table. Competition for available water is so great that these desert "trees" cannot grow close together and survive; so from the air the general effect of their distribution is that of groves or orchards with the individual plants spaced at fairly equal distances one from the other. To the east and north the stippling graded into a denser vegetation, which they knew was the rainy-green shrubland, and it in turn dissolved into the evergreen shrubland. In the farthest distance, inland, were the blue-green ridges covered with the forests of the Ecuadorean jungle.

The landing field at Piura was a shock. Unless one has seen the North Peruvian coastal strip in its intense aridity, no words can picture the contrast in its appearance produced by the heavy vegetation that follows the rare downpours of rain. The landing field actually had to be mowed with a scythe.

From the air, and at a considerable distance, they had seen that the Piura and Chira were out of their banks, but had no conception of the volume of water that was running. The Piura was a deep, menacing flood, flowing exceedingly fast and full of sand and debris. The soft banks were constantly crumbling as the river cut deeper down into its channel and then pushed out to undermine its feebly constraining margins. Later on Harvey flew over the Río Chira. Only four sections of the steel highway bridge could be seen; the other three had been torn out and washed downstream. Traveling on the same plane was the engineer who had built the bridge. It was his contribution to the Pan American Highway. According to his statement, the bridge piers went down thirty-six feet and rested on sandstone. Most of this coastal zone is composed of sandstone, clays, and stratified conglomerate that was uplifted from the sea bottom in relatively recent times, geologically speaking. It is said that these deposits carry evidence that periodic floods occurred in Peru in the far distant past.

Apparently the heavy rains were not uniformly distributed, and the vegetation that followed them was likewise variable in distribution. Plant growth in the area between Piura and Paita was particularly rank. Grasses and herbs made a veritable jungle, difficult to walk through. The number of species involved was not large, some fifteen or twenty being responsible for the larger share of the vegetation. The seeds of these plants must have maintained their viability over very long periods on one of the driest deserts on the earth's surface. Even cacti rarely appear on these exposed sandy wastes—they are shallow-rooted plants and begin to occur in quantity only on the eastern foothills, where a little moisture is condensed on the soil surface almost every year.

There are two common but very interesting plants that laugh at dry years on the desert. When the rains come they luxuriate and spread wide mats of green on the sands. When it is dry they simply retire underground. One is called *yuca de caballo* (*Proboscidea altheifolia*). It develops a large storage root, usually three or four inches in diameter and over a foot long, which retains moisture and food so efficiently that the plant will survive for several, perhaps many, years without putting leaf and stem above ground. As the name indicates, it is relished by horses. Burros and goats also fancy it. Like pigs rooting for truffles, all three paw the earth in likely spots to dig out the roots of yuca de caballo. Travelers in the desert when overtaken by thirst are said to emulate their four-footed friends and to obtain some relief by chewing the succulent roots. The other plant whose underground storage organs permit it to defy a limited amount of total aridity is known as *yuca de montaña* (*Apodanthera biflora*) because its roots can, in a pinch, be substituted for the true yuca (*Manihot*).

On the north coast the most important native desert food supply for animals is the algarroba. When Harvey and Bob were there, these small trees had matured an abundant crop of long green pods. They have a sweetish taste and are sometimes, but rarely, used for human consumption. For animals they take the place of corn, oats, and hay, and, in fact, constitute a complete diet, either fresh or dried. All over the desert the harvesting of the pods was in full swing. Sacks of them were carried in to Piura on the backs of men and beasts. Free-ranging burros and herds of goats were making the most of this year of plenty and eating their fill. As was to be expected, the goats were the most consistent and effective gorgers and all but climbed some of the trees whose limbs were lowest.

The oddest sight of all was the impromptu agricultural operations in the environs of Piura. At the first evidence that this was to be a year of rains, patches of maize, beans, squash, melons, and even cotton had been planted on depressions in the desert floor where water would be likely to accumulate. Each of these scattered desert plantations had to be fenced against the invading hordes of goats and burros. Fences were improvised from any material that came to hand, mostly brush struck in the ground, and the plantations had little regularity of outline. Normally the extreme north coast of Peru is hot as well as dry, and the addition of moisture had turned the desert into a gigantic hothouse where the hurriedly planted crops were growing at a great rate. There seemed to be no doubt that a mature cotton crop would be achieved, because in 1932, a less favorable year, the desert cotton planters had considerable success.

The flora of the rainy desert showed a great sameness, and it was not long before they felt that they had collected most of the relatively few species which had sprung up in the Piura area as a result of the abnormally heavy rains. It was therefore decided that Bob should go still farther north along the coast while Harvey went eastward into the foothills, so that a thorough canvass of the vegetation of "deserts afloat" might, if possible, be made. Coastal travel was relatively easy, but to get across the flooded deserts to the east was not so simple. However, Harvey had introductions to hacienda managers at Pabur, Serran, and Canchaque. It would be a day inland by truck to the first stop, another day by mule to Serran, and then another day on muleback to Canchaque.

Bob's diary gives an amusing account of their efforts to leave Piura:

"Wednesday. Harvey found that there was a truck going inland to Pabur this very afternoon. I was not so lucky and cannot get a truck to Talara until tomorrow. So after lunch I bade Harvey farewell and then trotted off to the Faucett office to express a bundle of wet plants by next morning's plane to Lima, for Harper to dry. Settled down for a dull wait, only hoping that my truck would be sure to go and not put off its start until day after tomorrow or later. After dinner, went to the movie house and sat down and pulled my feet under me to keep the fleas from traveling up from the floor. When the light came on after the first reel, imagine my surprise when I turned around and there sat the supposedly departed Harvey E. Stork, Ph. D., in person. His truck had traveled all over the town to pick up a little cargo here, and another passenger there, checked out at the *guardia civil*, and, at last, made a start toward the eastern hills. After a half hour the *chofer* drove more and more slowly and finally stopped. He then addressed himself to the passengers and, with many gestures and torrents of adjectives, called attention to what he said were rain clouds ahead, to the early approach of nightfall, to the dangers of automobiling in general and in particular, and ended by expressing a desire to turn back and wait until early the next morning, when a fresh start would be made. Five of the passengers were insistent that he go ahead. On the other hand, a Chinese merchant, convoying boxes of "Made in China" goods, and one other passenger agreed with the driver. The majority being against him, he was forced to start on again, but after a couple of miles he lost his nerve completely and without a word turned around and headed at top speed for Piura.

"Thursday. After bidding Stork another good-bye at 9:30—he was supposed to leave at 7:00—I caught my own truck, Talara bound, and we went through the usual procedure of touring around town, gassing up, drumming up more passengers, and, finally, visiting the *guardia civil*. Of course, we had to make a last stop on the business street. Whom should I see but Harvey! We then engaged in a third but not final farewell, because my truck made another aimless swing around the town and I had a chance to shout a few parting wisecracks at Harvey whose conveyance, when last I saw it, actually looked as though it was getting under way!

"Instead of heading directly north toward Talara we went west over the new, oiled road to Paita; since, according to report, the direct road to Talara was washed out. A good, warm morning, but windy enough to be cool in our speedy, uncovered truck. In about an hour we were in Paita. It seemed a friendly little town, nestled beside a natural harbor but one which is too shallow to allow the close approach of ships. Then we turned north to follow a coast road that wasn't a road at all. Just as the bumping, banging ride had reached a peak of misery for the passengers, a short but snappy thundershower added the more than final touch. In thirty seconds I was soaked to the skin.

"The desert floor, like that near Piura, was sprinkled with shrubs and low trees and a few flowering plants. An hour and a half after leaving Paita we dropped down the steep cliffs bordering the Río Chira. Since the bridge was mostly out of sight downstream, we had to cross the soupy waters on an extremely doubtful-looking lighter, similar in design, but not in size or strength, to those used in unloading freighters along this coast. The trip across the Chira floodwaters was exciting. The lighter was so overloaded with passengers and cargo that the brown water kept slopping over the sides. This floodwater was heavily charged with coarse sand. Too often, big logs and up-rooted trees came shooting by. A few days ago, this same lighter swamped and five passengers were drowned. They didn't have a chance because, in the water, your clothes almost immediately become sand-laden.

"On the other side we had to wait three hours for the Talara bus to flounder through muddy roads and pick us up. Then it took a long time to get to Talara because the new road—part of the Pan American Highway—was apparently built in the notion that it never rains along this coast and so is mostly washed away. After climbing out of the Chira River valley, the vegetation increased immediately and the roll-ing sand hills were absolutely covered with a luxuriant growth of grasses and herbs. In places they were from hip to shoulder high. Is it possible that this is the absolute desert we saw not so long ago? The bus ran north to the foothills before turning west to Talara. These foothills, also, are covered with an exciting green flora and I am keen to get my hands on it."

Unfortunately Bob did not have much chance to collect in the green fields the heavy rains had left behind. The reason is revealed by the entries in his diary that refer to the next few days:

"Monday. Talara. I planned to drive on north to Tumbes for a day or so but find that the roads are completely washed out. Could fly, but there are only two planes a week, Tuesday and Friday, so that's out and I still have a day's collecting to do here and I don't have to join Harvey in Piura until Friday. Hence, plan to fly south Wednes-day and put in a day's collecting at a hacienda north of Piura.

"Tuesday. Talara. The weather is so hot that I consume untold quarts of water and fear that the results are something akin to the 'Rocky Mountain trots.' At any rate I felt quite in the trotting mood all day. Spent six hours working along the bluffs east and south of town and still no indication of *Nicotiana*, although managed to pick up a few plants not found before.

"Wednesday. Talara. What a night! Sleep out of the question on account of I was so busy. Violently sick at my stomach and had bind-ing cramps all night. Was supposed to take the plane at 7:30 but knew that I couldn't remain away from a convenience the thirty minutes necessary to reach Piura and, as I am ahead of schedule, decided to rest up today and take tomorrow's plane.

"After a makeshift breakfast I went to the hospital of the American Petroleum Company in the hope of getting something that would stop my bellyache and the other thing. The American doctor suggested that I take the amoebic dysentery test. I agreed, although I feel sure that my condition is the result of too much hot weather plus too much ice water. Dropped by the Faucett office to arrange for reservations for tomorrow's plane and found there was nothing doing, so made arrangements to drive back. Spent the rest of the day trotting.

"Thursday. Talara Hospital. Another bad night. The doctor informs me that I have picked up a lot of amoebae and should start taking treatment at once. The treatment consists of five daily injections, a special diet, then ten days of rest accompanied by pills. A Grace 'Santa' boat is going south on Monday, so by taking my first injection today I can have the fifth Monday and finish treatment in Lima. After sending telegrams to Harvey and the Goodspeeds, I moved my belongings from the hotel to the hospital."

After four days in the excellent Talara hospital Bob was well enough to get aboard the ship for Callao. After a week of rest, diet, and pills in Lima he was as chipper as ever. Some weeks later, he was entirely free from amoebae.

Harvey's route to Hacienda Pabur led through algarroba-covered terrain into territory that normally receives more and more rain as one goes eastward, until some twenty-five miles inland some rain falls each year. With a little moisture the columnar cacti could live, along with algarroba and other small trees and shrubs, which together began to form an increasingly dense shrubland. Most conspicuous was *overal* (*Cordia rotundifolia*), a common shrub bearing masses of bright-yellow flowers. At the base of the foothills *gualtecas*, or *Bombax* trees, began to appear. They are relatives of the cotton plant and their seed pods are full of a brown wool. The trunks are smooth and spindle-shaped, with the greatest diameter halfway up. Another dominant tree was *Bursera graveolens*, called *palo santo*. It closely resembled *Bursera gummifera*, which in Central America is called by the natives "naked Indian" and by the Jamaican Negroes "birch," because it has a brown papery bark. Below these taller trees were smaller tree species, then shrubs, and finally a very dense stand of annual plants, the latter making it difficult to detour around the ponds of water that stood in the single-track truck road.

Pabur is situated on the river, and as they came nearer their destination the roar of the water could be heard a mile and more away. Boulders were rolling along just under the surface, trees and shrubs whirled by on the yellow flood, and the riverbanks were constantly crumbling. In fact, the banks had eroded so far back that some of the shacks occupied by peons employed on the hacienda were endangered. The road passed an old, spreading algarroba that had lost its moorings and was toppling over. It was only a question of hours until the angry current would work under the landside roots sufficiently to start the poor tree downstream to the Pacific. The unbridled power of this wild river whose banks were utterly powerless to restrain or direct its flow was immensely impressive.

Don Augusto, local manager of the hacienda, was not at home but was expected to come in at any time. When he had not returned at midnight, Harvey carried to bed the certainty that all chance of getting mules and making an early start toward Serran was gone. That evening and well on into the night the rain came down in torrents. There was some thunder and lightning. Listening to a continuous near cloudburst pounding on the roof and to the increasing roar of the mad river, it was hard to believe that during most of the year this region was a dry, brown, dead desert except where parts of valleys could be irrigated to produce some cotton and rice.

In the small hours of the morning Don Augusto and his foreman returned. They had worked most of the night to extricate their Ford truck from a mudhole. At breakfast they were excusably tired and cross. Don Augusto was impolitely positive that a trip to Serran would be impossible because the road was either washed out or under water. He made it clear that no one in his right mind would even think of making such a trip.

During the afternoon the rain somewhat decreased in intensity, and Harvey started out to begin a search for *Nicotiana—tabac cimmarón* —reported to be growing somewhere across the river. A big dugout canoe looked safe enough. Four men paddled and two poled, but their competition with the current was not very successful and the party was lucky to make a landing only a quarter of a mile downstream. Then the boatman walked along the bank and towed the canoe upstream for a considerable distance, so that when ready to return they would be able to land the dugout at the starting place on the other side of the river. Ashore, Harvey soon found that the going was too bad to make collecting profitable. However, he stuck to it long enough to assure himself that there was no tobacco near the river. His pertinacity so far as collecting was concerned must have impressed Don Augusto, who worked himself into a state of sufficient enthusiasm to order Miguel, his leading arriero, to get three of the hacienda's best mules ready for an early morning start toward Serran and Canchaque.

The next day Harvey and Miguel spent ten hours in the saddle, on brushland roads and trails that consisted of a continuous alternation of mudholes and small lakes. Every now and then they had to leave the flooded track and strike across country through a tangle of shrubs and annual vegetation. Canchaque is excellent orange country, and several trucks bringing out ripe fruit had bogged down. The approach to each of the stranded trucks was signaled by quantities of orange skins, remnants of a feast which every passer-by had enjoyed. At Palo Blanco the road, for a quarter of a mile, led through a lake of shallow water. The mules were *muy fuertes*, but toward the end of that grueling day were only with much violent persuasion forced into a lope. Finally they rode into Hacienda Serran. A few moments later, the heavens opened. This time there was no question that it was a cloudburst and a first-class one.

The hacendado, Don Félix, and his foreman gave Harvey a hearty welcome. It was their opinion, however, that a trip farther on toward Canchaque was impossible on account of the high stage of the Río Pate and the Río Piura, both of which would have to be crossed. After another night of downpour, one of the river men was sent out to the Pate to ascertain its condition. He returned to say that no man or beast could possibly cross. Making the best of it, Harvey settled down to collecting in the hills behind the hacienda. From these hills he could see the broad yellow flood in the valley and was willing to agree with the reports of its impassability.

At various points along the road Harvey was continually being mistaken for one of the long-awaited highway engineers. The almost impassable condition of the road, following the heaviest rains in many years, had brought numerous petitions to the provincial officials in Piura asking that "the government do something about it." Two engineers had been sent inland to make a report. They had disappeared somewhere along the way, and no one had heard from them. On the second morning of Harvey's stay at Serran they appeared at the hacienda with the story that they had found the rains and roads not to their liking and so had laid up for a couple of days at a small town off the main route. When things did not get better they had come ahead.

Early the next morning, when the engineers examined the river, they thought there were indications that it had started to fall, and announced their intention of trying to cross. They invited Harvey, with Miguel and the mules, to join them. Several other travelers had accumulated at Serran, and when they rode out of town anxious citizens and complacent goats stared after a small cavalcade of eleven mules carrying riders and freight. Two black river boys who were to help in the crossing trotted alongside. On nearing the river the party rode upstream for about a mile through dense shrubland to a point where the river fanned out into several wide channels. The two river guides then waded out naked to get the feel of the current and to search with their feet for the shallowest spots. When they had determined the proper course to steer, each took a mule on a long rope and led him across. The mules went cautiously and at each step felt carefully for safe footing. The current was strong in the middle of the channels but nowhere quite deep enough to make the mules swim. The crossing continued until all the animals and their riders or cargoes had safely reached the opposite shore. Then the river boys carried across on the tops of their heads those portions of the cargoes that had to be kept perfectly dry.

The next river was not so wide as the Pate and was crossed without difficulty. During the remainder of the journey the road was in many places under water, and in hilly terrain was often washing away. Along the river valleys it had been built on shelves above the streams. In places these shelves were entirely gone, and then the cavalcade had to take to the slippery hills and flounder about in the dense undergrowth.

Canchaque, which they finally reached after a long, punishing day, lies at an altitude of about thirty-seven hundred feet. It proved to be a rather inviting mountain town where the visitor is utterly detached from the outside world and finds employment only in communing with wild nature and studying the peaceful life of simple villagers. But let him visit Canchaque in the dry season only. When they arrived the town was *muy triste*. The oranges were rotting on the trees of the informal groves scattered in the environs. Trucks had ceased to ply over the mountain road down to the coast, and such few staple foods as the townspeople had come to depend upon from below were getting scarce. Worst of all, there was legitimate doubt whether the road would ever be rebuilt, so completely had the floods obliterated much of a roadway that has taken many years to build.

On the night of Harvey's arrival a meeting of prominent townsmen was convened to discuss with the government engineers the increasingly serious emergency. All the experts could do was give estimates of the length of time that would be required to reëstablish highway communication with the outside world when the rains had finally stopped. This was cold comfort, because it appeared that the rains were never going to stop. The streets were brown floods. Thatched roofs had become so sodden that they sagged, and little streams were penetrating them to make the insides of houses almost as wet as their outsides. The better-built residences, provided with tile roofs, were none too dry. People went about wearing drenched clothes and long, wet faces.

Even lighthearted Miguel, Harvey's *arriero,* succumbed to the universal pessimism and for three days could think of nothing but getting home to Pabur before the road should become impassable even for mules. He kept reminding himself, Harvey, and anyone else who would listen that he had a wife and three children and that they must be considered as well as the desires of the *botánico.* He painted a sad, but still somewhat exciting, picture of the river leaving its banks near Serran and washing his shack and contained family down to the ocean. When a Peruvian peon is really gloomy he challenges the world's champion pessimist. During the first day of his lamentations Harvey persuaded him to stay on with the promise of extra pay. On the second day even this inducement had no appeal, and Harvey was forced to become exceedingly hard-boiled and to threaten dire consequences if there were any signs of desertion. On the third morning Miguel looked so excessively sad that Harvey purchased a large bottle of *pisco* and directed him to drown his sorrows and homesickness with some cronies he had picked up in the town.

Looking northward from Canchaque, a mountainside some five miles away showed a vertical white streak—the foaming waters of a great waterfall. A local dignitary named Simón was recommended to Harvey as one who, for a consideration, would act as guide to the

region near the falls. Next morning they started out. After crossing
the Canchaque river, a narrow mountain torrent at that point, the
path led through orange groves and over a turbulent tributary stream,
and then began to climb rather abruptly toward the level of the falls.
It was no path, but just a mud slide, up which they progressed by grab-
bing such shrubs and small trees as were still firmly anchored in the
softening clay and sand. Finally it appeared necessary to cross a deep
ravine. But its sides had already begun to slide and in the bottom there
was a moving mass of mud carrying boulders, shrubs, and small trees—
the whole rolling down the narrow valley like a lava flow. At sight
of this strange phenomenon Simón became extremely agitated and
demanded that they return to Canchaque as quickly as possible. Such
a terrible thing he had never seen in his life and these awful rains would
probably continue until all Peru turned into mud and flowed into the
sea. To make matters worse, the clouds thickened at noon and a drizzle
started that grew into a steady downpour and finally assumed cloudburst proportions. There was nothing to do but hasten back. Before
they reached the town the press full of soggy plants was so wet that
the paper folders were fast returning to their pristine pulp stage.

Although he had not, of course, communicated the proposal to
Miguel, Harvey had from the beginning hoped to push on beyond
Canchaque to the city of Huancabamba. He had written me to this
effect, and I received the letter in Lima on the same morning that
I heard rumors of a severe outbreak of bubonic plague in the Huancabamba region. There appeared to be nothing that I could do to warn
Harvey of what he was getting into. Because of the floods all telegraph lines were down and no messages could be sent from the coast
up into the back country through which he was traveling. No one
could suggest a method by which I could make contact with Harvey.
Finally I discovered that the "plague squad" was leaving that afternoon by airplane for Huancabamba, or as near the city as a landing
field could be found. One of the doctors on the squad agreed to take
a message to Huancabamba. It was then to be carried by an Indian
runner down the trail to meet Harvey. This sounded like a very long
chance, but it was the best I could do. A few days later I received a
reassuring telegram from him. It was a great relief.

What had actually happened was this. On the day after the futile
collecting expedition to the falls, the rain came down in a continuous
torrent, Miguel's hangover made him dangerously nasty and positive

that the time had come to desert, and all reports indicated that the road to Huancabamba was thoroughly washed out. Nevertheless, Harvey was determined to wait another day even if he had to sit on Miguel's head to keep him from disappearing. Early in the afternoon word went about that a messenger was looking for the *botánico norteamericano*. After some exploring of grogshops Harvey finally located a drunken Indian who handed over my message about bubonic in Huancabamba. In another hour the mules were being loaded for the return to Serran.

On the way up the principal burden of one of the pack animals had been two sacks of algarroba pods for mule feed. By this time the sacks were empty and Miguel, seeing an opportunity for a little business on the side, filled them with Canchaque oranges. He asked Harvey's permission to transport them back to Pabur, where they would command a scarcity price. Harvey agreed, but had a distinct feeling that rough roads and detours through the brushland would reduce the oranges to juice and pulp long before Miguel's market was reached.

The return journey to Serran was wet, muddy, slow, but without mishap except for one baptizing of a plant press in a flooded river. The rivers had lowered considerably and the crossings were not difficult. In Serran a supply of algarroba pods was bought so that the mules might eat, and after a night's rest the journey to Pabur was resumed.

Harvey insisted upon an early start from Serran, because he wanted to collect the flora of the *Bombax* forest through which they would be traveling and still arrive in Pabur by daylight. For a change it was a fine morning with sunshine and bird notes in the air. The piping of a singer called *chilalo* was with them all the way down to Pabur. Its nests were built of mud, grass, and pebbles plastered together on the ends of slender twigs of the algarroba trees. They were more or less globose, about eight inches in diameter, and looked like small termite nests. Strong winds did not dislodge them, nor did continuous rainfall disintegrate them.

The road was terrible; the mules needed rest at frequent intervals. Thus there was opportunity to collect specimens. Despite rests, the animals tired rapidly, and not until noon did Harvey and Miguel reach Buenos Aires, one of the hamlets along the road. It must have received its name before the goats which swarmed in it had been acquired. They bought more algarroba pods for the mules and in one of the thatched huts were served with what passed for luncheon.

In the afternoon the animals poked along more and more slowly. Even a strong mule tires fast on a slippery road where mud has to be fought every inch of the way. It soon began to look as though darkness would overtake them before they reached Pabur. While they might do the last stretch of road after dark, it was doubtful whether, without some daylight, they could hope to cross the great lake of river overflow near Palo Blanco, unless the water had gone down considerably since they navigated it some days before. Miguel, with a sort of whistling-in-the-dark courage, kept saying that they would make it easily. They met a traveler who had come from Pabur that day. He claimed that the lake was a foot deeper than before and that it was becoming continually more difficult and dangerous to cross the rising expanse of water. The sky began to be heavily overcast, and it grew darker rapidly. Then the mosquitoes came out in full force. Harvey knew that this was bad malaria country. He put on a raincoat, hung leafy branches over his bare knees, and, with another branch, attempted to fan the mosquitoes from his face and neck. By the time they reached a small settlement a mile or so from the lake, the darkness was almost complete.

Their voices and the splashing and wallowing of their mules on the muddy road brought most of the citizens to the doors of their shacks. Inquiry gave most positive assurance that it was dangerous to cross the lake in the daytime and that at night it was definitely impossible. A garrulous old man invited them to stop with him. He boasted of having the largest house in the settlement and that to him always came the good fortune of entertaining travelers when night had overtaken them in the neighborhood. So to Pablo's establishment they went.

It consisted of a crude corral, containing two cows and some pigs, and an attached shack. They turned the mules into the corral and laid out an algarroba-pod supper for them. The pigs grunted a welcome and watched for a chance to squeeze into the house, as Harvey, Miguel, and Pablo shook off the muck of the corral on its threshold.

At this point Harvey's diary must be quoted: "Two flickering candles revealed a low room, partially divided by a bamboo partition. A dozen chickens had draped themselves for the night on poles along the walls. Two ducks waddled about and quacked vigorously in response to the general excitement that had pervaded the household at the advent of visitors. With difficulty two large, lanky hounds and a small, dirty white cur were quieted. Pablo's wife, son, and daughter busied themselves with preparing hot water for our tea. I shared my canned beef and 'dog biscuits' with the family, and they contributed hominy from a big black kettle.

"They were very curious concerning us. Whence had we come, and where were we going? Miguel, tired as he was, rose to the occasion. In his best oratorical manner, he did all that he could to impress his audience with the importance of our mission. I had only to listen in order to learn what a remarkable scientist I was and how I had come all the way from the *Estados Unidos* to visit this particular region where one found such plants as no other corner of the globe contained. Indeed, I learned that we had in our collection many specimens that would command sums upwards of hundreds of sols in the United States. The family proved, however, to be much more interested in our two sacks. Miguel had thrown them in a corner and piled the other baggage over them, hoping that they would not be noticed and become the object of an orange raid. But Pablo was suspicious. He asked point-blank what was in the sacks. Miguel replied that they contained some of the samples of plants that the gringo had gathered to take back to the *Estados Unidos*.

"While I was still taking inventory of the various forms of animate nature that had congregated in this Noah's Ark, I began to take council with myself concerning what might be done to secure a peaceful night's sleep. To make the situation almost ludicrous, a red deer sauntered out from the back room, blinked her large dark eyes at all the commotion, and retreated to her corner. She had been captured as a fawn and adopted as a member of the household.

"The old couple offered me their bed, but I declined, with no reluctance. It was merely a wooden platform covered with a cowhide that had been tanned with the hair. Miguel made his bed on the saddle blankets. After considering various alternatives, I brushed clean a space on the floor, laid out my sleeping bag, and improvised some uprights to support my mosquito tent. I knew malaria too well from firsthand experience, and was taking no more chances than were necessary. My activities had the greatest interest for the family. In fact, a neighbor was called in to enjoy the show. I finally retired beneath the mosquito netting, all of the spectators lending a hand to tuck the edge of the net well under the sleeping bag. Then they stood about viewing the body, as it were, and discussing at great length the advantages and disadvantages of sleeping bags and mosquito tents. Laid out to public view in that fashion, with a candle eerily flickering at my feet and another at my head, I began to realize how old Pizarro must feel as the tourists file by his dessicated form lying in the glass cage in the Cathedral in Lima.

"Morning came, and, with it, evidence that Pablo knew that our sacks contained oranges. How he had found out during the night Miguel and I could not imagine, because the protective layer of baggage had not been disturbed. He announced that he knew how to make excellent *ponche,* the 'o' pronounced with a very broad sound. From an Englishman he had learned the trick. It was particularly excellent before breakfast. Thereupon he produced a tall tin can, for which he had whittled a crude wooden plunger. Into this he would have to put some orange juice and some milk. The milk was in the corral. Perhaps we might have some oranges—no? This was directed at Miguel who, with a look of resignation overspreading his dark features, proceeded to untie one of the sacks. For the milk, Pablo produced a kettle and sent his wife out to do a little milking. It was not exactly milking time in our sense of the term, but milking time for these people was simply an occasion upon which they needed milk.

"The milk and orange juice were put into the churn and the dasher worked up and down until an emulsion resulted. Then Pablo produced a bottle with a spot of pisco left in the bottom. With a generous sweep of his arm he dashed it into the emulsion, put on an elaborate stirring act, and finally dealt the punch into three calabash shells. We drank and pronounced it good. Pablo then insisted that more punch was indicated and gave me no rest until I had sent Miguel out to the local drunkery for a bottle of pisco. Thereafter we made free with the punch. The family must have canvassed the settlement's henhouses, because we actually had an abundance of fried eggs for breakfast. Following the meal, Pablo decided that more punch was indicated. After a while Miguel and I found ourselves thoroughly fortified for the crossing of the *laguna* at Palo Blanco. When we finally said goodbye, Pablo was still at the churn and it was a question whether he or the pisco would hold out the longer.

"Arrived at the lake, it was necessary to swim the mules and so we had to find porters who would carry our baggage over a route that was not so deeply inundated but where the mules could not go. They, sensing that home was near by, actually broke into a trot. Miguel was delighted with the small fortune—three dollars U.S.—that I bestowed upon him, and was exceedingly rejoiced to find both his family and his shack still intact. I presume that for many days he was the center of attraction at the Hacienda Pabur, and that his account of our trip was better embroidered at each succeeding recital."

From Pabur, Harvey's coastward journey was uneventful, but he was thankful to reach comparatively dry ground once more. At Piura the news of Bob's hospitalization awaited him. He caught the next plane for Talara, where he stayed a day or two to cheer up the invalid and assure himself that he was being well cared for. Then he flew south to Lima.

On the whole, this expedition to northern Peru for botanizing on "deserts afloat" did not pay so much in the way of exciting dividends as we all had expected, for the combination of amoebae and high water precluded extensive collecting. Nevertheless, the plants that we received by air from the north and succeeded in drying gave an adequate picture of the vegetation that grows on the floating deserts.

11

TO CAPRICORN AND BELOW

To CARL AND JOHN had been assigned an eighteen-hundred-mile journey southward along the coasts of Peru and Chile. First they were to collect in what I hoped would prove to be verdant lomas in southern Peru, and then to follow the spring flowering as it advanced southward down the Chilean coastal strip. They would be tracing the southern extension of the Peruvian Nicotianas concerning whose distribution not much was known. In Chile they would come across other *Nicotiana* species and map their distribution southward. They would see the vast Atacama Desert and the living things, both vegetable and animal, which succeed in existing on its western margin. Below Atacama the vegetation would increase in amount and variety and culminate in the Vale of Paradise at the height of its spring blooming.

The southern coast of Peru can be even more barren and desolate than the northern one. From the port side of the coastwise Chilean steamer *Mapocho*, Carl and John watched the lifeless desert hills during those first days of their journey from Lima south. The fog was there, so much of it that sometimes the coastal hilltops were encased in a shining gray mantle. More often it was broken into ranks of little clouds or spun out into tendrils that floated light and high over the ridges. But the green film that meant the ephemeral, fog-engendered vegetation was never there. As mile after mile of coast line passed in review they saw only the reds, the browns, and the yellows of ridged outcroppings of barren rock and desert sand glowing against the clear blue sky.

The *Mapocho* swung in to the insignificant coastal towns wherever

185

freight or passengers were to come aboard or go ashore. All the ports were open roadsteads where big double-bowed lighters transported the freight, and fast launches the passengers from anchored ship to shore and vice versa. In these anchorages the long Pacific rollers, which were almost imperceptible when the steamer was under way, joined a heavy ground swell, and the *Mapocho* rose and fell, and lay heavily to one side and then to the other, in regular but disquieting sequences.

Their tickets read to the port of Lomas, and, although the collecting had looked most unpromising all along the coast, Carl and John decided to go ashore there. The village of Lomas proved to be typical of the many desert communities they were destined to see during the following weeks. The low houses, built of adobe or wood, were flush with the cobbled sidewalks. The streets were deep with sand and rutted by the passage of heavy trucks, and everywhere were the small, neat hoofprints of pack burros.

The low hills that backed the village proved to be absolutely bare of vegetation, nor was there any evidence that plants had ever grown upon them. Behind the outmost ridges they saw only a barren, stony plain, infinitely arid. It was obvious that the neighborhood of Lomas was going to do nothing for them and that they might as well hunt transportation to the south.

They found a truck about to get under way for Yauca, a coastal town some twenty-five miles in the proper direction. The cab of the truck was full up with two old ladies and the driver. The body of the truck seemed rather well filled also. There were household goods, produce, and general merchandise, with a top-dressing of bunches of bananas. Since two passengers had already perched themselves on top of the load, and since the truck driver was willing, Carl and John climbed up among the bananas.

After the customary delays, the truck began to churn the sandy streets of Lomas, which ended abruptly at a gravelly bank. The heavily laden vehicle pitched and rocked its way up. The steep pitch ended in the ancient uplifted beach. At that time there was not the slightest semblance of a road, nothing but an incredible jumble of large rock masses, flattened sand dunes, and big and little boulders. Every truck that passed that way must have picked out its own special route because double ruts led in all directions. On every hand was evidence of the severest kind of wind erosion, and none that rain had ever fallen. Wherever there was a comparatively level stretch, all fine earth material had been swept with the wind's gigantic broom into dunes and piles which lay against the low hills and spilled down into the narrow quebradas. Under its high, gray canopy of fog, the wide expanse of rough desert was a scene of gloomy grandeur.

It was a long twenty-five miles from Lomas to Yauca, lifeless except at one spot. In the bottom of one wide, sandy quebrada, the runoff or seepage from the fog-covered hilltops nearer the sea supported a thin growth of stunted trees and scraggly underbrush. In the scant protection of this wind-blown grove a bit of a house had been built, and there a family lived by selling from a pitifully meager stock those supplies of food and drink that travelers in the wasteland might require. The road down into this inhabited quebrada was so nearly vertical that the truck, with set brakes, slipped and skidded over the loose sand-and-gravel surface. After a few miles the landscape changed. Stiff sandstone cliffs replaced the rounded contours of low hills and gave the scene more character. High, conical piles of partially decomposed pinkish granite lent some color to the distant view.

Yauca proved to be a three-streeted village. Near by they found a green oasis where a small stream issued from the coastal hills to irrigate fields of alfalfa, truck crops, and small orchards. The sight of vegetation was a welcome one to the two *botánicos*, and along the margins of the cultivated areas and on the hillside behind they hoped for native plants to collect. They were disappointed. Just as near Lomas, so here there was nothing, not even vestiges of vegetation of former years. In the violent overlighting of the clear desert afternoon the Yauca hills were stark and harsh, and the lengthening shadows and softer light tones of early evening did little to dissemble the crudity of their outlines.

The next morning Carl and John pushed on south, to Chala. Their arrival in Yauca had provided a much-needed source of gossip and thus had been well advertised. Local owners of automobiles were waiting for the *yanquis*. All quoted the same outrageous price to Chala and there was nothing to do but pick the car with the best-looking tires and the driver who looked the most intelligent.

The road ran through the village toward the sea and then to the left up onto a bench that sloped gradually down to the beach. By contrast with the roads they had traveled for two days, this one was remarkably good. Indeed, it was so good that the paying passengers began again to complain about the fare. They called attention to the fact that if this were a hard and difficult road there might be some excuse for charging such an exorbitant sum, whereas actually it was almost a highway. The driver looked at the protesters, smiled pityingly, held up a graceful hand, and said, *"Paciencia, señores, paciencia."*

For a mile or two the road traveled parallel to the beach, which was three hundred yards away and one hundred feet below. The road surface was good enough to justify thirty-five miles an hour, or a little more, but to a Peruvian driver it was a challenge to step on the gas, and soon the car was pitching and swaying at fifty. Without warning and as though the car had gone out of control, they curved sharply to the right and careened away on a mad dash toward the sea. The car seemed to sail over the slanting surface of the drifted sand, miraculously missing outcrops of rock and the hummocks built up around both the rocks and the occasional bits of strand vegetation. Finally it glided past the last obstruction and found the hard, packed sand of the seashore.

The beach stretched ahead for three miles in a wide crescent and ended abruptly in massive cliffs on which the surf broke high and white. The tide was coming in fast. The driver stepped up the speed and swung his car back and forth to follow the water's edge where the surface was most firm. Apparently he was gambling on reaching the end of the beach before the waves drove him back into the soft sand, where the car would be trapped. Perhaps the driver had a little private bet with himself on the outcome. Anyway, he won, but not until he took another long chance by turning sharply to the left at the edge of the cliff and putting the car at top speed up an almost vertical goat-path. Pulling with every ounce of its power, the poor car struggled on, bouncing and jolting, and finally flattened out on the road that they originally had been following.

A bad detour carried them around some road work and brought them out to a completed section of the Pan American Highway. As the car met it, the driver relaxed with a contented sigh and opened up the throttle. The highway was wide enough for two cars, surfaced with gravel, and beautifully engineered. There were dozens of small quebradas and larger ravines sunk into the desert floor, and the road crossed them on neat, functionally simple stone bridges that blended well with the landscape. The turns were carefully banked and the car took them at sixty miles an hour. Well on in the morning, thankful to be alive, they rolled into Chala.

From a distance the hills behind Chala looked green, but grazing animals had long since done their worst. Still, there was some collecting, and after the days of lifeless desert Carl and John fell to with enthusiasm. Just at the line of juncture of the coastal plain and the hills, between lichen-encrusted boulders, they came upon thin rosettes of long, slender, deep-green leaves. From the centers of some, tenuous, foot-long flowering stems had been pushed up. Topping each were two or three deep wine-red, tubular flowers, obviously of an amaryllid and the first of that charming plant group which South America had exhibited to them. Often thereafter, on coastal mountains and Andean foothills to the south, we were to find equally attractive relatives of this first amaryllid.

On the lower slopes of the hills were two species of *Oxalis*, the sorrel, one of which grew abundantly but was rather inconspicuous and small-flowered. They found only a few plants of the other *Oxalis*, but it was a more attractive species, with large, creamy-white to pale-yellow flowers. Like most of the other species of this genus that we brought back from South America, this one proved to have little ornamental importance in competition with the attractive races already listed in garden catalogues.

Above the amaryllids and *Oxalis*, the hillsides steepened rapidly and were green; the collecting was fairly rewarding, but nothing to become excited about. On the whole, Chala's vegetation was rather disappointing.

Dinner at the town's one hotel, the "American," was served at eight-thirty. The guests sat with the proprietor and his family at a long table on a balcony overlooking the ocean. At the head was the venerable padre of Chala, and at the foot Señor O'Donnell, the proprietor. All had scarcely been seated before loud shouts of "Dolores! Dolores!" were raised. In a moment or two the soup appeared in Dolores' small brown hands. She was a short, chunky, dark-skinned twelve-year-old girl, a member of a family that did most of the work in the hotel. Her mother was laundress, her elder sister was cook, she was waitress, and a younger sister was chambermaid. This hard-working group of four owned only one pair of shoes and they were not Dolores'. Her bare feet had worn a smooth path from the cookshack, up the wooden stairs, and onto the outdoor dining room.

Next morning the lower slopes of the fog-drenched hills and the near-by sandy plains some ten miles from Chala yielded an abundant harvest of plants. Of these the most colorful was the blue-flowered *Nolana*, quite like the garden one. We found many other Nolanas and near-Nolanas on the dry coasts of Peru and Chile. Most bore flowers in shades of blue. The yellow-brown sand they preferred provided them with an effective background. A few were white-flowered and exceedingly attractive.

Just as in northern, so here in southern Peru the presence of lomas, those fog-determined vegetational oases in a coastal strip as arid as any place on the earth's surface, is a constant source of surprise. Near Chala their composition was quite varied. The blue *Nolana*, a low, woody borage, and a tuberous *Solanum* with white or bluish flowers were the dominant species, while a near-*Grindelia* and a few different legumes were also common. In addition there were sparse grasses, some cacti, a wild tomato, one or two inconspicuous members of the Lily family, one valerian, an *Oxalis* or two, and a *Tigridia*.

In the afternoon they succeeded in routing out an old villager who agreed to guide them into the low mountains to the south. The old man, accustomed since childhood to climbing the hilly terrain near his home, set off at a stiff pace that taxed their capacity. The lower hillsides were worn almost bare by the feet of the villagers and the hoofs of their stock. Only in the bottoms of deep quebradas was there any vegetation. Then the slopes became rapidly much steeper, and scattered shrubs and herbs began to appear. This so-called *chaparralita*, or little chaparral, plant association consisted of low, dense composites, a shrubby yellow *Calceolaria*, and small, stunted trees probably related to the mesquite. The open ground was surfaced with a compact, lawnlike sheet of prostrate grasses and herbs, mostly a red-flowered clover.

Then, suddenly, a thousand feet above the sea, they came into the fog. At one moment it was merely the gray, gloomy roof of the world; at the next it was an all-enveloping, milky-white mist into which everything began at once to disappear. The nap of sweaters and the inside and outside surfaces of spectacles were instantly covered with millions of tiny droplets. The vegetation at the same time became denser. To tear a path through the high brush meant the bringing-down of cold cloudbursts at every step. The clayey surface soil was completely saturated. Rivulets ran down the steep cattle paths to fill the many depressions left by the hoofs of grazing animals. In the openings of the brush, the soaking, grassy slopes were impossible for wearers of hobnailed boots that had picked up a slick coating of wet clay. All this would not have mattered if there had been anything to collect. The plants were there, new and interesting ones, but only one or two of them in flower. Buds were just forming and it would be a month or more before the sun, breaking through a thinning fog mantle, would stimulate their development into flowers.

Two wet and discouraged botanists turned about-face and began to slide and fall down the mountainside. The old man had long since vanished in the mist and probably was waiting far above for them to reappear. As they came out from under the veil of moisture the sun was hanging low out over the misty Pacific. It warned them to hurry down and begin the return drive to Chala.

Halfway back to Chala the road was full of cattle. At the driver's first toot, the hard-bitten *vaqueros* who had been riding in front of the herd turned around and tried to clear the road, pushing through the cattle with shrill shouts and pistol-like cracks of their short, heavy lashes. Slowly a tortuous path began to appear. Down it the driver guided the car with its horn at full roar. For a desert chofer who rarely could find valid excuse to use his horn, this was an opportunity not to be overlooked, and he made the most of it. The unfamiliar and deafening noise increased the terror and fractiousness of the poor animals and largely counteracted the vaqueros' efforts to clear the road.

At last, however, the cattle were left behind and then the car passed the hacendado to whom they belonged. His señora was with him, and together they made a charming picture. He was a big man, with a bright, colorful poncho over his shoulders, and rode a bay horse, light-footed and nervous. The shy, petite, dark-haired lady was mounted on a large black mare and sat daintily on a high sidesaddle. In the early evening the couple arrived at the Hotel American and tied their horses at the hitching post beside the kitchen door.

Years before, Chala had been an important cattle-shipping center. Herds of range-fed steers were driven down to the port from the more remote mountains near the coast and from the distant Andean foothills, to be shipped on the hoof up and down the coast by water. Most of them went to the nitrate fields of northern Chile. There the aridity is complete and extensive. By contrast, on the South Peruvian coast a dozen watercourses flow down from the Andes, cross the dry plains in deep channels, breach the coast range, and finally reach the sea. Along these rivers, and especially where they run through coastal hills, domesticated animals and the wild, cameloid *vicuña* have always found abundant pasturage. Correspondingly, the condors wheel above the coast range in numbers said to be far greater than can be seen in the high Andes that lie to the eastward. The great birds, carrion feeders, live well on the carcasses of cattle and vicuña and on the bodies of dead sea birds washed up on the ocean beaches.

During the evening they took stock of their situation after listening to all kinds of advice from the other guests in the hotel. It was obvious that this year the season for plants was going to be an early one, at least in the lower altitudes. Therefore they must go south fast or the vegetation of the generally less foggy Central Chilean coast would be gone before they reached it. Apparently there were only two ways to get on to the south. The first meant an overland journey of one hundred miles or more by automobile and muleback to one of the more important ports where southbound ships might call—in other words, the traversing of still more of the desolate wasteland they had seen. The alternative was to fly to Arequipa and then go by train down to the port of Mollendo, where almost all coastwise shipping was certain to call. They flew, the next day, and at Mollendo went aboard the southbound *Orduña* of the Pacific Steam Navigation Company.

As we have seen, the coast of South America from the point where the continent stretches farthest west, almost at the border of Ecuador and Peru, to the southern limits of the latter republic must be called a desert. But this desert does not end at the Peruvian border. Rather, it continues on into Chile along eight hundred miles of coast line. At the beginning it broadens greatly to the east and in certain areas approaches the absolute in terms of aridity. Behind Antofagasta, Chile spreads its maximum width, approximately two hundred miles. This eastward bulge is Atacama, a dry, salt-encrusted waste thousands of square miles in extent.

The whole of Atacama's great extent is rainless and waterless, and therein lies the explanation of the vast surface deposits of sodium nitrate. Such an accumulation of salts represents complete evaporation in the dim past of an impounded arm of the ocean. Perhaps tremendous masses of seaweeds were imprisoned in the ancient inland sea and added their organic remains to the saline layers. Possibly guano beds of a size and extent to dwarf those found today on the near-by coasts and islands were involved in the origin of the deposits on the floor of this great desert. Be that as it may, Atacama's past and present aridity is responsible for the production and preservation of her saline wealth. For Chile saltpeter is highly soluble and therefore could have accumulated in such quantity on the Atacama Desert only in the almost complete absence of rainfall.

Fabulous fortunes have been made on Atacama from *salitre*, the Chilean saltpeter, that was only waiting to be scraped from her desert floor. Arica, Pisagua, Iquique, Tocopilla, Mejillones, Antofagasta—these nitrate ports are names to stir the memories of men who loaded the clean, white salt into the holds of their ships and carried it back to revive or enrich the heavily cropped soils of the Old World.

Antofagasta is commonly a port of call for passenger steamers on South America's west coast. Most of the trippers who go ashore there during the usually short stop are unaware that this rather bright and attractive little city lies on the margin of the rainless nitrate desert where water and soil must be imported. It is a tribute to the enthusiasm of the citizens that such relatively good-looking parkways and private gardens have been developed. Recently a large and rather unexpectedly pretentious hotel has been constructed on the beach, away from the docking area. Presumably it reflects increasing prosperity in a region which in the past appeared to be very impoverished.

The immediate vicinity of the nitrate deposits is plantless not only because of lack of moisture but also because of a lethal concentration of salts in the upper soil layers. Just west of the nitrate desert, however, the hills and low mountains next the sea show vegetation during the foggy season. Therefore the two botanists expected to find something to collect, perhaps not close to Antofagasta, but certainly somewhat farther south. Local information suggested that Taltal would probably be the most important center of operations and they decided to go there at once. By sea Taltal is a little more than one hundred miles south of Antofagasta, but by the railroad, which they used, the distance is half as much again.

The Longitudinal Railway extends a total distance of two thousand miles north and south through Chile and has numerous branch lines, most of which serve the ports. Railhead in the north is somewhat above the coastal city of Iquique. Thence the railway runs on a line roughly parallel to the ocean along the high and more or less level plains that lie between the coast range and the Andes. The Atacama Desert represents the northern part of this wide valley, but well south of its great nitrate fields the railway still traverses only arid terrain.

A train ride in northern Chile is likely to be a hot, dusty, and generally disagreeable affair, although the service is remarkably good. Always the wind blows hard and steadily. For hundreds of miles it has blustered across the floor of the desert and thereby acquired a high temperature and a load of sand and dust. A part of this load is deposited in the cars, which become hazy with a fine suspension of superdust. It can work its way through the stoutest cloth to irritate covered as well as uncovered skin. Despite the intense dryness, enough moisture clings to one's skin so that the dust particles are held and fused upon the body. In a short time you look and feel like a glacé fruit. When a sudden movement cracks the glaze, you shiver!

From midday onward through the stifling afternoon the desert flings at your eyes a blaze of hard, yellow light reflected from its shining, salty crust. As the sun begins to fall below the rounded hilltops of the coastal ranges, soft pastel contrasts, miragelike paths of shadow, begin to float across the barren plains. Gradually they increase and flow together to spread a gray-brown mantle over all the cooling sands. The last streamers of golden light strike horizontally from the serrate crown of the western hills. Toward the Andes the sky is delicately flushed with a rosy light. Slowly the shadowy eastern horizon is rimmed with a deep band of pink and lavender. Then, as the eastward-rolling earth thrusts more and more of itself into the pathway of the sun, the pink horizon flows skyward on the surface of an increasing cloud of aquamarine. The light fails fast, the desert comes to bear a dome of dull turquoise, and Atacama's day is at an end. Through the pale-blue sky the stars begin to shine and gather brightness as their background deepens.

Along the railway across the desert are many isolated stations. Whom or what they serve, one never discovers. Usually there is only a single building, rarely more than two. But the train always stops, and each time something is loaded and unloaded. Invariably a poorly dressed, deeply tanned, and wind-blown woman stands in a doorway. She carries a baby on her hip and children cling to her skirts. With a hand shading her eyes against the desert glare, she intently watches the operations of the train crew at the baggage car. Without the train there would be no food or water at these desert stations. Small wonder that she watches it so intently. She must be certain that it leaves behind that which will supply the simple needs of her family for the days until it returns again.

The next day, in the Quebrada de Taltal they began their first serious Chilean plant hunting. In past time heavy rains had cut this deep gorge in the coastal hills. Today the stream bed rarely carries water, and it was entirely dry on the October morning when they saw it. But hillslopes high above were covered with vegetation. Here again was that now familiar but still almost unbelievable contrast between the arid lower altitudes rising from an incredibly dry desert floor and the moist, fog-drenched, green hilltops.

John's diary gives a firsthand account of what they found on the margin of the desert and on the foggy hillsides above it:

"At lower and middle altitudes the cacti were abundant. Massive, candelabra-like *Trichocereus chiloensis*, called *el quisco*, grew everywhere and overtopped a whole series of lesser spiny relatives. Where this great cactus extended its distribution upward into the foggier, moister regions, festoons of lichen hung from its long, tough spines. Sometimes the red stems and flowers of a parasitic plant changed its green surface to an unnatural color. One particularly large quisco was almost completely covered by a vigorous climbing nasturtium, *Tropaeolum tricolor*, sparkling with brilliant, red-and-orange, orchid-like flowers. Between the rocks we saw our first plant of *Cruckshanksia*, that curiously beautiful genus of the Rubiaceae, or Madder family, which was often to thrill us in our Chilean collecting.

"This species, *Cruckshanksia pumila*, was the smallest and the only annual member of this striking genus that we came across. The plants were compact and, in rocky crevices, made small, rounded tufts three to six inches high. Their bright green leaves formed a clear, fine background on which were displayed the large, brilliantly yellow bracts that surrounded the relatively inconspicuous flowers. In Cruckshanksias the small true flowers are borne several together in the center of a flat, colored disc formed by much-modified leaves or bracts, which, at first glance, can readily be mistaken for petals. The individual flowers were about one half-inch long. At the base slender tubes, at the tops they flared out to form little, five-pointed stars. As we got up from our knees after analyzing this first *Cruckshanksia*, we looked ahead and saw that a few rods higher in the quebrada the rocks were everywhere painted yellow by this low annual. Collecting promised to be good.

"We turned up a narrow, rocky gulch to the north and began to climb a bit. On this hillside the first plant seen in any abundance was *Balbisia*, which happens to be a member of the plant family to which the Geranium belongs. This *Balbisia,* or *Ledocarpum* as it was called by the early writers on Chilean botany, was a tall, rounded shrub, reaching when mature a height of six to eight feet. At this season of the year, the gray-green bushes were heavy with erect, bright yellow flowers about an inch across. In the loose soil below this decorative plant we noticed a small lupine with pale yellow and white flowers. For some obscure reason, we could find only a single plant of this tiny *Lupinus microcarpus.* There was also a beautiful lilac-colored species of *Cristaria,* a genus of the Mallow family which is very widespread in Chile. Along the edges of the rocky slopes we began to find several little, hairy, white-flowered plants of a borage, *Cryptantha.* They called our attention to the similarity between elements of the Chilean lomas flora and the annual flora of the coastal hills in California.

"We worked our way along the rough hillside for a while and then suddenly our path was blocked by a huge mass of *Loasa bertrandi* that was climbing through the tall cacti. The shiny, bright green leaves of this *Loasa,* and its beautiful white flowers, striped with bright yellow and red, make you keen to strip great streamers of it from the spiny cacti and get busy putting them in the presses. Such a desire is almost immediately curbed. How stupid to be so careful to avoid the obvious spines of the cacti! They are just spines and only make puncture wounds in one's flesh. But this white-flowered serpent of a plant, with its marvelously glossy leaves—what a vicious thing it is! Each hair, those glistening white threads on stems and leaves and flowers, is a stinger of such authority that the pain from the worst nettle sting is less than a pinprick by comparison. Loasas can be collected, but heavy gloves or large forceps must be used.

"Here, in the coarse scree above the trail, we saw our first Chilean violet. It was a tiny, reddish rosette, with half-inch-long, slender, pointed leaves, closely packed in geometric fashion to produce an intricate design. Small, red-and-white flowers peeked out beneath the lower leaves of the flat-topped rosettes. In color this reddish-leaved violet so closely matched the rocks in which it grew that we had to crawl on hands and knees, with eyes close to the ground, in order to find enough specimens for the plant press.

"We climbed higher, and then, without preliminaries, the openings in the scrub took on color and we were looking at *Alstroemeria violacea,* one of the most attractive plants that grows on the west coast of South America. By this time we had climbed almost into the fog and just overhead was its swirling, cottony cloud of grayness. It began to send out tentacles all about us, and in a few more steps we were lost in its cool, soft embrace. In this fog-swept zone, the character of the vegetation changed completely and all plant life grew luxuriantly. Below, the plants existed only in dry, rocky soil and depended for moisture upon some hidden supply of ground water or the combination of nightly fogs and the low evaporation rate. It must have been the latter combination of factors which determined the continued existence of such shallow-rooted plants as *Cruckshanksia,* the rare lupine, and the other species of annuals. In the upper, fertile, fog-swept zone, the same factors obtained but with much greater emphasis. In the ever-present fog, a fine mist bathed the soil and everything above it. Under the apparently benign influence of this thick, wet mantle many beautiful and interesting species grew on the high hillsides. There were many low annuals reminiscent of home; for example, a *Bowlesia,* so like a California relative that it was hard to believe that they were distinct species. It spread its pale-green leaves and opened its tiny, white flowers in the half shade of a group of columnar cacti. Near by grew a few plants of *Pectocarya dimorpha,* another genus well known in California. Its inconspicuous, four-parted, spiny-edged fruits were ripe, but we could find no flowering specimens to put in press.

"Higher up we found two Calceolarias. The first, *Calceolaria paposana,* a straggling shrub with erect branches which bore an abundance of yellow flowers, was quite common among the large rocks in the very bottom of a high, narrow ravine. The second *Calceolaria* was extremely rare and grew only where fog moisture had collected in little rocky depressions. We saw only three plants. This species produced a few big, bright, orange-red spotted flowers and large, pale green basal leaves."

The two *botánicos* had gone to Taltal primarily because *Nicotiana solanifolia,* a tobacco relative, was reported to grow in the vicinity. This shrubby species is one of the few Nicotianas in North Chile and its distribution is restricted to hills near the coast. It is a choosy plant and demands just a certain combination of soil and atmospheric moisture, of sun, and of fog shade. When we grow it in Berkeley, the dry, sunny California summer has a discouraging effect and the plants mature slowly and flower sparingly.

As they worked up toward the foggier heights, a few plants of the sought-after *Nicotiana* began to appear. Stunted, scrawny, and poor as to flowers, these plants were, apparently, just able to survive in the bottoms of small, rocky, exposed gulches where they found some moisture in the subsoil. Much higher up, at about eighteen hundred feet, where the fog was thick and wet, the same species was quite a different thing. The plants were five feet high, straight and strong, and covered with big, gray-green, heart-shaped leaves; the stems ended in stately, foot-high pyramids of pale yellow-green, tubular flowers which shone through the fog with a faint, delicate light.

In Taltal they were joined by Rodolfo Wagenknecht, who was to act as guide and assistant during the remainder of their North Chilean collecting. He is an enthusiastic naturalist, and, as often as his duties in the Chilean highway service permit, he studies the vegetation and, particularly, the insects of both northern and southern Chile. Throughout the many years of our botanizing in his territories he has assisted us effectively.

The next day, when Carl and John had taken all the plants they needed from Quebrada de Taltal, they were ready to move southward. After some discussion with Rodolfo they decided to go by train to Copiapó, an inland city on the southern edge of the Atacama Desert. Establishing a temporary headquarters there, they would be in striking distance of Andean foothill as well as coastal collecting grounds.

The monotony of their eighteen-hour train ride across the desert was somewhat relieved by distant, indistinct glimpses of the great Andes, whose outlying ranges stretch nearer to the sea as one enters the central zone of Chile. Increasingly the wide plains were uplifted into low cross ranges and isolated peaks. As they approached Copiapó there were occasional patches of prostrate, flowering vegetation in the bottoms of shallow draws. The city itself lay cradled in a valley through which ran one of the few small rivers that succeed in crossing the Chilean desert to the ocean. As the train skirted the rim of this valley preparatory to winding down into it, their eyes, for the first time in weeks, came to rest upon the grateful green of riverside masses of Lombardy poplars and weeping willows. In a small, artificial forest, the uppermost trees were silhouetted sharply against the brownish scarps of the opposite valley wall.

They had left Taltal with presses full of recently collected and thus very wet specimens. Therefore their first duty at the hotel in Copiapó was to start plant drying. They were now some distance back from the coast. The sun shone all day long, and the air was hot and dry. Soon the floor of the hotel patio was mosaicked with dark-gray blotters and tan rectangles of corrugated cardboard, all heavy with the moisture that, in the presses, they had begun to extract from the Taltal plants. In the warmth and dryness of the patio this moisture soon left the driers and back they went between the plants.

The first collecting trip out of Copiapó was to Caldera, on the coast. They went by automobile, rather than by train, in order to collect whatever was to be found along the road. Instead of a road, however, they traveled a medium-good mule track. Great numbers of pack animals had used it over the decades during which their backs were the only means of transporting ore to the coast and foodstuffs back to the mines in the Andean foothills. No one but a west coast chofer would ever have attempted to drive an automobile over such a trail.

As the car careened crazily from side to side, the desert landscape took on an inexpressibly wild and desolate appearance. The land began to fall away toward the coast in a jumble of ledges, spurs, and isolated masses of rock. The driver headed his machine between and among these constant hazards with steady and practiced hand. His three passengers bounded up and down between the defunct springs of the seat cushions and the car roof, which was greasy and worn by contact with the heads of many previous unfortunates.

Near approach to the sea was signaled by a hint of moisture in the air and by the flowering of desert shrubs and herbs in the few flat, open spaces between the great boulders. The dominant plant was the lilac-flowered, yellow-green leaved *Cristaria*, which they had first seen near Taltal. With this attractive plant grew abundant blue Nolanas, Loasas (provided as usual with stinging hairs), and some species of *Argylia*. The rather scattered collecting led them on and on until, passing over a last rise, they saw the town and port of Caldera, and beyond it the dull-blue Pacific stretching out with ever-diminishing color to the foggy western horizon.

They had gone to Caldera because near by there were two collecting areas of some fame and importance. In one, Quebrada de León, I wanted them to search for a species of *Nicotiana* which had been reported to be growing there. It was said to be related to, or identical with, *Nicotiana solanifolia* which they had found in the coastal hills to the north. The second collecting ground, Morro de Copiapó, was a tall headland jutting out into the sea just south of Caldera.

Following an appeal by Rodolfo, the resident *carabineros*, local representatives of government, agreed to provide not more than two horses for the trip to Quebrada de León. It then appeared that one of them must be ridden by an officer who was to go along in order that the party should acquire a thoroughly official and dignified character. This meant that two more animals had to be found. After much scurrying about, the owner of two miserable mules was cajoled into renting them for the following day.

The next morning, horses, officer, and mules appeared before the hotel. The horses were fine, strong, well-gaited animals, but the less said about the mules the better. Of all depressed, ramshackle, bony-backed, cross-grained, and thoroughly unreliable quadrupeds, these Caldera mules were the worst.

It proved to be a distinctly divided trip. The horses trotted, the mules walked, and soon the horsemen were out of sight. At the edge of the Quebrada de León, the party was finally reassembled. A considerable disappointment awaited the three *botánicos*, for most of the vegetation in the quebrada consisted of perennial species and only a few of them were in flower. However, the *Nicotiana* I wanted was actually there in quantity and some of it in flower. They collected it and photographed it, but were unable to find mature seeds. I would willingly have exchanged a pinch of seed for all the pressed specimens and the photographs they made.

Of the few other plants that were flowering, the most conspicuous and unusual was the giant *Oxalis* (*O. gigantea*). The other *Oxalis* species they had found in the north had been small and rather delicate herbs. By contrast, this Quebrada de León *Oxalis* was a six-foot-tall, semiwoody perennial, with yard-long, slender, snaky branches—something quite beyond expectation for *Oxalis* and, in general, a decidedly peculiar-looking species. The leaves were sorrel-like, but very small for such a large plant. The flowers were bright yellow.

When they had collected this and a little *Oxalis* with orange-yellow, scarlet-tipped petals, and a few other more or less interesting plants, there was nothing more to do. With blasphemous references to the luck of the seasons—too early here and too late there—and while the afternoon was still very young, they mounted horses and mules and began the ride back to Caldera. The two horsemen again forged ahead and in a few minutes were lost to view. The mules reacted to the homeward journey, not by any improvement in their gait, but by developing a complete unwillingness to permit their riders to get on or off their backs. This was a disappointment, because in the morning John and Rodolfo had seen a number of trailside plants they wanted, and had planned to collect them on the way back. They did stop once or twice, but it took so much time to leave the rearing mules and to escape hoofs and teeth when they tried to regain their saddles that any hope of real collecting had to be abandoned.

Rodolfo hired a launch to take them next morning to Morro de Copiapó. They met it at the foggy dockside about seven o'clock. It was an old but sturdy craft and not too offensively odorous, even though it had long been used for fishing. Along the coasts of Chile and Peru the fishermen are on the fishing grounds before daybreak. Only a few hours after it has left the water, their catch of *congrio*, corvina, and other delicacies of the Humboldt Current, carried over the shoulder on a strip of rawhide, is offered for sale in the streets of coastal cities. Almost perfect freshness is one of the reasons why fish, especially corvina, is such a popular item for tourists on the menus of west coast hotels and restaurants. These fishermen had a steady job but a poorly paid one, and therefore the chance to earn eighty pesos by taking some gringos on a half-day excursion was very attractive.

The launch was powered by a big gasoline engine that drove them rapidly over the quiet surface of Caldera's inner harbor. They rounded a sharp, lighthouse-topped promontory into the rougher waters of Bahía Inglesa and hugged its southwest shore. Breakfast was then in order and exceedingly welcome. The younger of the two *lancheros* produced the ubiquitous five-gallon oil can. This one was a quarter full of ashes, with the lower part of one side cut away to provide a draft. With wires, a grate or grill had been hung down in the can. A bit of kindling under the grate soon produced heartening odors from the spout of the coffeepot. When it had boiled and been removed, the halves of good Chilean breakfast buns went on to toast.

Variations in the origin and topography of the Chilean coastal strip can best be observed from the sea. North of Tocopilla, near Chañaral, south of Taltal, and elsewhere, lofty, almost perpendicular cliffs and headlands rise directly from the water. At other points—for example, to the north of Caldera and from Caldera south to Huasco—there may be a terrace uplifted above the sea or a series of mighty steps that end in the coastal hills two or three miles from the beach. The power of the Pacific surge is magnificent, and that morning on the protected side of Bahía Inglesa they watched mountainous breakers crashing against the steep scarp of the eastern terrace. The sea was almost calm in the protection of the Morro, whose massive bulk grew rapidly larger, straight ahead.

They went ashore on a rocky ledge of the great headland. The launch immediately turned back into the bay so that its crew might do a little fishing while the botanists were at work. The vegetation, reputed to be very interesting, did not come up to expectation. In addition, once more it was too early in the season for the flowering of the shrubs and herbs that grew on the upper levels of the cliffsides. But to reward them for their climbing *Alstroemeria violacea* was there. They had seen it first at Taltal. But here, under the brow of Morro de Copiapó, they saw it in its full beauty. The many stems which come up from the long, slender, fleshy roots were not so tall as those of the familiar yellow-flowered *Alstroemeria aurantiaca* or of the so-called *chilensis* hybrids. They were, however, stiff and strong, with many broad, highly varnished, dark-green leaves. At the stem apices were the flowers, six to twelve of them.

Although a luminous lavender-blue color is their most unusually distinctive and attractive feature, the shape and size of the flowers is also outstanding among Alstroemerias. The petals are broad, somewhat ruffled on the margins, and together form a wide, spreading, salver-formed flower. The narrow bottom of this lavender-blue cup is colored yellow to orange, with a fringe of long, narrow, purple stripes.

Below the higher levels where this fine *Alstroemeria* was growing they found a number of interesting plants. There was a lilac-flowered species of *Astragalus*, a member of the Pea family, and two species of *Cristaria* different from the ones in the north. There was, too, a low, white-flowered *Schizopetalon*, of the Mustard family, botanically the most interesting plant they saw near the Morro. The petals were lacy, and in general the plant was almost a miniature edition of one of the swamp orchids of the northeastern United States. On a steep, sandy slope was a large patch of another *Alstroemeria*, quite a different one from *Alstroemeria violacea* but with considerable charm. It lay prostrate in the sand and was covered with small, clear-yellow flowers that almost hid the scant foliage. In the loose earth it was easy to dig the fleshy roots, which in most Alstroemerias are buried deep in heavy or rocky soil.

The broad vista of sea and sky well repaid them for a hard climb to the summit of the Morro and offset to some extent their disappointment over the meagerness of the collecting. The fog masses which in the early morning had enveloped sea and shore were drifting slowly inland. The surface of the sea, illuminated where the sun's rays struck through the mist, was a clear, mild blue, flecked now and then with white where the long, deep Pacific swells crested and broke. Almost at their feet the launch with the two fishermen at their tasks lay at anchor in the calm protection of the promontory. Far out to sea, wheeling and diving, thousands upon thousands of sea birds—gulls, pelicans, cormorants, boobies, and petrels—gave animation to the horizon.

For the plant hunter the neighborhood of Copiapó, at about 27° South, and that of Caldera, on the coast at the same latitude, marks the southern limit of the North Chilean desert. The hills surrounding Copiapó are dry, and the sandy wastes that stretch away behind them are barren. But each mile that one travels southward from this margin of the true desert marks a minute increase in moisture. It may be that only one twenty-fifth of an inch of rain falls each year, but even this small alteration in moisture conditions makes it possible, in favorable seasons, for a transient vegetation to appear. Thus, south of Copiapó, such a minimum will bring about the germination of grass seeds. If there chances to be an additional shower or two soon enough thereafter, then the brown hills are covered with a green mantle, a thin one but sufficient to provide temporary forage for grazing animals.

The railway runs southward from Copiapó through a perceptibly decreasing aridity, in terms of vegetation at least. Gradually you begin to realize that there are a few more cacti per acre. Increasing numbers of low shrubs wage a ceaseless and successful struggle with drought and wind. Ever so gradually do the distances between the individuals which combine to produce this shrubby vegetation decrease. As the main line turns west from Vallenar toward Coquimbo and the sea, an ever more continuous green covering smooths and softens the rough silhouette of the increasingly massive coastal mountain ranges.

With one of its sources in the snow fields of the eighteen-thousand-foot Cerro del Volcán, almost on the Chilean-Argentine border, the

Río Limari runs swiftly to the west, and, after it has left behind the interior city of Ovalle, enters the Pacific south of La Serena. In its valley west of Ovalle occur the northernmost known stands of the famous *palma chilena* (*Jubaea spectabilis*). This stately palm, indigenous to Central Chile, is found from the Limari to the Maule in the south, or through less than five degrees of latitude. Always a conspicuous element in its landscape, to me it is most attractive when it rises from a shrub-filled valley bottom and is seen against the tan surfaces of the distant Andean foothills.

The largest specimens are said to attain a height of almost one hundred feet. The trunk is swollen for one half to two thirds of its length, and then above that point the diameter decreases rather abruptly and thereafter continues upward without diminution until it terminates in the long, much-dissected leaves. The heavy leaf-crown often forms an almost complete sphere. In the coastal cordillera, at altitudes below one thousand feet, palma chilena was in years gone by an important element of every landscape. In the neighborhood of Valparaiso and for a hundred miles south it once existed in extraordinary numbers. Charles Darwin speaks of a census which was taken in 1830 on the lands belonging to a hacienda near the town of Petorca and was abandoned after some hundreds of thousands of palms had been tallied. Today its numbers have everywhere been greatly reduced; indeed, some of the local botanists speak of the possible extinction of this most attractive and typical Chilean plant.

Man has, of course, been responsible for its partly complete disappearance. Unfortunately for this palm, the abundant sap has a high sugar content. Boiled down, it yields *miel de palma*, palm honey, which is a commercially valuable and esteemed sweetmeat in Chile. To obtain the sap, the palm must be cut down in early spring. If possible, it is felled uphill so that the top will be higher than the cut end. Then a crosscut is made below the crown of leaves and the flowing sap is collected. A fresh slice of wood is periodically removed in order to maintain a constant flow. The exudate continues for six to eight weeks, and a total of from seventy-five to one hundred gallons of sweet sap is often secured.

How significant in the history of the race the palms have been, still are, and doubtless always will continue to be! They have rivaled every other plant in their importance and utility to man. Over great areas of the tropics and semitropics the date or the coconut palms are relied upon to provide food, drink, clothing, and shelter, as well as being among the most valuable articles of commerce that their areas produce. Among native Chilean plants, *Jubaea spectabilis* is certainly pre-eminent, at least in terms of the value of its products.

Many years later, Paul collected back and forth over much of the North Chilean coastal terrain that John, Carl, and Rodolfo had traversed. Between us, he and I spent from October to March in Chile on the fifth South American expedition. I was there at the request of the Chilean government to encourage the development of a national botanical garden and agricultural research station near Valparaiso, a project with which I had been concerned for some time. Paul, a specialist in cacti and other succulent types of plants, was to make a survey of the not-too-well-known and reportedly rich and varied cactus population of the northern coast and adjacent Andean foothills. In a truck we had brought from California, and with an Anglo-Chilean assistant, he covered much ground and made extensive and valuable collections. The most significant of them were shipped as living plants to Berkeley and made an important addition to the cactus collection in the Botanical Garden, where already were numerous species sent back from our earlier South American plant-hunting forays.

Cacti, like many other groups of flowering plants, are likely to exhibit in their native environments a range of variation which causes considerable confusion for those who study and name them. Few botanists who collect in foreign lands have enough time or opportunity to take more than a specimen or two of the apparently new or rare species they come across. This seems to have been particularly true of cacti because it takes extra time and attention properly to prepare a pressed, dried specimen of a fairly sizable spiny and succulent plant. In addition, the plants may not be in flower when the botanist finds them; if they are, there will probably be no ripe seed capsules; and both flowers and seed are essential to give a complete picture of the particular cactus you collect. Years later, other botanists working in the same area will find cacti they think are different in appearance from any previously reported from that area. The result is that, ultimately, the cactus specialist at home will be faced with a series of dried, pressed specimens, more or less complete ones, that appear to him to be divisible into a number of separate entities, and so he gives each subdivision a new and different specific name. Actually, they may all be basically the same species, the various specimens showing small individual distinctions which are due to hereditary variation, to seasonal growth responses, or to more or to less favorable habitats.

To make a long story short, you have to spend enough time in a given collecting locality to determine on the spot the range of natural variation owing to the causes just mentioned. This Paul did for a considerable number of Chilean cacti. Sometimes the plants involved were not in flower or fruit, and then they were sent back to Berkeley where they ultimately flowered and made seed in the Botanical Garden. The result of this intensive research was a demonstration of an often wide range of natural variation, and proof that within this range fell the plant characters which previously had been used to subdivide a composite species into distinct units, to each of which had been given a new and different name. Last year, Paul spent many months in making much the same type of studies of the remarkable cactus flora of Peru.

Just after this was written, Rodolfo, whom we have encountered earlier in this chapter, left his headquarters in La Serena, well down the Chilean coast toward Valparaiso, to collect for me in an area virtually unknown botanically. It lies more or less due east of Antofagasta on the Chilean-Argentine frontier, at altitudes of from twelve to fifteen thousand feet in the Andes. I asked him to make this rather difficult trip because in that area *N. longibracteata*, one of the two South American Nicotianas I have not seen in the living state, was discovered, for the first and only time and just one hundred years ago, by Dr. R. A. Philippi during his celebrated *Atacama Journey*. In his day-by-day report of that pioneering and extended collecting expedition the famous Chilean botanist gives much too vague a reference to where in the highlands he collected the dried specimens of *N. longibracteata* which are preserved in excellent condition at the Museo in Santiago.

In Antofagasta Rodolfo got nothing but discouraging reports concerning the remote *longibracteata* region. Even the *carabineros*, who maintain law and order throughout Chile, and who knew the region, shook their heads when they heard that Rodolfo was looking for transportation to it. Actually, the season was pretty well advanced for high-altitude collecting; indeed, a few days after Rodolfo arrived in Antofagasta the first of the late summer snows began to fall on the North Chilean Andean summits.

Rodolfo feels sure that at an earlier and generally more favorable season he can complete his *longibracteata* assignment, and I hope that he soon will. On his way back and forth from Antofagasta he made valuable collections of coastal Chilean cacti in some areas previously little known botanically.

Not so long after he started his return journey to La Serena, heavy rain fell for almost half a day on Antofagasta and near by. Telegraph lines went down, transportation was at a standstill, and the city was virtually isolated. Probably nothing quite equal to it has ever happened in northernmost Chile, for many generations drier than the Sahara. I wonder whether anyone measured the amount of strontium 90 that was added to the already highly mineralized nitrate desert.

12

VALE OF PARADISE

CHILE IS a long and extremely narrow country. Something like the airplane distance between San Francisco and New York separates Arica, on Chile's northern border, from Tierra del Fuego, its southern extremity and the southernmost point on our sister continent. North Chile is desert or semidesert; South Chile is extremely wet, and cool to quite cold; between them the climate is generally delightful. A semicircle based upon the Pacific whose seventy-five-mile radius includes Santiago, Chile's capital, and whose center lies in her important port, Valparaiso (literally, "Vale of Paradise," whereas the city is only a part of it so far as this chapter is concerned), encloses what corresponds amazingly in aspect, rainfall, and sunshine to middle western California.

The city of Valparaiso has been built on a narrow coastal plain which, after running back from the sea wall only a few city blocks, comes to a full stop against precipitous cliffs and steep ridges. On this coastal plain you wander along well-paved, not-too-narrow, rather well-kept streets beside stores, banks, office buildings, and apartment houses and through plazas large and small. If you have come to Chile by sea and if your time ashore is limited, you are unlikely to wander too far from the main plaza, which you enter soon after leaving the dock. This plaza and the near-by streets contain a few shops filled with the trifles that tourists buy. The characteristic "come-on" in these Valparaiso tripper emporia is likely to be a window display of pseudo Easter Island wooden images that are not only undraped but also prominently decorated with anatomical grotesqueries, both fore and aft.

There is today a distinct air of prosperity about Valparaiso. When I

208

first knew the city it was a rather shabby place with almost no modern structures in the business district. With regret, but with no hint of hard feeling about the responsibility of the United States for the building of the Panama Canal, my Chilean friends explained that before the opening of the canal Valparaiso was an exceedingly busy port and the city correspondingly prosperous. In those long-gone days all the ships from Europe and North America bound for the Far East and back had to round Cape Horn. Usually they put in to Valparaiso to break the long journey and restock with food and water. In particular, the clipper fleet carrying Australian wheat to England always made the port, and sometimes on the voyage home also. Those must have been great days in Valparaiso, with sailors by the hundreds on leave in the first port they had seen, perhaps, in months.

A short excursion will take you down the Calle Condell, which runs along the inner edge of the coastal plain. Every now and then you will pass a small ticket office next to the sidewalk, and behind it an elevator-like car that runs on tracks and a cogwheel almost straight up the hillside to a small box perched far above. Into that box an ascending car suddenly disappears, while at the same instant a descending one pops out. This is one of the famous outdoor *ascensores,* or elevators, on which most of Valparaiso's population goes home at night and down to work in the morning. If you live in Valparaiso you will have your office or shop on the coastal plain, while your home will hang on one of the hillside streets so far above that the only thing to do is to take the elevator, to go up or down.

Steep, cobbled roads wind back and forth up the rocky sides of the ravines that break the continuity of the hillsides and, above, cross the series of terraced residence streets that follow the contours of the hills. On the abruptly ascending roads the up and down traffic of foot passengers, strings of loaded burros, private automobiles, taxis, autobuses, and trucks weaves in and out with noisy good-nature. A little boy with packages to deliver from a store below kicks a tennis ball up the hill to make his journey really worth while and thoroughly interesting. A greengrocer with his stock in trade on a burro's back comes to a sudden stop at the shrill call of a housewife; and behind him brakes squeal and grind, horns protest, the bus driver springs out with imprecations and with a wooden wedge to fortify his brakes. From the level streets below it is impossible to appreciate the construction of the city of Valparaiso or to see anything of what is going on above.

In addition to the collections of dried plants, seeds, bulbs, roots, and cuttings which we were making in the Vale of Paradise, I kept constantly receiving more of all these kinds of plant material from the other collectors, who were scattered a distance of from two to five hundred miles both north and south.

The handling of thousands of plant specimens requires plenty of room. It is always a mussy job, usually a dirty one. We first began the work in our hotel room, and before each day was over the tables, dressers, beds, and finally the floor were entirely covered with plants. Every now and then we found ourselves penned in a corner, unable to move for fear of stepping on something valuable. At least once every twenty-four hours everything had to be cleared up in order, first, that we could get a little sleep and, second, that the maid could come in and at least go through the motions of cleaning up the mess. At this juncture our friend "the General" came to the rescue, just as he has done on many other occasions.

"The General," Dr. Edwyn P. Reed, one of the best-trained medical men in Chile, is an Anglo-Chilean whose father came from England to Valparaiso many years ago, later to become prominent in pioneer studies of the natural history of his adopted homeland. Mentally and physically he is one of the most vigorous men I have ever known. Better still, he is wonderfully good company and all that a real friend could possibly be. His title was bestowed upon him long ago and was a consequence of his enthusiasm for recounting stories or using expletives acquired from officers of American and English ships docked in Valparaiso, with whom he has had a long and wide acquaintance. On a particularly warm day he greeted us with, "It's as hot as Jesus Christ and General Jackson!" So "General" he straightway became.

The General let us establish ourselves on a wide first-floor balcony overlooking the garden of his hillside home. There were big tables on which our specimens could be spread out. All about we accumulated great piles of corrugated boards and pieces of felt; with these we dried our collections and completed the drying of those that were sent in to us too wet for packing and shipping. Once a day, and often twice, we had to change the plant driers and then carefully lay out the moist ones on all garden paths. When the hot Valparaiso sun had done its work and the driers were thoroughly dry again, we had to pick them up one by one and put them back into the presses or store them on the balcony against the evening dew.

The drudgery of what we did for many weeks on the General's balcony was each day lightened by our pleasure and interest in the plants we spread out before us. Sometimes they were my own collections made the day before, or perhaps many weeks before. Each plant brought back a memory of a bit of landscape and often some experience, amusing or the reverse. When a shipment came in from the collectors, I began to feel real enthusiasm for the work. The first question was, "Did he get the particular thing he and I hoped that he would come across in that special area where he has been collecting?" This question led to a quick search through the specimens, but I had to curb my impatience, for fear of mixing up the plants, and would then set about a slow, methodical examination of each one. Until I came across the desired plant, and I almost always did, a certain suppressed atmosphere of excitement prevailed. Then we would relax, apply ourselves to the old routine, only now and again commenting on some specimen that attracted our attention.

During the past forty years I have spent much time examining the specimens of *Nicotiana* which, along with those of all other genera of plants, are to be found in the great herbaria of the world. An herbarium is, of course, a collection of dried, pressed plants, and in the larger herbaria every section of the globe is well represented. To each specimen is attached a label on which the collector has written the date and place of collection, a variety of information concerning the conditions under which the plant was growing, notes on plant characters —such as color of flower—which may disappear when a plant has been killed and dried, and any further data he may have secured. The botanist, or the interested and informed layman, can obtain from an herbarium a remarkably accurate picture not only of the character and composition of the floras in any part of the world, but also of the environmental conditions that characterize any particular area.

At the beginning of my herbarium work I came across specimens of many species and varieties that were not represented in my accumulating living collection of *Nicotiana* in the Botanical Garden in Berkeley. Most of the dried Nicotianas in which I was particularly interested had seed capsules containing seed; but in the majority of cases the specimens had been collected so long ago or had been so thoroughly poisoned against destructive museum insects that the seed which I took from them failed to germinate. To insure my botanical colleagues against similar disappointments I have always tried in South America to take seed from the dried plants, not only of *Nicotiana* but also of all other genera. This has proved to be a rather large order. Rarely was the seed large and easily removed without injuring the dried specimens; more often it was small and in many cases minute, as, for example, in the species of *Calceolaria*. Then, with the greatest of care, we had to seek and find the mature seed pods among the dry and brittle flowers and leaves, and open them carefully to extract what seed they contained. Sometimes the seed pods were so hard and woody that a hammer was required.

In my youth, our family spent each summer in northern Wisconsin. In addition to fishing, one of the favorite family occupations was blueberry picking. In openings in the pine forests there were acres of blueberry bushes and we had soon charted all the most important patches. I happened to be the only child in a combined family of fifteen. When we undertook a blueberry excursion I was supposed to pick only from those bushes that were lowest. Thus, only the higher bushes required the attention of the rest of the family and a minimum of stooping on their part would be involved.

Nevertheless, I might have enjoyed blueberry picking except that constantly in my mind was the aftermath. This consisted of picking over the blueberries and examining each one on the chance that the small stem had remained attached to the fruit. After a successful visit to blueberry areas, the succeeding day or two was largely devoted to this process of "picking over." The entire family assembled about large baskets of blueberries and each one dipped in and proceeded to examine his handful, this sequence being repeated indefinitely. To lighten the labor, one member of the family, almost always my father, was assigned the task of reading aloud to the group. The only respite came when the reader paused for breath or a drink of water. I was sustained through the long hours of picking over primarily by loyalty to my father, who was troubled whenever he was interrupted in his reading. This was bound to happen when older members of the family noticed that I was becoming at all derelict in my duty—a dereliction often caused by pleasant visions of pies into which ultimately the blueberries would become incorporated. Even this anticipation could not, however, banish from my mind the experience which I knew I was

Machu Picchu, that amazingly preserved Inca stone "City of a Thousand Steps," so well known to tourists, falls off sheer for two thousand feet down into the canyon of the Río Urubamba.

A series of Machu Pic-
chu's rooms walled with
beautifully fitted blocks
of stone—a characteristic
niche in the farthest
wall.

From a Machu Picchu
corner, the turbulent
waters of the Urubamba
are seen far below.

A calling card cannot penetrate the joints of these Machu Picchu ashlars.

Like a great white snake the road to Machu Picchu lies on the sheer mountainside.

At eighteen thousand feet this blue lake nestles in a fold of the Bolivian Andes.

On these reed boats the Peruvian highlanders sail Titicaca, world's highest lake.

going to have during the succeeding night. After a day of picking over, my dreams pictured a series of backgrounds, usually steep hillsides, on which I was constantly threatened by larger and smaller blue spheres which approached me at tremendous rates of speed. Part of the night I spent dodging these missiles and during the rest of it my dreams involved an exhaustive examination of a great collection of blue balls, which continuously moved before my eyes and arranged themselves in a variety of constantly altering patterns.

After concentrating on the General's balcony each day for many weeks on seed extraction and examination, our sleep was similarly troubled. Before our eyes passed constantly in review a succession of seeds of various sizes, colors, and shapes. Sometimes we found ourselves approaching a large object that ultimately proved to be a gigantic seed pod which, when attacked, proceeded to disgorge a large number of objectionable objects that chased us for miles across imaginary countrysides.

To the north and south of the Vale of Paradise the coast range consists primarily of high hills, but between Valparaiso and Santiago and for a considerable distance north of an imaginary line connecting these two cities the hills become mountains. In this portion of the Cordillera de la Costa, the topmost peak, Cerro Cache, rises somewhat over seven thousand feet above sea level, and there are ten or more other mountains whose altitudes exceed six thousand feet. The most famous is La Campana, the Bell Mountain, which is a few miles northeast of Limache, one of the most climatically delightful, garden-filled towns in the Vale of Paradise. In 1832 the young naturalist of H.M.S. *Beagle*, Charles Darwin, climbed the mountain. It had attracted his attention as an isolated portion of the Cordillera de la Costa which rose more or less solitary from the broad coastal plain. One hundred years later, the Valparaiso Scientific Society prepared a bronze plaque commemorating Darwin's visit and with appropriate ceremonies placed it permanently near a spring where, on the slopes of La Campana, he spent the night.

The varied character of the vegetational habitats which these mountains in the Vale of Paradise provide leads one to expect a correspondingly varied plant population, and this expectation is abundantly fulfilled. The peaks themselves may be covered with upwards of four inches of snow during the southern winter, and a part of this white mantle may extend down to the three-thousand-foot level. Rains that fall, but often sparingly, preceding and following the snow, add further moisture to the rocky soils of the mountainsides. In summer the lower altitudes are regularly bathed in fog, while the peaks and high ridges are drying out in the bright sunshine and clear atmosphere. In the quebradas and on the gentle, lower mountain slopes, especially on those facing south, where soil moisture is longest preserved, some of the characteristic trees of heavily forested southern Chile reach their northernmost limit of distribution.

In midsummer the higher elevations, the broad valleys, and the exposed plateaus become almost arid; but there are still many deep, moist quebradas in the Cordillera de la Costa, in the bottoms of which slow-flowing rivulets meander around huge stream-bed boulders and on whose sides tall trees festooned with "Spanish moss" rise high above a dense undergrowth. On north-facing slopes, where maximum exposure to sunlight produces maximum evaporation, or on mountainsides too steep to hold a heavy layer of fertile soil, this forest is abruptly replaced by *monte,* or dense chaparral. This is characteristic of thousands of square miles in the mountains of Central Chile just as it is of similar terrain in the Far West of the United States.

Of all the coast range mountains in the Vale of Paradise, Las Vizcachas, some six thousand and fifty feet in altitude, has time after time yielded large and varied collections of plants of ornamental as well as botanical interest. The mountain is named for the elusive *vizcacha,* whose shrill, piping cries echo along the most inaccessible rock slides and cavernous defiles in the evening afterglow, or as the dawn first touches the highest peaks of the Chilean ranges. A larger edition of its relative the chinchilla, the *vizcacha* resembles a rabbit in shape and size but differs from it by possessing the large, fluffy tail of a squirrel.

The first time we botanized Las Vizcachas we drove to the village of La Dormida, which lies at the foot of the mountain, and found the man who had been engaged in advance to act as our guide and horse wrangler. His name proved to be Diógenes, and those who at his birth bestowed it upon him must have possessed clairvoyant powers. Although carefully instructed some days before to provide riding horses and pack mules, Diógenes had apparently made no effort to procure them. We immediately proceeded to work up a violent rage on the subject and finally a few animals were brought round.

At four in the afternoon we began to ride up the lower slopes of Las Vizcachas. For the first two thousand feet Diógenes led us along the side of a deep quebrada in which such handsome trees as the *boldo*, the *peumo* (*Cryptocarya peumus*), and the *patagua* (*Crinodendron patagua*), formed the dominant feature. The vegetation also included *Escallonia rubra*, other shrubs, and a multitude of ferns as a dense understory of the open forest. The *Escallonia* is locally called *siete camisas* ("seven shirts"), in allusion to the readiness with which the bark of this shrub scales off, soon to be replaced by another loose integument.

Along the margins of the quebrada, where its forest was replaced by *monte*, the fountain-like sprays of a near-bamboo formed impenetrable thickets. Often the upper surfaces of these brownish-green thickets sparkled in the sunlight with hundreds of the deep orange-red flowers of a species of *Mutisia*. The climbing species of this genus of the Sunflower family are familiar and attractive elements of the landscape in not-too-dry, brush-covered areas in both Peru and Chile. They prefer to aggregate their plant bodies under shrubs or small trees, clasping the branches with long arms and pushing out into the light, among the leaves of the supporting plant, only the extremities of their leafy, flowering shoots. Unfortunately, we found only a seed or two per plant, and sometimes none, because the insects had always been there before us. Apparently their eggs are laid within the bud or flower, and as the fruits begin to mature the larvae follow suit and devour the ripening seed. As we rode upward the forest became thinner, with more and larger openings where the sunlight could reach the earth through its green canopy. In these sunny spots we saw the first of the Alstroemerias which were to make memorable our collecting on Las Vizcachas.

In recounting our plant-hunting experiences along the northern coast of Chile and in the Andean foothills behind it, I have mentioned a number of species of *Alstroemeria*, and particularly *A. violacea*, which was one of the real prizes of our early South American plant hunting. On the slopes of Las Vizcachas, *Alstroemeria haemantha* first appeared. In contrast to some of the North Chilean species, which were relatively low-growing, these plants were tall and stately, the long straight stems clothed with slender, bright green leaves and terminated by clusters of ten or more golden-yellow, broad, bell-shaped flowers.

When we reached the three-thousand-foot level on the west side of the mountain, we left the quebrada up which the climb began and started the weary ascent of steeper, treeless slopes on a rough and zig-zag trail. Somewhat higher, a small grove of trees appeared. Diógenes informed us that this would be our first *descanso,* or resting place. The bit of scattered woodland consisted of small trees of *Quillaja saponaria,* a member of the Rose family; the bark is prized because of its richness in a soaplike substance. Beneath these trees, species of *Berberis, Escallonia,* and *Cestrum* formed a loose underbrush. We walked about examining the vegetation, stopping now and then to look upward toward the peak far above our heads and the steep slopes just below it. On them we detected here and there faint films of pink laid upon the prevailing tan and gray of dried grasses and rocky ridges. The next day, when we reached the high slopes, these pink patches proved each to represent hundreds of square yards of rich, rocky soil covered with *Schizanthus hookeri.*

Diógenes insisted upon a second *descanso* after we had climbed only another thousand feet. Here on the open mountainside, in veins of loose, rich, black soil, first appeared *corymbosa,* the alpine and subalpine species of *Nicotiana* which we were particularly in search of. It is an unattractive and unpleasant little plant, with a multitude of glandular hairs on its epidermis which are ready at a touch to exude a sticky, resinous, strong-smelling gum, but it has had a prominent place in our South American *Nicotiana* plant hunting. We were soon to find it again, and in greater abundance, higher up on Las Vizcachas.

Our proposed camping place for the night was what had been reported to be a relatively level area immediately below the peak of the mountain; but we began to despair of reaching it before dark because Diógenes called for a *descanso* twice more before the climbing was over for the day.

The first plant we saw in the early morning light was a superb species of *Argylia.* This genus belongs to the Bignoniaceae, of which one of our most familiar garden representatives is the "trumpet vine." In the lomas flora along the North Chilean coast, we had already found another species of *Argylia,* as well as a third species in the *Alta Cordillera.* This Las Vizcachas species was much the best of the three. Over patches many feet square and usually in broad pockets among huge boulders, it spread a continuous, deep-green, varnished carpet on the mountaintop scree. From this shining surface rose short flower-stalks on which were borne numbers of large, tubular, trumpetlike flowers whose mottled corollas came in shades of yellow, orange, and salmon.

With the General, we have visited a number of haciendas near Valparaiso owned by some of his numerous friends. We were once entertained at one of the larger of these baronial establishments. One Sunday morning I stood with the *patrón* of this hacienda in an open field behind his large, rambling, one-story, patio-enclosing ranch house; immediately behind to the east was a range of low hills, and far in the distance in front of us light-gray fog masses marked the shore of the Pacific. I asked him to point out the extent of his landholdings. He thought for a moment and then said, "My property begins in those hills to the east, and it runs to the ocean on the west, but just how far it extends north and south I cannot show you." Later in the day we rode over a part of his domain and found that for convenience the numerous employees on the estate were concentrated in more than one little hamlet. This dispersion enabled them readily to reach outlying agricultural operations instead of having to travel a number of miles to and from the headquarters of the hacienda. Since it was Sunday, the entire population was on display at the hacienda buildings and in the villages.

After lunch the General and I tried a little plant hunting in the hills that formed the eastern border of the great estate. There he promised to show me some extra fine specimens of *Puya*, one of the most impressive of all Chilean plants. The genus *Puya* belongs to the Bromeliaceae, or Pineapple family, and has representatives in both Chile and Peru. They are essentially plants of arid terrain and grow successfully on barren ocean cliffs and on rocky shoulders thrusting out through the thin soil that covers the coastal mountains; they form one of the most characteristic elements of the vegetation of the Vale of Paradise.

As usual, the General did not disappoint me, for soon we began to see on the sky line above the low ridges a serrated fence of unequally spaced, dark-green posts which, on closer approach, looked more and more like the gun swabs of Civil War days standing at attention. They were, actually, the flowering stems of Puyas which rose five to eight feet, each one from its own round, green bed of long, leathery, straplike, sharp-pointed leaves whose edges are dangerously keen as well as spiny. For over three quarters of their length the thick flower-stalks run up clear; and then abruptly comes a compact, cylindrical head eight inches in diameter, in which are closely set hundreds of inch-and-a-half-long, half-inch-wide, vaselike flowers.

They showed silvery gray-green stems, with flowers colored a somewhat unfamiliar but nonetheless attractive shade of light blue-green. Farther north and nearer the sea we found, later, the still more decorative species or variety in which the equally tall flowering stems are brilliant scarlet, while the flowers in the tight heads are a bright, shining steel-gray. These massive Chilean pineapple relatives sometimes are grown in California and fill a garden corner impressively, give height to a slight eminence, or provide an accent point on the margin of a large rockery.

In the late afternoon displays of horsemanship were arranged for our benefit. First, the Chilean cowboys, or *huasos*, did a little plain and fancy riding; later, they arranged an informal rodeo. They wore the typical Chilean poncho, and since it was Sunday they had on their best. The poncho adds a great deal of animation and color to a Chilean rodeo because, as soon as the horseman gathers speed, this red, green, or variegated shoulder-covering begins to rise, front and rear, and flaps vigorously in the wind. The riding exhibition soon changed into something different. Horsemen in twos and threes began to rush at and jostle one another, not with intent to unhorse an antagonist but rather to demonstrate how, by clever manipulation of the horse and pressure applied at the right point and right moment, a rider's course could be effectively altered.

The rodeo that followed reminded us of a more elaborate affair we had seen some years before in the Santiago section of the Vale of Paradise. On that occasion we had been invited to go with the Santiago Scientific Society on their annual excursion. We accepted in the expectation that the party would inspect some near-by region of particular interest either for the botanist, zoölogist, or geologist. On the appointed day some twenty members of the Society and guests left Santiago by bus. After an hour and a half we arrived at the outskirts of a large hacienda. It was then explained to us that the Society had decided, instead of engaging in scientific pursuits, to devote the excursion to enjoying a rodeo which was being held by the *patrón* of the hacienda we were approaching. This particular rodeo was to be the one big event of the year for the countrypeople for miles around and involved a two- or three-day celebration, of which the rodeo itself was the culminating attraction.

Near the hacienda building a semicircular line of booths had been set up. Some of the booths were outdoor bars, and others were hucksters' establishments. Some were small dance floors roofed over with branches and leaves, while a few booths served as picnic places provided with tables and benches. In one of these last our party established itself and then promptly dispersed to take part in the festivities.

This was my first opportunity to watch the Chilean native dance called the "cueca," which was actively under way in all the dancing booths. It requires the maintenance of a certain rhythm and full acquaintance with a complicated series of figures, while the feet keep up a continuous combination of a shuffle, a certain amount of clogging, and a great deal of heel-and-toe work. The music is provided by a violin and small harp, and the dancers receive encouragement from the spectators who continuously pound their feet on the dusty dance floor and clap their hands. First, a man and his lady come out and each raises one hand above his head. In this raised hand is a handkerchief, preferably a green or a red one. After a moment of moving of their feet to catch the rhythm, the couple begin to engage in a series of stampings, kickings, and hoppings, sometimes face to face, sometimes back to back, sometimes whirling, with the upraised handkerchief kept constantly twirling. The tempo of the dance depends upon the amount of alcohol that has been consumed, particularly by the musicians; the duration of each round is equivalent to the strength and lung capacity of the participants. At the beginning and end of each performance the dancing couple quaff large glasses of cider, to which has been added a considerable amount of wine. From the sale of this beverage those in charge of a dance floor and the musicians receive their remuneration.

Our whole party, dressed in city clothes, attracted considerable attention, and Florence and I received the larger share since it was soon noised about that we were *norteamericanos*. In line with my consistent attempt in South America not to remain merely a spectator but to observe national customs and share enthusiasms, I decided to take part in the cueca. This was an error of judgment, because not only did I know nothing of the dance save what I had observed in the last half-hour, but I had also entirely failed to appreciate some of the ceremonial niceties connected with the performance. Thus, my appearance on the dance floor and my selection of a charming country girl as my partner at first aroused great enthusiasm among the spectators. This was soon followed, however, by an embarrassing silence, particularly on the part of the musicians. It finally occurred to me that buying a drink might ease the tension. A motion of the hand was sufficient, and I was promptly provided with a quart-size glass of grape chicha. I immediately handed it to my partner, and the applause indicated this was the proper gesture. I expected, of course, that another glass would then be provided for my consumption—but not at all. My partner, after having taken a generous drink, handed the glass back and I discovered that I was supposed to drink, from the original glass, with all present, while an attendant stationed at my elbow refilled the glass as often as required. Apparently the North American custom of passing along the word that somebody is "buying" also exists in Chile. At any rate, in a few moments I was faced with the probability of having to share the glass with an increasing number of Chilean agriculturists. Hygienic inhibitions soon became so strong that I ignominiously retired, after providing sufficient funds for the entertainment of the entire company.

Our party of scientists had, as I have said, made headquarters in one of the picnic booths. After my unfortunate experience with the cueca I returned to this booth to find that the party was preparing to eat luncheon. A rather strong wine punch made its appearance first, and full glasses were served all around; but having just come from the consumption of a considerable amount of alcohol, my enthusiasm for more was much reduced. While I was being rallied on my meager capacity a messenger arrived with an invitation for Florence and myself to be guests of the patrón of the hacienda at a special luncheon. At first we declined, since we were already guests of the scientific group. They, however, urged us to accept and we did so.

The patrón was a man of about thirty years, good-looking and charming. He was dressed in the height of huaso fashion, including tight-fitting trousers, covered from shoes to knees with heavy leather leggings. Under a short black velvet jacket he wore a white silk shirt, and over the jacket a small, bright poncho made of finely woven soft wool on which large roses were embroidered in silk. We were subsequently told that such a poncho was probably a valuable heirloom. His hat was the typical broad-brimmed, low-crowned felt affair, decorated with a brilliant hatband from which extended strands of wool tipped with colored woolen balls, reminiscent of an Andalusian type of headgear.

He told us that he had seen our pictures in the Santiago papers and when our scientific party arrived had immediately identified us among the Chileans. After we were introduced to the other guests the whole group began to wander off to a near-by grove of trees where a large luncheon table had been spread.

From the character of the decorations and table service I saw that this was not a picnic but, rather, a decidedly formal luncheon, even though most of the ranch owners and some of the city guests were dressed in huaso costume. At each place were bottles of both white and red wine, and no invitation was necessary to start it flowing as the first course. Thereafter came a series of courses, the principal one being a choice of barbecued beef, sheep, or young goat. All the men knew each other quite intimately but they vied with one another in trying to make us feel a part of the occasion. They explained the intricacies of a Chilean *asado*—the barbecuing of meat, and repeatedly asked for an expression of our reactions—hopefully pleasant, of course —to Chile and its inhabitants. Many toasts were drunk, including one to the United States and another to the success of our Chilean plant hunting.

Indeed our healths were proposed so repeatedly that finally we hesitated to raise our eyes for fear of catching those of someone across the table who would immediately propose a health. In a weak and thoughtless moment I referred to the various ceremonies connected with the drinking of a "skoal" in Sweden. I was then called upon to stand and demonstrate the ceremony—eye to eye, glass up to the third vest button, drink, glass down to the fourth vest button, and so on. Before I knew it I found that I was being asked to carry on an individual demonstration with most of the others present.

When the last health had been drunk we left the table and proceeded to the rodeo. A circle of level ground about an acre in extent had been surrounded with a barrier made of eight-foot uprights heavily surfaced inside with saplings and brush. A small segment was similarly walled off with openings left at either end of the wall to give access into the larger area. Within this segment twenty or thirty lively calves had been driven. For the patrón and his guests there was a small, high grandstand behind the calf corral, and across from us, on the far side of the circular rodeo field, was another, larger grandstand for the country-people.

When the patrón and his guests were seated, the mounted huasos who were to take part in the rodeo arranged themselves in a line in front of us and acknowledged the patrón's presence by removing their hats and bowing. Then they lined up with their horses backed against the outer side of the calf corral. At a signal from the patrón the rodeo began. Two huasos left the line, saluted, rode into the corral, forced their way among the noisily protesting calves, and proceeded to "cut out" the animal of their choice. When they had succeeded in forcing him to one of the exits from the corral the excitement began. The calf promptly attempted to break away into the arena, whereas the huasos had something quite different in mind. They proposed to drive the calf three times back and forth along the circular barrier without permitting him to escape them, the performance being carried on at top speed. While one huaso began to drive the calf with whip and yells, the other member of the team rode at the calf's shoulder and attempted to keep the animal running continuously beside the barrier. Just before the calf reached a point in front of our grandstand he had to be turned about and started back in the opposite direction. This job fell primarily to the huaso who had been riding beside the calf. Putting on a burst of speed he advanced a half-length ahead of the calf and, turning his horse sharply at right angles, rode head on into the barrier. This immediately checked the forward progress of the calf which, if wise, turned directly about and began to retrace his steps. Thereupon the huasos reversed positions: the one who had been riding at the calf's shoulder now pursued the calf and the other one took the shoulder position. Just before reaching the calf corral they engineered another about-face and so reversed their positions again. When they had successfully repeated this performance three times the calf was permitted to escape through an opening just beneath our grandstand. The two huasos then returned to their positions in the line and were greeted with groans or cheers, depending upon whether or not the calf had escaped them for a moment or two or whether they had or had not successfully demonstrated certain refinements in the correct technique, which we were unable to appreciate. With varying fortunes all the other huasos, in teams of two, carried out a similar performance.

For the spectator the excitement was almost continuous and for the huasos it must have been a strenuous hour and a half. The calves were big, tough, fast, and very fractious, and knew their own minds from start to finish of each round. Obviously it needed much practice, as well as a special timing and perfect coördination between horse and rider, to turn the calf without letting him get away. Most of the huasos in the rodeo were older men, large and powerful, and, in some instances, seemingly too heavy for the horses they rode. The best strains of Chilean horses have a certain amount of Arabian blood and appear to be rather light in the legs. One particularly large cowboy, when he drove his horse into the barrier, must have put too much weight on its front legs; at any rate, the horse stumbled and the rider was thrown. He got up almost at once, caught his horse, mounted it, and completed the sequence of three turns back and forth. We noted, however, that he did not return to his place in the line, and we learned afterwards that he had broken his hip in the fall. How he managed to mount his horse and carry on is hard to understand. When the rodeo was over prizes were distributed, with much enthusiastic comment from the persons seated in both grandstands.

For those of us who have, over the years, worked in Chile, Santiago, the republic's capital, has frequently been headquarters for weeks at a time. It is a much larger city than Valparaiso, and has most of the best hotels and shops in Chile. The foothills of the Andes begin to rise rapidly behind Santiago, which lies at an altitude of a little over fifteen hundred feet. In the wintertime these first ridges of the Andes, as well as the far higher, serrated backbone of the continent on the horizon, are snow-covered; and in summer when the snow is gone from the lower ridges you can sometimes see behind them the great range, covered with perpetual snow, standing out sharp and clear. After living a while in Santiago the visitor almost unconsciously glances up each eastward-running street to catch a glimpse of the city's tremendous, snow-capped Andean backdrop.

Today, Santiago has a considerable tourist appeal, in part because there are now a number of rather superior hotels and one which would rank high anywhere in appointments and service. On the uppermost of its many floors there is a terrace restaurant surrounding a swimming pool below which is spread a rather breath-taking panorama of the city, the extensive valley in which it lies, and the magnificent cordillera to the east. Years ago, some of us stopped in one of the city's much less pretentious hostelries. Our room faced one of the main streets, not wide, along which flowed a continuous stream of traffic and on which one-way streetcars were constantly running. The noise was pretty bad, but we managed to adjust ourselves to it except when it continued far into the night.

A considerable proportion of the Chilean population is much addicted to gambling—in lotteries and otherwise. Late at night when

other, more spohisticated opportunities for wagering failed, the die-
hard remnants of the sporting fraternity gathered to bet on streetcar
numbers. Four or five car lines originated on our street, later to branch
out into other parts of the city and suburbs. Thus a sequence of different numbers might be expected to appear. This desirable condition
of affairs plus proximity of the hotel bar resulted in a gathering every
few nights on the sidewalk beneath our windows. From ten to twenty
men would assemble, place their bets in rather loud voices, and then
in noisy anticipation listen for the approach of a streetcar. As soon as
it was spotted, the number would be shouted out by the keenest sighted.
A great uproar followed as the winners congratulated each other vo-
ciferously and the losers very audibly commiserated with one another.
At first there was a certain novelty about this performance and we
would hang out of our windows to follow the course of the betting.
The novelty rapidly wore off as need of sleep asserted itself. We therefore provided a pitcher of water on the window sill and when once
well awakened proceeded to pour it over the assembled gamblers. This
treatment was temporarily effective and was accepted quite good-
naturedly by those below. I felt constantly worried, however, because
in the rather dim light it was difficult to determine whether or not a
policeman was among the group. If this ever occurred he must have
accepted our technique of noise abatement as good-naturedly as the
gamblers, for we never received any official reaction. However, nothing permanent was accomplished by the sprinkling method. Within a
few days much the same group, to judge by their voices, once more
took up headquarters underneath our window.

Many of my days in Santiago have been spent at work in the Museo
de Historia Natural, which is to be found in the Quinta Normal, a park
about a mile from the center of the city. Long ago, Dr. Philippi during his extensive term as Director of the Museum planted around it
an interesting and unusual collection of trees and shrubs. Many of
the species became well established and grew rapidly in the exceptionally favorable climate of Santiago. Although the park is now
somewhat abandoned as a botanical garden, a considerable number of
fine, mature specimens of native and introduced trees are still preserved.

I worked in the rooms in which the collections of dried plants are
housed. These collections have great importance for the students of
floras of the Andes and the Chilean coast, particularly because preserved in them are the original plants which Philippi collected during

his numerous extended journeys throughout Chile. Many of his plants had previously been unknown, and he gave them names and described them. Subsequently, other botanists collected in the same areas where Philippi had made his collections and oftentimes, as we did, chanced upon many of the plants which Philippi first named. Usually his published descriptions of new species are sufficiently detailed so that other botanists have been able to identify the plants they collected as equivalent to his. But sometimes there is considerable doubt, and then it is important to be able to see the actual dried specimen which Philippi named, called the "type" specimen. This was particularly important for me, because Philippi collected and described many species of *Nicotiana*, and I have been able to see the original specimens in every case. At the request of botanists in the United States and elsewhere I examined and reported upon his type specimens in genera other than *Nicotiana*. In the case of the Nicotianas and some of their relatives— *Petunia, Salpiglossis, Nierembergia,* and *Fabiana*—I found that many of the questions I had asked myself about the species Philippi had described were answered.

When I first knew the plant collections in the Museo they were in a somewhat deplorable condition, due primarily to their unmounted condition—the plant specimens loose in paper folders, rather than permanently affixed to light but strong sheets. Oftentimes plants of a number of different species had been placed in the same cover and the little labels, with the names and the collecting data that Philippi and others had attached to each specimen, had fallen off. Sometimes it was easy to determine to which particular plant in the folder a given label should be returned and sometimes it was not.

In Chile during the war years, I succeeded in doing something about the situation. Properly to preserve the thousands of specimens a large supply of mounting paper and a considerable crew of mounters would be required. This would be only a preliminary; then a trained botanist would have to attack the major problem of matching labels to specimens and reorganizing the entire collection. The fact that exactly the right botanist, Dr. Carlos Muñoz—today the leading authority on Chilean floras and long associated with the plant collections of the Museo—was available made it eminently worth while to attempt to arrange the preliminary.

It was apparent at once that a government appropriation for purchase of paper would not be forthcoming. I then appealed to Washington to secure the paper and ship it to Santiago, gratis. The appeal was made through a group of North American businessmen resident in Santiago who were in a position to recommend to the Department of State the disposition of certain funds allocated to Chile. Thereupon, the wheels of Washington bureaucracy began to turn in a favorable direction, but slowly. Somehow, word of what was in progress reached the ears of the leading Chilean paper manufacturers. They immediately informed us that they could produce as good a quality of mounting paper as could be obtained in the United States and that they would willingly donate the necessary supply to the Museo. This generous gesture, inspired by local pride, stimulated the Chilean government to agree to hire the mounters. Long since, the mounting of the most scientifically important portion of the collections has been completed, and today, through the effective and sustained efforts of Dr. Muñoz, the herbarium is in excellent condition, correctly named and organized, to the great benefit of local and foreign botanists.

I have inserted this now historical note because it illustrates one method, if the approach is correct, of assisting our South American neighbors. Thus, the problem of preserving one of their most valuable scientific collections was entirely solved by the Chileans themselves once it became apparent that we believed in its importance and were prepared, in part, to finance its solution. This was, of course, a minor problem and there always have been and there will continue for many years to be numerous major problems to be met in South America. Undoubtedly, it will be necessary that we—alone, or together with international agencies within the free world—underwrite or share with South American republics the cost of major projects clearly essential for economic development leading to the attainment of some measure, at least, of the freedom from want which we, as a nation, are privileged to enjoy. Although I have evidence that makes me critical of the organization and implementation of certain types of foreign aid in South America, I have equally good evidence that, over all, it is paying ever larger dividends toward strengthening of the ties that bind free peoples together. For one example, why, otherwise, should the Communists who are dedicated to breaking these ties and destroying individual freedom be constantly more aggressive in their subversive activities in the other America?

During my early periods of study in Santiago the late Ricardo Latcham was Director of the Museo. He was primarily an archaeologist. On display were remarkably complete evidences of the life and culture of the ancient peoples who buried their dead in the coastal deserts of North Chile. I was especially interested in the corn that Don Ricardo had found there in twelfth-century burials. Remarkably enough, it consisted largely of a variety of popcorn. Those pre-Inca inhabitants of Chile who grew it must, doubtless entirely by chance, have learned that application of heat caused the kernels of this kind of corn to explode and become transformed into delicate white material. They must have highly esteemed this popped corn, or it must have had ceremonial significance for them, because Don Ricardo often found little bowls or cotton bags filled with it beside the mummified bodies. Some of the ears, midget ones with every kernel in place, were also found in the graves. Don Ricardo was good enough to give me a fine one, along with a few pieces of the popped corn.

One evening, at home in Berkeley, it occurred to me to try an experiment with my kernels of pre-Inca popcorn. I placed a few on a pie tin and heated them on the electric stove. Much to my surprise, that corn which had been gathered nearly a thousand years ago popped as readily as did last year's crop that had come in a box from the shelves of the neighborhood cash-and-carry store. Today a tin pie-plate on an electric stove; yesterday the campfire or primitive hearth and a flat stone or clay bowl. I thought I could catch a glimpse of those faces dimly seen in the flickering light of that fire which burned so long ago—the strong features, the high cheekbones; and in the shadows I thought I saw the long, brilliantly embroidered robes of cotton, the bright scarves of llama wool, the feathered headdresses, and the golden breastplates.

Later, I put the ear of ancient popcorn in one of the Inca bowls that adorned our Berkeley living-room table. I exhibited it along with other South American antiquities and recited to my friends the little story of where it had been found. As friends always do under such circumstances, mine took a courteous if not too sustained or intelligent interest in the little ear of corn. They did, however, feel impelled to test the firmness with which the kernels were fixed upon the cob. I soon discovered that there were more kernels off than on it, and promptly withdrew the corn from exhibit.

One morning I took the newly popped corn to my eight o'clock class at the University. The lecture was supposed to be concerned with something quite apart from Chilean antiquities, but I found a spot at

which my corn-popping experiment could be dragged in and its result displayed. At the end of the lecture a number of those students
who are always willing to humor the vagaries and enthusiasms of the
professor gathered round the lecture desk to examine my popped
corn. One asked permission to sample a few kernels. Since this appeared
to be a natural request and one that might sustain interest for a longer
period, I agreed. The rest of the students came closer and watched
the mastication with interest. At first, the experiment seemed to be
going well when, without warning, a horrified expression appeared
upon the face of the experimenter; he violently expelled as much of
the popcorn as he had not already swallowed, and showed signs of
desiring to be rid of all of it. It suddenly occurred to me that since the
corn had originally been in a museum it might have been impregnated
there with poison to discourage insect attack. Fortunately, however,
the unpleasant outcome of the student's scientific curiosity was due
to nothing more serious than camphor with which, as I somewhat
tardily recollected, the ear of corn had been sprinkled before shipment
to California. During the remainder of the semester I sensed a certain
reserve in the camphorated student's personal attitude toward me,
and it came into my mind that he actually thought that I had per-
petrated a practical joke.

Dr. Gaulterio Looser is one of the best-known, nonprofessional
botanists in Chile. For many years he has collected South American
plants, of which he has a large and valuable herbarium. He has always
generously shared with us many of his duplicate specimens and given
us advice about collecting areas and the seasons during which they
could be most profitably visited, and more than once has gone into
the field with one or another of us.

One hot day early in December, Looser and I made a collecting trip
into the dry, hilly, plateau country that lies a little northwest of Santiago. I wanted to find out whether the subalpine species of *Nicotiana*
came down from the foothills of the Andes east of Santiago into this
lower altitude, and also whether the coastal species so often found
near Valparaiso extended their distribution any great distance eastward. In Central Chile, except in the mountains, where, of course, it
is considerably later, the height of the blooming period of native plants
occurs during October in a normal year. The rain, which falls only
during the southern winter—from April or May to September or
October—rarely amounts to a total of more than fifteen inches each

year, and in dry years rainfall may be reduced to only seven or eight inches. This happened to be the second of two dry years, and as a result the countryside in which we were botanizing showed few plants in flower.

In Central Chile I am continually reminded of California, and that day I could easily have imagined that I had been suddenly transferred to the foothills of the California Sierra in summer. I saw the same intensely brilliant, vivid blue sky. There was the same brittle quality in the atmosphere, the same warm, brown mantle spread over hills and valleys and plains—a mantle striped in the same fashion with thin bands of green to show where declining streams or deep-shaded canyons alone supported a vigorous growth of trees and shrubs.

The region we were in was familiar ground to Looser where he was certain that some years before he had seen plants of the Nicotianas that I sought. At first we tramped along rough country roads leading through broad valleys. Then we began to follow cattle paths out into the uncultivated, hilly countryside. In the bottoms of deeper valleys and along the lower contours of southward-facing slopes we saw clear evidence that an herbaceous spring vegetation had been in bloom a month or two before. Now the plants were dead and dry, but their rapid desiccation and the lack of rain since their blooming had preserved them in remarkably lifelike condition—ghosts of their former splendor so perfectly intact that often it was possible to identify them long after death.

On this mummified vegetation there was an abundance of mature fruits, and Looser and I filled many envelopes with seed of some of the handsome Chilean plants which in early October are in full flower nearer Valparaiso. It was easy in imagination to transform the brown landscape into its spring background of green, on which would be painted sky-blue fields of the Chilean lily called "glory of the sun"— sky-blue fields that would be rimmed and veined with the rich dark-blue of *Conanthera* and, in the lush valleys, with a mist of delicate lavender *Godetia*.

From time to time, bulbs of *Leucocoryne—ixioides* and other unnamed species of the genus, all of which are called "glory of the sun" —have been introduced into cultivation. A good many years ago, Clarence Elliot, the English plant hunter and horticulturist, dug large numbers of *Leucocoryne* bulbs from the hillsides of Central Chile and grew them in his Thames Valley nursery. Since that time the average wild plant of *Leucocoryne* has been greatly improved by repeated selection for vigor, flower size, and flower color. For me, these improved strains have never had the charm that their wild relatives possess. I have seen them growing close together and blooming by the hundreds, perhaps thousands, in more than one part of the Vale of Paradise, and a single glance revealed a wide range of variation in all plant characters, but particularly in flower color. Beginning with pure white or cream, there was a graded series of soft, pastel lavenders and blues which culminated in the brilliant, hard sky-blue which is the horticulturally popular but to me least attractive shade for *Leucocoryne*.

The dusty heat did not seem to bother Looser, but it bothered me considerably. Finally I asked for a respite and we decided to stop and eat an early lunch. It was not easy to find a shady spot, since the hillsides in the more mountainous and more arid country we had begun to traverse were covered with nothing but columnar cacti, while the valley bottoms were overgrown with tangles of spiny shrubs, among which I recognized species of *Acacia, Adesmia,* and *Proustia.* We therefore struck off to the west toward a stream which, true to Looser's promise, we found on the other side of a ridge. Although it had long since completely dried up, its sandy bed was bordered by a few small trees.

I picked out the shade of the first of these trees and was on the point of settling down beneath it when Looser warned me off. He explained that my tree selection was the much feared *litre (Lithraea caustica),* from contact with which many people receive a quite serious dermatitis. It belongs to the Anacardiaceae, a plant family of which our poison ivy (*Rhus toxicodendron*) of the Eastern States and Middle West and the equally dangerous poison oak (*Rhus diversiloba*) of the Pacific Coast are also members.

Farther down the dry wash we found shade under *Peumus boldus.* When well grown, this treelike Chilean shrub is attractive, with its deep, compact crown. The dark-green leaves resemble in shape those of the California live oak and, when crushed, emit a pleasant, spicy fragrance. In Chilean homes one may be offered a choice of after-dinner beverages—coffee or *boldo,* the latter a cup of boiling water in which a dried leaf or two of *Peumus boldus* is steeping, sometimes with a smaller leaf of "lemon verbena" added. I usually choose *boldo* because it is remarkably refreshing and sleeplessness does not lie in its cup.

As we consumed the contents of our knapsacks, conversation turned to the remarkable occurrence in north central Chile of a few small, isolated areas in which grow many of the plants otherwise found only far to the south where the climatic conditions are entirely different. The most famous of these vegetational "islands," which we later visited, is the so-called "forest" of Fray Jorge which, like a green oasis, lies surrounded by the semidesert of the north-central coast, some three hundred miles above Valparaiso.

The vegetation of that region is not abundant, and the low growth-form and the compact structure of the plants that compose it show an obvious adaptation to drought conditions. It is, therefore, more than a surprise to find in the midst of such a vegetation a small forest made up of fairly sizable trees, with numerous ferns on the forest floor, and vines connecting it and the tree crowns above. Even more startling is the fact that almost all the elements of this out-of-place forest belong to southern Chile, where they grow in abundance in a uniformly cool, wet climate. For example, at Fray Jorge you find such typically South Chilean plants as *Aextoxicon punctatum*, a tree of the Euphorbiaceae, or Milkweed family, *Mitraria coccinea* and *Sarmienta repens*, two beautiful vines, and even *Nertera depressa*, the "bead plant."

We fell to wondering how these vegetational "islands" came into existence. One explanation might be that in past time the climate of southern Chile, with its heavier rainfall and lower temperatures, must also have been the climate of middle and, at least in part, northern Chile, which today is so dry and warm. Moreover, the fact that the Fray Jorge plants are identical—species for species—with those which today grow farther south means that from a geological standpoint the change in central and northern Chile from a cool, wet climate to a warm, dry one must have occurred relatively recently. We reasoned this out in the following way. Suppose such a distinct climatic alteration had taken place at an early period in the earth history of that part of the west coast of South America which we today refer to as central and north central Chile. Then, evolutionary processes, which are always at work everywhere, would certainly, during the long interim, have produced visible changes in the form and structure of those groups of plants that survived the climatic alteration in the environment. But today the relics, like the forest at Fray Jorge, of the vegetation which we assume to have once covered central and north central Chile show no such distinction in form and structure—no adaptation to their present warm, dry surroundings—when compared with the same species in the south. It seems fair, therefore, to say that the climatic alteration that took place up the Chilean coast occurred too short a time ago to permit evolutionary processes to do their work. . . . It was, however, too hot a day to prolong this somewhat academic discussion, and Looser and I soon replaced it with a siesta, to which in Latin America the hour following luncheon is universally dedicated.

Toward the end of our discussion and just before the siesta, my attention wandered to a group of plants growing on the opposite side of the dry stream. As from a distance I had suspected, they later proved to be plants of *Nicotiana acuminata*, the coastal species, and precisely what we had been looking for all the morning. Growing in almost pure sand on the banks and in the dry bed of the stream, the Chilean habitat of these tobacco relatives corresponded to that of the places near the coasts of California and Washington where this typically Chilean species is now and then to be found. The seeds of the tobacco plant and its relatives are extremely small and light, and have rough, catching surfaces. Lodged in and under the feathers of some of the birds that annually make the tremendous round trip from almost the northern to almost the southern extremity of the western edge of the two Americas, the seeds of *Nicotiana acuminata* have been carried to the Pacific coast of North America. Probably you can still find, as I did long ago, this Chilean *Nicotiana* growing in small quantity but quite happily in the dry, sandy summer bed of Niles Creek, which empties into the southern end of San Francisco Bay. I found it, also, north of San Francisco, again in dry, sandy soil, on the banks of the Napa River. Others have collected it near the mouth of the Columbia.

On the Australian continent there are a number of native species of *Nicotiana*, each of which has a somewhat distinct geographical center of distribution. The early plant hunters found these different Nicotianas only in or near these centers of distribution. Today, however, some of the species have spread considerably beyond their original domains and have intermingled extensively. As already mentioned, this recent plant migration undoubtedly took place during the period when the cattle industry was beginning to assume importance in parts of Australia and when herds were driven across country for great distances in search of pasturage or to market. On the rough, shaggy coats of the cattle the small, clinging seeds of trailside plants of *Nicoti-*

ana were caught and then were transferred from their original habitats to others far distant; and there, now and then at least, they fell on fertile soil and, if the climate was favorable, grew and even flourished.

Man has consciously, and for a variety of good reasons, shifted plants back and forth from one part of the globe to another, but some of his plant introductions have been entirely unconscious ones. In ancient times and down to recent days, ships were ballasted with rocks, rubble, and soil gathered up on the shores of those distant harbors where their cargoes were discharged. When in some other port another cargo was found, the sailors threw the ballast out to add to the debris accumulated near the dockside. With each exchange of ballast between the ports of the world went seeds of a variety of plants. Many were cosmopolitan weeds of ancient lineage, but some were hardy representatives of a local flora; and all of them that could survive in any of the climates to which they had been given free transportation grew and bloomed and shed their seed on the ballast heaps. As such "ballast weeds," a number of South American *Nicotiana* species have appeared in various warm-temperate portions of the world; and often they have extended themselves far beyond the port to which they were originally brought.

The most widely traveled or at least the most climatically adaptable of South American Nicotianas is a species called *glauca*. This species is referred to as "yellow tree tobacco" in California, where it has so long become naturalized along highways near the coast that present-day Californians, who sometimes grow the plant in their gardens, consider it a part of the native vegetation. On the lower west coast of Mexico it probably arrived somewhat later; but at any rate it has found conditions so much to its liking that it has taken over considerable tracts of land and is looked upon as a most undesirable visitor. In parts of Australia it has gained a substantial foothold, and a reward is now offered for its destruction on the ground that it is poisonous to stock. It has been collected on all but the most tropical coasts of South America, in the Canary and Cape Verde Islands, and in Egypt, and doubtless can be found growing in other regions equally distant from its Argentine home. For, despite local claims upon it as a native plant elsewhere, *Nicotiana glauca* for many centuries lived only in the foothills of the Andes in northwestern Argentina; and it was man who carried it with him to the sea and thence in his ships to the wide world.

Speaking of *glauca*, I once heard that there was a red-flowered variety, as contrasted with the common yellow-flowered one, very rarely seen in northwestern Argentina. I did not believe it but the Prince found the red variety, and in seed, just about where it had been said to be growing in the foothills of the Argentine Andes. Its flowers vary somewhat in intensity of color and its growth habit is also variable. After a good many years of selection I have a race which is bushy, with dark-maroon flowers. Perhaps California seedsmen may become interested in it as a garden subject.

Looser and I followed a different route on our return journey. Along it we slowed down to watch an amusing affair which doubtless is being continuously repeated wherever in Chile, and Peru also, goats and the tall columnar cacti of the Cereus group are living in the same region. Goats, by the way, came to the west coast of South America with the conquistadors and during the intervening four hundred years have destroyed a lot of native vegetation. In places where they are pastured—and in how few they are not—the plant hunter despairs of arriving early enough in the spring or getting up early enough in the morning to anticipate the goats which nibble every green thing down to the very level of the soil. As a result, at the end of the summer season there is a very limited supply even of dry forage. The goats then proceed to eat cacti and especially the somewhat less well-armed bromeliads, except those species whose spines are long and tough enough to penetrate horny hoofs and leathery mouths.

On the barren hillsides which we were crossing, thousands of tall cerii—slender, fluted, dark-green, spiny columns—were coming into bloom. These majestic cacti, giant candelabra, were often fifteen feet high and a foot in diameter at the base. The long yellow-green buds and large white flowers were borne at intervals up the leafless trunks and opened in sequence, beginning a few feet up from the ground.

On a steep slope a small herd of goats wandered in seemingly aimless fashion through this scattered forest of green columns. After watching them for a while I realized that there was a definite purpose behind this wandering, because whenever a goat passed one of the tall cacti he cocked an eye upward. The goats were methodically examining every plant to determine whether there were any buds or flowers within the limit of their maximum capacity to stretch upward. Finally an old ram decided that he could reach the lowermost of a series of fine fresh flowers high up on the side of a big cactus which, unfortunately for him, happened to be growing on one of the steepest parts of the hillside. From long practice he thoroughly understood the technique required. Stationing himself as near as he could to the base of the plant he settled his hind hoofs into the soil and sprang straight upward, to come down with forefeet resting well up on the side of the spiny stem. Then, stretching against the plant, he began to elongate himself. First his hind legs visibly increased in length, then his thin body, finally his neck and head. Again and again he alternately stretched and relaxed, stretched and relaxed, but always the flower was just out of reach of the long, nibbling lips. Without warning, his hind hoofs began to slip and he slid down rapidly, leaving tufts of hair from his belly and the inner surfaces of his front legs along the heavily spined ridges of the cactus stem. Without pause the old gentleman returned to the attack, and as long as we had him in view he continued his apparently hopeless effort to secure that tempting bite of soft, succulent plant tissue.

Later on in the afternoon these great cerii gave me something of a shock. After being continually present all day they no longer possessed individuality and had completely merged into the general landscape. Looser and I had now left the hilly country and were following roads that ran through broad valleys. On their rather distant hillsides my eyes picked up unfamiliar dots of color which I certainly did not associate with the tall cacti I knew must be growing there. Soon our road began to wind up a ridge, and as I approached the cacti I realized that something had happened to them. Always before, they had been shafts of continuous green from soil line to apex, but now their tops and sometimes their sides were painted a brilliant scarlet. On closer examination I saw that this added color was provided by the flowers of a species of *Phrygilanthus*, a parasitic plant or nonpaying guest, most of whose body was within the cactus feeding upon the stores of food and moisture conserved therein by its unwilling host.

During the following months I saw this phenomenon again and again. It remained, however, for me one of the most startling and in many ways one of the most attractive elements in the landscape of the Andean foothills: tawny, barren hillsides forested with gigantic cactus candles each one burning with a steady scarlet flame, or ridges dark against the evening sky fretted with black columns whose pointed apices glowed in the sunset light with living fire.

13

ROBINSON CRUSOE'S ISLE

IN NORTH AMERICA most of the dwellers in outlying areas have long since adjusted themselves to the chance naturalist—botanist, zoölogist, or geologist—who pokes about, apparently more or less aimlessly, in their mountains and forests. The mountain man or backwoodsman has learned that these are quite harmless individuals impelled solely by a consuming curiosity about the animate and inanimate elements of his environment. He does not share this curiosity, but he recognizes it as something real and legitimate. In South America, on the other hand, native populations are not familiar with the collector and his somewhat bizarre equipment. Nor are they at all ready to accept his explanation of his presence in parts of their domains which they know contain little of interest for the ordinary tourist. The natural resources of their homelands have for centuries been vigorously exploited by the foreigner; and so, quite naturally, they suspect the scientist from overseas of searching for something of great intrinsic value, presumably gold. That a plant, and often an inconspicuous or undesirable one, can be sought because of its scientific importance is beyond their comprehension. Even the more intelligent interpreted our explanations as indicating that we were professional gatherers of medicinal herbs which would ultimately be exposed for sale somewhere in *Norteamerica*. This inability to understand what we were about, and the certainty that a pot of gold was directly or indirectly buried under each plant we collected, inspired a news item which appeared in a Chilean newspaper and in translation reads as follows:

"On the Juan Fernández Islands grows a variety of the tobacco plant, the rarest plant in all the world. It is worth five thousand dollars and a scientific institution in the United States offers this sum to the man who will present to it a plant of this tobacco."

This statement, which doubtless surprised and interested its Chilean readers, approaches the truth only in one regard—there *is* a wild relative of the cultivated tobacco plant on the Juan Fernández Islands. Concerning its rarity we shall see later on in this chapter that it is a plant exceedingly difficult to find. The fact that I was the "scientific institution" referred to should have automatically discouraged anyone from attempting to collect the reward. Nevertheless, I did want this plant very much, and after an explanation of why I wanted it I shall tell you some of the things that happened when we went in search of it.

Well out in the Pacific, almost due west of Valparaiso, lie the Juan Fernández Islands—Más a Tierra and little Santa Clara side by side and three hundred and sixty-five miles from the mainland, and Más Afuera ninety-two miles farther west. Insular floras are likely to contain plant species peculiar to their island homes, and the Juan Fernández group is remarkable for the large number of such endemics which grow upon them.

In 1854, the then Assistant Director of the Museo de Historia Natural in Santiago made one of the first important collections on the outermost island, Más Afuera. Among many new plant species discovered by this pioneer naturalist was a tobacco relative, later named *Nicotiana cordifolia*. He reported it to be a rather scraggly shrub growing to six feet in height, with large, velvety-white, more or less heart-shaped leaves, and bearing masses of inch-long, reddish-violet, tubular flowers. Although other botanists visited Más Afuera in the interim, it was not until 1891 that this remarkable plant was rediscovered by a Chilean botanist.

In 1908, and also in 1916–1917, the eminent authority on insular floras in the South Pacific, Dr. Carl Skottsberg, then Director of the Botanical Garden in Gothenburg, Sweden, visited Más Afuera and found *N. cordifolia* again. He collected its seed and, remembering my interest in growing all the Nicotianas I could lay my hands on, was good enough to share the seed with me. In the Botanical Garden in Berkeley I succeeded, over thirty years ago, in growing a few plants from this seed. They represented an important addition to my increasing collection of *Nicotiana* species. Through some mischance the remainder of the original seed was lost and, even more unfortunately, I somehow failed to save any seed from the plants we grew. Since *N.*

cordifolia was almost the only important known species of *Nicotiana* which we were not growing in the Botanical Garden in California, I was extremely anxious to secure the seed again.

I asked the "General" to arrange that one of his botanically inclined associates should make a collecting trip for me to the Juan Fernández Islands. As will appear later on, this voyage can be a highly unpleasant adventure. Perhaps for this reason, the General found no one in Valparaiso willing to volunteer his services. The best that he could do was to send a man who was permanently established on Más a Tierra, "Robinson Crusoe's Island," across the ninety and more miles of open ocean in a small fishing boat to Más Afuera in search of *Nicotiana cordifolia*. This friend of the General's went to Más Afuera twice, but on neither trip was he able to find the plant. After the first trip he reported that the wild goats had exterminated it. After the second trip he declared that it must have been the hummingbirds—of all things— that had destroyed it.

I was so certain that *Nicotiana cordifolia* still grew on Más Afuera that I determined, during our second South American expedition, to go myself or arrange for one of our party to go there. Early in February our collecting in northern and central Chile was progressing so successfully that John could be spared for two weeks. He was glad to make the trip because the opportunity for a young botanist to see and collect the famous and relatively little-known vegetation of the Juan Fernández Islands was alluring.

In those days a lobster-fishing company with headquarters in Valparaiso owned two small schooners, the *Iris* and the *Gaviota*, which plied back and forth from the islands during the lobster season from December to March. We made a reservation for John on a February sailing of the *Iris*. This, we thought, would give him a week or ten days on Más Afuera to find the much-desired *Nicotiana* and to increase knowledge of other elements of the flora of this rarely visited island by intensive collecting on its lofty mountainsides and in its deep gorges. I knew that in late December and early January the vegetation on the Juan Fernández Islands is at its best, and that John would be a little late for the wave of flowering there, which passes rapidly. Nevertheless, there would be many plants in good condition, and if *Nicotiana cordifolia* were in seed and not in flower, so much the better, because it was primarily seed I wanted.

How many times, over the years, have we discovered new or little-

known plants of potential scientific or ornamental importance clinging to ocean cliffs, half hidden under rocky outcroppings on foothill
slopes, glowing on high scree or talus slopes, or dyeing shady walls
of deep Andean valleys with warm color—and how often they have
given us only flowers and leaves and stems and colored photographs
to take back to California. How many long, backbreaking, and knee-
wearying hours have we spent going over every plant of these prizes
in the hope of finding a few seeds, so that as living things and not alone
as dead, dried specimens could they be seen at home.

For anything but a sizable vessel the ocean between Valparaiso and
the Juan Fernández Islands constitutes always a trial and often a menace. The little *Iris* on the homeward voyage before John's scheduled
outbound one was badly buffeted by a storm. Sails were torn, masts
were loosened, and running gear was damaged. Quick repairs were
promised, but day after day went by, each one filled with renewed
promises. Finally, sailing day arrived.

After agreeing on the inevitable last-minute decisions concerning
what should be discarded from the assembled collecting equipment,
John and I went down to the quay with the still large accumulation of
plant presses, duffel bags, and cameras. The uncertain light of an early
Valparaiso evening made our descent of the barnacle-incrusted stone
steps to the waiting skiff a dangerous operation, but at last we and
the luggage were loaded. Since the *Iris* was supposed to sail that night
she had been anchored well out in the stream, and the oarsman had a
long pull through the crowded harbor where, from almost water level,
the ships and lighters, larger and smaller, loomed enormous in the half-
light. We were, therefore, the more unprepared for the diminutive
size of the *Iris*, and when our skiff approached her we felt certain that
our oarsman had made a mistake. It was by all odds the smallest of
the seagoing vessels in the harbor, and my heart sank when I realized
that John was going to entrust himself to her on a voyage so long
and dangerous. Could I have foreseen all that was in store for him
I would have ordered the oarsman to return us both *pronto* to the safety
of the Valparaiso quay.

Covered with luggage, we struggled up the side and tumbled onto
the deck just at a point where steel water-barrels were being hauled
aboard. A glance around the deck made it immediately apparent that
the *Iris* was not going to sail for a considerable number of hours. Car-
penters were still at work, but not too busily, and a halfhearted effort

was being made to complete the repair of one of the sails that had been torn in the storm. The aft deckhouse, which housed both officers and passengers, was in a state of extraordinary but quite typical confusion. In addition to John the passengers consisted of two families, one a mother with three small children and the second a mother and grown son. The total space available for the captain, the engineer and his assistant, and these six passengers was hardly equal to that of a good-sized cabin-and-a-half on a transatlantic liner.

The deckhouse was divided into small cabins for the officers and three cubbyholes for the passengers. Of the latter, one was apparently for John since it had a single bunk. A second was filled with ship's stores—dried meat, barrels of flour, dried vegetables, and so on. A third, about as wide as an ordinary writing table, with narrow upper and lower bunks, was to be occupied above by the mother and son and below by the mother and the three small children.

The *Iris* finally pulled out of the harbor at about one-thirty in the morning, propelled toward the open sea by her all-too-small diesel engine. Immediately she ran into a severe head wind and a high sea that had been lying in wait for the one-hundred-ton schooner. John never had much to say about what happened to the vessel and to him during the next sixty hours, but his diary contained the story:

"The little schooner had a most amazing spiral, gyrating motion which was absolutely devastating to one who had been to sea only on sizable craft and usually in fair weather. On an approximately even keel, the ship would rise like an elevator on the long steep slope of a great wave and when the crest was reached would lunge downward with the deck listing sharply to starboard. When the next crest was attained we took a correspondingly abrupt list to port. Soon I lost track of the seconds of comparative calm, and the sequence of listings, first to one side and then to the other, seemed to merge into a continuity of horrible, jolting lurches. I lay flat on my back without even a pillow to break the horizontal line of contact with the bunk. Probably I dozed a little. Gradually a vague grayness penetrated the dirty little porthole above my head and I began to hope that the dawn would bring some respite; but as the morning hours dragged along I realized that the sea was still rising. The pitching and tossing of the schooner became so incredible and unbearable that I rose a little on my elbows to turn over and attempt to find a more comfortable position, one which would protect me somewhat more from being thrown out of my bunk. Even as little movement as this was disastrous and immediately I was disgustingly sick.

"With the dawn of the second day I gathered a little courage, attempted to sit up, drink a glass of water, and eat a few raisins. The result was immediately forthcoming and doubly painful, but at least I had the doubtful satisfaction of knowing that I had made a noble experiment. Late in the afternoon, after forty hours almost continuously in my bunk, the dirty and inefficient but quite sympathetic steward brought a mug of tea. It was unexpectedly hot and gave me the momentary strength to climb out of my bunk and try to stand erect. At that very instant the poor *Iris* began to take aboard even heavier seas and the decks no sooner achieved the greatest possible slant to starboard than the vessel gyrated wildly and plunged to port. My bunk was the only comfortable place, really the only reasonably safe place, and once in it I could cover my head and shut out, in part at least, the horrible sounds emanating from the other seasick passengers.

"During the succeeding night the sea became a little calmer. By morning I gathered the necessary strength and fortitude to go out into the cabin for breakfast. The table was so small that only three chairs could simultaneously be drawn up to it, but I had no competition from the other passengers, who apparently proposed to stay in their bunks until we reached land. After eating something I decided to lie down, but after a few hours I roused up and went on deck. The storm was blowing itself out and the horizon was beginning to clear. To the west I saw a misty silhouette which one of the sailors told me was Más a Tierra. All the rest of that day we had the island in view but our few knots per hour made this part of the voyage exasperatingly slow. Late in the afternoon I was able to make out some details of the geography of the island and could identify Cumberland Bay, which was to be our anchorage, and the lofty hillsides behind it."

From a distance on the sea Más a Tierra, the "Nearer Land," is an isolated, serrated mountain range rising clean and sharp from the Pacific, whose giant rollers ever surround it with first higher and then lower ranks of foothills. In its lee the eye travels almost vertically upward to the cloudy, three-thousand-foot apex of El Yunque ("The Anvil"), and from deep notches on either flank of this highest peak rise lesser eminences—to the one side El Pico Central and to the other La Damajuana ("The Demijohn"). Más a Tierra, although possessing a land surface of only about twenty-two square miles, consists of a complex mountain system that centers in El Yunque. From there two ranges branch out, one extending to the east and one to the north. At its extremity the latter is uplifted to form El Cerro Alto before it ends precipitously on the north flank of the island, while from one face a third range extends toward the southwest. Within this complex of ridges and peaks, El Yunque dominates. A ponderous block of stone, a lofty sentinel facing alone the high-swirling, down-racing, gray-white cloud masses, the sight of it for more than three hundred years cheered the heart of the mariner on his approach to that verdant isle, toward which his thoughts had been at full stretch since first he hazarded the dread passage of Cape Horn.

The Juan Fernández Islands are volcanic in origin and no sedimentary rocks are found. The layering seen in the sea cliffs and steepest mountain slopes, which so strikingly simulates a series of sedimentary accumulations, represents the result of an alternation between compact lava residues and looser, lighter volcanic materials. This horizontal layering is conspicuous from the sea on the north side of Más a Tierra, where the bluffs that rise straight up from the water show in addition innumerable vertical dikes of lava which cut across the layers and represent intrusions of the former after the latter had been laid down.

Discovered in 1563 by the Spanish sea captain whose name they bear, the Juan Fernández Islands, and almost exclusively Más a Tierra, served the early merchantmen from the Old World, but especially pirates, privateers, and the navies of the great powers, as havens of refuge in the southeast Pacific or as a base for nefarious or semilegitimate naval operations. Sufficiently far out to escape the coastwise prowl of Spanish men-of-war, Más a Tierra offered temporary sanctuary in addition to a well-established rendezvous for convoys on one route from Europe to the "Isles of Spice." Moreover, from their isolation the fast-sailing buccaneer might overhaul the treasure ships hurrying toward Spain from Panama, Peru, and the Philippines. Possessing a relatively commodious and protected anchorage, they also offered at all seasons abundant stores of fresh water and supported a luxuriant vegetation for "wooding and watering" and the refreshment of scurvy-ravaged crews. Here, too, the crews had a chance to replace "salt horse" with fish and lobsters readily taken from the reefs and shores and, finally, with great herds of wild goats to be killed and salted down over against the months of voyage still ahead. It is small wonder that as long as sailors sailed, Más a Tierra was much in their thoughts and mouths.

On a morning in October of the year 1704, the *Cinque Ports* galley, part of a small British squadron operating in the South Seas, rode peacefully at anchor off Más a Tierra. Aboard the *Cinque Ports* all was not peaceful. For months the Scotch sailing master, Alexander Selkirk, had been at odds with his superior, Captain Stradling, and that morning an open quarrel broke out between them. In the heat of it Selkirk demanded to be set ashore on the then uninhabited island in the lee of which they lay at anchor. His anger cooled and he bitterly regretted his demand when he found that it was about to be complied with. Nevertheless, he was put on the beach at the point which is today called Cumberland Bay. Beside him on the sand lay only "his clothes, bedding, a firelock, one pound of powder, a hatchet, cooking utensils, some tobacco and his books." Doubtless the twenty-eight-year-old Scotsman, and certainly Captain Stradling, who had taken such cruel advantage of a word spoken in the heat of argument to rid the *Cinque Ports* of a shipmate he disliked, believed that before many weeks, or months at most, another British ship would chance to put in at the island and a rescue would follow. Could either of them have foreseen that four years and four months would pass before a friendly sail approached, their quarrel might have been temporarily mended and they might have sailed away together, to quarrel again another day.

The story of Alexander Selkirk's difficult and lonely life on the island comes partly from his own account of his experiences, but principally from Defoe's version of the story, *Robinson Crusoe*. He built two huts, thatched them with long grasses and lined them with goatskins. One served him as living quarters and the other as cookhouse. From the beginning he hunted the wild goats, and when his meager supply of gunpowder was exhausted he learned to catch them. Before his rescue he managed to dine on some five hundred and slit the ears of a like number which had been caught in excess of his needs. When his clothes became too ragged to wear he replaced them with goatskins and hardened his feet until he could run barefoot over the jagged volcanic rocks that composed the ridges and summits of his island home. There were no dangerous land animals or venomous reptiles to guard against, but Selkirk was much annoyed by rats. They, together with cats, had originally escaped from ships and had considerably multiplied, especially the rats. According to his account, the cats were at first exceedingly wild and shy, but he finally succeeded in redomesticating enough of them to keep the rats away from his huts.

On January 31, 1709, a British squadron again approached Más a Tierra. Under command of Captain Woodes Rogers and with Captain Dampier as pilot, the men-of-war *Duke* and *Duchess* cruised off the island while they sent a yawl ashore. Darkness came before a landing could be made and, a fire being seen on the island, Captain Rogers suspected the presence of Spanish ships near by and promptly recalled the boat. It is easy to picture Selkirk's thanksgiving as he watched the approach of ships which he recognized and which might carry him away from his prison island. How frantically he must have gathered and kindled the fire that should draw the boat to a safe landing-place. What suffering he must have endured when he saw its bow turned back toward the ships.

His hope of rescue was renewed at dawn, when his eager eyes again saw the sails which he feared had borne away the British ships during the night. Later in the morning Captain Rogers, finding no ships of Spain near Más a Tierra, decided to send the yawl ashore again, to scout a Spanish garrison that might have been established there. When the yawl failed to return he followed it with an armed pinnace, which scarcely reached the landing place before it hastened back to the ship. Aboard was Alexander Selkirk, whose goatskin-clad figure, long hair and beard, and rusty voice combined to produce an impression both wild and pitiful.

Captain Dampier recommended Selkirk to the commander of the squadron, calling him the best man who had sailed in the *Cinque Ports*, with the result that Captain Rogers "immediately agreed with him to be the mate of our ship." With some hesitation and not until he had determined that the officer whose quarrel with him had ended so disastrously was not a member of the ship's company, Selkirk came aboard and "found all to his liking."

Thus, in the second month of 1709 was rescued and "restored to the society of his kind" the last and most celebrated of a long line of "Crusoes," who had lived, better or worse, for longer or shorter periods on Más a Tierra. Today, more than two hundred and fifty years after, it is still called Robinson Crusoe's Island. In competition with islands similarly designated, Más a Tierra alone deserves the name because, however geographically hybridized and fancifully embroi-

Along the nineteen-thousand-foot ridge, down which this glacier flows, runs the frontier: Chile to the left, Argentina to the right. (Photograph by Manuel Bazan.)

The "Christ of the Andes" with twenty-thousand-foot Cerro Juncal in the background.

The backdrop of Santiago, Cerro Altar in the center. (Photograph by Manuel Bazan.)

A precipitous staircase trail on "Robinson Crusoe's Isle" (Más a Tierra).

The serrate silhouette of Más a Tierra as John saw it from the *Iris*.

Forbidding, fog-shrouded Quebrada de las Vacas, where John searched in vain for *Nicotiana cordifolia* during his one day on Más Afuera.

dered, it is Alexander Selkirk's account of his surroundings and activities on this lonely isle in the South Seas with which Daniel Defoe continues to thrill successive generations of boys and girls.

Tradition has it that Juan Fernández himself landed the first goats on the islands, but whoever was actually responsible for their introduction could scarcely have anticipated how successfully they would adapt themselves to a somewhat remarkable environment. They multiplied exceedingly, and from that day to this have represented a never-failing meat supply. For more than one hundred years the goat population on Más a Tierra has been relatively scanty; but on minute, barren near-by Santa Clara and on far-off Más Afuera it is apparently undiminished. In the seventeenth century it occurred to the Spaniards that the availability of fresh meat on Más a Tierra might be a reason for the effectiveness of the forays on their South American shipping made by various categories of foreign naval vessels that used the island as a base. Therefore they attempted to exterminate the goats, first by intensive hunting and later by loosing dogs. The dogs promptly returned to a state of nature and, running in savage packs, soon killed a large proportion of the goats and drove the residue to the security of the highest mountainsides. The transient foreigners retorted by shooting dogs as well as goats.

In the evening of the third day out of Valparaiso, the *Iris* finally dropped anchor in Cumberland Bay. The voyage had been an unusually long and peculiarly nasty one, although John has no basis for comparison except the homeward voyage he took some weeks later, which was bad enough. Some of the crew promptly went ashore. During the long, stormy trip from the mainland no wine had been consumed on the *Iris*. Soon the sailors returned and brought with them bottles of good Chilean red wine. Since John's was the only corkscrew available, he felt justified in exacting tribute from each bottle. The anchorage was calm, and he decided to spend the night on the *Iris*.

In the morning John went ashore for what, according to schedule, would be a day's collecting before the ship sailed for Más Afuera. Half a hundred houses, a radio station, and wharves and sheds filled with the lobster fishermen's boats huddled on the shores of Cumberland Bay between the ocean and the almost vertically ascending mountainsides; this was the village of San Juan Bautista, the only permanent settlement on the Juan Fernández Islands. Two streets paralleled the beach and two at right angles to it ran up the steep hillsides. Torrential rains falling on the heights above descend the mountainsides in stony watercourses which produce, in drier seasons, rough trails that lead to high, deep quebradas where the villagers cut their wood supply.

John had a letter of introduction to one of the oldest fishermen on the island and was entertained by him during his stay ashore. He also got into touch with a German who had lived on Más a Tierra off and on since 1915. This man had been a sailor on the German cruiser *Dresden*, which was sunk by the British near Más a Tierra in that year. Some of the crew drowned, but he and the others who escaped landed on the island and for a time were interned there by the Chilean government. He had the typical German flair for natural history and, among other collections, had accumulated a small one of the flora of Robinson Crusoe's Island.

During the first afternoon John began botanizing, accompanied by the German, two small boys, and two dachshunds. From the German's cabin they climbed a path carved along one of the steepest ridges. This trail was nothing more than a staircase in which rocks and the trunks of tree ferns constituted the steps. Quoting from John's diary:

"Tired and a little weak after my miserable days aboard the *Iris*, I made pretty heavy work of the staircase trail, but managed to do better than the dachshunds, who were either underfoot, or had to be assisted up a particularly long step, or succeeded in tumbling off into the brush on the trailside, requiring a rescue. Up a few hundred feet, I began to notice fallen flowers of a dark mulberry-voilet tint. They looked extremely odd. Soon we came upon the plant which bore them. It was a tree belonging to the Verbena family and known by the islanders as *Juan bueno* and by the botanist as *Rhaphithamnus venustus*. This species, closely related to the *espino blanco* or "white thorn" of southern Chile, is the only tree native to the Juan Fernández Islands which has spines.

"The trail rapidly increased in steepness and we began to haul ourselves up from step to step by grasping the trunks of tree ferns and the larger rocks which bordered the stony path. Out of breath and weary almost to the breaking point, I dragged myself around a particularly perpendicular series of steps and without warning came suddenly out into the open on the knifelike edge of the island's main divide. Here the rough, rocky ridge was so narrow that I had to hunt for a space large enough to rest upon comfortably. Almost directly below me lay tiny Santa Clara, a low, barren islet set like a brown dot in the surface of the deep-blue ocean, less than a mile from the south-western extremity of Más a Tierra. As I looked out through the tree-fern branches down to the thundering surf breaking against the cliffs and over the outjutting rocks in the channel between the two islands and then raised my eyes to the horizon, I tried to translate myself into Alexander Selkirk and to think some of his thoughts as he sat perhaps in exactly that same spot where I was sitting, or on what is called his lookout, on the northwest shoulder of El Yunque, ever longing for the white gleam of the sail which was so long in appearing.

"I climbed a short distance up the incredibly steep slopes of La Damajuana and soon convinced myself that the report that this peak has rarely been achieved is undoubtedly correct. Everywhere there was evidence that it was too late in the season to find many plants in flower on the high ridges, but I did succeed in collecting a few. There was an attractive Campanulalike plant (*Wahlenbergia fernandeziana*) quite abundant among the rocky outcroppings and, in looser, rocky soil just below, a single specimen of *Colletia spartioides*, a curious leafless plant with much-branched, yellow-green stems.

"From the village on the shore of Cumberland Bay, the two-mile-long trail which we had achieved, and which brought us to the notch between El Yunque and La Damajuana, had seemed sufficiently steep in most places; but the approximately vertical drop on the other side of the narrow divide produced a shrinking feeling as I looked down the fifteen-hundred-foot mountainside to the sea, less than half a mile away. Finally, gathering courage, I worked my way down a few hundred feet to collect a plant of the endemic potato (*Solanum fernande-zianum*), which had been described as producing edible tubers. This potato is a sprawling perennial growing in moist, shady woods, and the only specimens I saw were in fruit, the unripe capsules looking like miniature tomatoes."

It is said that Daniel Defoe when he wrote *Robinson Crusoe* had the impression that the Juan Fernández group were desert islands. In order, therefore, to provide a more favorable background for his hero's activities and to furnish the surrounding area with a native population of cannibalistic tendencies, Defoe devised a West Indian locale for Robinson. Far from being desert islands, Más a Tierra and Más Afuera support a dense vegetation. Although geographically and climatically they are by no means tropical, the tangle of low forest trees and dense

underbrush that fills the greater and lesser gorges on their mountainsides is definitely reminiscent of the equatorial jungle. During the
winter season, from May to October, the rainfall is heavy, and lack
of precipitation during the rest of the year is compensated for by a
generally foggy climate.

I have already pointed out that the floras of oceanic islands tend to
be rich in plant species that occur nowhere else, and that the vegetation
of Más a Tierra and Más Afuera is noteworthy because of the unusually large number of such endemics which it contains. John had
his first glimpse of one of the most beautiful of them almost as soon
as he landed. In a deserted garden, where the trail to the highlands replaced the village street, grew a stately palm whose tall, slender, pale-
green trunk was ringed at regular intervals with bands of darker green
and bore at the very apex a dense, flat crown of bright green leaves.
This attractive palm (*Juania australis*), the so-called "chonta" of the
islanders, produces small, edible fruits which doubtless represented a
share at least of Alexander Selkirk's food supply during his years on
Más a Tierra. These fruits and the soft, edible bases of the leaves furnished a fresh salad to many a scorbutic English mariner, and the
plant was therefore known as the "cabbage tree." At one time this palm
grew in quantity on the mountainsides above Cumberland Bay, but
ships' crews have long since destroyed them all. The chonta is, fortunately, still quite abundant in less accessible portions of the island.
To a limited degree it has been successfully introduced into gardens
in parts of the world where climatic and other factors are congenial.
Polished sections of the trunk made attractive souvenirs to sell to
visitors who landed from a South American tour ship that, until some
years ago, made an annual side trip to Más a Tierra. Foreseeing the
ultimate extinction of this palm, the Chilean government has made
cutting of the chonta unlawful.

The most famous of the plants of Más a Tierra was the sandalwood
tree (*Santalum fernandezianum*), which undoubtedly grew there in
abundance when Juan Fernández landed on the island. Probably it was
first cut for wood and ship repair, but soon the value of its beautiful
and fragrant wood, previously available only in the Far East, was
appreciated. During early Spanish Colonial days on the west coast of
South America it still grew in quantity on Robinson Crusoe's isle, and
a lucrative trade in sandalwood was carried on for many years. Gradually the trees became scarce and finally none could be found, and, long

ago, the sandalwood was reported to be extinct. In 1906, however, a single specimen was discovered which, unfortunately, died in 1916. The General thoughtfully shared with us a piece of the wood that had been cut for him from this last remnant of a botanically and commercially valuable member of Más a Tierra's remarkable flora.

The geographically nearest relative of the Juan Fernández sandalwood is *Santalum freycinetianum* of the Hawaiian Islands. There are a number of other species of *Santalum*, all Eastern, of which the most important is *S. album*. This grows in dry regions of southern India and on the East Indian archipelago, whence for centuries it has been exported, chiefly to China where its wood is used for incense, perfume, and carving.

For the lay naturalist, as well as for the professional botanist, the most lively interest always attaches to the discovery anywhere of a plant that grows nowhere else. But on those two relatively insignificant uplifts of volcanic earth in the South Seas, Más a Tierra and Más Afuera, not one species but actually eleven genera of plants are endemic; there and only there throughout the length and breadth of the world may they be seen growing on their native heath. Among the ten endemic genera of flowering plants and one endemic genus of ferns are some of the most ancient of all the living plants known to man. One of them, *Lactoris*, is the only genus of its family. Another, the chonta, is only distantly related to other genera of palms.

Of the eleven endemic genera, seven are monotypic; that is to say, they have only one species each. Four genera—*Robinsonia, Rhetinodendron, Centaurodendron,* and *Dendroseris*—are members of the Compositae, the Sunflower family. The four Juan Fernández Compositae, as the names of two of them point out by the suffix "dendron," are trees or treelike, a growth form one never associates with the plant family to which they belong.

An Italian physician in 1830 made one of the best of the earlier collections of the plants of Más a Tierra. It was from the dried specimens which he sent back to Europe that botanists first learned of the existence of these tree Composites, which immediately were recognized to be among the rarest, most ancient, and most interesting members of their plant family.

Among the ferns two species stand out prominently in the remembrance of those who have climbed the steep ridges or torn their way through the dense, matted forests of Más a Tierra and Más Afuera.

Both are tree ferns and warrant that designation. One of them, *Dicksonia berteriana*, grew abundantly along the route of John's first botanizing on Crusoe's isle. In deep quebradas it luxuriated, and where low-lying fogs maintained high atmospheric humidity it formed extensive and charming groves. On Más Afuera the ascent of high mountainsides is made almost impossible by compact stands of this tree fern.

The other outstanding tree fern, *Blechnum cycadifolium*, might be called the "cycas fern" because it resembles so closely the sago palm of conservatories—or, in California, of front lawns—that the uninitiated refuse to believe that it can actually belong to an entirely different subdivision of the plant kingdom. It shuns the moist shade of leafy gorges and forested slopes, and prefers to populate the dry, barren ridges. There, in the rocky wasteland, silhouetted against the burnished blue of the sky or framing a glimpse of the darker-blue ocean far below, it stands out as one of the most characteristic elements of the somewhat bizarre and even sometimes a little otherworldly vegetation of the Juan Fernández Islands.

I expected John to be away at the most ten days and spend most of his time on Más Afuera, where alone grew the *Nicotiana* I was determined to have. The fourth morning after John's arrival in Más a Tierra, the chambermaid was just bringing in the meager breakfast which our Valparaiso hotel provided, when the telephone rang. It was the General on the other end of the line and his first words were, "Have you seen the morning newspapers?" He then went on to explain that a radio message had been published to the effect that the *Iris* had been wrecked on the Juan Fernández Islands, but with absolutely no further details. He kindly agreed to keep in touch with the owners of the *Iris* and with the newspapers, and to pass on to us any later news. When noon came without any, we tried to radio John on Más a Tierra, asking for a report on his personal safety. The radio company would not give us much satisfaction, however, because the abbreviated condition of the original announcement had been due to a breakdown in the radio station on Más a Tierra, something usually followed by a day or two of silence. We received no answer to our first radiogram, and sent two more during the next twenty-four hours. Finally, on the second morning, the newspaper announced that the *Iris* had been refloated. Since the account again gave no details we were forced, with lingering doubts, to assume that everyone was safe and that no particular damage had been done; we had to wait until John's return two weeks later to get any account at all of what had happened. The following is the story.

The *Iris* was to leave for Más Afuera on the second evening of John's stay on Crusoe's isle, and sailing time was set for late afternoon. After the crew finished their supper, the redheaded German-Chilean engineer and his Chilean assistant retired below to the engine room, the bosun took his crew of four forward to the winch, the steward left his galley and climbed into the chain locker to coil the anchor chain, and the cook took over the wheel. When everyone had reached his proper station, the captain shouted to the bosun to take in the anchor. At the same time he signaled the engine room "full speed astern." The bosun and his crew threw themselves against the winch and slowly the anchor freed itself from the rocky floor of Cumberland Bay. Then, without warning, a strong onshore wind sprang up and immediately the little schooner started to drift toward the shore. Again and again the captain furiously signaled the engine room, when suddenly he and everyone else realized that the diesel engine was not running. Any doubt on this subject was dissipated by the engineer, who popped up on deck screaming in his mixed German-Spanish that the diesel would not start. With windmill arms the cursing Captain scampered about and repeatedly commanded the bosun to drop the anchor. Before anything could be done, the bow of the *Iris* began to grate on the rocks fifty feet from shore.

Most of the population had gathered to watch the departure and had, of course, observed the whole operation. Sailing had been scheduled for high tide, and the ship went on the rocks just after its crest had begun to recede. If anything was to be done to save the schooner, obviously that something had to happen before high tide entirely passed. Immediately fishermen began to launch their large boats which were provided with outboard motors. The captain ordered his one lifeboat to be swung out, and two members of the crew entered it with a collection of heavy hawsers. Soon the fishing boats were attached one to the other and to the *Iris* and, strung out in a long line, began a strong pull on the heavy lines. The captain, who was obviously responsible for the disaster because he had not assured himself that the engine was running before ordering the anchor up, lost control over the crew. The cook assumed command. As the tide rapidly lowered it became clear that the *Iris* was not going to be pulled off the rocks that night.

Only the bow of the schooner was on the reef, but it was firmly wedged between great, upjutting rock-masses. All night long she pitched and heaved in dangerous fashion, but the motion did not suggest that the bow was being driven farther up on the reef. By the greatest good fortune the onshore breeze did not increase in severity and it was only the long Pacific swells that were rolling the ship from side to side. At daybreak the crew made another unsuccessful attempt to refloat the *Iris*. A final try was then planned for that evening during high tide. This was to be the last good tide for a number of days, which meant that unless the ship could be refloated with its aid a week might pass before any passage from the island would be possible. Meanwhile, if even a moderate blow developed, the ship would go to pieces on the reef.

There were spare anchors in the warehouse ashore, and during the day the sailors managed to get four of them aboard the *Iris*. By half past five, as the tide began to come in, the anchors had been lowered behind the ship, two on each side, and these, by gently pulling on their hawsers, had been tightened on the rocky bottom. One by one, the twenty or more fishing launches were pushed off the shore and again slowly arranged in a long line. Hawsers passed out from the ship were strung through the procession of launches until they formed a continuous strand. As the tide began to approach its crest, the launches pulled full speed ahead and the crew at the winches on the *Iris* began to put pressure on the anchors. The little schooner trembled, rocked, and finally lurched violently to port—only to settle into a new berth on the reef. The combined force of launches and anchors was repeatedly applied, but with no effect, and the *Iris* continued to swing slowly from side to side as the long rollers flowed under her.

On the near-by shore everyone not allowed a seat in the launches had assembled to watch what was for them the show of the generation. A German schoolteacher from the mainland, spending his holiday on the island, was taking pictures in all directions and predicting in a loud voice that the *Iris* would never be moved from the rocks. Little boys weaved in and out among the crowd and dashed back and forth along the beach to work off by exercise the nervous tension they shared with the older spectators. Suddenly, as the tide surged to its final height and the small waves broke just a little closer to the feet of the company assembled on the shore, a final pull was given and the schooner slowly, quietly, slid clear of the rocks and in a moment was towed to safe anchorage.

The launches then gathered around the *Iris* and people began to come out from shore in rowboats. Soon there was a considerable group on and near the ship to begin a discussion that lasted for a long time. First of all, responsibility for the wreck had to be assigned. The captain and the engineer were both considered to be at fault, a decision against which they violently protested. In a moment everyone began to shout his opinion. Epithets were hurled, the lie was passed, fists were doubled, and the quiet anchorage reverberated to a din which the surrounding hillsides echoed. In the end, they arrived at the conclusion that the tank containing compressed air essential to the functioning of the diesel engine had been entirely exhausted during the voyage out from the mainland. Although either the captain or the engineer was obviously in duty bound to examine the condition of this tank before sailing for Más Afuera, the fact that both had forgotten to do so pointed to the final conclusion, with which all were in agreement, that the wreck of the *Iris* was an act of God.

It had taken the assembled company more than an hour to arrive at these various conclusions. Now that everyone was thoroughly talked out, the crowd dispersed to the mainland or to their bunks aboard ship. During the following morning, radio communication was established for a few moments with Valparaiso and the *Iris* learned that the other lobster schooner had left the mainland on its regular trip to the island and was carrying an extra cylinder of compressed air. With good weather, and better equipped as to sails and engine than the *Iris*, late that afternoon the *Gaviota* appeared. Now that the extra tank was aboard the *Iris* and its diesel behaving properly, there appeared to be no reason why a start for Más Afuera could not be made by the next morning at least.

Because of wasteful methods of fishing, storage, and transportation, the lobster grounds of Más a Tierra had long been since become badly depleted. Más Afuera then became the more active fishing ground, and a small fleet of launches was operated about that island during the lobster season. The launches and their crews, consisting of two or three fishermen each, were carried from Más a Tierra to Más Afuera by one of the schooners. The attempt to land was often risky, and sometimes days and even weeks were spent cruising on and off the only possible landing place. Never going ashore except in case of accident or other emergency, the fishermen lived from twenty to forty days in their launches. A shore party prepared bread and other food and transferred it to the cruising fishermen via a little boat which was pulled back and forth on a rope attached to a barrel anchored a short distance off shore. The reader will see later on what could happen during the trip from barrel to shore and back again.

The lobsters caught by the Más Afuera fishermen were stored in large, floating "live-boxes" until they could be removed to the schooners when these came on their regularly scheduled trips back and forth from Valparaiso. Because the stores for the sea and land parties were closely calculated to last only until the next arrival of a schooner, any interruption in the schedule worked a real hardship on both fishermen and shore crew. This was a well-known fact both to the crews of the two schooners in Cumberland Bay and to the Más a Tierra fishermen, but it did not in the least deter the former from prolonging for two days an argument having to do primarily with which ship should proceed to Más Afuera. Finally, and for no apparent reason, it was decreed that the *Iris*, not the far better-equipped *Gaviota*, should make the trip. At long last, they got under way.

A brisk breeze had by this time sprung up and the cumbersome sail was hoisted in an effort to supplement the efforts of the diesel engine. When the last of the running gear was finally stowed, one of the deck crew took over the wheel from the cook, who then undertook the preparation of some doubtful tripe and ill-cooked chick-peas which together constituted the evening meal aboard the *Iris*.

Shortly after daybreak Más Afuera, the "Farther Land," appeared on the horizon. It is a much more compact, much smaller island than Más a Tierra, yet the crest of Los Inocentes, its highest peak, rises to almost twice the altitude of the loftiest spot on Más a Tierra. The surfaces of this volcanic extrusion in the South Pacific are scarred with deep, eroded canyons. From twenty miles away one can make out only the general outline of Más Afuera, but as the *Iris* slowly came closer two V-shaped gorges stood out prominently on the mountainside near the middle of the island. In the mouth of the larger of these two, the Quebrada de las Casas, a number of tumble-down adobe houses gradually took shape. The other, almost as large, and deeper, the Quebrada de las Vacas, showed incredibly steep walls that reached up into the wreath of fog hanging about the top of Los Inocentes and spilling down to cover the summits of the two great quebradas.

At a snail's pace, the *Iris* pitched and tossed through heavy seas to within a mile or two of the shore. One of the fishing launches appeared around a promontory and rapidly approached. Almost before their shouted words were distinguishable above the roar of wind and waves, the fishermen aboard the launch began vehemently to call for an explanation of why they had for many days been left without sufficient food. When they learned of the wreck on Más a Tierra their attitude grew belligerent. Who, they demanded, had been responsible? Why had not the culprit been punished? Since question and answer called for great lung power to carry the words from boat to launch and back again the discussion gradually died for lack of breath. The heavy seas made it impossible to load into the *Iris* the lobsters in the floating tanks or to send ashore any of the much-needed stores; so the schooner swung sharp to starboard and proceeded to the extreme northern end of the island, where in the lee of sheer volcanic cliffs she found some respite from the storm.

The so-called Juan Fernández "lobster," *Palinuris frontalis*, is actually a large salt-water crayfish which lives only around the islands west of the Chilean mainland. The lobster pots were made of wire and cord and shaped like huge rat-traps. Baited with dead fish, decaying cheese, and other malodorous materials, they were placed in shallow water where they attracted the attention of the lobster. Once inside, he found that the cone-shaped channel through which he had entered prevented his escape. The fishermen took up their traps periodically, and removed the lobsters and stored them in live-boxes to await the arrival of the schooner that would transport them to the mainland. The sides of the schooners were pierced midships with ports that permitted the sea water to wash freely back and forth. The constant washing in and washing out of the water could become an effective method of aeration; if the sea was sufficiently rough, a large part of each cargo of lobsters reached Valparaiso alive.

From the moment of sailing from Valparaiso it had been impressed upon the captain that the principal objective of John's voyage was collecting on Más Afuera. During the trip between the islands John once more pointed out this fact. When, however, the *Iris* came to lie off Más Afuera, the captain denied any knowledge of John's desire to land there. After a long and stormy argument, John succeeded in convincing him that he proposed to go ashore with the first launch carrying supplies to the landing place.

The seas were now running a little lower, and in the lee of the cliffs the ocean was fairly calm. An hour or more was spent in leisurely loading a fishing launch with fruit, meal, flour, vegetables, the mail, and other things required by the shore party and the fishermen. John's plant presses and cameras went in last and then he swung over the side, clad in oilskins borrowed from the crew.

The powerful Swedish motor drove the launch smoothly through the quiet water, but soon the protection of the cliffs was lost and they swung southwest into the teeth of the wind. Waves crashed against the bow, sending spray over the entire boat. Now the full force of the storm caught them and began to toss the launch violently about. As they approached the landing place, off the mouth of Quebrada de las Casas, the waves appeared mountainous as they broke over the great lobster-filled live-boxes moored near the shore. The drone of the motor died to a whisper as the fishermen maneuvered up to the floating steel drum anchored two hundred yards offshore. From the beach a narrow mole had been built by driving two parallel lines of piling about thirty feet out into the ocean. On each side of these pilings massive rocks were piled as an added bulwark against the crashing seas. Between the rows of pilings each breaker roared far up on the sandy shore and then drained away rapidly to expose great ragged boulders at the mouth of the mole.

From high on the shore three men pushed down a small boat toward the bit of beach between the pilings. As they launched it in the swirling surf curling halfway up the narrow mole, the fishermen in the launch pulled on the rope, one end of which was fastened to the boat and the other to the steel drum. The little boat took one bad lunge that just escaped the pilings and then, buoyed up by the next roller and dancing like a cork on the water, it was quickly pulled out to the launch one-quarter full of water. First the precious cameras were placed in the center of the stern seat, then plant presses went in on either side, followed by mail, baskets of pears, fresh vegetables, and miscellaneous stores, and finally all was covered with a tarpaulin.

John was ready to jump into the boat and begin the obviously precarious trip to the shore; but the fishermen restrained him and, as the launch and the loaded boat pitched and rolled in the breakers, each in turn attempted to dissuade him. While the first man, a swarthy, stocky chap of twenty-five, shouted his advice, the backwash of the heavy seas started to drag one of the live-boxes over the life line to the shore. The second man was a tall, slender Jew who spoke French in addition to fluent *castellano*. He was certain that there was nothing on Más Afuera for John to collect, certainly nothing valuable enough to justify the risk of landing. The third was an old fisherman who had seen many seasons in the rough waters around the island. His only comment was that if John actually proposed to land he might just as well begin to do so. John tumbled in and seated himself amidships of the little skiff.

The two younger fishermen straightened the line along which the boat had been pulled out from shore. The old fisherman steadied the boat and shouted instructions to those on the beach who were to pull it toward them when he gave the signal. At last, when the waves seemed a little less wild and high, the old man waved his arm and the men on the beach pulled for all they were worth, running back with the rope up the beach as the boat came in. The three on the launch paid out their line slowly in order to hold the skiff as nearly on an even keel as possible. The taut line allowed them to check its forward movement the moment the boat seemed to be reaching the entrance to the mole too soon or too late to ride the crest of a breaker over the treacherous rocks. A hundred feet outside the mole they stopped the boat and it hung suspended among mountainous waves sloping in all directions; then, when a great swell surged beneath it, and with a last strong pull from shore, it was dragged the length of the mole to touch the sand in the trickle of the expiring wave. John jumped out into six inches of water and helped pull the skiff beyond the reach of the breakers.

We had agreed that, if possible, John should remain for a week or more on Más Afuera and return to Valparaiso on the succeeding trip of the *Iris* or *Gaviota*. But this was not to be. In the course of the arguments that he overheard during the long delay at Crusoe's isle, John gained the impression that because of the lateness of the season, the poorness of the lobster catch, and the disruption of the schedule caused by the wreck it was probable that this would be the last of the season's voyages to Más Afuera. The captain of the *Iris* estimated that it would take him approximately twenty-four hours to load the available lobsters. This meant that John had only an afternoon and part of the next morning on the island, instead of the many days which he had looked forward to and during which he had proposed an exploration of one of the most interesting and relatively little-known botanical treasure-houses in the world. In the circumstances he decided to confine his efforts to collecting *Nicotiana cordifolia* and to mapping its distribution on those portions of the island that he had time to traverse. It never came into his mind that after all the discomforts, delays, and disappointments he had endured the satisfaction of finding this plant that I so much desired would be denied him.

Upon landing John was cordially greeted by a remarkable individual. This man was tall, bespectacled, gray-haired, and academic-looking, dressed in a worn but well-cut tweed suit, and in general appeared thoroughly out of place in his wild and rough surroundings. He proved to be the representative of the lobster-fishing company on Más Afuera and was in charge of the stores and all arrangements connected with the lobster fishing. He had set up headquarters in the less dilapidated half of an old adobe and wooden structure, one of a number built in the first years of this century when the Chilean government maintained a penal colony on the island. With his señora and his young nephew he managed to exist on Más Afuera during the brief lobster-fishing season.

The three botanists who, beginning in 1854, found the much-desired *Nicotiana cordifolia* on Más Afuera had given the impression that the plant was fairly well distributed in the great canyon near the landing place and was, indeed, growing on the margin of the landing place itself. The manager claimed that he had made a complete exploration of the island and given some attention to its vegetation. When John described *Nicotiana cordifolia* to him and the places in which it had been collected, the manager shook his head and contended that he had never seen a plant of that description anywhere on Más Afuera. Together they made a rapid survey of the cliffs near the tumble-down encampment but found no sign of it. John then decided that since the previous botanists who had found *Nicotiana cordifolia* had all of them collected it in the Quebrada de las Vacas he would devote every available moment that afternoon and the next day to a careful search there.

Unlike Más a Tierra, where steep cliffs rise sheer from the sea with practically no level coast line, on Más Afuera there is a bit of beach almost all the way around the island, so that it is possible to pass beside the sea from one of the deep gorges to another. From the landing place along this narrow beach, John, accompanied by the manager and his nephew, hastened toward the "Canyon of the Cows." At one place the sea approaches to within a few steps of the sheer cliffs, and when one has scrambled past this point he understands why it is called by the islanders "El Paso Malo." The Quebrada de las Vacas is one of the steepest and deepest of those V-shaped depressions that raging torrents have cut in the sides of the great mountain which is Más Afuera. A low stone wall built many years ago across its mouth contrasts strikingly with the utterly wild and desolate appearance of the great gorge itself. A slender, cone-shaped hill fills its south side and forces the rapid stream to run close along the vertical cliffs of the north wall. Deep pools and sudden sharp curves mark the boulder-strewn passage of the stream down from the heights above.

Climbing with difficulty up the treacherous grassy slopes, they carefully explored the walls on either side of the mouth of the quebrada. Nothing remotely approaching *Nicotiana cordifolia* was to be seen. Darkness came early here on the east side of the island and deep in the gorge, and they soon had to abandon their search. Just as the last light was fading, a great herd of wild goats was silhouetted against the evening sky on one of the lofty ridges. The manager took an unsuccessful shot at the big-horned leader. In the half-light, with the rising tide and breakers, the journey back along the narrow strip of beach and across the Paso Malo was an experience John says he will certainly long remember.

He was glad to accept the manager's hospitality for dinner and the night. At daybreak the next morning he set out alone for the Quebrada de las Vacas. The whole top of the mountain was covered with a heavy mass of cloud, and small tongues of fog drifted down into the quebradas. The immensely rugged character of the island's coast was more apparent in the morning light. At the edge of the beach, ten to fifteen feet from the water, cliffs rose straight up five hundred to a thousand feet. Winter storms that dashed high on these cliffs had pitted their flanks with shallow caves and worn deep fern- and moss-lined hollows under overhanging rocks. Where through the fast-drifting clouds a glimpse above could be obtained, the highlands showed a solid mantle of trees and underbrush. In the morning light the quebrada still maintained a grim and forbidding atmosphere. As on Más a Tierra, so here also John was too late for good collecting. The grasses and other herbaceous plants on the lower slopes were dry and brown. Only *Physalis peruviana*, the introduced ground cherry, from which the islanders make a delicious cider, was still in bloom. Every moist and partially shady area on the walls of the gorge was filled with ferns and mosses. Higher up were straggling trees, outliers of the dense forests that grow in the more humid atmosphere of the upper mountainsides.

A half hour, an hour, two hours went by, but never a sign of *Nicotiana cordifolia*. More or less in desperation, John worked his way down again to the stream bed and then up onto the opposite slope of the gorge. On this south-facing slope there were practically no green plants to be seen. Nevertheless, he made a thorough examination of the cliffs and ledges, slowly descending toward the base of the conical hill at the mouth of the quebrada. Having had considerable experience with the irresponsible attitude of the captain of the *Iris* and his crew, John knew that he must take no chance on being late at the landing place. Tired and sore from the hard, rough climb, and utterly discouraged, he turned back about noon.

Although the waves rushed less violently against the mole than they had the previous afternoon, John discovered that the trip out to the launch that awaited him at the anchored barrel was psychologically a worse ordeal than the passage to the shore had been. He seated himself in the little boat and, powerless to aid or direct its progress, watched the crests of the turbulent seas rush toward him, break on either side of the narrow mole, and, surging backward and forward, toss his helpless craft violently from side to side. Wave after wave dashed in, and for a time the boat did not seem to gain an inch, but the fishermen in the launch pulled strongly and in a moment more the passage was over.

The deck of the *Iris* was piled high with half-dried, stinking carcasses of wild goats. Scores of equally stinking lobster traps were thrown everywhere. Slung on either rail were the launches of the fishermen who were returning to Más a Tierra after their forty-five days' stretch of cruising the rough waters round Más Afuera. The heavy seas of the previous day had almost abated, and when the *Iris* pulled away from the island she ran into a calm, so that for headway she had to rely upon her ineffective diesel engine. As a result, the voyage back to Cumberland Bay was a slow and, for the lobster-fishing company, a costly one. Because on the calm sea the ship did not engage in its customary rolling and spiral wallowing, very little fresh seawater with its life-sustaining oxygen was washed into the hold where the live lobsters were stored. The *Iris* was equipped with a motor-driven pump to force out water and thus to permit the intake of at least a certain amount of fresh sea water; but for some reason the captain never thought of using this pump. By the time the schooner reached Más a Tierra, therefore, hundreds of lobsters were dead and floating on the surface of the lobster hold.

As the *Iris* entered Cumberland Bay, boats filled with fishermen put off from shore, and no sooner was the ship anchored than they swarmed aboard, tore off the hatch covers, and began to count out the lobsters from the hold. The living ones were quickly put over the side into live-boxes and the dead were stacked on deck. The dried goats and the lobster pots went over the side into waiting boats. The fishing launches were unslung and their crews left immediately, doubt-less anxious as soon as possible to feel land under their feet again.

Late in the afternoon the final loading of the lobsters began. One full live-box after another was floated to the side of the ship, and baskets of lobsters were passed up to the deck. Two by two, the lobsters were then handed down to men in the slatted hold below and, in layer after layer, were put into position. It seemed to be an abso-lutely endless task, but about ten o'clock the complete load was aboard. A number of the islanders had meanwhile come out for a visit on the *Iris*, and soon the captain and the crew started to persuade the visitors to go ashore. More than an hour was spent in seeing the last one over the side, but finally the last *hasta luego* was shouted, the anchor was weighed, and the lights of the village slowly dimmed as the ship moved out into the open sea. Because the sea was somewhat calmer, the re-turn voyage to Valparaiso was more comfortable than the outbound as far as seasickness was concerned.

There is plenty of room for speculation concerning the origin of the Juan Fernández flora and the relationships of its species to those of other portions of the Pacific area. Apart from endemic genera, the flowering plants of Más a Tierra and Más Afuera often are, as might be expected, related to some of those that today are growing on the mainland and perhaps more particularly on the central Chilean coast. Some that grow on the highlands of Más Afuera have their affinities in the Magellanic flora of South Chile. Among the flowering plants, but especially the ferns, some appear more nearly related to species of northern and others closer in relationship to those of southern Chile. These mountainous islands appear to be wholly volcanic, and it has been suggested that they arose during the period when the Andean

backbone of the continent underwent its most recent and extensive up-
heaval. On this assumption Más a Tierra and Más Afuera may, geographically speaking, be thought of as quite young. Presumably they
would gradually have been populated by those mainland plants whose
fruits, seeds, or spores were capable of being transported by air or
water, and which, once arrived, were able to maintain themselves.
If we accept this theory, then we must propose the practically un-
tenable postulate that a few million years is a sufficient period for the
evolution of the extraordinary series of distinctions between the islands' present-day floras and the plants not only of the Chilean mainland but also of Pacific floras in general.

An alternative and somewhat more attractive suggestion has been
made to account for the origin of the islands and their peculiar plants.
We are asked to assume that many millions of years ago the Chilean
mainland was far more extensive than it is today and that on it and its
volcanic mountains grew many ancient plants. Later, the larger part
of this land subsided and only the Juan Fernández group and a narrow
coastal plain below the Andes remained above the surface of the sea
to perpetuate at least part of the ancient flora. On what is now the
Chilean mainland this flora failed to survive, whereas on the Juan
Fernández Islands, owing perhaps to lesser competition and a less
altered climate, a few relics of that once extensive vegetation of the
dim past have been preserved for our eyes.

Man, the universal despoiler, has been most largely responsible for
those alterations in the composition of the Juan Fernández flora that
are known or are suspected to have occurred during the past four
hundred years. He has brought goats, rats, cats, and finally rabbits,
each one undesirable and each having a larger or smaller share in destroying or restricting the perpetuation of a series of plant species. The
crews of early buccaneers, naval craft, and merchantmen cultivated
vegetables grown from seeds that came from their ships' stores and
planted the stones of fruit trees in the native forest. Along with cultivated plants, man has brought with him those ubiquitous weeds whose
origin in the dim past is more obscure than his own. They flourish
in the thoroughly friendly soil of Más a Tierra and Más Afuera and
help to rob the native vegetation of its rightful place in the sun.

By giving the islands somewhat the status of our National Parks,
the Chilean government some years ago took a first step in attempting

to preserve what man has not already destroyed there. Unfortunately, this gesture was not followed by appropriations adequate to maintain trained naturalists or, at least, interested and active caretakers on Más a Tierra and Más Afuera.

Long after John's attempt to find *Nicotiana cordifolia* on the "Farther Land," a new one was made by Rodolfo Wagenknecht, our former Chilean assistant. A set of complications, somewhat different from those that delayed John's arrival at Más Afuera, brought Rodolfo there so late in the lobster-fishing season that again there was doubt whether he could get away at all if he did not return with the schooner that had carried him to the island.

With only an afternoon and the following morning for collecting he was forced, as John under like circumstances had been, to give all his attention to finding *Nicotiana cordifolia*. I had told Rodolfo to hunt for this much-desired plant in some of the other gorges, the mouths of which could be reached from the landing place by following around the towering cliffs on the Playa Ancha, or "Broad Beach." He therefore started off to the south and, passing the Quebrada de las Vacas which John had thoroughly and unsuccessfully explored, came to the Quebrada del Varadero, or "Shipyard Canyon." It proved to be an even wilder and more rugged gorge, and was formed by the union of two smaller, narrower ravines whose perpendicular walls limited exploration to the restricted stream beds between them and to a few ledges near their bases.

Failing to find any trace of the plant he wanted, Rodolfo began in a rather desultory fashion to scan the higher, inaccessible ledges and cliffs. Suddenly, he saw a low shrubby bit of vegetation which seemed to correspond to the description of *Nicotiana cordifolia*. There were no flowers, but the shape and color of its leaves and its growth form were exactly right. In considerable excitement Rodolfo began to consider how to reach the plant. There was no route by which even a goat could have found its way to the cliffs above. At last he had the bright idea of trying to lasso the plant and drag it down to a point to which he could climb. He found some heavy string in his pocket and some bits of rope on the beach. Piecing them all together, he made a strand with a terminal loop long enough to reach the plant. Then began a long and tiresome series of casts, one of which was finally successful, and at his feet there fell a branch or two and a few leaves. Examination of the specimens in California a month later left no doubt that Rodolfo had proved that *Nicotiana cordifolia* still grew on Más Afuera.

The next morning he had a few hours for collecting before the schooner sailed and was in high hope of finding the plant in flower and seed, now that he had "gotten his eye on it." He began at once an exploration of the Quebradas del Mono, del Ovalo, and del Pasto; all three were deep ravines that run up into the forested mountainside north of the landing place. He saw no sign of the much-sought-after tobacco relative, but his time was so limited and he was so fearful of being left behind that he was unable to make a really careful search.

Assured that *Nicotiana cordifolia* could be found on the Juan Fernández Islands, I made another attempt to obtain seed of it. Besides a perhaps too obstinate unwillingness to be beaten in such a quest, there was a special reason for growing this plant in Berkeley. The external appearance of *Nicotiana cordifolia* suggested that it was closely related to two other *Nicotiana* species which today are found only near the desert coasts of northern Chile and southern Peru. Of these two species of the mainland far above the latitude of the Juan Fernández Islands, I had collected seeds, and from the seeds I had grown plants and studied their cell and tissue anatomy. If now we could make equivalent studies of living plants of *Nicotiana cordifolia*, I would be able to compare the results with those obtained from research on the two apparently related northern mainland species. Then there might become available for students of plant distribution some significant evidence concerning the fundamental relationship of a characteristic member of the Juan Fernández flora with species growing today far to the north on South America's west coast.

At a season when the seas were least stormy and flowering should be at its height on the islands, Pablo Aravena, a Chilean schoolmaster and knowledgeable amateur botanist, went at my request to Más Afuera, to operate on the cliffs from which Rodolfo had lassoed *Nicotiana cordifolia*. The hazards of ship to shore and vice versa were much the same as those that John had encountered. On the other hand, the lobster schooners were running on schedule, so that Pablo could spend days rather than hours on the "Farther Land." Successfully rope-laddering himself up the seaside cliffs, he explored the wide plateaus they margined. On them *cordifolia* was present in some abundance, and he put in press many flowering specimens and filled envelopes with enough seed to plant a dozen acres.

In succeeding years the plants grown from this seed in the Botanical Garden in Berkeley were "given the treatment" necessary to extract from them evidence concerning their evolution and relationships. That which came from the hybrids that I made between Más Afuera's *cordifolia* and the South Peruvian and North Chilean Nicotianas is my best proof of a common origin of the three. Would you care to speculate, as I have, on just where this common ancestor of remote antiquity grew and by what evolutionary mechanism were derived from it a group of different, but definitely related, species? If so, you might also care to suggest how and why one of the descendants of this ancestor can be found today on a remote South Pacific island and the others in the foothills of the Andes over a thousand miles to the north and nowhere else. The reward for your correct answer would be the satisfaction of having solved some rather fundamental botanical and geological problems.

Almost fifty years after his first period of collecting on the Juan Fernández Islands, Dr. Skottsberg, to whom reference has already been made in this chapter, revisited them. Accompanied by Mrs. Skottsberg, he spent a total of many weeks on Más a Tierra and Más Afuera, only to find that a majority of the botanically most interesting species he had studied earlier were almost or quite extinct. During his two previous contacts with the remarkable flora of the islands he saw relatively little evidence of the alteration in its original composition induced by the successful competition with the native plants on the part of cultivated species and weeds of European origin, initially introduced some hundreds of years earlier. In the last twenty-five years, however, a number of species widely distributed on and native to parts of the near-by Chilean mainland have invaded Juan Fernández in quantity and are rapidly becoming dominant.

The effects of this invasion and the extent to which it has progressed are described in the following quotation from a letter written to me by Dr. Skottsberg from Más a Tierra. The species to which he refers came from South Chile, where in favorable situations they, and in particular the European blackberry, luxuriate. "This is a terrible place now. The island has become a cattle and sheep farm; animals are in all the valleys and forests, in which today there is nothing but maqui (*Aristotelia maqui*, family *Elaeocarpaceae*), murilla (*Ugni mo-linae*, Myrtle family), and everywhere *Rubus ulmifolius* (the black-berry) in places so thick that you cannot get through. From a distance the forest looked good and dense, as it did years ago, but when we got there it was a jungle of maqui and, higher up, a close stand of *luma* (*Myrtus luma*, Myrtle family) and canelo (*Drimys winteri*, Magnolia family), and under them absolutely nothing, the ground covered a foot thick with withered red *luma* leaves. And I have little hope that we shall find Más Afuera, where we go soon, any better. People set fire there to large areas just for fun, and of forest there is said to be only one patch of any size."

On Más Afuera I asked him to keep an eye out for *Nicotiana cordi-folia*. I needed evidence concerning the extent of its distribution on the island because none of the various expedition members who had succeeded in landing had been able to go inland any distance from the coast. Dr. Skottsberg's report confirmed my assumption that *cordifolia* is a rare plant in its native home and, in addition, refers us back to the opening paragraphs of this chapter, in which are described the excitement created, some twenty years ago, by an announcement in a Chilean newspaper. He says: "When we sailed for this forlorn place I was sure that I could find your *Nicotiana* without difficulty, but that was not the case; it has, in fact, become very scarce. Ever since you organized a hunt for it and finally succeeded in finding it, all the Juan Fernández fishermen know it and it is always spoken of under its Latin name! So much for botanical publicity! Previously, I knew it from several different localities and hunted for it unsuccess-fully for several days. As I said, people here know it and they pick the flowers and bring them home—this they do with everything known to them to be rare and in this way they contribute to the extermina-tion of such species." Later, *cordifolia* was reported to grow in a rather inaccessible quebrada on the north side of the island, and by offering a suitable reward Dr. Skottsberg found a goat hunter who would go there for it. He returned with an ample collection of flowering, fruit-ing, and seeding plants which, ultimately, came to me. So far as I per-sonally am concerned, this brings the saga of *Nicotiana cordifolia* quite definitely to an end.

14

TOP OF THE WORLD

O UR EXPEDITIONS have done a lot of collecting in the central Chilean Andes. This magnificent mountain barrier, separating Chile from Argentina, is the top of the world for the two Americas because it contains Mount Aconcagua which, with an altitude of 22,835 feet, is the apex of both continents. For neighbors it has Tupungato, Juncal, and the Mercedario, thrusting toward the sky to altitudes a little above twenty thousand feet. It is reported that in the Chilean cordillera there are at least seventy-five peaks approximately as high as the three just mentioned and more than two thousand at least sixteen thousand feet above the sea.

Among the unforgettable days of my life is the one when I stood at the foot of Aconcagua. It was early in January, which means the beginning of the short alpine summer at above eight thousand feet in the highlands of Central Chile. We had spent the night at Puente del Inca, where the cold, blustery winds off the snow peaks round about continually threatened to shake the little wooden hotel to pieces. The much more elaborate hostelries which have long since replaced it are far stouter buildings.

Puente del Inca has been headquarters for most of those who have attempted an ascent of Aconcagua, and from it less arduous excursions can also be made. The most popular takes you to the "Christ of the Andes," the famous statue that stands on the lofty border between Chile and Argentina. During the almost sleepless night in our creaking, rattling hotel room, we discussed plans for the following day and decided to combine a visit to the *Christus* with such plant collecting as could be done near by. In the morning, however, we found that the trippers at the hotel had already booked all seats in the available automobiles. I was not so disappointed as I should have been. I was confident that a day would come when I could see the "Christ of the Andes," but not with a crowd of tourists; see it standing alone on the bleak, rough mountainside, and read, but not over the shoulders of other travelers, the words that are inscribed in Spanish on its pedestal: "Sooner shall these mountains crumble into dust than the peoples of Argentina and Chile break the peace which at the feet of Christ, the Redeemer, they have sworn to maintain."

There are those who like to scoff at this inscription. They insist that no one, either in Chile or Argentina, ever looked upon this pledge as representing more than a typically Latin gesture, something for the world to watch. I like to think otherwise, and to believe that such an affirmation reflects at least a little of the spirit of the two republics whose territories are joined beneath the figure of the Prince of Peace.

From Puente del Inca we tramped up the highway in the wake of the tourist-filled automobiles. At first, I thought that we might manage the ten miles or so to the pass that leads to Chile and the near-by statue, and then hitchhike back to the hotel. Puente del Inca lies at almost nine thousand feet and the road eastward begins to climb rapidly on its way to the 12,800-foot pass. The wind that had blown through the night was still strong and, as the road swept in wide curves up the mountain slopes, it blew alternately in our faces and on our backs and was equally disagreeable either way. The combination of wind, grade, and altitude made progress slow. After a mile or two I knew that we would not reach the frontier or see the statue that day.

Collecting in the wind is difficult, but I managed to put many plants in the presses. Except on the steeper ridges, the soil was moist; along little valleys and in most of the lesser depressions it was boggy, sometimes exceedingly so. In such spots, the yellow and red flowers of a delicate *Mimulus* shone brilliantly against the dark background of the bog. Thin, brittle stems, only a few inches long, appeared to be highly insecure supports for the flaring, gaudy trumpets nodding at their tips. Behind ridges or in the lee of boulders on drier ground, small groups of shrubs were flourishing. Most conspicuous, and the only one in flower, was an excessively spiny species of *Adesmia*, which sometimes grew to five or six feet.

Farther on we came to the broader valley of the Río de las Cuevas and began to traverse increasingly barren plains that ended abruptly in steep mountain walls. At first glance these sandy, rocky expanses appeared destitute of vegetation. Actually, however, they supported a variety of rather remarkable plants. Many of them were composites, members of the Sunflower family. All were dwarf, hugging the ground to escape the wind and enjoy such warmth as the soil retained at night. Most of them suggested the common dandelion gone a bit crazy. Their flat rosettes were often massive, and either woolly or provided with a coating of wool plus glandular hairs, the latter making the plant exceedingly, and sometimes unpleasantly, sticky. These true alpines were perennials and grew from partly woody and partly fleshy roots, deep-seated in the soil. Beneath the heavy winter snows such underground organs retain vitality, and each year, with the melting of the white blanket and the first warming of the soil that comes with the highland spring, they send up new leaves and short, thick stems. Abundant food, with its contained energy, flows from the storehouses in the roots to make successful the competition of these perennials with the rigors of their environment. Growth has to be very rapid so that maturity, with its flowers and seed, can be attained before the short summer season is at an end.

These prostrate composites were devilish things to bring to press because the ruffled margins of the strong, stiff leaves were set with short, sharp bristles eager to stab you. To take a proper specimen meant that one side of the broad, prickly rosette had to be held up with the left hand while the digging tool was manipulated with the right. On such occasions Florence retired upwind, where only faint echoes of the imprecations in which my anguish culminated might reach her ears. In rocky outcroppings I saw a charming plant with big, white, bell-like flowers half hidden in masses of much-divided foilage. It was such a contrast to the monstrous "dandelions" that I turned to it with pleasure. Too late, I realized that I was handling a species of *Cajophora*, a near relative of the loasas whose violently stinging hairs have taught us many a sharp lesson in the foothills of the Peruvian and Chilean Andes. At the start the pain seemed to be almost unbearable, but it decreased fast, only to rise again and again, but with diminishing intensity. Later on I learned that this *Cajophora* is well but not favorably known to Chilean alpinists who call it *ortiga caballuna* which, freely translated, means "nettle with a kick like a horse."

As we walked up the highway, the character of the terrain began to change. The curves became steeper and narrower as the road followed along one side of deep gulches and then turned back along the opposite one. On open hillsides I saw my first alpine nasturtiums. They grew from tubers, or, perhaps better, from corms, which I discovered were securely hidden below massive boulders or in rough scree. From this security they trailed for two feet or more over the rocky soil like dark but shining, flat, green feather boas. Each was tipped with a tight nosegay of cream to reddish-orange, nasturtium-like flowers. This was the plant I had hoped to find. On somewhat shaded slopes it was still in bud, but in more exposed areas, where the hot alpine sun had full sway, the flowers were open. With their deeply divided margins, reminiscent of the foliage of the California poppy, the leaves are quite different in appearance from those of our garden nasturtiums. There was no ripe seed, so I began to dig the tubers. My digging tools consisted of a light, short-handled, double-headed pick and two scratched hands that, alternately, glowed red and then paled to a white-pustuled surface, as the venom of *Cajophora* reduced or increased its authority.

The succulent stem of the nasturtium was three fourths of an inch in diameter where the leaves grew densest, but farther back it rapidly decreased in diameter and, slender as a thread, disappeared among the rocks. This meant that only with the utmost care could the layers of rock be removed without breaking the delicate, leafless lifeline to the underlying soil. Once broken, it was almost impossible to find the point where the white thread extended farther downward. After a number of tedious and unsuccessful attempts to burrow through the rocks, I began to work on plants that grew in what appeared to be sandy soil, beside big boulders. It seemed to me that the tubers could not be very far back under the boulders. I was entirely mistaken. The sandy soil-surface was a sham, nothing more than six inches of covering above hard-packed scree. The sand was a light, almost dustlike product of decomposition of granite and sandstone. At the slightest disturbance it rose in the wind and filled eyes and nose with an irritating mist. Keenly disappointed, I finally had to give up the attempt to bring home alive one of the finest alpines of the Andes.

From time to time we had been turning our eyes northward up the increasingly large valleys that crossed the highway. Somewhere behind the high ridges in which each of these valleys ended was Mount Aconcagua. Then, around a turn of the road, we looked up again, and there she was—a tremendous, glistening-white, truncated cone, rising in majesty above a jumble of lesser peaks. On an air line we must have been about fifteen miles away from the crown, which rose only eleven thousand feet above us, so that Aconcagua's height and breadth were not so impressive as they would have been had our view been a closer or a much more distant one. Nevertheless, there was some mysterious, some detached quality about that mass of snow and ice glowing and shimmering against the intensely blue sky. It made this sky and all familiar things seem a little unreal, and the very air took on a new, headier quality.

Growing thick and strong on a wide, gentle slope, the alpine nasturtiums made an almost completely green foreground for the surpassingly beautiful picture. Beyond, a long, broad, barren, boulder-strewn valley led directly to the dark ridges from which Aconcagua sprang. Near us, the valley walls were very high and almost vertical, and the morning sun was strongly reflected from their tan, orange, and rosy rock surfaces. All this made a brilliant frame for the vista of the great white peak.

While we were attempting to appreciate and evaluate it, something new began to be added. At first there was a very distant, almost imperceptible, humming. Rapidly this faint breath of sound came nearer and increased in intensity. Was it a bumblebee that, with noisy flight, might be visiting the golden nasturtium flowers? There was no bumblebee. Simultaneously we put back our heads and stared straight up into the bright sky. I saw it first. Directly overhead a shining silver insect raced across the zenith, halfway between us and Aconcagua's white shoulder. Almost at once it began to disappear eastward, and went behind a distant ridge. A gradually diminishing hum floated in the air long after it was lost to view. It was only one of the airplanes that in good weather fly daily, both east and west, over the pass and beside Aconcagua. But, for the moment or two during which that silver thing was in the sky, it became a part, almost a natural and appropriate element, of the very top of the world, and not a familiar man-made and man-directed machine.

I began to feel the magnetic quality of great eminences—the urge to pit feeble human strength against the immensity of the forces that hinder their ascent; the urge to demonstrate again that high courage and the driving power of the human will can successfully transport the body beyond its normal sphere, that resourcefulness of mind can circumvent the limitless powers of nature. All this the Fitzgerald party demonstrated when they made the first ascent of Aconcagua, in 1897. We tried to identify the nineteen-thousand-foot saddle, beneath the summit, where they established their highest camp and from which a number of attempts were made to climb the remaining four thousand feet. On both of the two successful ascents Fitzgerald was forced to give up at about twenty-two thousand feet. One of the Swiss guides who accompanied him was the first man to stand on the top of Aconcagua. Later on, Stuart Vines, a member of his party, with another guide, also reached it. On this second ascent almost eight and a half hours were required to conquer the summit from the nineteen-thousand-foot camp.

The summit itself proved to be a square plateau, measuring seventy-five paces each way, sloping at an angle of seven degrees toward the southeast. In Fitzgerald's book, *The Highest Andes*, Vines describes the unparalleled panorama lying at his feet:

Northward over the cloudless expanse my eye wandered down the great slopes of the mountain, over glaciers and snow fields . . . to where the great snow mass of the Mercedario, towering above all the surrounding heights, barred the way. . . . In the enormous distance to which I could see beyond, numerous giants reared their mighty heads, many of them in the shape of perfect pyramids. . . . Over Argentine territory, range beyond range stretched away; colored slopes of red, brown, and yellow, and peaks and crags capped with freshly fallen snow.

Away over the surging mass of white cloud that lay on the glacier at my feet, rose the southern frontier chain, Torlosa and the Twins, on either side of the Cumbre Pass, like colossal sentinels guarding the great highway between the two republics . . . the lofty glaciers lying between the rugged crags of Juncal . . . and some sixty miles farther on, the magnificent white summit of Tupungato.

No lens or pen can depict the view on the Chilean side [as] I looked down the great arête, past the western peak of Aconcagua . . . over ranges that dwindled in height . . . to where, one hundred miles away, the blue expanse of the Pacific glittered in the evening sun. . . . The sun lay low on the horizon and the whole surface of the ocean . . . was suffused with a blood-red glow.

Such is the soul-stirring reward of the alpinist.

I have twice crossed the pass at Aconcagua's feet from east to west, in part by automobile and in larger part on foot. The alternative is to fly or take the "Transandino" train from Argentina to Chile. Limitation of time has required my using both on a number of occasions and in both directions. Of course, for the botanist intent upon collecting Andean vegetation, the car-foot mode of travel is indicated and is almost certain to be as rewarding as it is strenuous.

The old road over the pass, which I first traversed by car in 1935, seemed in my then limited experience of Andean "highways" to be a trifle on the dangerous side. I shall never forget one spot where the rough, one-way roadbed wound around the walls of a deep valley. The almost sheer drop over the unprotected edge was well over a thousand feet. A mountain stream, tumbling down from the heights above, crossed the road at the apex of a hairpin turn. Below, the stream became transformed into a long waterfall. A strong upward current of air lifted the spray and carried it, as a dense cloud, over the road. The narrow track at the head of the turn was swallowed up in this mist and the driver had to run dead slow, with horn at full blast, as we splashed and rolled through the ford and made a sharp turn against rocky walls. For an hour a succession of fast-moving trucks had been meeting us at highly inconvenient spots along the narrow road. I prayed that another would not come roaring into the mist as we moved slowly out of it.

A week or so before our arrival at Puente del Inca a young compatriot had appeared at the hotel with the announcement that he proposed to climb Aconcagua. According to the hotel proprietor, this youth confessed to practically no mountaineering experience. Nevertheless, he was absolutely determined immediately to begin the Aconcagua ascent, which is one of the most difficult in the world, at least so far as physical strain is concerned. He had left a ship in Valparaiso only a few days earlier, and certainly needed a week or two to become adjusted to high altitudes and to harden himself by preliminary climbing, before attempting an assault on the highest American peak. The proprietor had been able to put him off for two or three days by claiming that trained guides were not available. Finally, however, the young man became so demanding and generally obstreperous that the guides were forthcoming and the ascent was begun. After reaching about eighteen thousand feet, the poor chap collapsed; he died before he could be brought down to a lower altitude. Over the intervening years Aconcagua has more than once been conquered, but by no means by all those who have attacked it; indeed, it has continued to take its toll of human life.

Once through the long tunnel and out on the Chilean side, the railway runs along natural and artificial ledges that hang on gigantic mountain slopes. The rock scenery just below the tunnel has been said to be the grandest in the world. It certainly is stupendous, and more impressive than anything I remember in Europe and the Rockies, American or Canadian. I have often watched it pass the windows of the Transandino observation car, and have spent days on foot in the midst of it.

I have not yet decided whether a near view of the incredibly rugged, broken complex of two- to four-thousand-foot rock walls, toothed ridges seamed with tightly packed snow, steep, ruddy scree slopes pimpled with immense boulders, and, finally, the group of white peaks is more impressive than the view at a lower altitude, upward toward this complex. From below, you watch a superb panorama of rough plains between confining mountain slopes rise in unbroken sweeps of four, five, and six thousand feet to a black ridge against which presses a semicircle of snowy peaks. These white pyramids carry the eye another five thousand feet up into the brilliant blue sky of the Chilean highlands. The almost impossibly steep angles of repose of the mile-long scree slopes, the piling of one rock mass upon another and then upon another, the snowy crown almost directly overhead, combine to create something scenically unique. Imagine, if you will, a steep gorge high in the Rockies or Sierra Nevada expanded a hundred times, preserving all geological features and relationships, but each of them enlarged to a monstrous degree.

The spring and summer vegetation on the Chilean side of the pass has been for me an object of special interest. Since altitudinal changes are abrupt in this broad, rapidly ascending, vertical valley that the Transandine Railway skirts, the zonation of plant species is as striking as it has proved to be in the deep canyons of southwestern Peru. I have been particularly concerned with the reactions of *Nicotiana* species under the influence of altitude. On both sides of the pass, *Nicotiana corymbosa*, a previously little-known, low-growing tobacco relative, was here and there abundant, and particularly so near corrals and along the trails used for cattle on their way to market in Chile. On the Argentine side these plants began to appear at about seven thousand feet and continued to occur until the altitude reached a little over nine thousand feet. Over the pass and on the way down the Chilean side they reappeared at ninety-five hundred feet and disappeared at sixty-five hundred feet. After an additional drop of two thousand feet an entirely different species, *Nicotiana acuminata*, takes up the westward distribution of this genus, which can then be followed down to the shores of the Pacific in Central Chile.

Later on, I was surprised to find *Nicotiana corymbosa* rather common at much lower altitudes, on the southern edge of the Chilean coastal deserts, and in the Cordillera de la Costa that rims the Vale of Paradise. Still later, when we followed the Argentine Andes southward for hundreds of miles into lower Patagonia, this diminutive *Nicotiana* most strikingly demonstrated its adaptability to environmental distinctions by growing vigorously all the way from the highlands down to practically sea level. Its total distribution spread is somewhat remarkable—from far south in Argentina on the Atlantic edge of the continent, northward at middle altitudes on the Argentine side of the Andes and west over the Uspallata Pass into Chile, and, finally, for three hundred miles farther north along the Pacific freeboard.

Not only to examine at first hand the *Nicotiana* situation on the Chilean side of the pass, but also to collect seeds of the fine ornamentals that we had seen in bloom, toward the end of one alpine summer I started up into the highlands. The "General" went with me. From Valparaiso we took a train to Los Andes, and there engaged a car with driver. I never discovered just what kind of agreement the General made with the driver. Certainly he proved to be most obliging, and throughout the trip there was no acrimonious bickering about where and how often the car should be stopped along the roadside to permit botanizing.

From Los Andes the automobile road over the pass into Argentina has its official beginning. Although on the Chilean side there were spots along this Pacific-Atlantic highway that might give the average touring North American a bit of the jitters, it is a remarkable accomplishment, and on it, at a proper season, a steady procession of automobiles crosses the Andes and back again.

Until we had passed Río Blanco and risen above five thousand feet there was not much that was new or exciting in the way of plants. Thereafter, the first of the vegetation that attracted my attention was scattered growths of something resembling tall, loosely growing, single-flowered garden stocks, except that the color was wrong. They proved to be a species of *Malesherbia*, belonging to a South American plant family. It is a quite charming plant with long flower spikes covered with flat, inch-and-a-half-across, navy-blue disks. Elsewhere in the Chilean Andes I saw this same *Malesherbia,* and often in shades of paler blue. Sometimes the petals of the dark-blue flowers showed an intricate design of faint white lines that added considerably to their attractiveness.

Along with *Malesherbia* was *Schizanthus,* well known as a garden plant. I was glad to see it, again, on its native heath and in its original, unimproved condition. It is commonly grown in California, but usually as a pot plant, and is called "butterfly flower" or, sometimes, "poor man's orchid." We collected seed of a number of *Schizanthus* species in Chile. The one which the General and I came across was the familiar *Schizanthus* that bears bluish-magenta flowers marked with orange stripes at the base of the petals. The particular virtue of the plants from our alpine seed is their robust habit, either field or pot grown, and the size of their flowers, almost that of the hybrids offered by the seedsmen. The hybrids tend to become weak-stemmed and usually need support when full grown, while our plants put up three-foot-long flowering stems that are strong and stiff and stand considerable abuse without breaking.

Another *Schizanthus* we brought back is also a robust plant, but its importance comes from the delicious, if faint, fragrance of its pure-white flowers and their unusual shape and form. In place of the rather flat-faced blossom we expect in *Schizanthus,* the flower of this species has become a tube. At the end of the two-inch flower the tube broadens to form wide upper and lower lips, from which hang delicate, deeply cut, white fringes.

The Malesherbias and *Schizanthus* occupied a definite altitudinal zone, and when we got above it the vegetation became sparser. In a few protected areas I saw silky, brown, foot-long stems rising in twos, threes, or fours directly from the sandy surface of the soil. Each was topped by three dark-brown balls that popped open at a touch, to shed neatly packed rows of flat, black seeds. This was obviously some sort of amaryllid, and I gathered seed in the expectation of having to wait until flowering-sized plants had been grown in Berkeley before seeing its bloom. Soon, however, I saw the smooth brown stems crowned with flowers instead of seed capsules. These flowers showed that it was a species of *Placea.* They were large, shell-pink trumpets, held so strongly in horizontal position that they jerked stiffly back and

Seaside vegetation near Valparaiso: pink *Alstroemeria* and *Oxalis* among white *Mesembryanthemum*.

The plant hunter at work: Rodolfo putting into the press specimens of a minute swamp buttercup found at La Vega Escondida.

This climbing *Mutisia* spread its crimson flowers over the crown of a low tree.

Lovely to look at, dangerous to touch, is this high Andean *Cajophora*.

One of the beautiful Argylias that adorn middle altitudes in Chile's coastal range.

A *Cruckshanksia* in porphyry scree at ten thousand five hundred feet, Chilean Andes.

Earthquake: walls and cornices bury those who flee their homes and churches.

Concepción's Cathedral was shattered in the earthquake of January, 1939.

forth when the quick-thrusting breezes from the snow fields over-head slipped around the protecting boulders, to blow across their delicately colored surfaces.

Over a considerable distance the highway ran in wide curves across a broad, up-tilted plain. Above, in the rapidly narrowing valley, the foreground ended abruptly in a two-thousand-foot wall. This barrier was so steep that the full course of the snakelike track on which the highway climbed to an upper plateau could be seen only from above. As we began the ascent, the automobile entered a rubble-filled trough, on the sides of which the wheels began to spin and continued to do so until they reached a firm, rocky bottom. In other words, the highway was nothing more than a boulder-free depression in the gray, powdery, decomposed rock. In some places it had been worn down to a depth of six feet. Today, this rather unique piece of highway engineering has been greatly improved.

In a westward direction, the beginning of the descent on this trans-Andean highway is spectacular. The upper plateau is large and not too steep. As you motor down and rapidly approach the wide cliff-edge, the road ahead suddenly disappears. Beyond, there is absolutely noth-ing for miles, until the high mountains far down the valley rise against the sky. The combination of this distant background and the tre-mendous height of the vertical rock walls around the upper plateau make it seem certain that a glider, rather than an automobile, is the proper conveyance from that point onward. In another moment you dive over the knife edge and catch one quick glimpse of the road-spiral below and of the far-off valley floor at your feet, before the car begins the steep descent.

Once I walked toward the edge to determine the impression that this first descent over the cliff would make on a foot passenger, and also to take a longer look at what lay below. It proved to be a strategic point from which to obtain the sum of all the impressions of grandeur and immensity that crowd upon the traveler who passes over this portion of the Andes by train or automobile. The rock masses to the east were almost overpowering in their sheer bulk, in the crudity of their silhouette, and in their total lack of natural arrangement or symmetry. Directly above them, the peaks of Aconcagua's neighbors showed only as white apices, but the fact that they were able to ap-pear at all above the near-by vertical foreground left no doubt that the summits were supreme in altitude. To the west, down the valley, a more distant background of softer horizons made the view easier to understand, even though it, also, was on a monumental scale. From my vantage point on the cliff edge I tried to form some estimate of the steepness of the mountainsides. Seen in profile, it was almost impossible to believe that their rock surfaces could long remain in position, and it was easy to understand why in that region no hour of the day or night goes by without the distant rumble of rock slides. However, as many times as I stopped to scan the surfaces of those almost vertical slopes, I never detected rock movements until I was in the midst of one myself.

The General and I put up at what was in those days a small and not too comfortable little hotel near the station at El Portillo. This is the railway stop below the tunnel on the Chilean side. From it an easy climb leads to Laguna del Inca, which all passengers from east to west on the "Transandino" know, because the train gives them a brief look at what can be one of the most beautiful alpine lakes in the world. It lies at about ten thousand feet, spread narrowly in the bottom of a deep cleft between immensely steep mountain slopes, with the snow-mantled peaks of the Aconcagua range in the background. At high noon the sun briefly illuminates its deep, still waters, on whose surface the gray, brown, and red rock walls and the white peaks are reflected. At other hours of the day, and especially once when I saw it in the half-light of early evening, Laguna del Inca is a forbidding place of giant shadows thrown across black depths, with inhospitable walls of dark rock everywhere about.

Below the lake, we walked down the track to find a spot where the long scree slopes could be entered. This was not easy, because on the mountainsides the railway ran along shelves and through cuts, the inner sides of which were in most places too steep to climb. The General, armed with his big butterfly net, was out for certain rare, fast-flying insects peculiar to higher altitudes in the great valleys below the Andean crests. At one moment we were walking slowly, picking our way over the surface of the rough scree; at the next, the General was thundering away as fast as the footing would permit and with net extended toward something that was either so small or so fast as to be invisible to any but the trained eye of the entomologist. Thereafter, he came into view only now and then, in the nearer or farther background, and rarely were we in hailing distance.

During previous journeys by train and car down the Chilean side I had made mental note of a series of areas in which the alpine nasturtiums grew abundantly. Following my first sight of them near Puente del Inca and appreciating their unique character and ornamental value, I was determined to obtain their seed so that they might be grown in California.

The General and I entered the scree and boulder slopes about a mile from one of the nasturtium areas. I worked over to it as fast as I could. At a distance, the surface of the steep mountainside appeared to be smooth and rather uniform in composition and in angle of repose. Actually, however, it was a sea of smaller and larger blocks of stone and an undulating one, with broader or narrower depressions, steeper in one part than in another. In the depressions, massive boulders, tons in weight, stood at crazy angles, either alone or in a loose arrangement. On the low ridges between the depressions the rocks were smaller, mostly from fist to head size, tightly crowded together and sometimes covered with a thin skin of coarse-grained gravel. Now and then this rough, but comparatively even, scree surface had shifted and loosened, to exhibit layer after layer of rock and rubble extending down toward the bedrock. That, in a few spots at least, this solid bed beneath the rocks could be near the surface was soon and most convincingly to be demonstrated to me.

Forward progress over the mountainside involved climbing obliquely upward and then downward. The powerful autumn sun poured upon my back and was strongly reflected from the rock surfaces. I often stopped to wipe dust from my black goggles. During these halts a sense of insignificance as a physical element of that stupendous mountain panorama began to oppress me. Even my immediate surroundings were on such a formidable scale that I felt out of place. Above my head the mountainside rose many thousands of feet, even though the angle of its inclination was too steep to disclose more than a third of its upward extent. At my feet the rocky slope fell away abruptly for three thousand feet to the broad secondary terrace of the great valley. In the light of succeeding events it now seems strange that I was impressed only with the incongruity of my presence as a part of the gigantic mountainside and not at all with what might happen if all, or my portion, of its surface should begin one of those downward shifts in position that I knew so often occurred.

During my slow progress I began to see on the rock in the foreground more and more greenish-yellow splashes. They proved to be the much-desired nasturtium. In most cases the plants were long past flowering. Their masses of drying stems and foliage made a faint rustling, scraping sound as the rising afternoon wind, blowing fitfully down the mountainside, tossed them lightly back and forth across the scree. The first group of plants I handled bore only one or two ripe seeds—light-brown spheres almost a half inch in diameter. They were attached, insecurely, to the dried ruins of the flowers. The remainder of the seed had already fallen, and once the little balls rolled down into the scree it was impossible to find them. This I soon learned when I hunted for them on the rough surface beneath the plants. It was, however, with a pleasurable sense of achievement that I heard those first few nasturtium seeds rattle down into my paper seed envelope.

Intent on nothing but collecting as many seeds as possible, I moved slowly from one group of plants to another. They were disappointing. Often a dozen plants yielded only a single seed, sometimes none. Finally I realized that the majority were almost completely sterile, with shrunken, undeveloped seed-bearing parts at the base of the dried petals. During the next hour I must have handled a thousand plants, and still the seed envelope was only two-thirds full. Oblivious of my surroundings, I moved up and down and across the first low ridge on which I had found the nasturtiums. As I gradually descended into a broad depression, the plants became more scattered and decreased in number.

I straightened my aching back and surveyed the possibility of finding more nasturtiums. On the next rise there seemed to be a few spots of color, and so I clambered up big boulders and started out across the smaller rocks beyond. Working slowly out toward the low ridge I noticed that the rocky surface seemed looser, and I found it necessary to climb more carefully than before. If I had been less intent upon seed collecting, I would have realized that when rough scree lies loosely on a steep slope it is dangerous. At any rate, I was entirely unprepared for a slow but definite shifting downward of the surface under my feet and did not fully appreciate what it signified. Indeed, I merely tried to settle my boots more firmly into the increasingly insecure footing while I continued to pick seeds from the more fertile plants that I was now beginning to come across.

In the next instant the rock surface went out from under my feet. Struggling to stand erect, I was dimly conscious of a deep, grinding note that rose from the churning rocks about me. To this undercur-

rent of sound was added the dull smacking, sharp crashing of larger
boulders that were beginning to leap from one impact to another,
faster and faster, higher and higher, longer and longer, down the almost vertical mountainside. Stumbling and falling, I tried to keep on
the top of the rapidly developing rock slide. I can remember seeing
the bedrock through the moving rock-cover and realizing what this
meant—that I had been climbing over a rock surface not many feet
deep, as it elsewhere had been, but very shallow and most insecurely
held on smooth outcroppings of the solid rock foundation.

Fortunately, I had not crossed much of the loose surface before it
began to move, and so was near the edge of the slide. Of even more
importance was the sudden division of the moving rock mass, one
part of which carried me into the lower end of the hollow filled with
big boulders which I had just left, while the rest went crashing down
the slope for a thousand feet or more. How much of the time I was on
my feet and how much of it I spent on hands and knees, I cannot say.
I must have fallen a number of times because my knees turned out
to be pretty raw.

My friend, Dr. Joseph Rock, the famous plant hunter, who directed
the University of California's 1931–1932 expedition in western China
and Tibet, once told me that when, without warning, you find yourself
falling forward on a rocky surface you must remember to close your
fists. You then receive the impact of the fall upon your fists rather
than upon the palms of your hands. He said that, in falling, a person
unconsciously thrusts his arms outward and flattens the palms of the
hands, as though to ward off the equivalent of a blow. With the fists
loosely closed, the impact is cushioned a little and, of greater importance, the more delicate tissues of the palms of the hands will be protected. I must have remembered Dr. Rock's advice at least part of the
time, to judge by the small amount of epidermis left on my knuckles.
Unfortunately, however, there must have been other times when I
forgot to close my fists, for when I got around to looking myself over
the palms as well as the backs of my hands were bloody. Deep-seated
and apparently permanent injuries developed later. Strange and unpleasant things also happened to my back and hips. Ever since that
day I have been aware of them.

An entirely unexpected aftermath of my experience on the rock
slide was the discovery, in a hip pocket, of the paper packet of nasturtium seeds. How it got there, I have not the slightest idea. It should

have been in my hands when the slide began, and should therefore have been dropped and ground to bits or carried down the mountainside.

That night at the El Portillo hotel I had a light attack of siroche, or mountain sickness. It must have been the result of unusual exertion, plus the late unpleasantness, because the altitude was only about ten thousand feet. From previous attacks in the Peruvian Andes, but at much higher altitudes, I knew the symptoms. This time the gradual onset of a severe headache was followed only by a remarkably slow heart action; something that was, however, singularly distressing. Half awake for hours, I listened to one heartbeat and then seemed to wait an eternity for the next one. The General, who was sleeping near by, came in at least once during the night. What he said or did, I do not remember. Probably I slept a reasonable amount. At any rate, in the morning everything was normal.

Near the hotel I found an extremely fine plant. It was an *Alstroemeria*, but so altered in size and general appearance as a result of its alpine habitat that I hardly recognized it. Growing on thin, light scree, the rather stout stem had to push up only six or eight inches to expose the plant to the light. Often its rosette of small, fleshy, light-green leaves, four to five inches across and heavily powdered with white wax, lay flat on the finely divided rock surface. From the center of the geometrically disposed mosaic of leaves there arose a compact knot of wine-red flowers. Each of the three to four in the knot was an inch-and-a-half-long tube that broadened toward the top and ended in a shallowly lobed margin.

Later on we found many of these same attractive, dwarf, succulent-leaved Alstroemerias, both under the pass and on Andean hillsides farther to the north. In no case, however, was their seed ripe. The General and I took the hotel proprietor at El Portillo out on the scree slopes, made him gaze intently at the Alstroemerias, and then extracted from him a solemn promise that he would periodically examine them and collect the seeds when ripe. We made it abundantly clear that ripeness would not be attained in less than a month. A week later, in Valparaiso, I received a small box containing nothing but withered *Alstroemeria* flowers, accompanied by a letter from the proprietor expressing gratification that he had been able to coöperate so successfully in our most important botanical investigations.

We have often collected along the higher slopes of the central

Chilean cordillera over a north-and-south distance of three hundred miles—approximately one hundred miles south of Mount Aconcagua and two hundred miles north of it. In addition to the more intensive botanizing on both sides of the pass under the brow of the great mountain, a part of which has just been described, we collected in the Andes east of Rancagua, Santiago, Petorca, Illapel, Ovalle, and Rivadavia. Sometimes the luck of the seasons was with us, sometimes it was not, but altogether we took abundant loot from the Chilean highlands.

The grandeur of the Andean crest near the twenty-two-thousand-foot peak of the Mercedario is perhaps more impressive than in the Aconcagua area, because the Mercedario massif is very extensive and involves a large number of snowy peaks, between and below which, on the Chilean side, vast snow fields and glaciers are exposed to view. Within the shadow of the Mercedario the Chilean frontier swings sharply to the east for a number of miles, and then west again to form a small dimple on the Argentina side. In the depths of this dimple members of our expedition have worked with considerable success. Carl, John, and Rodolfo rode into it one December morning.

The rough trail ran beside the rushing torrent in an irrigation ditch. When the party tried to cross, the horses, fresh and a bit skittish, shied badly at the foaming water, and so they had to go downstream to a quieter ford. They skirted the base of high hills, crossing and recrossing small ditches that led the precious water from the melting snow fields of the Mercedario over the rocky slopes to small plots of arable land.

The trail began to follow a river. At a sharp bend it had been piling up alluvium for centuries. A progressive farmer had laboriously cleared away the larger boulders and with his incredibly slow oxen he was scratching the soil with a primitive wooden plow. Later on, they saw a little boy driving a small mule which dragged a sizable pile of brush back and forth across this "plowed" land. The primitive harrow was supposed to break up the cloddy soil, so that potatoes, a little wheat, and a few vegetables could be planted. These crops, together with eggs from a motley collection of multicolored hens around the little farmhouse, milk from a small herd of goats pastured above, and meat from kids and lambs, represented practically all the food that this family unit required.

For a time the party followed one of the numerous small streams that flowed together to form a river. Then the trail started to weave in and out of quebradas, as they followed up each little tributary until a suitable ford could be found. Their *vaqueano*—horse wrangler and guide—began to look at the sun, something he continued to do all day long as though to estimate the number of hours that still remained for their journey. He led the cavalcade and soon opened a gap of several hundred yards between his horse and Rodolfo's. John followed close behind Rodolfo, and Carl brought up the rear. Realizing that the animals were accustomed to spurs and that he alone was provided with them, the vaqueano stopped and cut sharp switches from the shrubby mesquite beside the trail. He insisted that the other horsemen use them constantly and maintain his pace, else the party would never reach the high country in time to do any serious collecting.

At an elevation of thirty-five hundred feet they passed the last farmstead. All the country above and beyond, so vast an area that one can ride for days without seeing any sign of human life, was devoted solely to pasturage. With a scanty rainfall and raw, rugged mountainsides, there was little level ground and certainly no soil, in the farmer's sense of that word, above four thousand feet. They had entered a rocky wilderness. It stretched away to the Argentine border, and far beyond.

After another hour's ride the path took them on a long, slow climb across rough hills, toward the highlands. Near the streams, they had been riding through tangles of that curious leafless vine or straggler, *Muehlenbeckia*, with its inconspicuous flowers. Here were also thickets of *Escallonia* and an occasional tree of *Quillaja saponaria*. Soon after beginning the climb the vaqueano paused for a brief descanso in a clump of small Quillajas into whose thin shade the horses crowded close. Ahead, the rock-bound foothills of the Andes rolled higher and higher toward the snow, like brown waves piling up to be shattered into foaming white as they broke against the highest, snow-clad mountainsides.

The wet mountain meadow for which they were bound, La Vega Escondida, lay at an elevation approaching ten thousand feet, which meant that there were still five thousand feet to climb. Ahead was nothing but the stony, zigzag trail, which here and there cut gashes through the low, gray-green chaparral, or monte. The rock formations were, in general, sedimentary, of sandstone-like quality; occasionally shale ledges and outcroppings of quartzite occurred. The vaqueano, who fancied himself a prospector, insisted upon carefully inspecting all these outcroppings. The sparse, low chaparral consisted of *Baccharis*, a tough, resinous-leaved species with pale greenish-white flowers, *Acacia cavenia, Adesmia,* and others of the more common shrubs or diminutive trees of the Andean foothills. They competed with the highly specialized Puyas and columnar cacti for the scanty moisture held in the rocky, sandy soil. Among these woody or succulent plants, in exposed bits of thin soil, they found a red-flowered *Stachys*, or mint, with woolly gray leaves. There was, also, an occasional pink-flowered *Alstroemeria.*

At sixty-five hundred feet they approached a high black crest. Over it a stream tumbled in a fine little waterfall. There they called a halt in order to collect flowering specimens of the dry, shrubby flora through which they had been riding. In addition, they tried to persuade the vaqueano to stop for lunch. He, however, insisted upon continuing to the *vega*. Although pressed, he refused to give any estimate of how much longer luncheon would be postponed and, as if to close the subject, began to climb to the plateau above the falls. Ahead was a wide scarp, hiding the *vega*. Its situation was reflected in its name— *escondida*, or hidden. To the northeast rose a great conical peak, on whose southern flank lay a large, circular, dishlike depression filled with snow. The trail soon began to climb steeply again. The terrain became even rougher, if that were possible, and the monte ever more scattered and poor. At one o'clock they finally reached the meadow and immediately fell to preparing the midday meal.

This vega owed its origin to a quantity of small springs and many seepages of water in the bottom and on the walls of a wide valley. Grasses and sedges were common over the deep, green, wet, cushiony surfaces, and among them grew many showy plants—delicate orange-red *Mimulus, Epilobium, Trifolium,* Gentians, Calceolarias, and many other less familiar genera. All grew in some abundance. Around the margins were other ornamentals, and among them the botanists saw their first Andean violet, a dwarf *Malesherbia*, and a number of brilliant Argylias.

After lunch Carl decided to climb the scree slope above the vega, and John and Rodolfo collected furiously on the marshy surface and over the near-by slopes. In two hours they had put almost sixty species in press. Later Carl returned and told of finding the snow line at ten thousand feet. This meant that they were too early in the season for any collecting on the upper Andean slopes in the Mercedario region, but they consoled themselves by recalling that this was only a scouting trip. Besides, the vegetation in and near the vega had been more than up to expectation.

The afternoon was well advanced when they finally heeded the vaqueano's urgent requests that the homeward journey be started. Rodolfo explained that their guide had just been married and wanted to get back to his village before dark, because encamped near by were some "*muy malos, muy molestos*" miners. For Rodolfo the Andes held certain terrors. Whenever we were outdoors after dark, he informed us that the mountains were liberally infested with miners who butchered and robbed everyone they came across. Doubtless there were some professional prospectors about, but no one of us ever saw any.

Later in the southern summer, John and Rodolfo botanized at twelve to fourteen thousand feet on the slopes that culminate, far above, in the snowy crest of the Mercedario. In a foothill village they had secured the services of a vaqueano and his string of mules. They planned to spend three or four days above ten thousand feet.

First they had to cross the dry lower slopes of the foothills, a tan-to-brown landscape except for scattered gray-green *Acacia* and *Prosopis*. These uninteresting wasteland plants had been transformed by the parasitic *Phrygilanthus* into masses of broad, thick, dark-green leaves, set with rich red flowers. Because of a late start, seven hours in the saddle brought them only to an altitude of sixty-five hundred feet. They camped on the edge of an extensive vega covered with grass. Scores of fat cattle were pastured there, grazing with a vicious thoroughness that was killing the thick turf in many places. After the grass is dead the hoofs of animals break up the dry vegetation, and soon a circular spot of black, crumbly soil is exposed.

The next morning they set the vaqueano to rustling dried dung and the resinous "vegetable sheep" (*llareta*) so that there might be plenty of fuel for the cooking fire. After some collecting on the vega that yielded much the same species they had previously found at La Vega Escondida, John and Rodolfo rode out toward higher altitudes.

For hours, rapidly shifting, ever-darkening clouds had been sweeping down from the crest of the continent toward which they were proceeding. Without warning, the clouds closed in upon them and brought a rapidly rising wind. First it carried a few drops of rain; then a downpour. The rain was cold, sharp, stinging, and held a threat of something more severe to come. The mules did not seem to mind, and plodded slowly up the ever-increasing gradient. Soon the sky became still darker, and the rain gradually changed into a cutting sleet. Faces burned as it lashed them with icy whips. Then came a hailstorm, and in an instant the muddy trail was full of big white marbles. The pounding of the hard pellets and the uncertain footing annoyed the mules, who struggled hard to turn their rumps to the storm. But John and Rodolfo relentlessly forced them onward and upward, and finally, at twelve thousand, five hundred feet, the ridge was topped.

No sooner had they crossed it than a thick snowstorm developed. It walled them in so completely that, for a few moments, they had to halt. The snow had come so rapidly that they had had no time to take stock of the foreground or the background, and for a time they lost all sense of direction. Then, as suddenly as it had come, the storm was at an end. The wind fell to a gentle breeze; the clouds burst open to permit the passage of shafts of sunlight and then dissolved to clear the blue sky. In a few moments the snow began to melt, steam arose from the backs of the mules, and their riders felt warmth flowing back into clammy, shaking limbs.

They dismounted to wring some of the water from their soaking coats and sweaters and to stretch cold, cramped muscles. Rodolfo examined the mules, found that their softened hoofs were showing signs of soreness, and insisted upon starting for the camp. John decided to go forward on foot, while Rodolfo led the animals back. On the return journey he was to stop and dig as many tubers as possible of an alpine nasturtium they had come across on the slopes of the first ridge. The plants had begun to wither before they were old enough to flower, but the leaves suggested that these might be something different from the Tropaeolums previously collected.

John climbed higher and higher through the slush, until he stood upon the last and highest of the foothill ranges. There, at over thirteen thousand feet, he looked across a deep, glaciated valley to the magnificent Andean peaks. Around him the hail and snow were fast disappearing, but, on the farther wall of the valley, a wide belt of whiteness swept up from ten thousand feet to the permanent snow fields that began at sixteen thousand feet. Through his binoculars the soft, brilliantly white, new-fallen snow, which looked to be half a foot deep, contrasted strangely with the glazed, blue-green surface of the almost limitless fields of perpetual snow, from which rose one glittering white eminence after another. He identified Cerro las Lanas (15,700 ft.), Cerro la Mesa (20,440 ft.), and, dominating these and many lesser summits, giant Cerro Mercedario. Great white cumulus clouds began to float up behind its mighty massif, and made shifting patterns of light and shade on the white expanses.

He unshipped cameras and recorded, in black and white and in color, the unsurpassed panorama that stretched away, north and south, only fifteen miles from his lofty coign of vantage. Hardly was the picture taking at an end before the sky became heavily overcast once more and another snowstorm threatened. In addition, there were no plants to collect; the unusually early drought had seen to that; in short, a rapid retreat to the camp, three thousand feet below, was indicated. Cutting across the zigzags of the trail, John slid and floundered straight down the loose, rough talus slopes.

At the camp it had rained much more heavily and for a longer time, and the vaqueano was lying prone in order, periodically, to blow into flame the damp chunks of dung and llareta (*Laretia compacta*) over which the *cazuela*, or stewpot, was suspended. Mountain menus, although they never varied, did not pall. For breakfast there was tea, some sort of breadstuff, and charqui (jerked meat, sometimes suspected of being horse) toasted crisp over the coals. For lunch there was tea, a big stew of charqui—to which had been added any wild game that came to bag—and a few pieces of dried fruit. Dinner always proved to correspond exactly to luncheon, except that another two hours' cooking had reduced the contents of the cazuela to delicious shreds and a rich gravy, which went into the mouth via slabs of bread. Then the serious tea drinking began and oftentimes two big kettles full of the dark-brown brew would no more than satisfy the demand. If the day's work had been unusually taxing, a little cocktail of raw aguardiente increased interest in the evening meal.

When the last cup of tea had been consumed, the bedrolls were opened and spread on the least rocky areas that the fading light revealed. A large waterproof ground-cloth was found essential, because, however rapidly the burning alpine sun dried the rocks or surface soil wetted by a mountain shower, there always seemed to be a residue of moisture ready to dampen the bottom of a sleeping bag. During our many days in the Chilean highlands, no matter how rainy the daylight hours might be, the stars were almost certain to shine unclouded all night long. Thus, a tent or other protection was superfluous. After a night or two of watching those glowing constellations that, in the pellucid Andean atmosphere, seemed to have gained scores of brilliant stars, no one could want to substitute a close, canvas sky.

To try for pictures of the unclouded morning Andean crest, John arose early and rode still higher up the lofty ridge he had climbed the day before. Under the clear sky and brilliant morning light, the Mercedario and its satellites seemed to have decreased the distance that before had separated him from their glaring white slopes, now sparkling and glittering like living things. Just below the peaks, and some ten miles across the deep, U-shaped valley at his feet, a higher ridge marked the Argentine frontier and hid the Aconcagua massif.

The collecting on the high range had been meager. They found a number of hardy grasses, one of which was probably *Stipa chrysophylla*, and a few prostrate editions of some of the shrubs that sparsely populate the lower foothills. Frequent above twelve thousand five hundred feet were the "vegetable sheep" already mentioned. One soon begins to take them for granted, despite the fact that these umbellifers are strictly top-of-the-world plants, rare elsewhere, which exhibit rather remarkable adaptations in form and structure permitting them to withstand the most rigorous environmental conditions that plants attempt to meet.

For the camp that night they found a vega still moist enough to support a little vegetation on which the mules could be scantily pastured. The evening meal was a decided disappointment and consisted principally of the crumbs at the bottom of the charqui bag, washed down with tea. When John routed out his campanions at daybreak, they discovered that the only food remaining was a five-day-old roll apiece and that there was no tea. At the start of the eight-hour ride, all three were hungry, restive, and cross; but as the altitude decreased, and the heat correspondingly increased they lost interest in one another, in their surroundings, and even in the prospect of what the grubby little pension at their destination would supply in the way of food.

Plant hunting in the Chilean highlands has an enduring fascination. Where the vegetation is right, new or little-known species lead the collector across the vegas and over the ridges from one excitement to another. Even when the plants are few and far between there are sure to be some of them so charming or so scientifically impressive that their presence in the press excuses the fact that it is not so full as one could wish.

There are other compensations for all the long, hard, and sometimes hazardous climbing, the midday heat of the alpine sun, and the struggle against cold storms that arise so rapidly on the barren plains below the highest Chilean Andes. At the close of day all this is forgotten when, in the hush that comes at nightfall in high altitudes, the sunset transforms the horizon. A long, deep shadow rapidly unfolds, to creep across and above the tan foothills, to touch the snow line, then on to spread its gray cloak over the snow fields and glaciers, and finally to fall across the peaks that glitter against the pale sky of early night. Hardly is shadow's work accomplished before the ruddy sunset glow, for all too brief a season, brings a new and colorful existence to the rugged Andean crests. Their lofty white expanses become transformed into clouds of rosy light, which shades to deep magenta in the broad depressions on the gray-hued snow fields. Gradually the roseate panorama fades into the deepening violet of the evening sky, as though the final curtain were being drawn across the brilliant alpine stage. Then, suddenly, the highest peaks are touched with rich, warm light and begin to glow like beacons invisibly hung against a darkening background. Their light is so long sustained that the forward progress of time seems suspended, while one strains fully to comprehend the glory of the alpine afterglow and fix indelibly in remembrance a picture of the top of the world aflame.

15

EARTHQUAKE

D URING FINAL STAGES in the preparation of the new edition of this book, the first accounts of the terrible products of the 1960 seismic disturbances in South Chile began to appear in the press. Later information enlarged the area of material destruction and loss of life to nearer and more remote portions of almost the entire Pacific basin. Then, continued earth movements extended the range of devastation in southern Chile, and volcanoes long inactive or largely dormant came into eruption to add a crowning element of terror.

I was in central and southern Chile at the time of and immediately following the great earthquake of 1939. Much of the terrain affected in 1960 was the same as that which suffered equally or possibly more severely in the earlier year. As will appear in the following pages, much of the destruction of property in 1939—for example, in the city of Concepción—was a product of types of construction which could hardly have been expected to withstand earth movements of almost maximum known intensity. Loss of life and serious injury to Concepción's inhabitants—apparently greater in 1939 than in 1960—was, therefore, inevitable. During the last twenty years the city has in considerable part been rebuilt, and new structures have been added. Much of this construction is said to have been of concrete, suitably reinforced, and to this fact many of Concepción's residents owe their lives.

Up to the time that this was written, there has been no report of earthquake damage in Santiago or Valparaiso; indeed, the "General" writes that no appreciable tremors (in Chilean terms) were felt in the capital or the coastal city. By contrast, in 1939 the earth movements were extremely violent, in Valparaiso at least. Neither in 1939 nor in 1960 was there a tidal wave at the port city. However, between the two dates both cities have felt more than one quite appreciable *terremoto*. One, in Santiago, that I well remember was of sufficient magnitude to drive out into the street many of the guests in the hotel in which we were stopping at the time. The earthquake, which came late at night, gave the extremely disquieting impression that the hotel building was alternately being raised up and then lowered. Our room was near the head of a long flight of stairs leading to the street floor. Before the peculiar vertical movement had completely stopped, I heard a commotion outside our door. I looked out to see the stairs almost completely blocked by badly panicked men, women, and children, none of them with much of anything on, pushing and crowding their way downward. Since the introduction of animals into the hotel was strictly prohibited, I was a bit surprised to note that a number of dogs and even a cat or two were among those present. The next day we were told that a certain proportion of Santiago's residents had spent the remainder of the night in one or other of the big plazas.

In 1939 we occupied a big room in the Hotel Lebell, a modest hostelry far enough removed from Valparaiso's center to be relatively quiet. Our big-windowed room was on the ground floor of the two-storied building. Within less than a stone's throw, the traffic on horse- and burro-back as well as on foot was constant during daylight hours and immensely entertaining. The broad avenue upon which it flowed was constructed with two rather narrow lanes for all traffic and a broad, grassy promenade between them. This was one of the principal thoroughfares paralleling Valparaiso Bay, and along it early in the morning and late in the afternoon the countrypeople came and went. Their journey had begun hours before on some outlying farm and was approaching its weary end. The soft padding of tired feet had a deliberate quality as, with low-voiced commands, the farmers slowly guided their laden animals in and out of the wheeled traffic toward the city markets. But late in the afternoon the street sounds had a different tempo. The soft footfalls were quicker and lighter. On the cobbles the hard little hoofs of the burros provided a staccato accompaniment for the steady creaking of empty leather panniers and the soft, gossipy laughter of the countrypeople homeward bound.

There was an endless fascination in these parades that flowed past our window. Just opposite, in the promenade, a municipal water faucet had developed a leak. It was just sufficient to give a continuous trickle that had dug a little moist basin and spread beyond it to make a miniature marsh. Clearly it was a plumbing defect of long standing, and at first we wondered why somebody did not do something about it. Soon our question was answered. A hot, dusty muleteer would leave his line of loaded animals for a moment, paddle his bare feet in the little pool, and stand for a brief, delicious instant in the soft, cool, wet grass before he stepped out again onto the hard, hot roadway. And the tired lines in his face would be a little smoothed, as with a handful of water he would wash a part of the gray dust from them. What a simple explanation of a leaking faucet. How often in South America we saw such unobtrusive evidences of appreciation for the problems of the poor and underprivileged—regulations relaxed, their infringement overlooked, or some helping hand coming from an unexpected source. For us these proofs of an underlying social consciousness and generosity in South American life did much to counteract the unfavorable impressions which small natures in high places sometimes insisted upon making.

At about eleven o'clock in the evening of January 24, 1939, we were in bed and almost asleep. On the street outside our window only an occasional automobile rattled by. At last were quieted the high, shrill whistles of the launches that all the evening had been escorting coal barges across the bay of Valparaiso. The thin edge of consciousness was gradually wearing away; drifting visions of the day's exploits were merging into dreams. Suddenly stark, rigid reality seized us. Without preliminary trembles or that distant rumbling in the earth which to Californians is a preamble to its tremors, we were in the vicious grip of a violent earthquake. It did not begin gradually, as though tentatively feeling out the weakness of a fault line before accelerating to maximum movement. Rather, it engulfed us, mature and at the height of its power. The immediate transition from peace to horror was totally beyond normal comprehension. Something was happening which so transcended experience that full consciousness was instantly suspended. For an eternity of seconds we lived in another world. In company with two hundred thousand others in Chile that night we were struck dumb and rendered entirely incapable of action. Then consciousness flowed back, and with the others about us we joined our voices in agonized, frenzied protests and appeals that rang out above the deep, grinding roar of the earthquake. It was the first time that I had heard human voices reflect elemental terror in the high falsetto or deep bass of animal throats.

R.L.S. knew earthquakes. His frightened old buccaneer, lying sick in the Admiral Benbow, told Jim how in distant lands he had "seen the blessed land a-heaving like the sea." During those eighty seconds of earthquake we unconsciously affirmed the blessedness of a normal earth, an earth free from movement, but not this earth that now, like the stormy sea, was heaving, pitching, and twisting without respite and with obvious intent to bring complete destruction upon us.

In remembrance nothing that I did or thought during that overwhelming experience is clear. Almost from the beginning I must have realized the menace, not only of the land, but also of the sea, only a few hundred yards from our ground-floor room. I knew that we must escape to higher ground against the coming of a tidal wave, that frequent follower of earthquakes, which all too often has completed the destruction begun by them in Chilean coastal cities. With this thought came despair because, so long as the earth movements continued with their initial violence, escape was out of the question. Perhaps we were still in a state of partially suspended animation produced by the sudden onset of the earthquake. Perhaps we were suffering from a certain lack of muscular coördination induced by it. At any rate, by the time we realized the desperate need of action, we found ourselves so violently and so rapidly tossed about in our beds that leaving them seemed impossible. In addition, the beds and other furniture were beginning to move about the room in dangerous fashion. Finally, the ceiling plaster began to fall and, like the ostrich, we thought only of protection for our heads, something that the pillows alone would give. Each succeeding second seemed inevitably to be our last. It was impossible to believe that the building could longer withstand the continuous shaking—certainly any increase in its violence would bring it down.

Then, as suddenly as it began, the earthquake was over. We lay there side by side, without a word, each gathering together the shattered remnants of faith and courage, in a now motionless, noiseless world—waiting for the earthquake to return. A long minute passed, and with it the strain was released. Immediately our world awoke, we heard running feet and shouts in the street, above our heads there were tentative movements and then quick steps and strained voices, a subdued hum of activity traveled about us through the city, and we too came back to life.

There was no tidal wave and no further perceptible earth movement on that night or during our remaining two months in Valparaiso. But earth adjustments were not complete for many weeks. Gutter pools would one moment show a calm surface and the next be covered with shivering ripples to indicate the quick passage of a minute temblor. The city gave little evidence of what it had endured. Chilean architects of the last generation had insisted upon adorning their larger buildings with many elaborate cornices and heavily decorated window frames. Most of these architectural excrescences fell in the destructive Valparaiso earthquake of 1906 and some of the remainder came down in 1939. A few buildings were structurally damaged, much plaster fell, many walls were superficially cracked, and plenty of crockery was smashed. Probably a number of persons were injured in Valparaiso and in Santiago, where the earthquake was felt almost as strongly. But their misfortunes were forgotten in the news that next morning began to filter in, and that told of heavy loss of life and terrible destruction of property in Concepción and Chillán, some two hundred miles to the south.

The first reports made it clear that a major disaster had occurred in one of the more densely populated sections of Chile. The city of Concepción, the third largest in the republic, with a population of seventy thousand, was near the epicenter of the earthquake. Chillán, a city of about forty thousand, was even more disastrously located. Telegraph and telephone lines were down over a long distance within the earthquake area. Because of damage to roadbed and rails, train service ended at its margin. With all normal means of communication interrupted, preliminary estimates of damage had to be made from the air. Early morning editions of the Valparaiso newspapers carried estimates that amounted to almost complete destruction of Chillán and very grave damage in Concepción. On the basis of this evidence claims of loss of life in the devastated area were naturally placed at a high figure. Later, when radio communication was reëstablished and rescue parties by land, sea, and air reached the earthquake zone, these claims were somewhat reduced; but it was still believed that many thousands of persons had been killed or injured. An unfortunately long experience in Chile with the effects of serious earthquakes suggested to the authorities that the injured rather than the dead would make up the larger proportion of this total. As a result, all available physicians and nurses in the Valparaiso-Santiago region were mobilized, and coastwise shipping was requisitioned to carry them and medical supplies to Talcahuano, the port of Concepción. The General, of course, agreed to organize a medical unit, and went about it in his usual vigorous and effective fashion. John at once volunteered to go, and the General wangled an appointment for him as a male nurse in his unit.

The journey to Concepción was made on the coastwise steamer *Teno*. The *Teno* was not a large ship, and the sea was exceedingly rough. The only excitement during the thirty-six hours' run was the appearance of the cruiser *Ajax*. With the now equally famous *Exeter*, she had been lying in the harbor of Valparaiso at the time of the earthquake, and was at once ordered to southern Chile to assist in rescue work. A year or so later, when John read about the remarkably rapid and clever maneuvers of these cruisers in the battle off Montevideo, he recalled how the fifteen-knot *Teno* had seemed to be standing still as the *Ajax* sped by on the way to Talcahuano, the port of Concepción. They arrived there too late in the evening to permit passengers to go ashore, and so had to spend a second night on board. Early the next morning the party of doctors, nurses, and a few sightseers was landed.

They hurried up the landing steps on the quayside and then toward the port captain's offices. The port buildings showed little damage, but what they saw around the corner was pretty bad. Everywhere the adobe- and brick-walled houses had toppled into the streets, most of which had become a shambles of broken plaster, cracked tile, and splintered wood. Twenty-seven victims of the disaster had already been buried in Talcahuano and there were still more bodies to be dug from the ruins. Later on, they saw most of the population living outdoors in vacant lots and in the plaza.

John and the others stood about in the gloomy fog, trying not to look too often into the ruined town. Finally they were herded into a dilapidated bus to begin the ride to Concepción. The fog began to rise from the surface of the bay, and slowly its dense, shroudlike mantle was lifted from the desolate streets of Talcahuano to the tops of the wooded hills behind the port. The day was dull and cheerless. The bus wandered from street to street to pick out those that were passable. Most of them were narrow and had been choked from curb to curb with knee-deep piles of bricks, tiles, cement blocks, and rubble. Through a few of these streets, crews of road workers had cleared tortuous paths. Because there were so many different kinds of things to be done during the first hours after the earthquake, these channels through the ruins had been hurriedly completed, and, in consequence, were rough and narrow. John and his campanions were glad to get clear of what was left of Talcahuano.

The rolling, sandy countryside between the port and Concepción slipped past quickly, the driver skillfully steering his bus over smoother parts of the considerably damaged highway. Farms and little settlements that they passed showed the effects of the earthquake—fences were broken or out of line, and walls had fallen or been badly cracked. Half the tile roof of one house had slipped away to become a high heap of debris before the front door. John wondered whether the occupants had stayed inside or had got clear before the tiles came crashing down. Perhaps their crushed bodies still lay beneath the ruins of their roof. Many times that day he was to ask himself similar questions, and only rarely were those questions to be answered.

The closer they came to the city of Concepción, the greater was the degree of destruction. Whereas in Talcahuano two or three houses in a given block—or half the front walls of twice that number—had fallen, in Concepción they saw streets in which all the buildings were demolished. After many detours and a rough, jolting passage along the few partially cleared thoroughfares, they reached the center of the city and disembarked beside the great plaza where the twin-towered Cathedral looked across at the Intendencia, which housed the local governmental offices. Both structures gave evidence of the destructive power of the earthquake. The main plaza in any Latin-American city is normally the center of human activity. In Concepción it was headquarters for all the work of rescue and rehabilitation that was in progress.

John's diary tells the story of his brief stay in what, a few days before, had been one of the most attractive centers of population in Chile:

"At first glance, the great plaza appeared to contain only a milling mass of humanity. Actually, however, there was a good deal of organization. The largest crowd was assembled in the center around the bandstand, which had been occupied by the officers of government. They had moved what was left of the furniture and records from the ruined Intendencia. To the left of this government headquarters was a considerable area that had been roped off and filled with benches. Overhead, a large canvas sheltered part of this roped-off space. It gave to those who sat on the benches some protection from the rain that had been falling and threatened to come down again at any moment.

A number of pretty Red Cross nurses were treating innumerable superficial injuries, and men and women kept coming in to have their wounds dressed. Small wonder that some of these wounds looked dirty and angry! They had not received attention since they had been acquired, forty hours before.

"On the other side of the bandstand, registration booths had been set up by the local political parties of the Left-Radical, Socialist, and Communist. To these booths party members came to sign for work in clearing the city, and to obtain tools and work assignments. Each of them had the insignia of his party on an arm brassard or in his hat. At regular intervals, groups of these workers marched out of the plaza toward their assigned areas. The remainder of the plaza was given over to refugees. Everywhere there were families who had been sleeping outdoors either through fear of recurrence of the *terremoto* or because their homes had been smashed beyond immediate repair. One family, a mother and six children, had placed two benches about six feet apart, and in the space between had spread all the bedding they had salvaged. The mother and older children were cooking a light breakfast over a small fire, while the smaller children slept fitfully in the dim morning light. They all seemed dazed, oblivious of their physical surroundings and of the crowds around them.

"Everyone was talking about the extent of the disaster in terms of dead and injured. I spoke to an Englishman who said that three thousand had already been buried in Concepción and that the number in near-by Chillán must be as great. People were referring to thirty thousand dead in South Chile. It was obvious that under the stress of emotion accompanying such a terrible disaster no one could be expected to be conservative in estimating anything connected with it." The final record showed that a little over eight hundred people died in Concepción and not over ten thousand in the entire earthquake area. John continues:

"The residential area had been hard hit. There were many streets where every house had lost its cornices or other brick or stone ornamentation the architects had seen fit to design. It was a curious sight to look down a street and see every building standing, while the sidewalks in front were covered to a depth of three feet with cornices, gargoyles, and the like, all apparently thrown down at the first shock. About three blocks from the university we came upon a dozen English sailors from the cruiser *Ajax* methodically clearing away the debris in front of a ruined house.

"When we arrived at the plaza about eleven o'clock, the General had some official business to transact. I agreed to accompany his son Alfredo, who was also a member of the medical unit, to look up a number of relatives and friends. We walked down a narrow street past the skeleton of a large store that had burned after the terremoto. Two blocks beyond this blackened ruin, we found the two-story apartment building where one family of relatives had lived. From a man standing disconsolately on the curb, Alfredo learned that none of them had been killed or injured, and that probably some of them were still in the building.

"From the street, this building looked unharmed. It had not been provided with cornices, so that even the sidewalk was relatively clear. We opened the door to find the stairway deep in broken plaster. Dust swirled about us as we slowly and carefully picked our way up the stairs, which felt rather shaky under our feet. When we reached the second-floor landing, we discovered that outside appearances in Concepción were deceptive. Inside, this house was entirely ruined. Ceilings had come down, walls had fallen in or out of the rooms, everything was in a state of complete smash. We found one of Alfredo's cousins in a back room. In a dazed, hesitating way he was trying to gather together some of his belongings to take to his family. They were living with another relative whose home was less damaged. For Alfredo's benefit, he enumerated all the relatives then in Concepción. Many had lost their homes, some had suffered minor injuries, but none had been killed.

"We looked into the bedroom where this man and his wife had been asleep when the terremoto struck. How they had managed to get out alive, I could not imagine. All the rear wall, built of unsupported brick, had crashed into the room, and there were hundreds of bricks piled on the flattened bed and thrown about over the rest of the broken furniture. His explanation of how they escaped sounded simple enough: 'The instant we felt the house begin to move we jumped out of bed and ran for the stairs that led outdoors. Arrived at the front door, we stood under the casing for a moment until the plaster had stopped falling and there was no longer any danger that the surface of the building would fall into the street, and then we went out.'

"Alfredo and I walked slowly away from this ruined house toward the plaza. No longer were we interested in the ruins about us. That look behind the walls of an apparently undamaged home had given us a new conception of the extent of the terrible human catastrophe that had occurred. All damaged structures in this stricken city would have to be rebuilt from the ground up. Otherwise, the next earthquake, or the next, both of them certain to come, in one, or ten, or ninety years, would be even more destructive.

"We got our baggage from the Red Cross tent, and I took tripod and movie camera to get views of ruined Concepción before the black clouds reduced the light still more or ruined my day completely by giving up their rain. It was not easy to photograph such a disaster. One had to be a little hardhearted. To intrude upon the private affairs of grief-stricken people is difficult. Old men and women sat dejectedly on the curb in front of the remains of a home or little shop, and they were not much interested in a photographer. Under such circumstances tact must be used, and that is not so easy when one's Spanish is a little weak.

"As I started out, people began to stream from all directions into the plaza. There were well-dressed Chileans, Englishmen in boots and riding breeches, and many workmen with bare feet and ragged pants. As I stopped and looked about me to see what could be the excitement, Alfredo came over and whispered, 'Look, there is the President.' I looked in this direction and in that direction, expecting to see a platoon of soldiers or at least a guard of carabineros conducting the official party. But what I saw, almost directly in front of me, was Don Pedro Aguirre Cerda, the then President of Chile, walking slowly from a sedan parked across the street and unprovided with any guard or, so far as I could see, any official entourage. A man was walking beside him, and the President's head was bent as he listened to what this man was saying.

"The crowd opened a wide path as the President approached. He passed us and went on to the headquarters of the government in the center of the plaza. I could hardly believe my eyes. Here was a public figure of great importance walking, unprotected, across a plaza crowded with people of all kinds of political enthusiasms. Later on, we met his wife, the First Lady of Chile, walking resolutely about in the midst of the ruins, expressing interest and asking for information about her friends and her friends' friends.

"In the plaza again, the refugees were beginning to prepare the noon-day meal. One family, all grown people, sat in a circle on a path bordered by flowering hydrangeas. To judge by their clothes, they had been people accustomed to comfort, perhaps luxuries. With the corners weighted down by stones, a number of newspapers had been spread on the pavement to serve as a tablecloth. As I walked along on an adjacent path, one of the younger people in the family was staring intently at this improvisation. Suddenly, and as though remembering something neglected, she turned and broke off a flower, fitted it rather clumsily into the broken neck of a beer bottle, and then leaned forward to place flower and incongruous container in the center of the newspapers. I lingered a moment to watch this panto-mime. No member of the family smiled or spoke or moved. With apparently no realization for the moment of their surroundings, they sat there like statues and gazed unseeingly at their pitiful table decora-tion. I had no right to be watching them and, with smarting eyes, turned away in search of my transportation to the port."

When John ultimately reached Talcahuano, to return by sea to Valparaiso, he began to see another distressing aftermath of the earth-quake. From the port captain's office stretched a long line of ref-ugees. For hours they had been waiting patiently to be assigned to one of the various rescue vessels lying in the harbor. Most of these sad people had lost practically everything they possessed, and the govern-ment was transporting them to Valparaiso and Santiago, where rela-tives or friends would take them in. They had piled the remnants of their possessions along a high fence separating the quay from the street. John, rather overwhelmed by this final evidence of human want and suffering, got away from the waterside as soon as he could.

Among the regions of the earth that have been subject to destructive seismic disturbances, Chile has suffered very severely. Relative in-tensity is difficult to determine in comparing Chilean with Japanese or with Californian earth movements, but in total number of recorded earthquakes Chile has the misfortune to lead the field. It is said that for every one thousand earthquakes felt there, only slightly over four hundred occur in Japan and about eighty in California. Earth-quakes have been recorded in Chile since 1570, at least. On February 8th of that year, less than eighty years after the discovery of the Amer-icas, severe shocks destroyed Concepción.

Rain often appears to be a concomitant of Chilean terremotos. On that terrible night in January, 1939, rain began to fall in Concepción, Chillán, and near-by areas soon after the earth movement was at an end, although January normally represents the height of the dry season in south central Chile. Chileans sometimes insist that any unseasonable rains, especially those that occur rarely on the excessively arid northern coasts of their country, are always related to earth movements. This, however, is not the case. The torrential rains of 1940 and 1959 that caused destruction on the nitrate coast were not preceded by an earthquake.

The predicting of earthquakes is, quite naturally, a popular indoor sport in Chile. Since a large number of noticeable earth movements is practically certain to occur each year, the chances of picking the right day, now and then, are fairly good. Of course, erroneous predictions are promptly forgotten, whereas correct ones receive local publicity for years to come.

Charles Darwin visited Concepción several days after the disastrous earthquake and tidal wave of 1835. He called attention to the fact that on the same night volcanoes became active from southern Chile to Ecuador, including even Aconcagua, long quiescent. Whether this was merely coincidence, whether volcanic activity was responsible for the earthquake, or whether the earth movements brought the volcanoes into action are all questions for which there are apparently no final answers. Darwin also pointed out that the "very heavy and evil odor of brimstone," which was reported as early as 1570 to accompany earthquakes in Concepción, was probably the result of a thorough agitation by the earth movements of the foul bottom of the near-by harbor of Talcahuano. Certainly, vile odors arise when an anchor chain is dragged in that and in many other harbors.

I have been permitted to copy a few excerpts from the unpublished diary of a "forty-niner" en route to California from Boston on the brig *Rudolph*. They made the port of Talcahuano on May 29, 1849, one hundred and ten days out of Boston, 'round the Horn. The diarist saw the town of Talcahuano and also the city of Concepción, with the evidences of earlier terremotos in them. He includes some comment on the flavor of Chilean life a hundred and ten years ago:

"*May 29, 1849* . . . The Captain of the Port came on board, entered us at the customhouse, gave us the regulations of the port and directed us where to anchor . . . We find it a very fine harbor, protected on all sides except the north. The anchorage is good and there is a fine chance to get wood, water and provisions. The bay abounds in birds of all kinds but you are not allowed to shoot them. The hills on either side rise some five or six hundred feet above the level of the sea. They are verdant and highly susceptible of cultivation. There are but few trees on the hills but quite a number of huts, with a little piece of cultivated land, from which the inhabitants get their living . . . Plenty of fish in the bay, which are very good eating.

"We found the following vessels in port, bound to California: ship 'Panama' of New York, 115 days' passage, and stopped 9 days at Rio, with 202 passengers on board and all well; ship 'Hopewell' from Warren, Rhode Island, 105 days' passage and made no stops, 150 passengers and all well except the Captain, who is not expected to live; ship 'Christoval Colon' of New York, 145 days' passage, stopped 35 days at Rio to repair (having sprung her main-mast in the Gulf Stream), 15 days off Cape Horn; [and the] brig 'John Pette' of Norfolk, Virginia, 130 days' passage, stopped 11 days at Rio, 14 passengers. Two old whalers are preparing to go to California as soon as possible. A large Chilean man-o'-war ship, two Chilean brigs and one American brig which has been seized by the Chilean Government. The town looks like a dirty mass of huts.

"After dinner it was 'Hurrah for the shore.' At two o'clock the first boatload left, and in the course of an hour nearly all were on shore. There is no wharf in this port; vessels are obliged to lay at anchor and land on the beach with their boats. The houses, with two or three exceptions, are one story high and generally built of brick and plastered outside and whitewashed. But some have a kind of frame plastered up with mud. They have no chimneys. They build their fires to warm their houses in earthen pans. They do their cooking out of doors. The roofs are made of bricks of the same material that the walls are made of, called tiles . . . There are three two-story houses, one of them the customhouse, one-half of which is occupied by a hotel kept by an American by the name of Canfield who, by the way, is one of the most obliging and kindest men you ever saw, and sets a fine table . . . He has a Spanish lady for a wife, who is a very fine woman. This is the only hotel in the place.

"This place is probably one of the most corrupt and licentious places in the world. There are four females to one male, and about two-thirds of these girls are prostitutes and are driven to it perforce of circumstances. There are no factories and the Gentry do not employ females

for servants and in consequence they become bad and come to Talcahuano because it is a place where a great many whalers put in for
supplies. These girls are healthy and robust, capable of enduring
fatigue. They have generally black hair and eyes and round oval features and are very pretty and many play the guitar and sing very well.
I wish they were in old New England where they could find better
employment. The Spanish people are the most hospitable in the world,
especially the Gentry, and the government has done everything for
their protection that they could do. The streets are paved with small
round stones and the walks are stone and bricks but they are very
uneven and it is the muddiest place at this season that I ever saw. There
are six or seven Americans who trade in the place and do very well.
The principal amusements they have are billiards, tenpins, cock fights
and Dame Houses. Wild game is plenty but very shy; plenty of snipe,
curlew, teal, partridges, and so forth. We spent two days a-gunning
and had a very pleasant time."

He then mentions a hospital and certain Americans confined there.
"Mr. Hudson of Waterville, Maine . . . had his leg shot off acci-
dentally on board the 'Mary Wilder' from Boston . . . [He] is
getting well fast and has engaged passage in the 'Globe' to California.

"*June 3* . . . We made up a party and started to go to Conception. The way is over a plain covered with low shrubby trees and
the roads run all around among them. One place we stopped at they
were roasting a hog, which seemed very novel to us—I say "roasting,"
I suppose they were scorching off the bristles. They do not scald
them as we do in the States.

"Arrived at Conception at ten o'clock and took a stroll over the
city. Stopped in the American Hotel and got something to eat . . .
then visited the ruins of the old Cathedral and what they call 'Mother
of Mercy' . . . [We were] invited into several places and had a
good time, especially at the Bishop's [where] we sang several songs,
which pleased him very much . . . I thought the old fellow would
get drunk, he drank so much wine. We had a great time [and] at
twelve o'clock found all beds occupied at Mr. Brooks' hotel and I laid
down somewhere on the floor. I pulled one of the bricks out of the
floor for a pillow and tried to get to sleep.

"The next day we visited some more of the ruins caused by the
earthquake of 1751 which were very imposing and really worth one's
while to visit them. There are some ruins of the earthquake of 1835

but that was slight to this one of 1751; then it was almost totally destroyed . . . the one of 1835 killed 7 men and threw down a few houses. We have all taken specimens of the ruins; we intend to carry them home. To the southwest of the city is a very high mountain, which we went up and had a fine view of the city and surrounding country. [We] had the pleasure of picking oranges and lemons off the trees, besides having many given us. The trees about the city are principally orange, lemon and palm. The palm makes a very novel and pretty appearance. The houses are much better than those in Talcahuano but the same style. They have several cathedrals. They all have bells and when they are all ringing them they remind one of home and sound well.

"They are mostly gentlemen who live here and very fine people. The ladies are very pretty and very accomplished. They play the piano, guitar, sing and dance finely and they walk splendidly and I think I can spend a week here very well.

"The term by which the common people are called is *peon* and *choler*. If one of these trouble you on the road you are at liberty to shoot him, and the laws will justify you in it . . . [There] is a bay next up to Conception where it is fine sailing and fishing. Population, Conception 10,300, Talcahuano about 4,000 . . . Let me say one word in regard to the American Consul . . . [In] the language of another 'his wife is a fine man but he is a nobody.' He certainly is a very poor representative of our government and ought to be removed. He has been the means of reducing the value of American money 25 per cent, which is an outrageous thing and ought to be exposed. The British and French consuls are business men and perfect gentlemen.

"*June 11* . . . At four o'clock [P.M.] we are all on board and we are under way with a flattering prospect . . . and are glad to be on our passage again . . . [We] hope in fifty days to be in San Francisco." (It took them ninety-six days to reach their destination.)

The zones of destruction in the 1939 and 1960 earthquakes involved the center of one of the most important agricultural areas in Chile. From the Maule River northward toward the plains that surround the city of Santiago, a wide valley stretches between the Andes and the coastal hills. Its deep, fertile soils have for many generations produced rich crops of wheat and barley and fine stands of alfalfa. From its hillside vineyards come the wines that even the educated palate has difficulty in distinguishing from the better vintages of France. The annual rainfall of from fifteen to thirty inches, or sometimes more, is supplemented by irrigation water diverted from the coastward flow of rivers whose sources are in Andean snows. Thus, optimum moisture conditions prevail during the long, sunny growing season. Many of Chile's great landowners are here the lords of little agricultural empires and, in the past at least, were absentee landlords most of the time.

The broken topography of much of Chile's farmland, combined with the dependence and rather low intellectual level of the rank and file of her peon labor, makes anything approaching complete mechanization of Chilean agriculture neither feasible nor at present desirable. On the other hand, it should be possible to reduce, by at least one third, the amount of hand labor involved; the average farmer would then become more prosperous, or rather, would for the first time know a little prosperity. This prosperity he would inevitably pass on, in some part at least, to his farm labor. With increased profits from his estates, the larger proprietor could afford to improve the housing conditions and raise the general standard of living of his contract labor, with a consequent improvement in its efficiency. In other words, even a limited increase in farm mechanization will usher in a new era in Chile's most important agricultural areas.

16

LAND OF THE MONKEY PUZZLE

A s THE ANDES flow south from the American "top of the world" in Central Chile, the altitude of their peaks begins to decrease rapidly at about 36° South, which is Concepción's approximate distance from the equator. Thence, southward, the mountains that make Chile a narrow coastal plain rarely rise more than ten thousand feet above sea level. After knowing intimately the immensity of the Central Chilean Andes and the pass at Aconcagua's feet, across which an altitude of over ten thousand feet must be attained, it is a surprise to find that only seven degrees to the south the extension of that miles-high mountain range can be crossed at an altitude of less than thirty-five hundred feet. It is equally surprising to find that, both on the coast and in the Andean foothills, one's progress southward from dry Central Chile is accompanied by a rapid increase in rainfall which ultimately produces a land of rivers and lakes where the annual precipitation is above one hundred inches; in localized areas it may reach two hundred inches.

I have, a number of times, balanced collecting in arid northern Chile with expeditions into its climatic antithesis, southern Chile. In that rainy territory we collected in areas along the coast from Constitución to below Valdivia, and to the east in the foothills of the Andes and at higher elevations also—especially in, and north and south of, the forests of *Araucaria araucana*, the "monkey puzzle" or "Chilean pine."

Before the Spaniards came, considerable forests covered large portions of the central valley, the coastal mountain ranges, and the Andean slopes of south central Chile. Much of this forest was long ago destroyed to provide the large areas that, for a century or two, have

307

been devoted to crops and pastureland. The present-day forests of Chile are first seen farther to the south. They are largely confined to the Andes and cover the mountainsides to an altitude somewhat above five thousand feet. Still farther south and then for over a thousand miles toward Cape Horn, the forests become denser and denser along the diminishing Andean crest.

The Araucarias, their name derived from the Province of Arauco in southern Chile, have been among the most prized pot evergreens in cultivation. For one who is used to seeing stately trees of a number of *Araucaria* species growing outdoors in California, it used to be amusing to observe the enthusiasm evoked by a two-foot specimen which some years ago was likely to be decorating the center of a New England dining table. This pot plant was almost certain to be *Araucaria excelsa*, a symmetrical, light-green, little tree with two or three branch-stories, each formed by four or five horizontal branches arising in a ring about the scaly stem. Its popular name, "Norfolk Island pine," indicates its native home. There are other Australasian species also.

The hardiest *Araucaria* is *A. araucana*. It is probably the best-known member of the genus, because most widely grown. It thrives in cultivation not only in California, Florida, and similar climates, but also in some gardens in Great Britain and Ireland. Like its dinner-table cousin it becomes a symmetrical tree, with branches occurring in whorls. These branches, however, are not horizontal; they curve gracefully upward, and at regular intervals numerous branchlets stand out in pairs along them. This subdivision of the branching increases as the tree matures, ultimately developing a complex that might well puzzle any monkey who attempted to find his way to the top of the pyramidal mass. On its native heath the tree grows to between seventy-five and one hundred feet. The trunk, bare for well over half its height, supports a wide, flattened crown of long and symmetrically disposed but somewhat scraggly branches which often give the effect of symmetry gone wrong—a weird, bizarre effect almost without parallel among sizable plants.

Like our Sequoias, the monkey puzzle long ago was widespread in distribution, almost cosmopolitan, whereas today both genera occupy only minute fragments of the earth's surface. In South America, the Brazilian *Araucaria* covers a quarter of a million square miles, with its best development in the State of Paraná—whence its local name,

Mount Osorno, "Fujiyama of South America" is the gem of the Chilean lake area.

The "monkey puzzle" (*Araucaria auracana*) is characteristic of the south Chilean-Argentine Andes.

The long, glistening trumpets of el copihue (*Lapageria rosea*) are white, through pastel pink, to maroon.

The masses of the "fire bush's" (*Embothrium coccineum*) scarlet flowers make burning dots on the green surfaces of the temperate rain forest.

"Paraná pine." The only other species in our sister continent, the monkey puzzle, is today limited in total distribution to a relatively small area in the coast range south of Concepción and to a much larger but still somewhat restricted area in the South Chilean Andes and over their crest in Argentina. The Chileno calls this, his most famous conifer, "*el piñón*" or "*pehuen.*"

Tourists should never neglect to see Volcán Villarica with its perfect, snow-capped cone reflected in the azure waters of one of Chile's loveliest mountain lakes. On and near the nine-thousand-foot volcano are some of the finest stands of *el piñón*. For fifty miles south of Villarica and thirty north of it, forests of these Disneyesque trees are scattered in larger and smaller groves. They prefer altitudes of twenty-five to thirty-five hundred feet where the pressure of cordilleran winds reduces the extreme humidity characteristic of lower altitudes in the southern Andes.

Having had considerable knowledge of the vegetation of the characteristic and extensive monkey puzzle territory on both western and eastern slopes of the southern Andes, I wanted to know something about the botanical features of the only other, and limited, area of occurrence of *Araucaria araucana* in the coastal mountain range a little south of Concepción. The region is known as the Cordillera de Nahuelbuta. With an average altitude of about three thousand feet and eminences up to forty-five hundred feet, it has some climatic distinctions between its western or Pacific face and its eastern one. I had twice been on the margins of Nahuelbuta but neither time at a season propitious for plant collecting. During our fifth expedition Paul collected there briefly, and two years ago Walter spent some time among its Araucarias.

On both occasions, the long-established Methodist mission and agricultural school, called El Vergel, near the town of Angol, was collecting headquarters. For many years, on a large acreage of cultivated land, El Vergel has instructed the youth of southern Chile in agricultural techniques appropriate for that region. Also, imported trees and vines have been tested and acclimatized, and El Vergel has long been a principal Chilean source of superior horticultural varieties. The Rev. Dr. Dillman Bullock, for over half a century the guiding spirit of the Mission, is an accomplished naturalist as well as horticulturist. He has accumulated in his museum a fine collection of native birds, reptiles, insects, and many other sorts of natural history material

characteristic of southern Chile and has called to scientific attention
a large number of species previously unknown.

Reports of the 1960 catastrophe in southern Chile referred to
Angol as one of the centers of population which suffered severely.
Fortunately, El Vergel, at some distance from the town and at the
base of the coastal mountain range, escaped the worst of the destruction wrought by the successive earthshocks.

Dr. Bullock has always coöperated with me most generously by
offering hospitality and assistance to members of our expeditions and
providing valuable information on collecting opportunities. For Walter he arranged a sojourn at the large cattle ranch of a friend high up
in the near-by Nahuelbuta highlands and thus in monkey puzzle
country. The headquarters of his hosts, the Solano brothers, lay in
a well-watered little mountain valley at about fifteen hundred feet.
It was an exceedingly remote spot and the rare presence of a visitor
may, in part, explain the warmth of the Solanos' hospitality and the
sustained collecting assistance they provided during Walter's visit.

Just after his arrival, there was a roundup and he watched the cowboys drive a large herd of mountain cattle, including two extremely
large bulls, into a strong corral. The roping and branding was interrupted by lunch served at a fifty-foot-long table in a grove of large
"Chilean beech" (*Nothofagus*). Following the branding, the two bulls
were reduced to oxen. Walter observed this operation but was hardly
prepared for its aftermath. That night at dinner the bulls' testicles
appeared—plus the eggs of sea urchins, brought over from the coast
and considered an additional delicacy. In his diary, Walter remarks
that, "It is fortunate that I am used to eating almost anything and although I found that I had no relish at all for sea urchin soup and
bull's balls I told my hosts how good this food tasted and they were
highly pleased."

He found the Nahuelbuta cordillera "beautiful and presenting most
pleasing landscapes of open forests, mountain meadows, and, here
and there, little gardens around the simplest sorts of dwellings. Almost
everything is handmade or improvised. The heavy fences have strong
posts pierced with laboriously cut square holes through which the
poles are pushed." Echoing my reaction to the atmosphere of the
Andean Araucarias, Walter writes: "The Nahuelbuta *Araucaria* forests are remarkably interesting and bizarre. You cannot help feeling
that they are not of this world. You wander about in what seems to

be a forgotten land that belongs to a lost world of prehistoric monsters." For my own part, I am always entirely prepared to see one of those monsters come ambling through a monkey puzzle grove.

Unfortunately, neither Paul nor Walter hit the height of the flowering period either in the foothills or in the highlands of Nahuelbuta. Each made considerable collections and listed the vegetation types, but the total bag of both flowering and fruiting specimens was a little disappointing. However, we can, up to a point, compare the plants that grow in the Andean with those of coastal *Araucaria* terrain. It was also a bit tantalizing to see dried specimens of potentially valuable ornamental material without having its seed to grow and test under California conditions. In a few instances, Dr. Bullock was growing these same species and generously shared the seed or living plants with us for cultivation in the Botanical Garden.

Our most intensive botanizing in southern Chile has been carried on somewhat below the area where the Andean Araucarias are most abundant, in what is known as the Chilean lake region. There is, doubtless, a certain scenic analogy between it and the Swiss Alps that perhaps justifies the tourist bureau's appellation "Switzerland of South America." For me, however, that marvelous country of dense forests, foaming rivers, sparkling lakes, and snowy volcanic peaks has a distinction all its own. It is sufficiently unique so that it need not, indeed cannot, be described in terms of any other geographic area.

For some years now it has been possible to fly from Santiago to the Chilean lakes as well as journey to them by train. Incidentally, by air it is but a few hours more to Punta Arenas, the city "farthest south," separated only by Magellan Strait and Tierra del Fuego from the very tip of the South American continent. If you are to be in southern Chile in February, do not overlook this possibility of so easily and conveniently spending a few days at one of the "ends of the earth." Hotel accommodations are good and the picturesque little city is an increasingly thriving headquarters for the managements and products of the vast sheep ranches of southern Patagonia, some of which you can visit in a day's trip by automobile.

We have always traveled to Chile's lake region on the ground, and the opportunity to have pass in review from the train windows the gradual alterations in character of Chilean terrain, climate, and vegetation has, each time, compensated for the fatigue which follows a long ride on Chilean rails.

From the train you begin soon to see green and then greener land-scapes which are in striking contrast to the semiarid Santiago country-side. You will be going down the southern extension of the great central valley of Chile. The actual and, even more, the potential abun-dance which its geologic and climatic features confer upon it will be impressive. Increasingly you see wide stretches of cultivated soil and wider sweeps of pastureland. Often the fields are set apart, one from the other, by rows of straight, slender Lombardy poplars, through the stiff tracery of whose narrow crowns the distant Andes hang like a vague, dull-green, white-capped tapestry let down from the pale-blue, cloud-flecked sky.

Later on, the character of the terrain is somewhat altered. More and more often the right of way crosses rivers, large and small. The land becomes more rolling, and its greenness acquires that depth and in-tensity of shade which tells of almost too abundant stores of moisture in the soil. River margins and all depressions become increasingly marshy. At the same time the areas of cultivated land are less extensive, and thin, scattered groves of *Nothofagus*, the southern beech, begin to be a familiar element in the landscape.

On hilltops and slopes, neat and attractive farm buildings appear. They spell prosperity and evidence the pride that their owners take in the character and appearance of their establishments. There are well-constructed and well-arranged collections of hip-roofed barns, low silos, fenced corrals, and hints of flower and vegetable gardens around small but comfortable farmhouses. All the buildings are likely to be painted a dark red, and, like redded sheep on a Devon hillside, stand out in pleasant relief against their rich green back-ground. Casting about in remembrance, I am, each time I see it, also impressed by the extent to which this South Chilean landscape is reminiscent of a typically Danish one.

Actually, you will be travelers in Chile's most important dairy district. It has been developed by German immigrants who began to arrive in South Chile over a hundred years ago. Even today, when you leave the train at the spick-and-span little city of Osorno, the Teutonic atmosphere of business and society in Chile's southland is quite apparent.

The tide of German immigration into South Chile began in 1852, probably as a result of the favorable reports of the half hundred or so Germans who had arrived in the Osorno area some years earlier.

In November, 1852, the three-hundred-ton schooner *Susanne*, four months out of Hamburg, landed about one hundred Saxons and Silesians. In six years the port and town of Puerto Montt had increased in population from fifty to six hundred, and of this total almost one half were Germans. Thus, in southern Chile as in the United States, a fair share of the population which is of German origin has its roots deep in the beginnings of the economic and cultural development of its foster fatherland. And, of course, the same is true of other South America republics.

From Osorno as headquarters, we have made collecting trips to the coast, to the Andes, and into the heart of the lake region. Our first, many years ago, took us some twenty miles east of Osorno to the justly celebrated falls of the Pilmaiquen, below the point where the river leaves Lago Puyehue—most of the geographical names in South Chile have an Araucanian Indian origin and are more or less unpronounceable.

Just out of town we began to meet countrypeople on their way to market. Some were on horseback, sitting well forward of large panniers containing fresh vegetables and other farm produce. Others walked beside yokes of powerful oxen that were slowly but steadily pulling long, narrow wagons loaded with forage or lumber. Their plodding steps were directed by a touch of a long, slender goad. When we, in our hired car, appeared in the offing, shouts were added to the authority of the goad and the teams swung off into a grassy track that paralleled the graded road. Now and then a huaso trotted by us, dressed in his going-to-town costume—broad, low-crowned, stiff felt hat; gaily colored poncho; long, bright-buttoned, leather leggings; and big wheel-spurs.

The vegetation near the falls was said to be of some special interest for the botanist. So it proved, except that we were too early for the blooming of many of the species that were the most unfamiliar. After some persuasion the driver brought the car as close as possible to the falls. The water had grooved a rounded gorge into which the Río Pilmaiquen dropped, first sheer and then in cascades, for a sufficient distance to create a dull, rumbling roar and a cloud of mist that rose in waves of moisture, as though the cauldron of white water below the falls was at the boiling point. As often as the sun broke through the cloudy sky, the chasm was alive with rainbows.

At the bottom of the chasm the Prince and I had our first contact with that remarkable South Chilean vegetation that later we came to know so well. For hundreds of square miles the eastern surfaces of the southern Andes and parts of the near-by coastal mountain ranges are covered with a temperate rain forest. In general physical features such a forest, which occurs in only a few other areas in the world, corresponds to the tropical rain forest. In other words, the vegetational type and general plant complex near the falls of the Pilmaiquen, at forty-two degrees south latitude, were singularly like those we encountered in east central Peru, less than ten degrees from the equator. Near the falls and on the walls of the chasm the forest floor was spongy and knee-deep in green vegetation. The trees grew so thick that their crowns merged to form a lofty ceiling through which the sun penetrated only here and there, and then only in slender shafts of light. Rising from the ground among the tree roots, climbing plants clasped the trunks and, on long, bare stems, carried up their leaves and flowers to become a part of the green canopy above our heads. All this was on a smaller scale as contrasted with the Peruvian jungle, and the species of plants that constituted the two types of rain forest were utterly different. Nevertheless, the quality and spatial relations of the two vegetations and the impressions that they made upon us were remarkably alike.

We were hopeful that *el copihue* (*Lapageria rosea*), Chile's national flower, would be growing near the falls and be already in bloom. We could find plenty of copihue plants, but they bore nothing but immature flower buds. It is a typical South Chilean plant, which recently has been discovered in the wild state in, or near, the Vale of Paradise. For many years grown successfully in gardens in Great Britain and Ireland, it is little known in California, where, however, it finds a congenial home in favored locations around and north of San Francisco Bay, near the coast. At first glance its climbing habit and long, tubular flowers make it difficult to include it in the Lily family, but on closer examination it clearly belongs there. What appeals to one as most remarkable about the copihue flower is its substance. The petals are thick and firm, with a fine, shining granulation on their surfaces which makes them appear to be made of frozen red-tinted snow.

In the Botanical Garden in Berkeley a number of especially fine forms of copihue are now flowering. Some of them had their origin in living plants given to us on two different occasions by Dr. Bullock, of the El Vergel agricultural school. In soil-filled tubs the plants were carried to San Francisco as part of the deck load of Grace Line freighters when expedition members were passengers and could give constant attention to their charges during the long voyage home. To comply with plant quarantine regulations, all soil was washed from the roots just before docking; then, packed in wet sacks, the plants were rushed to Berkeley for repotting in the proper compost.

Transplanted from Chile to California, the copihues grew and prospered and, in due time, seeded. Later, some were planted at the bases of sizable Redwoods growing along a little stream in the Botanical Garden and have found entirely congenial such unfamiliar supports for their climbing stems. One plant has partially covered the lower surface of a Redwood trunk and extended itself along lower branches from which, during the winter season, hang hundreds of upside-down red trumpets.

When, some years ago, Paul enjoyed the hospitality of El Vergel during his collecting in Nahuelbuta, he admired a number of attractive forms of copihue cultivated in the school's plantings. At his request, Dr. Bullock sent us seed of them and of hybrids he had made between them. Recently the plants grown from these seeds have flowered, and a few prove to be exceptionally desirable as garden subjects. For example, one bears exceedingly large, long, pure-white blossoms; another, clusters of little, bell-like ones. On a third, the flowers are quite slender and of a delicate shade of pink. Others show a jagged red margin on white petals, or a lacelike petal pattern of light and dark red. Paul has given these various races, previously unknown horticulturally, such appropriate names as "White Cloud," "Pigmy Bells," and "Pink Dawn."

We return, now, to the Prince and myself as we began our collecting under the falls of the Río Pilmaiquen. We gave attention, first, to el copihue but soon found that all the plants in sight were still in bud. This was a disappointment, but a glance at the rest of what was growing in the humid chasm was encouraging.

The heavy mists floating across the downpouring water and over the pools that it formed were continually blown downstream, as well as up the steep chasm walls. In this gentle bath, ferns, mosses, and other lowly plants luxuriated. On every overhanging rock they hung in festoons that waved in the currents of air blowing up and down the gorge. Even the almost vertical gravel slopes were carpeted with green.

Where the spray itself splashed up into the forest, near the falls, immense near-tree ferns formed an understory in the forest. Today, alas, the Falls of Pilmaiquen, as we knew them, are no more; the river that produced them has been diverted, upstream, to become a source of electric power, and not much more than trickles slip down the sheer rock faces.

There was little sun and considerable rain during our days in Osorno and the near-by collecting grounds. It therefore seemed possible that the week or two we proposed to spend in the Chilean lake region might not yield enough sun for natural-color movies, and that collecting might be difficult as well as uncomfortable. Sometimes in December, and even January, tourists go through that aggregation of marvelous scenery without catching more than a glimpse of white peaks, blue lakes, and green mountainsides through low, drifting rain clouds. In normal years early February is the best tourist season. However, on the morning we left Osorno for Ensenada the sun was shining bright and we had high hopes for good weather.

For an hour or two the highway traversed the verdant, rolling South Chilean countryside to which we had now become accustomed. Straggling groves of *Nothofagus* covered the upper slopes of the higher hills and filled such stretches of level land as had not been cleared for cultivation. A settled atmosphere of comfortable prosperity was reflected by the substantial farms and by the fat herds of dairy cattle slowly moving across the rich grasslands. The warm sunlight began to dissipate the damp chill with which southern Chile had so far afflicted us, and the mountains to the east and south slowly took definite shape and form as the mists and rain clouds rolled away from the horizon.

In addition to the driver, the Prince, Florence, and myself, the large, glass-enclosed autobus had aboard a man and his wife and their servants. Obviously the couple were of German extraction, presumably prosperous South Chileans off for a holiday in the lakes or heading across them to Argentina. Soon they began to exhibit an unnecessary hauteur and even some resentment at our presence, and so we examined them more carefully. Their traveling clothes cut in the English fashion, their stiff and punctilious motions and actions, and their much-traveled and overlabeled baggage suggested that they were touring Germans—people of means, perhaps of title. The latter identification later proved to be the correct one.

From our windows we watched the pleasant panorama. On the hillsides appeared larger and larger outcrops of dark, soft rock, reminding us that we were approaching an actively volcanic region. The pasturelands decreased in extent until they became only small interruptions of a more and more continuous forest. Cultivated plots were few and were brilliant with white daisies that sometimes spread an unbroken carpet over them. In South Chile these imported daisies, along with blackberries, have become a trial to the farmer. On the margins of the forest and in small clearings the European foxglove had gone native in a big way. We saw thousands of purple, and some white-flowered, foxgloves around and in the lake region. Their introduction, also, has proved to be highly undesirable, and their distribution difficult to control. Even in remote parts of the rain forest we saw the big rosettes of leaves and tall, spiky flower-stalks competing far too effectively with native ground-cover vegetation.

As the road topped a low ridge we had our first sight of the blue expanse of Lago Llanquihue (which, if necessary, can be pronounced "Yankeé-way") and of some of the volcanic peaks whose pyramidal outlines add distinction to the mountain scenery throughout Chile's "Switzerland." Soon we were running beside Llanquihue's margin and over the lower slopes of Volcán Osorno, which at a distance seems to rise directly from the water's edge. The greatest number and many of the most beautiful of the South Chilean lakes lie north of the familiar tourist route into Argentina, and so the average traveler knows only Llanquihue, Todos los Santos, and, across the border into Argentina, little Lago Frías and the larger Lago Nahuel Huapí.

Ensenada, our destination, consisted of a hotel, its numerous outbuildings, and a few cottages. This little settlement lay near a bay at the eastern extremity of Lago Llanquihue. In the long-distant past the rushing river that flows westward from Lago Todos los Santos must have entered Llanquihue at a point where the hotel now stands. Doubtless in the days of Volcán Osorno's activity its vomit filled the original river channel and deflected southward the course of the river, which now enters the Pacific via the estuary of Relancaví.

From the road a long sidewalk led through gardens to the porch of the low, spreading, two-story wooden hotel. With the Germans and their entourage, we descended from the autobus and stood beside a mountain of baggage. Around it the Prince's duffel bag, our battered suitcases, and the ragged plant presses made a distinctly unimpressive fringe. The hotel proprietor and a couple of servants came hurrying toward us. Our traveling companions immediately stepped forward and addressed him in German. Paying no attention to us, he ushered them along the sidewalk with much bowing and scraping, while their servants and the hotel porters began to attack the pile of German luggage. Throughout this little scene Nazi salutes were freely exchanged, for in those days, just before World War II, a temporary but fervent devotion to *der Führer* was much in evidence in southern Chile, something which today the entirely loyal *Chilenos* of that region are anxious to have forgotten.

We were tired and hungry. Chill mists began to pour off the nearby lake. Rain appeared to be in the offing. We not only wanted, but needed, shelter. Under ordinary circumstances I would willingly have carried the baggage into the hotel, and, indeed, Florence and the Prince started to pick up some of it. When I refused to move, Florence took one look at my face and asked me whether I proposed to make a scene. I had not exactly decided what I was going to do, but her question gave me an idea.

At this moment the hotel porters returned and began to load more German baggage. I told them to put it down and pointed to ours. They quite naturally demurred, and we were beginning to argue the point when the proprietor hurried over. Under the stress of emotion I became unexpectedly voluble in German, and those deficiencies in grammatical construction that my harangue exhibited were compensated for by its vehemence. I produced my receipt for hotel accommodations, purchased in Osorno. Smiting it with my fist, I demanded to know why to our rooms we had not immediately been shown. Were we in the cold on his doorstep like dogs to remain standing while others within escorted were? These so important, so honored guests, who were they? This last question loosed a counterflood from the proprietor. Did we not know, had we not understood, that during our journey from Osorno a veritable, thoroughly authenticated German *Freiherr* and his *Freifrau* were our fellow passengers? The hotel was exceedingly honored by their gracious presence, and when his staff had made them comfortable he would gladly do the same for us.

During the course of these blasts and counterblasts the diminutive Prince stood at my side, intently examining the ground at his feet. As already explained, he had long been known in California only as James West, and his true identity had been revealed to only a few friends. I wondered whether in this emergency he would permit me to reveal it to the Chilean lakes also. I turned to him and said, "Jim, may I shoot the works?" He looked up at me with a doubtful smile, hung his head for a moment, and then nodded assent.

By this time the porters had departed with another load of German baggage and the proprietor was bending over the last of it. With an authoritative finger in the small of his back I straightened him up. What had he said, I cried, concerning some German *Freiherr?* Who were we to be kept waiting on such a pretext? Did he not realize that he was in the presence of Egon Victor Moritz Karl Maria, Prinz von Ratibor und Corvey, Prinz zu Hohenlohe-Schillingsfürst! How could it happen that this Prince of the Holy Roman Empire had been practically turned away from the door of a small hotel, while a mere *Freiherr* was given every attention by its staff?

Wildly the poor proprietor looked first at me and then at the Prince. After a moment of hesitation Jim stepped forward and, much embarrassed, made suitable acknowledgment of repeated genuflections, and waved aside the elaborate apologies that were instantly forthcoming. With a shout the porters were recalled and loaded with our baggage. A triumphal procession then formed—first the Prince, conversing amiably in German with our deflated host, then Florence and myself, and finally the laden porters. I caught the twinkle in Florence's eye and suddenly the humor of the situation took possession of both of us. The contrast between the elaborately outfitted six-foot *Freiherr* and our little, bareheaded Prince, in faded sweater and ancient khaki pants, was too much. We were purple in the face by the time the proprietor had bowed us through the hotel entrance.

The hotel at Ensenada was a pleasant and comfortable place. During what was left of the afternoon following our arrival, clouds lay thick on the heights above and mists filled the forests below, so that there were no views of nearby Mount Osorno. As we went to sleep, the rain began to rattle on the roof above our heads and I had premonitions of leaving the shores of Lago Llanquihue without pictures of the famous "Fujiyama of South America."

Something awakened me very early. A faint illumination was filling the room. Unconsciously, I was drawn toward the open windows. In a moment I found myself gazing, almost without comprehension, upon one of the most beautiful things in the world. In the first light of dawn, against a delicate, pale-pink sky, the mists were withdrawing from the white crown of the symmetrical volcanic peak of Mount Osorno. In the foreground, scattered groves gradually became continuous with the green bulk of the rain forest which flowed without interruption up the smooth and rapidly increasing gradient until it seemed to end in the snow, three thousand feet below the gleaming apex of the mountain.

The morning light strengthened fast, and a fiery glow began to encircle Osorno's peak. Suddenly, I thought of pictures, and moments later we were hurrying toward the mountain with tripod and movie camera. We set up our apparatus and then prayed that the film was absorbing a little, at least, of the marvelous perfection of the glistening, white, pink-tipped cone above our heads. But it could not record the delicious, moist breath exhaled from the awakening forest, the shivering coolness of the gentle breezes that ruffled the blue-gray surface of Llanquihue and spent themselves among the rough volcanic boulders over which we climbed; nor could it absorb the tiptoe-provoking stillness of earliest morning spread across all those miles of water and green canopy beneath our feet.

We watched a progression of lights and shadows fall across Osorno's summit. Clouds of pearl-gray mist swept in from the ever-deepening azure of the morning sky and then away again to permit broad shafts of sunlight to be reflected from the glittering snow. We alternately sighed as heavier clouds slowly crept all about the peak and gasped with wonder when they opened for an instant to reveal its entirety. Imperceptibly, the broad expanse of water below us gathered blueness from the clearing skies. Beyond was the hotel, and from its red roofs smoke drifted into the forest and slowly rose to create a broad stripe of blue-gray mist across the dark-green surface. On the far shore of the lake we could see the lower slopes of Volcán Calbuco, its shattered cone deep in heavy clouds which now and again blew apart to show the thin trail of smoke that floated up from the active fires deep in the bowels of the crater.

I have as yet been unable to verify the statement in the press that Mount Osorno was among the peaks which erupted violently during South Chile's ten days and more of horror in 1960. It is almost impossible for me to picture Osorno's perfectly symmetrical, snow-mantled apex—reflected so perfectly in Llanquihue's blue surface—uncapped, split, blazing, and surmounted by a mushrooming cloud of volcanic debris.

By comparison with the supreme heights of the mountain summits in Central Chile, the numerous volcanic peaks that add so much beauty to the Chilean lake region are altitudinally insignificant. For example, Osorno is a little less than nine thousand feet; Calbuco, about eight thousand; and Tronador ("The Thunderer"), something over eleven thousand feet. But the rains that fall almost daily upon them and the chill Antarctic winds that blow over them so much of the year combine to maintain a snowy cover on these and other, lower mountaintops. Long ago the glaciers scooped out deep depressions between spurs of the diminishing Andean ranges, so that today the peaks seem to rise isolated above the surface of the forest, or abruptly from the margins of the blue lakes that fill the glacial scars.

The temperate rain forest of southern Chile contains any number of remarkable and beautiful plants. Some of the best of the ornamental species have for many years been grown in famous gardens across the Atlantic. For example, *Embothrium coccineum*, the "fire bush," is not uncommon in them. It has never been in flower when I have visited the English and Irish gardens in which it is grown, but the size and general appearance of the introduced plants gave no promise of anything to approach the gorgeousness of their December blooming near Ensenada and along the western shores of Lake Nahuel Huapí. On a clear day the mountainsides above the blue lakes showed scattered dots of hard, brilliant, scarlet light that, at first glance, simulated the glow of a hundred little fires beginning to gain foothold in the green depths of the omnipresent forest. Where the density of this forest gave way to open glades or on the edges of cleared lands, *el ciruelillo*, as the natives call it, grew in small groves and as single specimens. They were rarely more than twenty feet in height, rather symmetrical but still somewhat loose and weak, and were, really, treelike shrubs. At the height of the flowering period the extremity of every twig bore its corymb of threadlike, scarlet-crimson flowers against a background of dark-green foliage. A dozen Embothriums in a mass hurl back the sunlight as a burning red haze, so powerful and so rich that the onlooker prepares to shield himself from its expected heat. Sometimes plants are brought into gardens in its homeland, where they prove to be adaptable and respond to cultivation by an increase in their naturally rapid rate of growth and development. Near Nahuel Huapí wealthy Argentinos have acquired large estates. On some of these, *Embothrium* and other ornamental species of the encircling rain forest are employed in informal landscaping about the buildings. One designer, needing material for a long hedge, experimented successfully with the "fire bush." Trimmed and clipped to a height of five and a width of three feet, it made a tight and colorful protective edging.

Other genera of the ancient family *Proteaceae*, in addition to *Embothrium*, are interesting and decorative elements of the rain forest. There are three species of *Lomatia* (*obliqua, ferruginea*, and *dentata*), none of them large trees and some with a tendency, like the fire bush, to be a bit on the loose side as far as branching and general habit are concerned. The second of these three species, called *el romerillo*, is the most important as an ornamental, and for the cabinetmaker provides a source of rich, close-grained wood that takes a high polish. Its large, shining, dark-green, fernlike leaves and its racemes of yellow flowers attracted the attention of early plant hunters. Related to the Lomatias is *Guevina avellana*, again a small tree. At the beginning of the southern autumn it is covered both with the red balls of its maturing fruit and the white racemes of its late flowers.

Certain introduced ornamentals luxuriate in the cool, wet climate of southern Chile. I have never seen such Rhododendrons elsewhere. In Osorno gardens were magnificent plants of the hardier species and hybrids. I remember particularly the *ponticums*. Some had become trees, and one could walk about under their wide-spreading branches. The surfaces of these giant Rhododendrons were decked with big, dark-lavender pompons, from some of which the flowers were being shed to cover the garden paths with a heavy, colorful mantle on which we hated to walk.

Like Rhododendrons, most types of roses luxuriate unbelievably in South Chilean gardens. The flowers are exceedingly large and full, and the substance of the petals and richness of the colors are remarkable. During the two months or so of spring and summer, bulbs and annuals grow rapidly and flower heavily. Also, I never ate elsewhere such flavorful raspberries.

The floor of the South Chilean temperate rain forest, dim and moist, is rich in mosses and ferns. Along the many rivulets and lesser streams that flow silently between the bases of the tree trunks, this ground cover grows to waist height. When the watercourses cross small, rarely occurring, treeless meadows, their banks are heavy with *Gunnera*. From creeping, rootlike stems embedded in the soaking, acid soil, its immense leaves rise from six to eight feet and carry a six-foot, circular blade.

Near one *Gunnera*-bordered meadow, and someday to become an extension of it, stood an acre or two of dead and dying trees. Some had fallen and were fast rotting on the saturated soil. Over their decaying tissues the small, round leaves of a variety of *Nertera depressa* made a smooth green carpet set with thousands of bright reddish-orange droplets. Grown in a two-inch pot, and sometimes called "bead plant," it used to be quite the most attractive item in the Christmas windows of some California florists. The minute leaves were almost completely hidden by tiny, round, pale-orange fruits that had a transparent, glassy, beadlike quality. By comparison, the South Chilean plant is a giant, with larger, almost succulent, dark-green leaves and orange-coral berries almost as large as marbles. On hands and knees I hunted the ripest of these attractive fruits, smeared the seed-containing flesh on bits of newspaper, and then stuck these seed collections in my hatband to dry. Months later, in the process of unpacking our Chilean collections, someone must have discarded as worthless those dingy scraps of paper—only long and diligent search discovered one of them with a few seeds still attached.

In Chile there are two kind of "honey." In most restaurants in the central section and in the north they offer *miel de palma*, which, as we have seen, is obtained from the sweet sap of *Jubaea spectabilis*, the Chilean palm. In the south a true honey, *miel de abeja*, is served. It is a pale-yellow, viscous, slightly grainy substance ready to be spread like peanut butter, and possesses a flavor to which a kiss should be blown. Its delicious taste and scent are derived from the aromatic nectar of *el muermo, Eucryphia cordifolia*. This tree, one of the most beautiful in all Chile, grows to a height of one hundred feet. Single specimens in open parts of the rain forest almost always have a columnar form, with heavy branches clothing the trunk nearly to the ground. Late in the summer this massive column is covered with goblets of snow—lovely fragrant cups like miniature white roses. They swarm with bees and other insects. On a still, warm, sunny day a cheerful humming announces your approach to this *Eucryphia*.

In addition to the copihue, there are a number of vines in the wet forests of southern Chile. The ornamental value of some of them has long been appreciated, but they are rarely, if ever, grown in California. Some of them, like *Mitraria coccinea*, usually flower unseen, high up on the trunk of a forest tree where thin shafts of light penetrate the leafy canopy above. This climber is called *la botellita*, referring to the flasklike shape of its reddish-vermilion flowers. Often we were aware of its presence overhead only by fallen petals at the foot of a tree.

There are a number of areas near the Chilean lakes where relics or remnants of the Magellanic floras, eight hundred miles to the south, are to be found. These little-known islands of sub-Antarctic plants provide evidence bearing upon the geologic history of the lower west coast of South America as revealed by the present-day distribution of its vegetation. In the coastal cordillera east of Osorno one finds on a long, high, moisture-laden plateau numerous species that otherwise are to be seen only much nearer the southern tip of the continent. They are growing among typical elements of the rain forest which are somewhat altered in form under the influence of increased altitude.

During our first expedition I attempted to reach this unique collecting ground. We started by automobile and were to continue on horseback. It had been raining intermittently all the day before and when we got under way the first stretch of country road was sloppy. As the hilly country was approached, the rain became continually heavier. The car skidded badly, and, without chains, appeared to have little chance of negotiating the increasingly high ranges, over the first of which we were slowly passing. The rain beat through the cracked and poorly fitted side-curtains, and gusts of wind blew muddy wheel spray into our faces. The car began to slip and slide on the heavy grades, and by the time we topped this first rise the driver had to stop so that all the water in the radiator should not boil away. In order to get a bit of exercise, and because nothing could be worse than the cold, wet inside of the car, I opened a door and crawled out under the curtain into the pouring, driving rain. Then I started to walk downgrade on the slippery grass that bordered the sea of mud into which the surface of the road had disappeared. Just beyond the crest I saw a horse standing on the green pathway and beside the horse a large bundle of some sort. Nearer approach revealed this bundle to be a South Chilean huaso in his best regimentals, curled up sound asleep almost under the hoofs of his fine horse. He had pulled his gaily decorated, heavy woolen poncho over his head, drawn his knees up under his chin, laid his broad-brimmed, low-crowned, black hat to one side, and let nature take its course. Apparently the effects of too much alcohol, acquired in Osorno, had overtaken him on his way home, and, being a hardy soul and relying upon his poncho and leather leggings to turn most of the deluge of rain, he decided to sleep off his jag on the spot. As I stepped off the grass into the muddy road, the horse slowly turned his head and watched me pass, but, aside from skin twitchings where rivers of water splashed down from the ponderous sheepskin saddle, no other part of his rain-soaked body showed a sign of movement.

I walked far enough down the grade to see that a lake had collected in the first hollow. Beyond it were other lakes. The hills were misty with the rain, which showed no sign of abating its intensity. Obviously we could not get much farther without danger of stalling the automobile, and the *fundo,* or farm, where horses could be obtained was still far away. I therefore ordered a retreat, and while the driver hunted a spot where he could turn around we went out into the dripping forest and managed to collect enough so that our abortive expedition was not a total loss.

Some years later, and at a slightly drier season and a better one for flowers and seeds, John managed more successfully to get into the Cordillera de la Costa. He saw virgin forests in which *alerce (Fitzroya cupressoides)* grew to extreme size. This conifer, peculiar to the southern Andes, is much prized locally for its handsome, easily worked, and lasting wood. Under its spreading branches masses of *Desfontainea spinosa* lightened the gloom of the rain forest with thousands of large, red and yellow, tubular flowers. He saw many rare plants in their most luxuriant and uncontaminated condition. The curious dwarf conifer, *Dacrydium fonckii,* only two feet high, grew in the boggiest depressions of the rain forest—an olive-green treelet with minute, scaly leaves covering the dwarfed branches. Near by was *Podocarpus salignus,* a tree that might be mistaken for a willow were it not for its brilliant red, yewlike fruits. The shadowy forest floor was here and there brightened by the reddish blossoms of *Philesia buxifolia.* Its local name, *coicopihue,* relates it to copihue, and its specific name refers to its boxlike leaves, bright green above and grayish white below. Although its flowers are smaller than and differ somewhat in shape from those of *Lapageria rosea,* its exceeding floriferousness and more shrubby habit recommend coicopihue as an ornamental.

In the garden of a *fundo,* John saw a low, woody plant with attractive, red, tubular flowers. It proved to be *Latua pubiflora*—the *palo de los brujos*, or "witch's stick," of the Araucanian Indians. From its leaves they have from time immemorial brewed a hellish concoction that, like hashish, produces mental disturbances—violent and lasting ones. At this farm he was hospitably received and soon found himself treated like a member of the family. At dinner one day the middle-aged German-Chilean proprietor recounted a part of the story of his life, most of which had been passed in south Chile. Many years before, he had become the junior partner in this *fundo*, and after marrying the senior's daughter ultimately became full owner. He said that his first wife died in her youth after bearing several children and was succeeded by the present mistress of the establishment who added three more members to the family. At this point she took up the tale and laughingly referred to the fact that in addition to his legitimate brood, her husband had "*cinquenta y tres niños afuera.*" The others at the table, some of whom were apparently among the fifty-three illegitimates, nodded vigorously and exclaimed, "*qué diablo*," "*qué macho*" ("what a devil of a fellow," "what a vigorous male"), as they gazed proudly at the head of the mixed household.

The Chilean rain forest is a never-ending source of delight and fascination for the plant hunter. At the beginning he must become accustomed to the ever-present *Nothofagus*, a tree much like a European beech and still not like it. He notes its variations—in size and form and in character of leaf—and attempts to distinguish between the four or more species that have been given recognition by botanists. He looks forward eagerly to coming across his first *Drimys winteri*, "Winter's bark," and hopes that the season has arrived when snowy flowers are clothing it from head to foot. With even greater anticipation he watches for the heavy, ragged crowns of those South Andean conifers, *Saxegothea* and *Fitzroya*, which rise solitary above the green surface of the rain forest's roof.

As an old friend he welcomes *Berberis darwinii*, but is amazed at its height and bulk, for in the shade of the moist forest this barberry grows to fifteen feet, and its orange flowers and blue-black fruits are suspended far above his head. Also familiar will be *Fuchsia magellanica*, at last far enough south to justify its specific name, and the Godetias, Epilobiums, Violas, and many more. Most of them will, however, seem a little less familiar when more carefully examined and will prove to be species known only from southern Chile. Of oddities there will be a number, among them *chupalla* (*Fascicularia bicolor*), the big bromeliad that lives in trees and at a distance suggests mistletoe on a scale unknown in the north.

Natural openings or clearings in the rain forest contain their own specialties. Among them we found many terrestrial orchids. Most of them were large Chloreas, with pale-green petals striped with bright green; but there were also other, lowlier species, more delicate and more complicated in flower form. Rarely, and in the partial protection of low shrubs, we came across *Asarca odoratissima*, its part pale-yellow, part bright-yellow flowers full of delicate fragrance. Soft grasses, easily crushed, tiny annuals with inconspicuous flowers, and harsh-leaved little ferns formed the cover through which the orchids and other attractive species pushed their leaves and blooms to accept all the sunlight that the short southern summer could allow them.

17

TAXI TO CALI

In a red taxicab I have just crossed the Cordillera Central, that tremendous Andean backbone of Colombia, from Bogotá to Cali—nearly 400 miles, over 11,000 feet, 18 hours. We wrecked the taxi and missed a bridge. It was the most utterly insane thing I have ever done or ever will do, and every time I think about it I laugh until I cry.

"Dr. Cuatrecasas and I had finished our orchid collecting in north-western Colombia and I was on my way by air to meet the Good-speeds in Peru: Medellín, Bogotá, Cali, Lima. On Friday in Medellín, Avianca, the Colombian national airline and subsidiary of Pan American airways, gave me 7:45 A.M. as departure time for the one Sunday plane from Bogotá to Cali. My Monday morning Pan Am reservation from Cali to Lima read 7:00 A.M., and, remember, this was wartime; if you missed your Pan Am plane in South America another reservation could be fifteen days, plus, away.

"Arriving in Bogotá on Saturday I checked in with the Avianca office. They told me, 'the airport bus leaves here tomorrow morning at 9:25 with departure for Cali at 9:55.' I could not reconcile 9:55 with 7:45 and said so; they were adamant, 9:55 it was.

"With Dr. Cuatrecasas to see me off, I was at the Avianca office at 9:15. It was closed. In succession 9:25, 9:30, and 9:35 arrived. Just as we started for a taxi, an Avianca man appeared. Yes, I had distinctly missed the boat—9:55 was the weekday departure hour, 7:45 the Sunday one: 'Quite a natural mistake—no, Señor?' In unison, Dr. C. and I said, 'Yes, Señor—and such a serious one that Avianca will never hear the end of it. What will lord-and-master Pan Am have to say when they hear about such incompetence?'

328

"By this time the general manager of Avianca had arrived. He called the district manager. The confusion was beautiful. Spanish, with gestures, filled the air, but it was far too rapid and idiomatic for me and so I just stood by and enjoyed the mounting excitement. Dr. C. accelerated it by announcing that Dr. Goodspeed was a very influential person and would undoubtedly sue Avianca, via Pan Am, for at least 10,000 pesos if I was not delivered to Cali by 7 o'clock the next morning. The district manager became frantic. He called the divisional manager on the Atlantic side. What to do? What to do? There was no rail connection for Cali, the bus took at least three days, another plane could not be readied because no other air crews were available. What to do? What to do? There was, of course, only one answer—an automobile to Cali. After a brief consultation with the staff, the district manager announced, 'In one hour, *Señor*, you will have the best taxi in Bogotá, the best mountain driver.'

"On schedule, a red late-model Pontiac appeared. Two new tires had gone on the rear wheels and there were three extra wheels, with new tires mounted, in the back seat. The significance of this additional equipment was pretty obvious, and rather discouraging. Still, I had more or less asked for it, the car certainly looked stout and serviceable, and the young driver thoroughly competent. Let's go!

"A rough calculation indicated that we would have to average better than 20 miles an hour, nonstop. Unfortunately, you don't drive nonstop in Colombia. On the borders of political subdivisions and on both ends of towns there are likely to be chains across the highway and usually credentials must be produced. We would be crossing borders and passing through towns.

"The first hour was easy, except that we lost time changing a tire. Then we hit the first ranges of hills. The pitch wasn't particularly steep and the curves were wide. This was a challenge to the driver, and the speedometer rose rapidly to thirty-five and then to a little over forty. Probably there was no margin of safety beyond thirty. To remain on the rear seat, at least part of the time, I had to wedge myself into a corner and hang on to a door handle. I couldn't free a hand long enough to light a cigarette. The dust rose in a high dense cloud behind us, and inside it was piling up fast.

"The ranges of hills became successively higher and we were continually spiraling up or down. The grades became steeper and the turns sharper. Going around them where there was nothing to bank against, the rear wheels chewed up the outer road margins. I was constantly, painfully, aware of the insecurity of the car on the gravel road. At the speed we were traveling gravity was just able to hold us down but we kept slipping badly and a blowout would have sent us head over heels, cornerwise.

"No South American taxi driver can be content for more than a block or two without his radio going full tilt. True to form, mine turned his on and it had to be full on to be heard. A program had just ended and the Colombian national anthem began. It's a stirring bit of martial music and we responded automatically; the driver laughed happily and pushed the accelerator to the floor boards. I began to imagine things. I was Genghis Khan at the head of the thundering herd, I was a French soldier rushing to the defense of Paris in a taxicab, I was a knight-errant galloping to the rescue of a fair lady.

"Then it happened. On that particular curve we didn't honk; neither did the oncoming truck driver. We promptly took to the inner wall at about twenty miles an hour. I managed to roll with the punch and ended up, intact, on the front seat. My companion, well braced behind the steering wheel, was also intact. The car looked a mess— bumper and grille gone, radiator bent over the fan, a fender wrapped around a broken wheel. The driver started the engine and it sounded good. He went into reverse and moved a foot or two. That was enough to jam the front doors, which meant that the frame was sprung. Then came the crowning blow—the steering mechanism was out of line, with a quadrant arm badly bent. We took it out and tried to straighten it with a hammer. The diameter of that steel rod wasn't much, but we might as well have tried to fell a Sequoia with a hatchet. Looking about for an inspiration, I noticed a nice little niche between two road-side boulders. Into the niche went the rod, under the bend went the jack and we were back in business.

"The shadows were beginning to lengthen when, three hours later, everything essential was back in place. I never saw a man work harder than that young driver did. He never rested long enough to light a cigarette. I thanked him, congratulated him, and we shook hands. Then, I had to decide—back to Bogotá, or on to Cali. We had smashed up after covering only about one fifth of our journey, we would have to drive at least as fast as we had been driving, and the great Cordillera Central still lay ahead. On the other hand, another smash was unlikely, the car seemed to be in pretty good shape and, except for that one lapse, my companion had certainly lived up to his reputation as an exceptionally good mountain driver. After a little more reflection, I got into the back seat and pointed up the grade.

"From then on we drove like crazy. Every so often we had to stop to show credentials. At 8 o'clock we reached a sizable place and took twenty minutes for dinner. It was the driver's home town and he met a friend who wanted a ride to Cali. I agreed on the theory that four eyes in the front seat were better than two. After it was all over, the friend said, 'Never again.'

"For a while we stayed more or less on the flat. The car was, miraculously, taking all the driver gave it and asking for more. Somehow the headlights had escaped in the smash but they didn't seem to be quite as effective as I could have wished. Perhaps that was the reason we missed the bridge. It crossed a considerable canyon and the road approached it at an almost impossible angle. The result was, of course, that we went straight ahead in place of making the approximately right-angle turn that would have taken us on it. Anyway, at the speed we were going we couldn't have made any such turn and stayed right side up. The next second the headlights showed no road ahead. How the driver stopped that car, I'll never know. I went halfway over the back of the front seat and the driver's friend ended up plastered against the windshield. Three feet more and we would have been in the canyon. For some time before we missed the bridge I had been relieving my state of mind with a bit of song, and I kept on singing after we missed it. This seemed to reassure the poor driver, who began to show some signs of panic. Possibly the acrid smell of abused brake linings was partly responsible. We examined the brakes with the aid of my cigarette lighter. I wished we hadn't.

"The climb up and over the Andes soon began. It was really something. I am looking forward to the day when I can see those panoramas that were invisible on that black and stormy night. As you approach the 11,000-foot pass they must be magnificent. The steepness of much of the grade slowed us down and so did the rain, which soon became torrential and kept up all night. Now and then there was a succession of splendid lightning flashes. They brilliantly illuminated the road, the car, and its three occupants. After each flash the blackness seemed more inky. We drove steadily until midnight and then stopped in a village for a short coffee break.

"Considering the condition of our brakes, the grade, and the rain, our spiraling descent was anything but monotonous. Some of the time the road must have been running along the edge of nowhere. Elsewhere it was cut through the rocky mountainside to form a comforting natural barrier on the outside. Probably none of it was quite as bad as my imagination pictured.

"Finally, we got down into the Cauca Valley, in which Cali lies. There was, at once, considerable doubt about which of a number of roads led most directly to the city. All of them were awfully muddy. We made the mistake of stopping to ask questions and got contradictory answers. As the light brightened we saw, at some distance, our destination. Then followed a final frustration, for the mud held us down to not over ten miles an hour. Fortunately, the road we had chosen passed the airport, and at exactly 6:50 A.M. I stood before the office. We had made it with ten minutes to spare after fifteen hours of driving and a total of eighteen hours on the road.

"The waiting room was empty. I couldn't understand it; certainly I wasn't the only passenger for the south on the 7 o'clock plane. I compared my watch with the official one up on the wall. Both read 6:55. Had I missed the boat again? If so, I didn't give a damn; the driver and I had done our part. I was almost too tired and discouraged to rout out a clerk in the room behind the counter. My appearance must have suggested something about what I had gone through to catch that plane, but he appeared entirely unconcerned as he announced that, for military reasons, the 7:00 plane had been held up in Miami and would arrive in about two hours. I was to go to a hotel and wait for a call.

"The reaction to those many hours of continuous strain was beginning to hit the young driver. He looked a wreck—covered with dirt, dark rings around his bloodshot eyes, bent over with back strain. I sat right down and wrote a letter for him to the Avianca people in Bogotá. It explained the damage to the car and confirmed his reputation as a mountain driver of remarkable skill and endurance."

The foregoing was written a few days after Roy Metcalf joined us in Peru; by that time he had fully recovered from the aftereffects of his nightmare ride from Bogotá to Cali.

I had known Roy first as an amateur grower of orchids and later as a postgraduate student of the University of California concerned with research on the growth requirements of those rather remarkable plants. On our fourth Andean plant exploration I wanted to make a preliminary survey of the orchid populations in parts of tropical South America. As someone who could effectively help me in this project I naturally thought of Roy. He was much interested because it would give him opportunity to study the plants he was addicted to in their natural surroundings. It was wartime, but Roy's draft board agreed to give him limited deferment so that he could go with me to South America.

In the first chapter I spoke of the eighteen months I spent, during the war years, in Colombia, Peru, Chile, Argentina, and Uruguay as a representative of the State Department's "Committee on Inter-American Artistic and Cultural Relations," directed by Mr. (now Governor) Nelson A. Rockefeller. To make such contribution as I might to the increase of mutual understanding between South America and the United States, I gave, in Spanish, over one hundred and fifty illustrated lectures on such topics as our National Parks and Botanical Gardens, the relation of scientific research to the improvement of California agriculture, and student life and work in our universities. As time permitted, I collected plants and mapped vegetation in the five republics in which I lectured; in Colombia and Peru I had Roy's able assistance and in Colombia that of Dr. José Cuatrecasas also. Actually, the two of them were largely responsible for what was accomplished, botanically, in Colombia during our fourth period of Andean plant hunting.

Colombia is literally the "Gateway to South America" because, bordering Panama, it is the farthest north of our neighbors on that continent. Among its sister republics, Colombia alone faces both the Atlantic and the Pacific, and this duality of exposure is in some measure responsible for its unique floristic condition. A plant hunter needs only a brief experience in Colombia to realize that he will grow old before he can come to know intimately its remarkable range of vegetation types and the most characteristic constituents of each of them. The vegetation of Colombia is one of the most luxuriant in the world, with great diversity among its elements, perhaps the greatest known diversity. Heavy to excessive rainfall over most of a land so near the equator is responsible for the luxuriance. In the geological history of the northern Andes lies the explanation of the diversity.

The face of South America was, over a long stretch of geologic time, subjected to monstrous upheavals alternating with the leveling-off of much of what had emerged. These sequences produced in today's Colombia three impressive and continuous Andean ranges. Between them are profound depressions and within them lateral valleys and elevated plateaus; to the eastward are vast plains. In addition, these sequences sometimes closed and sometimes opened the pathways along which traveled the prehistoric vegetation of northern South America. As Colombia's terrain gradually became stabilized, different segments of the ancient vegetation became confined to particular areas. Upon these segments, isolated by altitudinal barriers which they could not surmount, evolutionary forces began to operate. These forces, acting over long stretches of geologic time, brought into existence a considerable series of distinct races of plants, each adapted in form, structure, and physiological requirements to the particular environment to which its forefathers had been restricted. Doubtless, this process of adaptation was long continued, for major climatic changes accompanied stabilization. In particular, the final emergence of the high Andean crests deflected water-bearing air currents from the two oceans to induce excessive rainfall in certain regions and relative aridity in others.

An evergreen tropical rain forest is the dominant feature of Colombia's vegetation. It occurs over extensive areas, sometimes continuous and sometimes in broad belts. The true jungle, which is the extreme expression of the tropical rain forest, is characteristic of the Colombian lowlands, especially on the Pacific side, where the annual rainfall, between sea level and three thousand feet, approaches four hundred inches, and where the atmosphere is both unbelievably humid and excessively hot. As the rain forest mounts the Andean ridges, reaching an altitude of about ten thousand feet, there is a gradual decrease in total rainfall and average temperature, with the result that its character and composition change and distinct vegetational zones appear.

Most passenger ships on the west coast voyage northward toward Panama put in to pick up coffee at Buenaventura, Colombia's principal Pacific port. Unless it is raining cats and dogs, as it may well be, the passengers are likely to go ashore and, sometimes, taxi a bit outside the city. In Buenaventura itself they see something of what constitutes daily existence in the tropics; outside it, they get some slight idea of what a tropical rain forest can be. The former is downright nasty; the latter is rather impressive and also somewhat menacing. An extensive and rather intimate view of the tropical rain forest east of Buenaventura can be obtained from the train that runs from the port city to Cali on the other side of the coastal range. You ride through the rain forest for hours and note its response to increasing altitude by the gradual changes in character and composition.

The air is likely to be very hot and sticky, sometimes almost stifling in the train, and you begin to wonder how it would be to live and work under such conditions. I may not be an entirely typical example, but such contact as I have had over the years with the Colombian jungle and some other jungles in Central and South America suggests that light-complexioned and thin-skinned Anglo-Saxons do not adjust well to intense heat and humidity. My most recent experience with the combination was in Panama. After my return to California it took many weeks, plus plenty of cortisone ointment, before the itching stopped. In the tropics the sweat glands obviously have to operate in "high gear," as it were, and when you return to a cool, dry climate they become confused, particularly on the less-exposed areas of your surface, and every one of them begins to protest vigorously.

I said, above, that the tropical rain forest, in its most extreme expression, can be menacing. By this I mean that, at first glance, its extraordinary lushness, the luxuriance and density of its complex of interwoven plant life, alternating now and then with more open glades through which thin shafts of dim light filter down to the dank forest floor, produces a compelling atmosphere of unreality, of mystery. Then, almost at once, imagination begins to people this totally unfamiliar world with highly undesirable denizens—jaguars and other snarling cats, the bushmaster, the fer-de-lance, and other venomous writhers, and poisonous insects in quantity. For the plant hunter the menace is there, and very real. He is thoroughly alive to it but not deterred by it. For him the exuberance of the vegetation, the remarkable diversity of its elements, has an instinctive and absorbing attraction. Probably he has, up till then, known only the vegetation of temperate climes. He knows, for example, the coniferous forests, the hardwood forests, the prairies. Each one has shown him its typical aggregations of shrubs, undershrubs, grasses, and the more delicate plants that appear and disappear seasonally; and, just as the trees in a pure forest repeat themselves indefinitely, so do these associated plants. By contrast, in any given area of the jungle there is no such repetition; it is composed not solely of one dominant tree but rather of many kinds. When you have identified one of them you may not find another for a mile, and the same is true of their associates. Confusion is increased by the colonies of ferns, mosses, and other kinds of epiphytes with which every tree is loaded and which spray out from their bases to mound the decaying remnants of earlier generations. For the Temperate Zone plant hunter the multitude of "unknowns" is staggering. He is in a world that is botanically almost completely new to him.

The rain forest demonstrates impressively the extent to which the need and competition for light determine the configuration and the growth habit of a plant. The trunks of a tall tree will be bare of branches until near the summit, where subdivision after subdivision has formed an umbrella-like crown. The crowns interlace, and so, when you fly over the tropical rain forest, its roof appears to be an almost "wall-to-wall" carpet, a mosaic in shades of green. Certain of the leaves belong to the many kinds of climbing plants that are a conspicuous and characteristic feature of most jungle vegetation. Among them you will find members of plant families—palms, for example—most of which elsewhere are trees or treelike. The climbers coil, sometimes stranglingly, about tree trunks, propelling themselves upward to insert their leaves into the green canopy, there to absorb a share of the sun's radiant energy. From the air, areas of the surface of this canopy are often painted, usually in pastel shades, by the flowers of the jungle trees. The skyward location of these flowers poses a problem for the plant hunter. To make a proper specimen he must, of course, have flowers as well as leaves and stems. To get them he has to cut down a flowering tree, send up a native to whom climbing is second nature, or content himself with fallen blossoms which briefly illuminate the dusky shadows of the forest floor.

Probably at least thirty families of flowering plants, not to speak of lesser plant groups, can be found in the Pacific rain forests of Colombia. Almost one hundred genera belonging to them are known, and of those genera there must be hundreds upon hundreds of species and varieties. Most numerically prominent among the families are the palms, with some twenty genera; the family that includes the figs and their relatives is represented by ten. The botanist recognizes that any compilation of the total population of a tropical rain forest like that of Colombia will be out of date almost immediately, because there are many new species and even genera constantly being reported by the plant hunter willing to search unexplored segments of an inhospitable area that presents so many difficulties and hazards. It is fair to say that in temperate climates nothing begins to approach the richness and infinite diversity of the vegetation contained in the Colombian jungle even if you think in terms of far more extensive areas in those climates.

In Colombia only the more fortunate tourist may have opportunity to visit what is the most outstandingly interesting high-altitude plant association that I have ever seen or expect to see. Throughout the northern Andes there are many, often extensive, highland plateaus and alpine valleys lying at from 10,000 to 13,500 feet and higher, depending upon the point at which snow begins. In Peru and Bolivia, where they are collectively called "punas," you expect the highlands to be relatively arid, cold—excessively so at night, barren, and windy. Nearer the equator, for example in Colombia, the "paramos," as they are called there, are equally inhospitable—never warm, cold after sunset, and windswept. However, by contrast with the punas, the paramos are wet and therefore capable of supporting a somewhat limited range of peculiar vegetation types that show remarkable adaptation in form and structure to a set of environmental conditions that would make most plants decidedly unhappy.

For a correct and impressive picture of a typical Colombian paramo, walk into Hall 29 in the Chicago Natural History Museum. There you will see a mural by Arthur G. Rueckert of a high Andean valley with its bizarre vegetation. It might well represent an artist's conception of a scene from another world; actually it depicts faithfully a little-known paramo in the Cordillera Oriental of the Department of Boyacá, not far from the Venezuelan frontier.

What gives the landscape such a spectacular and otherworldly flavor is the presence of plants of extraordinary appearance, among which the *frailejónes* are outstanding. Quoting from Dr. Cuatrecasas' comment on the mural, which was prepared under his direction: "The name *frailejón* was given because of a fancied monk-like appearance of these plants, especially if seen in fog or mist, when from a distance they could be mistaken for men. . . . The *frailejónes* belong to the Composite family, which includes such common plants as the sunflower, chrysanthemum, and aster. Within this great family of such diversity in form and color, no plants are perhaps so striking in appearance as the *frailejón*. Technically it belongs to the genus *Espeletia*."

Some seventy species of *Espeletia* have been described, and what, for a Composite, makes them particularly distinctive is the way in which all the leaves accumulate at the top of the stem to form a massive rosette. Some species are low-growing; others are tall, with woody trunks, usually unbranched, that can reach a height of as much as thirty-five feet. The leaves are long, rather slender, thick, and leathery, and are covered with a dense coating of long hairs which sometimes gives them a beautiful silvery luster. Quoting again: "As the stem grows, new leaves appear and the old ones dry, but their persistent, densely overlapping sheaths cover and protect the stem—only in very old plants do these masses of dead leaves fall spontaneously. This produces the remarkable appearance characteristic of these plants—in a well-developed individual the lowest portion is the most slender part, a naked and woody stem: the middle portion is covered by the cylindrical mass; and in the upper portion below the rosette of normal leaves is a mass of dry and twisted leaves, giving it a thick club-shaped appearance." The branched flower stalks growing from the bases of the bunched leaves that top the stems are densely woolly, and the flower heads, often nodding, are usually yellow, sometimes white.

The people who live on the paramos or near by, says Dr. Cuatrecasas, strip the woolly covering from *Espeletia* leaves to stuff mattresses and pillows, just as the Peruvians on Andean foothills remove the under surface of the stems of certain types of cactus and employ it similarly. Earplugs of frailejón wool and entire leaves worn under the shirt or hat protect against the cold of the paramos, which can be biting.

Under the caption "Edelweiss of the Tropics," he emphasizes how remarkably well adapted to withstand the extreme rigors of their environment the plants of the paramos have become, and reminds us that "some alpine plants of Europe are famous because of their peculiar forms and similar adaptations. The celebrated edelweiss, with heads protected by a rosette of spreading bracts, is entirely covered with a thick white woolen coat and is a good example of adaptation; it belongs to the same family (Compositae) as the *frailejón*. The latter might well be considered a giant relative of edelweiss in the Andes that rise high above but within the tropics. Edelweiss, with its white elegance, adorns and characterizes the Alps; likewise, the stately stands of *frailejón* lend incomparable beauty and exotic majesty to the *páramo* landscape of Colombia."

Within the confines of Colombia there are a number of other distinct types of vegetation, botanically of great interest but less spectacular than those of the paramos. Thus, below the west coast jungle are the mangroves—amphibious evergreen trees that show amazingly effective adaptations in the form and structure of their roots to meet the problems of respiration and absorption of nutrients that face a plant which is, periodically, surrounded by brackish water when the tides of the

Pacific flood the coastal lowlands. To see a radically different vegetation type, you can visit Colombia's northern Caribbean coast, where long dry seasons are responsible for a semiarid type of vegetation—that is, cacti versus mangroves. Then, east of the Andes lie the vast *llanos* covering thousands of square miles of Colombia and neighboring Venezuela. Characteristic of them are the savannas—great stretches of grassland almost completely treeless. The llanos contain a combined animal, vegetable, and human segment of the world that has no equivalent elsewhere. If you want to feel their pulse, read Nancy Bell Bates's *East of the Andes and West of Nowhere* and you will be well repaid.

Our orchid hunting in Colombia took us into still another and quite distinct type of vegetation, the Andean forests which occur at altitudes of from about six thousand to a little less than eleven thousand feet. The lower stories of this tree-covered zone are actually sub-Andean rain forests with a considerably higher annual precipitation and average temperature than the higher stories. Just as in the tropical coastal rain forest, or jungle, so in the higher and less tropical forests there is a mixed plant community rich in the number of genera represented. The dominant genera of both forest stories are the same in a few instances, but in general they are quite different. As altitude increases, the trees gradually decrease in size and fewer and fewer genera are dominant. Incidentally, it is in the higher forest that one finds *cinchona*, that natural source of quinine which for so many years has successfully battled malaria, the scourge of the tropics.

The other day I came across the following: "Swelled with the sultry pride of its savage parents, the orchid radiates a strange, compelling charm which, as one thinks of flowers, is far from flower-like—sensuous blossoms with a brooding, physical beauty which has become a part of a strange something which no other flower can have, the orchid personality." True enough, the flowers of a great many of the extremely large number of species belonging to the family Orchidaceae do have something unique about them, but, for me, it is hardly charm, and it is certainly not their sultry pride. However, the plants that produce the highly priced and increasingly monstrous and ostentatious orchid blooms guarded under florists' glass counters *were* derived from wild (or "savage," if you will) parents that bear much more conservative flowers. In many instances those parents are Colombian.

The author of the quotation was, no doubt, talking about the *Cattleya* or "butterfly" orchids, the flowers of which make up most of the florists' displays. The native Colombian Cattleyas, most of which are now considered to be varieties of the composite species *Cattleya labiata*, bear flowers that in any company would be classed as large. The varieties differ in flower color from white to dark maroon, with lavender-flowered plants most common in the Colombian forests. The national flower of Colombia is the *Cattleya "dowiana aurea"*—rather famous among "Catts" because, as "aurea" implies, there are strong tones of gold, bronze, or orange in its flowers. In its own right its appeal is largely to the grower of "botanicals," but it has for some time been sought after by the hybridizer in the hope of introducing something of its unique flower color into the more commercially valuable Cattleya hybrids.

Over a long period, before we began a study of Colombian Cattleyas in their native habitats, hundreds of thousands, and perhaps more, of the most showy varieties had been torn from the tropical highland forests of the republic by native and foreign collectors. These went, first, to orchidists in England and on the Continent and, later, in North America to form the background of the commercial orchid trade. For many years the flowers produced by these "wild" orchid plants in the greenhouses of lands far distant from their native homes possessed sufficient attraction and appeal to satisfy popular taste and, thus, demand. However, almost from the beginning of their cultivation abroad, hybridization between the varieties was undertaken to produce new shades of color and increase the size and substance of the flowers. These early hybridizations also involved as parents quite different groups of orchids which had come from the Far East. Fortunately for the hybridizers, interspecific and even intergeneric crosses in the orchid family are remarkably successful. Along with the hybridization programs went continual selection of superior races of the Colombian natives. Both techniques of orchid improvement continue, of course, to be actively practiced today. One need not be surprised, therefore, to learn that the pedigrees of the—to my mind—monstrous and unappealing orchid flowers in florists' windows are exceedingly mixed.

By contrast with the modern, almost obscenely lush, and quite pretentious products of the plant breeder's art, the orchids seen growing in the hot, humid Colombian forests bear flowers that have, for me, an unassuming charm along with an exotic appearance and feeling sufficient, seemingly, to satisfy anyone's taste. I even have a predilec-

In full regalia, the dignified chief of a tribe in southwestern Colombia.

A shy little couple on the trail to one of Colombia's orchid forests.

On the high Colombian paramos the frailejónes (*Espeletia*) dominate the landscape.

Strips of the woolly skin of *Espeletia* protect paramo dwellers from the biting cold.

Dr. Cuatrecasas demonstrates that a jungle climber contains a reservoir of water.

Roy smiles as he carries one of the few plants of *Cattleya gigas* he could find in Colombia's ravaged orchid areas.

The Prince is about to photograph Cerro Tronador, "The Thunderer," highest peak in the "Switzerland of South America."

tion for that humble *Cattleya* which has been called "var. *chocoensis*," deriving its varietal name from the political subdivision of the western or maritime cordillera in whose foothills it grows. The flowers are relatively small and somewhat delicate, from white to light lavender in color, bending a little downward from the flower stalk and with flower parts never as fully reflex as in the "Catts" that you know. I think of them as shy, hooded maidens, hiding their faces. When you look under the hood, there is a splotch of orange added, in the throat, and the whole exhales a perfumed, ephemeral breath. Because of its lack of ostentation, *chocoensis*, has, of course, no commerical value, except locally. Now and then you see bunches of its flowers for sale in produce markets near its foothill home, and you can carry away dozens of them after payment of only a few cents.

Many years after exploitation of the orchid populations of Colombia's subtropical forests had so greatly reduced the number of plants that only a very few could be found in the more accessible areas, the government awoke to the realization that one of the country's natural resources of considerable commercial value was fast disappearing. Laws were then enacted which prohibited the exportation of native orchid plants except by a few local growers, to each of whom an annual quota was assigned. I obtained exemption from this regulation because the plants we proposed to airmail to California were to be used for scientific purposes only.

The city of Medellín has been called the "Orchid Capital of South America." It is, also, the capital of the Department of Antioquia and, some three hundred miles by air south of the Canal Zone, lies in the so-called "valley of perpetual spring." The climate of Medellín and the surrounding countryside I have always found so delightful that I have had no hesitation in urging at least a brief stop there by those of my friends sufficiently intelligent to allow themselves more than the minimum of days considered necessary to "see all of South America by air." Medellín is a progressive city, a center of some important Colombian industries, and you sense a drive on the part of its citizens not often duplicated in the tropical sections of South America. Indeed, anywhere in Colombia, if you meet a businessman obviously very much "on his toes," the remark is almost certainly to be made, "Oh, yes, he comes from Medellín."

The city fathers were so farsighted as to dictate that large manufacturing plants should be built only at a considerable distance from the center of Medellín, and it will be a long time before the city grows out to the peripheral ring of factories. This is, of course, quite in contrast with centers of population in this country which early engulfed factory districts, to everyone's detriment. One of the manufacturing establishments I saw was a small, self-contained city, with houses for employees and a clubhouse surrounded by playing fields for their recreation; medical and dental services were provided by the company. No wonder that the Colombian coffee planters complain that Medellín industries are siphoning off their best workers, who flock to the departmental capital to enjoy some financial independence and a congenial way of life, both previously unknown to them.

At the suggestion of orchid exporters in Medellín and the Colombian Department of Agriculture, I undertook a survey of the remaining orchid resources of areas in the northwestern section of the republic from which a maximum of exportable plants had been taken in the past. The results of such a survey were to permit the determination, with some accuracy, of proper export quotas which, in the future, would preserve sufficient plants to repopulate the areas that were found to be the most seriously depleted. I soon discovered that this was a much too ambitious project, only to be accomplished with far more time and assistance than I had available. Dr. Cuatrecasas and Roy made a small beginning, and their work was continued, during one of my subsequent visits to Colombia, with the help of colleagues of the College of Agriculture in Medellín. I planned to restrict the survey, at the beginning at least, to a determination of the distribution of what still remained of the *Cattleya* which, as has been noted, produces Colombia's national flower—"*dowiana aurea*."

Dr. Cuatrecasas and Roy made a good team, worked prodigiously in the far too limited time I could allow them, and collected some two hundred species peculiar to the Colombian jungle, a high percentage of them never before known botanically. This last statement was vouched for by Dr. Cuatrecasas, who probably knows more about the flora of Colombia than anyone else. Long a leading plant scientist in Spain, he was forced by his democratic convictions to seek another home. Invited by the government, he came to Colombia before World War II to teach and to continue the collecting and research, begun in earlier years, which is now culminating in a comprehensive monograph concerning what has already been referred to as a conglomeration of some of the most diverse vegetation types to be seen anywhere

in the world. Long since, he became established, with his family, in
the United States.

For me, the association of Dr. Cuatrecasas with my botanical projects in Colombia was, obviously, of large importance. For Roy, a
knowledgeable plantsman but unschooled in collecting in an extremely
tropical environment, the opportunity to work side by side with a
distinguished botanist of long experience with the vegetation they
encountered was unique.

They made Medellín headquarters for thrusts into parts of the
tropical rain forests through which run some of the Colombian rivers
that empty, northward, into the Caribbean. These areas had been considered, and were still locally reported to be, rich in orchids. Suffice it to say that they are so no longer, as the following quotation
from Roy's reports concerning one of their orchid hunts will prove:

"This time we were to be provided, gratis, with transportation to
the jungle. It appeared on time, an empty two-ton truck of not too
ancient vintage. We rode in it for nine hours at one stretch. My insides rubbed together so long and so hard they must have ended up
calloused—what a business! Just the same, it was great; never a dull
moment for me, the tyro, almost twisting his neck off to catch glimpses
of the astounding succession of new and often beautiful plants, first
on one side of the road and then on the other. Enjoyed every bit of
it—bumps, terrific heat, everything.

"We spent six solid days in the jungle, passed through different
vegetation zones, collected lots of valuable dried specimens. But, orchids—the trip was a complete bust. I was never so thoroughly licked
in all my life. We went through thorn brush which ended abruptly
and then came the not-too-awfully-dense rain forest—after that, virtual
oblivion. There were some openings into which the sun blazed so
fiercely that my unprotected thermometer never recovered after reg-
istering 125°. The rain comes down in bucketfuls; average annual
rainfall said to be three hundred inches, plus. We struck the so-called
'dry' season, but I couldn't notice it. Palms—cruelly thorny climbers,
some of them—were everywhere, along with Philodendrons and their
near relatives, and Caladiums and a great variety of more lowly plants.
Some of the most attractive jungle trees were myrmecophilous, har-
boring ants which are responsible for cross-pollinating their flowers.
I had read about such plants but never expected to see them. I never
want, again, to see any of their paying guests—the ones I tangled with

I nominate for the title of meanest s.o.b.'s on earth. There are still worse ants in the neighborhood, and especially the famous 'Conga,' a fat black rascal a little over one inch long, apparently more feared by the natives than any one of the poisonous snakes, and there are plenty of them.

"Although on this trip we covered only a small part of it, an immense area has apparently been completely sacked, so far as orchids are concerned. We took native climbers and 'fellers' with us, and whenever we saw something that might be an orchid in the cleft of a branch high up on a jungle tree, we either sent up a climber or had the tree cut down. What do you think our total bag was—two good orchid plants and two sad ones!

"Never doubt that fifty years ago this was mighty good orchid country. Some of the best evidence of this is the almost unbelievable knowledge that the natives of the region have about commercially valuable orchid species. Ask almost anyone and he will rattle off the scientific names of a dozen genera and will be able to distinguish most of their species on the basis of sound botanical characters. I could scarcely believe my ears. And do they know what a good orchid plant will sell for, not only in Medellín but also in the U.S.A.? Once, when our native helpers had for five or six hours been hacking a path for us through an awfully dense strip of jungle, one of them asked me what a particular orchid plant would be worth. I thought I would try him out, and calmly replied, 'Ten centavos,' and he, as calmly, asked, 'Per leaf bulb?'—in other words, up to ten or more times my offer."

After this first discouraging effort, they decided that to find orchids in any quantity, and to make any percentage estimate of their normal occurrence in unexploited terrain, it would be necessary to "go back," far into the interior of the heaviest jungle. They proposed to attempt a six- to eight-day muleback journey from Dabeiba, paralleling the course of the Río Arato and coming out, ultimately, at Turbo, on the Gulf of Darien. It would, according to local report, be good "*dowiana aurea*" country, and certainly it was unexplored botanically. Some further inquiry produced quite a discouraging report of what such an expedition would involve. It appeared that a party of rubber hunters had succeeded in getting through to Turbo, but just barely. One of them had said, "Each one of us needed two natives to beat out the snakes and other vermin beside the trail that we had to cut step by step. Every foot of the way stank of malaria, snakes, and alligators.

We were so badly frightened that we never could have made it if we hadn't stayed swacked the whole way."

Limitations of time and the difficulty of finding reliable helpers to go along, rather than this and other similar reports, forced Roy and Dr. Cuatrecasas to give up the Dabeiba-Turbo proposal. Later they did discover a small area where orchids could be found, not many but enough, *gigas* and not "*dowiana aurea*" Cattleyas. Altogether, their botanizing in the Colombian jungle proved that for finding orchids you must be prepared to penetrate the practically unexplored "back country" lying two to four days beyond the limits of the more or less accessible jungle, all of which has long since been stripped of every commercially valuable species. In the latter there is, however, a wealth of new, botanically important, and often beautiful plant species awaiting the scientifically minded plant hunter.

First and last, we sent back to Berkeley many Colombian orchids. Except, perhaps, to the growers of "botanicals," none of them would be particularly exciting to commercial orchidists; but most had some greater or lesser scientific interest, and all were reintroductions directly from the wild. There was a good golden-yellow flowered *Anguloa clowesii*, along with the better-known *A. uniflora*, of which the pendulous, freely swinging lower lip of the flower is responsible for its common name of "cradle orchid." Among others might be mentioned *Brassavola nodosa* and *Trichopilia backhouseana*, the former with succulent leaves and white flowers and the latter a rather fine white-flowered type. It was interesting to see a species of *Acineta* push its flowers out of the bottom of its greenhouse container just as Stanhopeas do. There were of course, a number of species of *Epidendrum*, some rather attractive in a modest way. We took quite a quantity of *Odontoglossum crispum* from the cool, wet foothills of the *Cordillera Central*—hard to grow unless you can produce greenhouse conditions that approximate its native environment.

Of Cattleyas we accumulated a representative assortment. The Medellín growers had assigned scientific names to the *Cattleya* species and varieties they sold, and we found a considerable amount of confusion in nomenclature among the different growers. I was asked to take home good specimen plants of all the named forms and, after growing and comparing them, attempt to produce a standard system of nomenclature.

As appears in the opening paragraphs of this chapter, Roy's botanizing in Colombia actually represented only a stopover on his journey by air to meet me in Peru for the beginning, there, of a much longer period of plant hunting. In those wartime days in South America, as has been seen, you never knew when your next reservation would be confirmed, if ever. He was, consequently, decidedly nervous whenever he had to be out of touch for some time with the Medellín airline office. By good fortune, he correctly estimated how long he could stay away on the last orchid hunt and returned to Medellín just as his confirmed reservation arrived. Then his troubles began.

Roy had only two days before he was to take off for Bogotá, and, he writes, "there were dozens of things that had to be done before my departure—cartons, boxes, paper, and string to be bought; three official permits for export of living and dried plants to be wangled; exit credentials to be made out and properly witnessed. It was the same old story: a key official had just stepped out, 'to return sometime this afternoon, *Señor*'; one tienda had cartons but no string; another vice versa, etc., etc.

"The second day my frustration was complete. A beloved archbishop had died; his body lay in state in one of the churches, and on that second day a procession was to escort him to the Cathedral. It was a beauty but, of course, was routed, at snail's pace, along the main street where most of my business had to be done. The street was solidly packed with the faithful; every doorway was jammed. All I could do was join the procession and break ranks opposite a store I wanted. I knew that I was getting far behind schedule and began to rave internally. All that saved my sanity were the flowers. Nowhere else in the world could there have been such a display of orchids. In one immense set-piece I counted seven different genera in a background of callas. In another, equally large, a mixture of orchids, roses, and carnations. Every now and then, a file of buglers played the most mournful music I have ever heard.

"The night before, I had gone to the church where the archbishop's coffin rested before the procession. The nave was draped with long blue, white, and black streamers. The fragrance of the flowers banked around the high altar and filling the shrines beside it was overpowering, and I soon had to leave. In the Cathedral it was the same and, just as in the procession, there was a mingling of classes—the rich, the poor, the beggars; jewels and rags. There seemed to be no show of emotion; the attitude was that of resignation. I am sure that everyone believed that the archbishop had gone where all good churchmen go and that their loss was only a material one. The spiritual fervor was there, but only as a light in their faces."

The next day Roy flew to Bogotá. There he began his wild ride by "Taxi to Cali."

18

BEFORE PERÓN—AND AFTER

I SAW PERÓN twice, once officially and a second time from the sidewalk as his big car was moving very fast down the Alem, one of Buenos
Aires' finest boulevards, surrounded by the largest flock of motorcycle
police that I had ever seen. A block or two ahead, the advance contingent with horns at full roar had driven all traffic to the lanes that
bordered the main one.

There was a strong hint of urgency about the whole thing, as though
something rather significant was in the wind. I offered this supposi-
tion to a fellow curbstander. After a glance that identified me as a
foreigner, he smiled a bit quizzically and replied, "Oh, he always
goes home like this from his office in the Casa Rosada." Then, up went
his hands and back went his head in a typically Latin and decidedly
meaningful gesture. In 1948 there was plenty of other evidence that
Perón, and Evita also, understood showmanship, and, correspondingly,
that many Argentines took for granted the joint dictatorship's accomplishments in that direction and were amused and even intrigued,
up to a point.

Over the years showmanship on an international scale has had a
strong appeal for governments, particularly Latin-American governments and their dictators. Inspired by local pride—perhaps also in the
notion that they may thus be compensating for their intellecutal deficiencies—the latter are willing to underwrite congresses in scientific
and other fields and the publication of elaborate volumes descriptive
of the floras and faunas of their countries. These volumes are intended,
in the first place, for distribution, gratis, to foreign governments and
to certain of their most distinguished citizens.

In 1948 Perón subsidized the meetings of the Second South American Botanical Congress in the city of Tucumán in northwestern Argentina. A few foreign botanists, of whom I was one, were guests, and so Florence and I once more traveled to South America, this time on Perón's largess. Soon thereafter, and with Perón's support, the first volume of *Genera et Species Plantarum Argentinarum* appeared. In format it produced a rather staggering effect, and the cost of publication must have been very great. Obviously designed to correspond in extreme size of page and type and in quality and weight of paper to some of the famous floras of other lands published a hundred and more years ago, the book was heavy and cumbersome. One Argentine botanist facetiously remarked that if he wanted, with its aid, to identify a tree in the countryside, he would need a truck. Then, he had a choice: to carry the book to the tree or the tree to the book. Originally, a series of such volumes was to provide detailed descriptions of the character and distribution of all the native Argentine members of numerous plant families. Publication ceased with Perón's overthrow, but the volumes that had previously been published contain valuable articles by local and foreign botanists and are lavishly illustrated, with numerous reproductions in color. If Perón could have lasted a little longer, the volume which was to include my account of the Argentine Nicotianas might have appeared.

Following the Congress, the guests and some others were flown to Buenos Aires to see its important botanical institutions and to be greeted by Perón, in person. The audience was held in a big room in the somewhat well-worn Casa Rosada, the government house that faces the Plaza de Mayo. Some twenty-five of us were assigned seats at a long table. We remained standing until Perón entered the room and seated himself at the head of the table. With eyes cast down, and somewhat haltingly, he expressed his pleasure at our presence in his country. He went on to speak of his own contact with botany, referring to a distinguished Argentine as his teacher. At this, I caught a hint of raised eyebrows among the Argentine botanists present. Then he described, at considerable length, the encouragement of higher education and scientific research under his regime, and the eyebrows definitely rose. Throughout, he chain-smoked a familiar brand of North American cigarettes and, in general, seemed to be rather ill at ease. After the audience we were each given a package containing about a dozen small, paper-bound propaganda pamphlets.

I sat within a few feet of Perón and, of course, studied him carefully. Afterwards, as we walked across the Plaza, I asked Florence what her impressions were. She said, "He looked to me just like an ex-football player, guard or tackle, who has been leading a pretty hard life lately." That sounded about right to me.

In the mid-thirties Buenos Aires and much of the rest of Argentina appealed to me as being, in a variety of ways, years in advance of the other South American republics I had seen. The Argentines have always seemed to be more like ourselves than other South Americans. There was, and still is, especially in Buenos Aires, the alert, progressive, and self-confident atmosphere of a nation on the march and knowing where it is going. Industrialization began early in Argentina and, although great wealth was confined to a relatively few, a characteristic middle class was evolving. I was impressed by the superior quality of instruction and research in the universities and by the contrast between the size, equipment, and staffs of the museums and other scientific institutions in Argentina and those elsewhere.

There were many other contrasts, and the explanation was not far to seek—the great extent of readily exploitable natural resources, particularly agricultural ones, and the origin and character of Argentina's population. It has recently been said that the latter consists largely of "whites of Spanish and Italian origin." In addition, there is a large group which emigrated from Germany and another group, smaller, of English stock; both became Argentine a number of generations ago. By contrast, in many other South American republics there is a marked preponderance of Indian and mixed Indian-and-white nationals; in more than one South American republic they may represent at least eighty per cent of the population.

In the Argentina that I saw three times in the years before Perón, my friends now and then referred to the *descamisados,* the "shirtless ones," and I knew from report that they were talking about a segment of the population which was underprivileged, usually undernourished, exploited, and politically unstable. My first days in Buenos Aires were at the height of the summer season and my hotel was near the center of the city's business activity. The first morning it appeared that most of the coatless men who passed my window wore something distinctly approximating the upper half of a pair of pajamas, buttoned only part way up or down. Until undeceived by my friends, I rather naturally assumed that I had been seeing descamisados and that they made up the majority of the population. The truth was, of course, that a thin, loose, smocklike upper garment was entirely *au fait* on the street during the capital's extremely hot and humid December weather.

Later on I saw plenty of cruel poverty and, along the water front, a degree of degradation equal to the worst that South European ports can exhibit. In provincial cities and towns the contrasts between rich and poor were not so striking but, for the majority, the standard of living was, on the average, quite low. In the countryside the situation was different.

Argentina is blessed with a considerable proportion of the world's richest agricultural terrain, especially appropriate for the growing of cereals and the production of beef cattle. In the past there have been periods when Argentina exported about as much of both as did any other country in the world. Well over one hundred years ago, in part to encourage immigration essential for the exploitation of Argentina's potentially almost unlimited agricultural resources, arable land throughout the republic could be had for not much more than the asking. As a result, over the years, tremendous acreages had come under the control of a relatively small number of *estancieros* who became the "landed aristocracy" of the Argentine. Report has it that almost twenty per cent of all land suitable for agriculture was, and most of it still is, in the hands of not more than five hundred landed proprietors and over eighty-five per cent of it in parcels of one thousand acres or more. All this obviously meant that the vast majority of the countrypeople were without land of their own or possessed plots too small to yield anything more than a substandard existence. The rest were sharecroppers or tenant farmers responsible to a landed proprietor, living under what has been called "institutionalized feudalism," with little or no hope of improving their economic status.

In other words, not only in the capital and the few other large centers of population but also in the vast stretches of *pampa* that separate them, there had accumulated a great body of the underprivileged by the time that Perón assumed undisputed power throughout Argentina. During at least the early part of the twelve years of an almost completely planned socialistic economy dictated by Perón and Evita, the Argentine masses were granted what to them were almost unheard-of, undreamed-of, benefits and privileges. In return for dictatorship they were offered full employment, wage increases and bonuses, paid vacations, severance pay, pensions, low-cost housing, nurseries, playgrounds, and, essentially, free medical attention. I believe that of even greater significance for him than the material improvement in his condition, all this meant to the descamisado that, for the first time, he could feel a sense of personal importance and that, to some degree, he had attained a recognized position in the community.

Approaching the zenith of their power over Argentina, when I was there in 1948, Perón and Evita stared at me from almost every wall in Buenos Aires. Other posters, here and there, aimed to illustrate what the two dictators had done or were going to do for the "common man." The latter was most frequently depicted as a sort of Laocoön breaking the chains with which, before Perón, inherited power, wealth, and privilege had bound him; sometimes only the severed chains were shown. Perón himself stood some forty or more feet high—in aluminum, I think—facing the Casa Rosada on the Plaza de Mayo. Excerpts from his many and lengthy exhortations to his people blared forth from sound trucks on their routes through the business district. Except that Spanish is a far more liquid language than German, he sounded much like the Hitler whose mouthings I listened to for a while at a Nazi rally in 1931; they both gave the impression, from beginning to end, of being exceedingly angry at everybody and everything.

Perón was the last of a series of presidents elected from among those high-ranking officers who had maintained a fascistic sort of military dictatorship for the three years before he took office in 1946. The record leaves no doubt that during that period there was collaboration with the Axis. So far as we personally were concerned, there was plenty of evidence that many Argentines agreed with such Axis leanings. Although on the street we were never roughed up, there was now and then a bit of jostling and sometimes spitting, never on us but unmistakably in our direction. We early learned to avoid the obviously biased crowds that stood before the newspaper bulletin boards on which strongly slanted reports of the progress of early campaigns of World War II were posted. On the other hand, there was no serious unpleasantness during the almost one hundred lectures, many of them illustrated with movies illustrating landscape features and life in the United States, that I gave throughout Argentina in the early years of the war before audiences ranging from school children to university professors. All my numerous personal friends in Argentina were anti-Perón and pro-Ally.

Although in theory Perón's election marked Argentina's return to a constitutional type of government, he became a constantly less and less "enlightened" dictator. He was aided and abetted by Evita—shallow, vain, an utterly unscrupulous demagogue, but undeniably beautiful and, up to a point, brilliant. Her intense personal interest in the organization of social reforms and services endeared her to the masses. Attired in the height of fashion, with flashing jewels, she often appeared before them to tell of all that she was doing for them, and they fell in love with her. There was, however, increasing evidence that chicanery of many sorts was being practiced, and I saw an indication of how petty it could be. As the equivalent of our Memorial Day approached, it was publicly announced that Evita was personally providing flowers at Buenos Aires cemeteries for those too poor to buy such tributes to their departed. I happened to know the florist whose shop was below the windows of our hotel room. On the day before the one which was to provide an additional evidence of Evita's thoughtful generosity, I saw an army truck piled with flowers pull up at the florist's door, and watched him make additions to the pile. For some reason, the explanation did not at once occur to me. When, some days later, I inquired about the episode and his part in it, the florist, without comment, handed me an order signed by high authority and calling on him to provide, gratis, a specified number of bunches of flowers, each tagged, "From Evita."

Organized labor in particular benefited greatly by the opportunity which Evita's exalted position gave her to accede to its increasing demands. The extent of her influence became apparent when her death in 1952 was soon followed by the loss of Perón's contact with the labor movement. This was one of the more serious cracks that, as time went on, began to appear in the wall of class prejudice Perón and Evita had constructed between the more and the less privileged. At the same time, the constantly increasing cost of maintaining the exaggerated type of social security which was the prime foundation of their personal popularity began to undermine the economic prosperity of Argentina. Increases in taxation, which bore heavily on the descamisados as well as on the wealthy, could not balance a budget which had to provide for the large-scale peculations of the dictators themselves and of their henchmen. Graft and corruption, on an almost unbelievable scale, were rampant among others in authority also.

It has been estimated that when Perón became president Argentina had resources of over a billion dollars in gold and foreign currency. When he escaped into exile twelve years later, the domestic debt was found to exceed four billion dollars, with reserves of only three hundred million. The rapidly accumulating products of mismanagement and flagrant dishonesty at the seat of government began to make themselves felt throughout the economic life of Argentina—especially by the middle class, but also by the masses. Disillusionment and discontent followed. Repressive measures, long in the background, began to operate openly. Indeed, at almost the termination of his rule and during his final struggle to maintain his authority, Perón publicly announced that his followers were to have what amounted to carte blanche to liquidate the opposition and destroy its property—thus, in a sense, legalizing those same types of terrorism that had been winked at for many months.

More than a year before his exit, the dictator had finally succeeded in victimizing and rendering largely impotent practically all the powerful groups in opposition to his regime except the Catholic Church and elements within the Navy and Air Force. In addition, and despite his best efforts, the strongly entrenched landed proprietors and certain others of large wealth had never entirely succumbed. As is well known, of course, Perón's constantly more active and obvious persecution of the Church, which he denounced as an oligarchical institution, produced international repercussions in addition to crystallizing the opposition of a certain proportion of his own followers and of many others who had previously wavered in their support of his regime. It was a colossal blunder and another striking illustration of how thoroughly a dictator will ultimately lose all sense of proportion. Large-scale and repeated hostile demonstrations, the weakening support of the Army, and, finally, armed revolt by Navy and Air Force unmistakably pointed down the path to exile.

Destructive as it was of major bases upon which Argentina's prosperity and progress had rested, Perón's regime taught certain lessons which, presumably, will not soon be forgotten. Thus, although dictatorship in one guise or another was not new to Argentina, it had never, before Perón, evolved into crude despotism. The Argentines will, I think, be slow hereafter to surrender to the former lest they may again become subject to the latter. Further, it has become apparent that, politically, the underprivileged but now somewhat more coherent substratum of the Argentine community must be taken seriously into account and will not permit itself to be exploited as before. Conversely, certain of the thoroughly justified elements of Perón's much overextended social security programs cannot be abandoned, and succeeding governments have recognized this fact.

Recently, I had a rather amusing and enlightening contact with Argentina's publicly supported system of medical assistance which, under Perón, reached a maximum in benefits and application. When I required a series of vitamin shots, my Buenos Aires physician gave me a prescription and suggested that any *farmácia* that could fill it would also administer the injections. He was mistaken, for the one I patronized would only sell me the ampules and directed me to a near-by branch of the national *Asistencia Pública* for the injections. The large, one-story building gave the impression of being among the oldest in the city, and Betty and I entered with considerable doubt about what we would find within. It was, therefore, a relief to see a quite spotless reception room, high ceilinged and tile floored. The attendant was cordial and pointed to a room down the hall. Arriving there, we were greeted in friendly fashion by an exceedingly buxom nurse whose white costume was pristine. At the moment she had no other patients and, motioning Betty to a chair, went over to a wall sink. Above it, attached to a board, was a collection of syringes, most of which appeared to be of prodigious capacity; indeed, for a fleeting instant I thought that, by mistake, we had wandered into a veterinary hospital. Selecting from the board one of the smaller models, the nurse looked up with an encouraging grin to find me baring an arm. After one look she burst into a roar of laughter and, simultaneously, slapped me hard on a buttock. I got the point and exposed myself to an extent that I hoped would be sufficient. Meanwhile, both the nurse and Betty were full of giggles—it was subsequently explained to me that the expression of shocked incredulity on my face during the exposure process had been too much for both of them.

A moment later I felt a distinct but not too severe puncture and twisted around to observe what was in progress. Then I had my second shock—nothing was to be seen but the needle up to the hilt in my *derrière*. I looked about wildly, and there was the nurse at the sink calmly filling a glass tube. She then screwed it on to the needle and began to press down on the plunger. When she had completed the injection and a vigorous massage of the area involved, I asked how much I owed. She seemed a little surprised and smilingly replied, "*Nada*." I thought, of course, that this indicated that the bill was to be paid in the reception room, and to show my appreciation of her attentions I offered her a gratuity. She shook her head, patted me on the shoulder, took Betty by the hand, escorted us to the door, and waved a cordial farewell. At the office I was politely informed that the cost of the medical attention I had received, and more, was in Argentina free to all, nationals and visitors alike.

In North America the individual is in a position through his own efforts to gain personal recognition, respect, and material advancement without regard to the social status or economic stature of his immediate family and its ramifying connections. In Latin America, on the other hand, the reverse is often true and, thus, opportunity and privilege as well as wealth and social position are, by and large, inherited; they are recognized to be the prerogatives of those whose families form the upper stratum in the local community. It is, therefore, inevitable that in Latin America the individual owes his allegiance first to the family and, by extension, to the clan which is composed of families of equivalent prestige, and only secondly to the government and its constituted authority.

This situation deserves to be more widely recognized than it has been, because it offers a partial explanation of some of the problems to be faced when efforts are made to promote democracy and a thoroughly constitutional form of government in a Latin-American republic. The cohesion and political and economic importance of the clan, in its widest sense, were exemplified by Perón's inability to victimize effectively the powerfully entrenched landed aristocracy and others of large wealth who, throughout, opposed and hated him. Their spokesmen became prominent members of the revolutionary party that overthrew the dictator. This party represented, politically speaking, a remarkably mixed bag in which the representatives of opposing ideologies were willing to submerge their individual viewpoints in favor of the common cause. However, when, after Perón, the reinstitution of a constitutional government was attempted and the necessity for active coöperation seemed to be at an end, the political insecurity of the alliance soon appeared. Those who spoke for the clans had, apparently, looked forward to a return to the days, actually long gone, when they had been virtually beyond the law and when the under-privileged had remained underprivileged. Directly opposed, of course, were those who represented the element in the revolutionary group which was more or less far to the left as well as those of the middle class who understood the necessity for considerable social reform. It was no surprise, therefore, to find that those who took over control from Perón were immediately faced with serious problems which were seized upon and intensified by the hard core of the *Peronista* party whose allegiance to the dictator had not diminished and who were determined to reinstate him.

In the opening chapter certain geographic analogies were drawn between Argentina and the United States. Although in individual instances the parallelisms cannot be sharply defined, we may liken the semiaridity of Patagonia to that of our Southwest, and the semitropics of Argentina's northernmost and northwestern provinces to Florida and near by, while sections of our North Atlantic seaboard are similar climatically to the northern South Atlantic coasts of Argentina. Agriculturally, and to some extent in climate, sections of our Great Plains area correspond to the pampa. Remember, too, that in the Far West of both republics massive mountain ranges occur, the Argentine one being, of course, of a far greater order of magnitude, altitudinally and otherwise, than ours. Finally, the sub-Antarctic area of the farthest south in Argentina reminds us of the sub-Arctic parts of our forty-ninth state.

In the course of five of our South American plant-hunting expeditions, we spent a total of many months in Argentina and collected in all of its climatic and vegetational zones. In most of the zones the occurrence of microclimates creates larger or smaller pockets of specialized vegetation which must be found and their contents catalogued floristically to give a true picture of the character and composition of the entire vegetational zone in question. A good many of these pockets, often isolated, had already been seen and studied by Argentine and foreign botanists, and the report on one of them focused my attention on the northwestern provinces and on southern Bolivia, next door.

The genus *Nicotiana*, as I have already said, contains a species, *Nicotiana tabacum*, which provides the tobacco of commerce, one of the world's most important and widely cultivated crop plants.

In the first chapter I noted that a good many years ago in the Botanical Garden in Berkeley we demonstrated that the tobacco plant, with its numerous cultivated races, had its origin in remote past time from a cross between two quite distinct species that were growing in the wild state in Andean South America, presumably somewhere in that extensive territory which includes corners of today's Peru, Bolivia, Chile, and Argentina. We were, also, prepared to suggest which of the numerous South American Nicotianas represented the present-day descendants of the two original parents that hybridized to produce *Nicotiana tabacum*. One of them we felt quite sure was *Nicotiana sylvestris*. It had previously been found growing only in a restricted portion of northwestern Argentina, and rarely there. I wanted to verify this isolation of *Nicotiana sylvestris* and was able to do so, but only after long and arduous explorations northward, southward, and eastward of its already known area of occurrence—to the west was entirely inhospitable terrain, the high and desolate semiaridity of the knees of the snowy Andes on Argentina's frontier in the direction of the Pacific. Our search extended *sylvestris'* distribution a little and, in addition, determined that this *Nicotiana* disliked man's intrusion into its domain—perhaps at one time extensive—and had isolated itself in a few bits of countryside inappropriate for agricultural exploitation and easily overlooked by the plant hunter.

In European botanical gardens *sylvestris* has long been grown, and its name has from time to time appeared in seedsmen's catalogues which wax a little lyrical about the heavy fragrance which its long, white, tubular flowers add to a garden plot. It was good, however, to see *sylvestris* in its native habitat and, for the first time, to have seed from wild rather than domesticated races.

The identity of the other South American *Nicotiana* whose ancestor was involved in the hybrid origin of the tobacco plant was not so easy to pinpoint. I felt certain that it belonged to a small aggregation of species known to be rather closely interrelated yet easy to distinguish one from another by differences in the form and structure of more than one plant character. This group which I thought must contain the suspect consisted mostly of tall, semiwoody plants—"tree tobaccos"—from which the modern tobacco plant might have inherited its quite considerable stature. The species of the group had other plant characteristics in common that set them apart, quite sharply, from all other Nicotianas.

When first I went to South America all members of the tree tobacco group were thought to be restricted to the south Andean part
of Peru and some distance over the border into Bolivia. I found this
distributional picture was substantially correct, although we extended
it somewhat in various directions in both Peru and Bolivia. Incidentally, this particular reconnaissance turned up a new *Nicotiana*,
never before discovered, near the Peruvian-Bolivian border.

If the ancestors of *sylvestris* and of a member of the tree tobacco
group actually had cross-pollinated to produce the hybrid we call
tobacco, those ancestors must, of course, have been growing rather
close together. So far as I knew, the tree tobacco growing nearest to
sylvestris was a long distance away, in Bolivia. My proposition required
that one be found much nearer to or actually in *sylvestris* territory.
Well, one had already been found, but I did not know of that
until, in preparation for one of my early expeditions, I went to Europe
again to survey the dried plant specimens of South American Nicotianas in herbaria I had not previously visited.

In one of them I found a specimen which I had never seen before.
It was labeled "*Nicotiana otophora*," and I immediately realized that
it was an additional species belonging to the tree tobacco group.
Equally exciting was the notation on the label that the plant had been
collected in "Departamento Santa Barbara, La Quinta, Argentina,"
for I knew that Santa Barbara was a political subdivision of the northwestern Argentine province in which *sylvestris* is found. This meant
that *Nicotiana otophora* probably was the species of the tree tobacco
group of which an ancestor had crossed with an ancestor of *sylvestris*
to produce *Nicotiana tabacum*, the tobacco plant of commerce. This
hypothesis was, of course, based upon the seemingly rather logical assumption that those ancestral species grew more or less where their
descendants grow today. All this meant, also, that I must have seed of
otophora from which I could grow plants in the hope of extracting
from them evidence in support of my hypothesis. Therefore, a major
objective of one of our early expeditions was a search for *otophora*.

We finally found it, in limited quantity, near where the label on
the dried specimen said it had been growing. A month or two earlier,
the plants had been flowering heavily and had borne hundreds of full
seed capsules, but by the time we arrived every capsule was entirely
empty. When, at home, I stood looking rather disgustedly at our
flowerless and seedless dried specimens of *otophora*, it suddenly oc-

curred to me that a seed or two might have adhered to the sticky stems. The seeds of all Nicotianas are quite small; those of the tree tobaccos are on the minute side so that I had to use a magnifier in searching for seed among the debris from my stem scrapings. One by one the little brown ovoids appeared between the dust particles and grains of sand and, finally, I had about a dozen of them.

Another year we went back to La Quinta and the Santa Barbara hills at the proper season for the flowering and seeding of *otophora*. The area in which it grows is one of those pockets of somewhat specialized vegetation to which I earlier referred as produced by a microclimate. Of decided interest was the discovery that *sylvestris*, too, was there.

From the seed of *otophora* grew, in the Botanical Garden in Berkeley, sturdy plants which added that species to our almost complete living collection of the Nicotianas of the world. Near by, we grew *sylvestris* and *tabacum*. We made hybrids among the three. Under the microscope we studied the chromosomes and their behavior in the hybrids. The results confirmed my belief that from hybridization between the ancestors of *sylvestris* and *otophora* our tobacco of today has evolved. Finally, by artificially doubling the chromosomes of the hybrid that we had made between present-day *sylvestris* and *otophora*, we produced something that looked a great deal like modern *tabacum* —in other words, a synthesized tobacco plant.

My first contacts with Argentina, many years ago, were confined mainly to the lake region in the south and the city and province of Buenos Aires. The former is equivalent in landscape and vegetation to the Chilean lake area, earlier described; indeed, the two form a continuous belt of scenic attractions, with the international frontier an indistinguishable line of demarcation between the Chilean and the Argentine contributions. Lovely lakes, large and small, extend finger-like into depressions of the Andean foothills which, like the Chilean ones, are deeply covered with temperate rain forest—the snow-covered Cerro Tronador, is reflected in Argentina's Lago Nahuel Huapí just as white-capped Volcán Osorno is mirrored in Chile's Llanquihue.

On the shores of Nahuel Huapí the resort town of San Carlos de Bariloche is just within the well-watered forest zone, but not many miles to the east you unexpectedly find yourself surrounded by desolate, wind-swept, cactus-dotted aridity. Looking back toward Bariloche, you see how abruptly the South Atlantic gales blowing hard over the Patagonian semidesert have halted, at the base of the Andes, the smoothly continuous eastward flow of the rain forest and completely altered the character of the terrain and its vegetation. To me it has always been reminiscent of the remarkably precise fashion in which the distribution of the California Redwoods is determined by the distance to which the Pacific fogs penetrate inland—a sort of analogy in reverse. Where forest and desert approach each other in southern Argentina a transitional type of vegetation might be anticipated but as yet I have never found it.

Just as the glowing accounts of your tourist bureau and its literature do no more than justice to what you will see in the Chilean lake region, so their enthusiasm for its Argentine equivalent is entirely justified. Two years ago Betty and I crossed from Chile to Argentina along the tourist route through the land of lakes. At Bariloche we stopped at Hotel Llao Llao about which most trippers have only good things to say and, in particular, about the tariff. For some reason and contrary to custom, North Americans were conspicuous by their absence during our stay and the hotel—unavailable except with reservations made long in advance—was filled with Argentines and other South Americans on holiday. We had an especially good time with a Brazilian family consisting of father, mother, and two subteenage children, who sat at the table next to ours in the huge dining hall. The parents were of German extraction and all four were, fluently, polylingual—German, French, English, Spanish, and, of course, Portuguese.

Each morning, from the breakfast room, we saw the serrated crown of Cerro Tronador at the head of a green-walled valley and watched the play of lights and shadows on the mountain's white peaks and glistening flanks. From another window we looked down upon the deep-blue expanse of Nahuel Huapí encircled by mountains rising, westward, to loftier and loftier Andean heights.

On one border of the great stretches of greensward surrounding the hotel you can see, below, two slender arms of the lake margined by dense rain forest. At the base of the nearer one were moored the motorboats that transported fishermen to the gigantic trout and sizable salmon that abound in the cold lakes and rapid rivers of the region. Every evening in the hotel lobby, above a placard inscribed ARCO IRIS ("rainbow"), the biggest fish of the day was displayed, along with the name of the fisherman and the weight of his catch. I do not remember what the biggest rainbow weighed, but all of them were monsters; had it not been for their distinctive markings, I would have refused to agree that they and the—by contrast—fingerlings of California streams belonged to the same clan. A local guidebook says that a distinguished British visitor caught a twenty-four-pound salmon, probably in the lake or the Río Traful, both noted for their supply of large and gamey ones.

Lake Nahuel Huapí has given its name to the largest and most impressive of the numerous National Parks set aside by the Argentine government in the various vegetational zones of the republic. A considerable area was reserved over forty years ago; a later addition has brought the total land surface to some one and a half million acres along the slopes of the southern Andes and near by. Most of this vast and magnificent territory is forested, almost exclusively a virgin forest composed of species native only to southern Argentina and its Chilean counterpart just across the international boundary. On an island in Nahuel Huapí the naturalists of the park's scientific staff have assembled a representative collection of the native vegetation placed in their charge. It has become, and rightfully so, a tourist attraction. There, one sees groves or specimen trees of a number of species of *Nothofagus,* the "false beech" of South America, together with *Libocedrus,* locally called *ciprés,* and the mayten (*Maytenus*), *Lomatia* (*radal*), and both *Fitzroya* and *Saxegothea.*

Some of our expedition members, at one time or another, have approached or reached the Bariloche area from different directions. Once, Dr. Adrian Ruiz Leal, the well-known Argentine naturalist, collected for me southward from his headquarters in Mendoza, just below the foothills of the central Chilean-Argentine cordillera, along a newly completed highway that wound, not too far from the international border, in and out of lofty valleys that lie between the eastern extensions of the southern Andes. I wanted to determine how far south toward Bariloche grew the rather diminutive *Nicotiana corymbosa,* a species I knew could withstand extremes of altitude and aridity. We have already come across *corymbosa,* in the Vale of Paradise, and also in and on both sides of the Uspallata Pass—the main gateway between Argentina and Chile, frowned down upon by the loftiest of Andean peaks.

Ruiz Leal searched it out here and there along his route, sometimes tucked away in spots difficult to approach. Later, Walter and Alan traced it far into southern Patagonia, almost to Magellan Strait. Other expedition members extended its North Chilean distribution well along toward the Peruvian frontier. We were, therefore, able to demonstrate that tough little *corymbosa* can be found by the plant hunter for almost two thousand miles from north to south along one side or the other of the Andes. He must, however, be diligent and sharp-eyed, because only in often out-of-the-way pockets, at altitudes of ten thousand feet or more, can *corymbosa* find the moist but well-drained soil and full exposure to the sun which its seed require for germination. The seedlings must, then, grow rapidly in order that the annual life-cycle, which culminates in the production of seed that will give rise to the next generation, may successfully be completed before the brief Andean summer comes to an end.

A few years before Ruiz Leal had followed *corymbosa* south along the eastern face of the Andes toward Bariloche, Walter and Alan ended there a Patagonian journey that took them almost to the very apex of the South American continent. The pages upon pages that might be written about the many aspects of the nearly two thousand miles that they traveled by truck—first along the Argentine coast, and then back beside and into the far southern cordillera, with crisscrosses over the Patagonian plains—must be compressed into a few lines.

I bought them a Ford pickup in Buenos Aires, and found a black-smith who could fabricate the necessary hoops and a sailmaker to sew the canvas cover to go over the hoops. What approximated a "covered wagon" ultimately appeared. In it Walter and Alan drove south for many days along the coast. Once, on one of the many stretches where the road was narrow and high-crowned, they went into the ditch and the truck ended up on its back. No real harm was done, and soon a road gang dragged them out and set the truck on its wheels again. However, when they started to reorganize their scrambled collection of personal belongings, food, bedrolls, and collecting equipment, it appeared that most of the contents of the emergency oil can had distributed itself here and there.

As they voyaged ever southward, the coastal roads became worse and worse, and those on the inland return journey were, at times, almost impassable. Once, a strip of sandy gumbo which looked relatively firm held them immovable for many hours until a team of sufficiently powerful oxen could be brought up. At an overnight stopping place, someone apparently needed the nuts that secured a rear wheel, as they discovered the next day when the wheel rolled off. They thought that the axle had been bent; the wheel certainly was. Fortunately, a huge truck loaded high with wool appeared some hours later, and Walter and Eduard Grondona—who was in those days, as already mentioned, a graduate student of botany in Buenos Aires and was a member of the Patagonian party—were given a lift to the next town and its garage, several miles away. Meanwhile, Alan stood guard on the arid plain, swept continuously by icy winds against which the truck cab gave little protection.

These and numerous other mishaps were rendered less serious by the ready and cheerful assistance of chance passers-by. When they had lost their way or been delayed until after nightfall far from one of the few, small centers of population, they were always sure of cordial hospitality if they could find a rancher's home. This was not often easy, because many dozens of miles usually separated one landed proprietor's headquarters from that of his neighbor. When they were there, Patagonia supported about one fourth of Argentina's sheep and from them came one half of all its wool. Most of the pasturage is so scanty that, according to report, a single animal requires ten times as many acres to survive in Patagonia as it would need on the pampa of Central Argentina. As a result, a single sheep ranch, especially in the farthest south, is likely to encompass hundreds of thousands of acres.

Much of the Patagonian terrain they saw was barren, even in January and February, the late spring and early summer of the southern extremity of Argentina. Low scrub, bunch grasses, and but little else can survive the heavy snows of the southern winter and the force of the southwesterly winds that, throughout the remainder of the year, never cease to drive before them the sands which cover great belts of semidesert. Where the winds are most severe, a windowpane soon comes to represent nothing but protection, because the violently driven sand will, in a season, etch the surface until it becomes opaque.

Above sixty per cent of Patagonia's ground cover consists of species of the grass genus *Festuca;* other herbaceous species seldom total over ten per cent. In the far south, the latter are uniformly dwarf to prostrate, and this growth habit, imposed by the rigors of climate, is also characteristic of the gnarled and twisted shrubs which may be either dominant or almost completely lacking in any particular area. The Nicotianas of Patagonia, which were the major objectives of our collecting there, represent striking illustrations of the effects of climatic extremes upon plant growth and form. All the five species are diminutives, limited in occurrence to isolated vegetational niches and, on both counts, difficult to track down. The two most interesting ones, *ameghi-noi* and *acaulis*, look like nothing more than small rosettes of slender, ruffled leaves appressed against the soil surface. During the month or so that stimulates flowering and fruiting in a sub-Antarctic environment, buds at the leaf bases send up short flowering stems; indeed, to find the flowers of *ameghinoi* you look for small white dots that sprinkle the dark-green leaves. Both species are unique among Nicotianas in dividing their bodies underground and sending out stems which appear aboveground at a little distance and form additional leafy rosettes. Repeated many times, the products of this type of vegetative reproduction will, obviously, form a small carpet made up of many individual plants. Following seasons that limit or do not permit sexual reproduction via flowering and seeding, such a vegetative alternative can provide for an increase in population of the two Nicotianas.

Beginning in the north with Lago Nahuel Huapí, five large or smaller lakes contribute greatly to the rugged charm of the Patagonian mountains; indeed, those that lie far below the snowy peaks and glaciers of the southernmost extremity of the continent-long Andean range represent an essential feature of a truly magnificent scenic complex. In Patagonia's lakes most of her rivers, flowing down to the sea, have their origin; rivers which have served as means and routes of distribution for those species of the Andean flora which can survive on the arid Patagonian plain. Like many partial or almost complete aridities elsewhere in the world, southern Argentina's dry steppe will grow field crops and ornamentals quite successfully when water is artificially supplied, but until large-scale efforts are made to impound the flow of the Patagonian rivers, the extent of irrigated fields will remain as limited as it was when our botanists traversed the "Magellanic Provinces."

Their farthest south was the little city of Punta Arenas across Magellan Strait from Tierra del Fuego. During his stay there, Walter bought at my request a sufficient number of skins of the South American sea otter to make a fur coat for Florence. The old and grizzled Cape Horn hunter who sold them had sprinkled the pelts so thoroughly with powdered camphor that they appeared to have snow sifted over them. Walter was ultimately to meet us in Valparaiso which meant that he must cross the Chilean border in the lake region after his return from Patagonia. He was determined not to pay Chilean duties on the sea otterskins and to this end decided to get them out of sight by stuffing them under his shirt. The result was, of course, that he immediately acquired an entirely unnatural rotundity which, seemingly, could not possibly escape the eye of the customs inspector, even if he failed to detect the aroma of camphor which was still very powerful. This was a good many years ago and the Chilean customs must have been a far more informal institution than it is today. In some manner Walter determined in advance that the inspector and his family were of recent German extraction. Nonchalantly walking in upon them at their "coffee break," he exhibited his passport and at once began a conversation in German, which he spoke fluently. After entertaining them with descriptions of his collecting experiences in various parts of the world while he shared their afternoon snack, he bade them a cheerful farewell and was off across the border. This was Walter's story. It is a little hard to believe. I suspect that camphor asphyxiation of his new-found German friends was the true explanation, because when he proudly deposited the big bundle of furs in our Valparaiso hotel room we had to leave at once, with a demand that he take it immediately to the flat roof of the building and spread out the skins to air. Months after they had been combined into a coat there was still a residual trace of the original camphor deposit.

The south and the north of Argentina contain the majority of the republic's more important forestral resources, and these are abundant. Some description has already been given of the far-spreading Argentine-Chilean temperate rain forest, limited to the southern land of lakes and on down the Andes toward Cape Horn. In the north, where Argentina touches Bolivia, Paraguay, and Uruguay, there is another and more extensive forested area. The native species that make up this northern forest are entirely different from those of the south. In addition, they are at present of much greater economic importance.

In terms of plant distribution the northern forest represents the larger proportion of what may be called the "Chaco" floristic assemblage. It is characteristic of the province of the same name and of the provinces of Formosa and Santiago del Estero, with large or small extensions in a number of directions. This very considerable "Chaco" area may be geographically subdivided into a distinctly humid zone as contrasted with a semiarid one. In both, the dominant plant species are sizable, broad-leaved, and, often, exceedingly hardwooded trees. Certain species that grow in the humid subdivision are particularly valuable because of their high tannin content. The red quebracho of the Chaco

(*Schinopsis balansar*) produces twenty or more per cent of tannin. Two other quebrachos (*Schinopsis lorentzii* and *S. haenkeana*), of the drier zone, show a somewhat lower percentage. In recent years the annual export value of the tannin has exceeded twenty million dollars.

Among the numerous other strictly Argentine tree species associated with the quebrachos are a number that are valued for the hardness and weight of their wood, which produces a superior charcoal. In many temperate parts of South America, charcoal is almost the only fuel employed for cooking and is also the source of the limited amount of heat that the population seems to require during the southern winter.

Never to be forgotten was my first contact, literally, with charcoal heating. We had been invited to a formal dinner in a Chilean home. On the streets of Santiago the winter evening was bitterly cold, and when we entered the living room at our destination I could not detect any appreciable increase in temperature. Our thoughtful host, who must have had previous experience with tender *norteamericanos*, suggested that I had best retain my ulster and scarf until we adjourned to the dining room. When we did and I had shed my outer wrappings, there seemed to be a touch of warmth in the air; this I attributed to the proximity of the kitchen, because there was no visible source of heat in the room.

During the first course or two my chattering teeth made conversation difficult and I tried, surreptitiously, to massage my hands in order to restore sufficient circulation to permit manipulation of knife and fork. Somewhat later I realized that my feet and legs were beginning to thaw. Thereupon, I made my first mistake. More or less unconsciously, I stretched out a foot to determine the origin of the heat. After some slow and tentative movements in one direction and another it banged up against a hard object. My curiosity aroused, I started, quite impolitely, to raise my side of the tablecloth. This was my second and far more serious error of judgment, because as soon as I began my investigation there were subdued exclamations of distress from the ladies, followed by hurried rearrangement of skirts that apparently had been upraised to obtain a maximum of comfort from what proved to be a fairly large charcoal brazier which had been placed under the center of the big, round dining table.

In addition to yielding tannin and fuel, the hard and resistant woods of northern Argentine forests provide most of the posts that fence the great and small estancias of the pampa. Because of their extreme durability, timbers cut from certain of the quebrachos and other "Chaco" trees find important uses as pilings and in underwater construction. The demand for the various forest products just mentioned began many years ago and has, of recent years, greatly increased. There has been little effort to control cutting, with the result that over extensive areas the valuable dominant species have almost disappeared, to be replaced by others of little or no economic importance.

In the *Chaco húmedo* the botanist who knows only the vegetation of temperate climes finds himself surrounded, as he does in other tropical and semitropical plant associations, by a variety of previously unseen and sometimes unknown species. Although, as indicated in earlier chapters, I prefer the vegetation, landscapes, and atmosphere in general of the nontropical portions of South America, what I saw of the forests in the *Chaco húmedo* proved to be somewhat appealing. Perhaps it was their rather open character which, for example, permitted palms to grow treelike as I want them to grow and not, as in the Colombian and Peruvian forests, be so altered in growth habit as to become long, straggling, spiny climbers propelling themselves upward into the rain-forest ceiling to obtain their share of light. In addition, the extent to which the forest floor was illuminated produced a variety in the growth and form of the ground-cover vegetation strikingly in contrast with the sameness of uninterrupted, dense, lush, soft, soil coverings to which I had, elsewhere in the tropics, become accustomed.

Turning, now, to Argentina's western face, the map shows that she and Chile each have their share of the crests of the central Andean cordillera which together form a mountain complex second in majesty only to the Himalayas. The line which politically separates the two republics may fall to one side or the other of the many peaks which rise to above fifteen thousand feet, some thus becoming Argentine and others Chilean. Scenically, the panorama looking eastward from the Chilean side toward the snow-covered frontier is far more spectacular than it is when viewed westwardly from Argentina. This distinction is largely a product of the abruptness with which in Chile the Andean slope rises to extreme altitudes. In Argentina the ascent is more gradual, range upon range of ever higher foothills ultimately becoming cordilleran. For the botanist, on the other hand, the Argentine Andes have more to offer than the Chilean. In Chile, north of Santiago Province, the extensive aridity of the narrow coastal shelf extends almost unbroken to the Andean snow line and, correspondingly, the vegetation which is restricted in amount and variety near the sea becomes more so as altitude increases. By contrast, on the eastward-facing Andean flank the ascending foothill sequence contains a series of vegetation zones. Only on the highest slopes and plateaus is there a barrenness and desolation corresponding to much of the Chilean foothill terrain.

There are a number of quite remarkable identities between certain of the plant species growing on the higher reaches of the North Chilean desert and on the semiarid portions of the Argentine Andes. Some of the most striking of these identities, or at least close relationships, involve the cacti of the two republics. The facts and implications in this situation would make quite a story, but I will note only the case of two species of *Trichocereus*—one that grows on the Chilean side of the Andes and is called *atacamensis*, the other found over the cordilleras on the Argentine side and called *pasacana*. If the two were growing side by side it would be difficult to say which was which; indeed, Paul, who knows intimately many of the South American cacti on their native heath and the remainder by reputation, is quite sure that they are one and the same. Does this mean that the distribution of the ancestors of these two *Trichocerii* was continuous during that long-gone era preceding the last shattering upraising of the Andean crest which today so completely separates them geographically? If so, the environmental conditions surrounding both halves of the divided tribe must from the beginning have been much the same. Otherwise, adaptive responses to distinctions in environment would have left their marks and today the descendants, one on the western face of the Andes and the other on the eastern, could rightly be called different species.

In any case, these descendants are, I think, the tallest, stoutest, and, generally, the biggest of all cacti. The little plant of *Trichocereus* we brought back alive from Chile many years ago has not really begun to get its growth but already is, outstandingly, the largest member of the extensive collection of cacti in the Botanical Garden in Berkeley. In their natural surroundings a plant of moderate size will well overtop a man and its diameter will exceed a foot, while the dimensions of a really large plant are, of course, much greater. A tough, woody skeleton supports this very sizable body. In their Chilean desert homes there are no other plants of equal bulk and so, formerly, they represented the only available source of timbers for use in the copper mines that lie high up on arid Andean slopes. On both sides of the mountains they are sawed into boards for house construction; they provide, also, some of the fuel for desert communities. The first time that I saw a pile of rather good-looking cactus planks on a railroad siding it was hard to believe that they had come from a member of an essentially succulent plant group.

As a final word concerning Argentina, let me recall that, before Perón, she was in the way of becoming a great sovereign nation, and let me express my belief that, despite the dictator's serious depletion of her moral, spiritual, and economic resources, she will regain, indeed increase, her stature in the world community.

Casting about for a theme upon which the concluding paragraph of this volume might be based, I decided that the one with which the following is concerned would be the most appropriate.

Mountains, of all the varied elements of landscape, live longest in remembrance. For me, at least, this is true. I am, for example, confident that today the lofty, white crests of the Dent du Midi appear, in memory, as sharply defined against the bright Swiss sky and as clearly reflected in the blue-gray waters of Lake Leman as they appeared to my eyes during those long-ago schoolboy days in Lausanne. Certainly, the individual features of contour and background that distinguish Ecuadorian Chimborazo, Peruvian Huascarán, Bolivian Illimani, and, on the Argentine-Chilean border, preëminent Aconcagua have left unerasable memories. For me, and I believe for all those valued companions who were with me in South America, such memories will long continue to represent some of the most cherished rewards of our plant hunting in the Andes.

INDEX

Bowlesia, 197
Brassavola nodosa, 345
Brazil, Nicotiana from, 6
Bubonic plague, 44, 179
Buddleia, 162
Buenaventura, Colombia, 334
Buenos Aires, Argentina, 19, 349, 360
Bullock, Dr. Dillman, 309, 314-315
Bursera, 117
    graveolens, 174
    gummifera, 174

Cachicadan, Peru, 30, 31
Cactus: collecting of, 72-74; extensive assemblage of, in the University of California Botanical Garden, 16; fiber for mattresses, 112; and goats, 234; and Phrygilanthus, 235; shipping of, 74; variation in, 205-206
Caesalpinia, 53
Cajophora, 269
Calbuco, Mount, Chile, 321
Calceolaria, 50, 99, 121, 161, 165, 190
    paposana, 197
    tomentosa, 151
Caldera, Chile, collecting areas near, 199
Calea, 106
Cali, Colombia: School of Subtropical Agriculture in, 15; trip to, from Bogotá by taxi, 328-332
Callao, Peru, 67
Canchaque, Peru, orange country, 176
Canna, 119
Cantua buxifolia, national flower of Peru, 165
Capparis, 29, 169
Carica candamarcensis, 120
    candicans, 50
"Carrion's disease," 87
Cassia latopetiolata, 157
Cattleya, 339, 345
    "dowiana aurea," national flower of Colombia, 340
    labiata, 340
    "var. chocoensis," 341
Ceja de la montaña (Peru): character of, 94-95; collecting in, 96 ff.; Carpis, 95, 130; Gaza, 95, 120, 121; Puno, 95; Utcu-yacu, 97-103
Centaurodendron, 249
Cerro Cache, Chile, 213
Cerro de Pasco, Peru, 111, 131
Cerro Tronador, Argentina, 360
Cerro del Volcán, Chile, 203
Cestrum, 216

Chala, Peru, 187; cattle center, 191
Chancay, Peru, 60
Chenopodium quinoa, 116
Chicha (native beer): de molle, 160; de platano, 127; of wheat or corn, 117-118
Chiclayo, Peru, 168
Chile: botanizing in southern, 311; dairy district of, 312; dense fogs on coast of, 48; farm labor in, 306; German immigration to the south of, 312-313; lake region of, analogy with Swiss Alps, 311; longitudinal extent of, 208; National Botanical Garden of, 15-16, 205; national flower of, 314-315; origin and topography of coast of, 201-202; people of, 18; rainfall in southern, 307; remarkable vegetation of southern, 314 ff., 321; reminiscent of California, 229; rivers and lakes in southern, 307; as a vacation land, 19; vegetational "islands" in north central, 231; wide climatic range in, 18
Chilean Andes: collecting in the central, 287-290; mountain highway, 273, 277; Mount Aconcagua, 267, 270-273; Uspallata Pass, 275; vegetation in, 274 ff.
Chilean flora, reminiscent of California, 196-197
Chilean National Botanical Garden, 15-16, 205
Chilean rodeo and festivities, 218-224
Chillán, Chile, earthquake in, 295
Chimborazo, Mount, Ecuador, 370
Chimbote, Peru, 51, 59-60
Chincheros, Peru, 164-165
Chota, Peru, bubonic plague in, 44-45
"Christ of the Andes," 267
Cinchona, 339
"City of the Kings." See Lima, Peru
"City of the Sun." See Cuzco, Peru
"City of Thatch." See Hualgayóc, Peru
"City of a Thousand Steps." See Machu Picchu, Peru
Clematis, 77
Cobaea, 101
Coca: chewed by natives for cocaine, 25, 27; cultivation of, 116, 120; proper quids of, 117; traffic in, 116-117
Colignonia, 80
Colletia spartioides, 247
Colombia, "Gateway to South America": national flower of, 340; orchid hunting in, 339-342; remarkable range of vegetation of, 333 ff.
Colombian Andes: geologic history of, 333-334; vegetational zones in, 334